Pro Asynchronous Programming with .NET

Richard Blewett

Andrew Clymer

Apress

Pro Asynchronous Programming with .NET

ISBN-13 (pbk): 978-1-4302-5920-6

ISBN-13 (electronic): 978-1-4302-5921-3

President and Publisher: Paul Manning
Lead Editor: Gwenan Spearing
Technical Reviewer: Liam Westley
Editorial Board: Steve Anglin, Mark Beckner, Ewan Buckingham, Gary Cornell, Louise Corrigan, Morgan Ertel, Jonathan Gennick, Jonathan Hassell, Robert Hutchinson, Michelle Lowman, James Markham, Matthew Moodie, Jeff Olson, Jeffrey Pepper, Douglas Pundick, Ben Renow-Clarke, Dominic Shakeshaft, Gwenan Spearing, Matt Wade, Tom Welsh
Coordinating Editor: Christine Ricketts
Copy Editor: James Fraleigh
Compositor: SPi Global
Indexer: SPi Global
Artist: SPi Global
Cover Designer: Anna Ishchenko

Distributed to the book trade worldwide by Springer Science+Business Media New York, 233 Spring Street, 6th Floor, New York, NY 10013. Phone 1-800-SPRINGER, fax (201) 348-4505, e-mail orders-ny@springer-sbm.com, or visit www.springeronline.com. Apress Media, LLC is a California LLC and the sole member (owner) is Springer Science + Business Media Finance Inc (SSBM Finance Inc). SSBM Finance Inc is a Delaware corporation.

For information on translations, please e-mail rights@apress.com, or visit www.apress.com.

Apress and friends of ED books may be purchased in bulk for academic, corporate, or promotional use. eBook versions and licenses are also available for most titles. For more information, reference our Special Bulk Sales–eBook Licensing web page at www.apress.com/bulk-sales.

Any source code or other supplementary materials referenced by the author in this text is available to readers at www.apress.com. For detailed information about how to locate your book's source code, go to www.apress.com/source-code/.

Contents at a Glance

Contents

About the Authors

Richard Blewett is a professional software developer and trainer living in Bristol in the UK. He has been writing software for over 20 years and has spent most of that time building distributed systems of one form or another. He first started writing multithreaded code in C on OS/2 and continued when moving to Windows, COM, and .NET. Over the years he has built software for banks, insurance companies, travel companies, emergency services, health companies, and more. He is a cofounder of Rock Solid Knowledge, a development, training and consultancy company specializing in .NET development, and a Microsoft Integration MVP.

Andrew Clymer is a professional software developer and educator living in Chippenham, Wiltshire (UK). Andy cut his teeth working in various startups and programming on a host of platforms, finally working for a small startup that was acquired by Cisco in 1997. Having worked for Cisco for a few years, the lure of the startup world was too much to resist. He is a cofounder of Rock Solid Knowledge.

About the Technical Reviewer

Liam Westley has been using Microsoft technologies since the days of Visual Basic 1.0 and is currently a Microsoft MVP in C#. He's a prolific speaker in the UK developer community, talking at user groups and community conferences.

After 15 years in the television industry, including working with BSkyB, Reuters Television, chellomedia, GMTV, and the QVC UK shopping channel, Liam moved into the world of tech startups in London.

He is currently one of a team of application architects at Huddle, where he works with some of the best .NET developers and UX designers to deliver world-class collaboration software. He quite likes working just off Old Street as there is some fantastic food and coffee to be had within a few minutes' walk.

Photo courtesy of Ian Battersby/DDDNorth.

Acknowledgments

We'd like to thank all the folks at Apress who have helped us ship this book: Gwenan Spearing for getting involved in the first place; Christine Ricketts for her patience and perseverance in keeping us on track; Tom Welsh and Matthew Moodie for their great editing; and James Fraleigh for his copyediting. We'd also like to thank Liam Westley for his technical reviews of the chapters.

Thank you and apologies to Michele, Carmel, Tegen, and Ewan for bearing with me as I paced around the house with writer's block. I couldn't have gotten here without your understanding and support.

—Richard Blewett

Thanks to Jules, Emily, and Joseph for putting up with me juggling so many things over the last 12 months and for picking up the things I dropped. Thanks to my Mum and Dad, who through the purchase of many home computers set me off on the most incredible of journeys.

—Andrew Clymer

CHAPTER 1

■ ■ ■

An Introduction to Asynchronous Programming

There are many holy grails in software development, but probably none so eagerly sought, and yet so woefully unachieved, as making asynchronous programming simple. This isn't because the issues are currently unknown; rather, they are very well known, but just very hard to solve in an automated way. The goal of this book is to help you understand why asynchronous programming is important, what issues make it hard, and how to be successful writing asynchronous code on the .NET platform.

What Is Asynchronous Programming?

Most code that people write is synchronous. In other words, the code starts to execute, may loop, branch, pause, and resume, but given the same inputs, its instructions are executed in a deterministic order. Synchronous code is, in theory, straightforward to understand, as you can follow the sequence in which code will execute. It is possible of course to write code that is obscure, that uses edge case behavior in a language, and that uses misleading names and large dense blocks of code. But reasonably structured and well named synchronous code is normally very approachable to someone trying to understand what it does. It is also generally straightforward to write as long as you understand the problem domain.

The problem is that an application that executes purely synchronously may generate results too slowly or may perform long operations that leave the program unresponsive to further input. What if we could calculate several results concurrently or take inputs while also performing those long operations? This would solve the problems with our synchronous code, but now we would have more than one thing happening at the same time (at least logically if not physically). When you write systems that are designed to do more than one thing at a time, it is called *asynchronous programming*.

The Drive to Asynchrony

There are a number of trends in the world of IT that have highlighted the importance of asynchrony.

First, users have become more discerning about the responsiveness of applications. In times past, when a user clicked a button, they would be fairly forgiving if there was a slight delay before the application responded—this was their experience with software in general and so it was, to some degree, expected. However, smartphones and tablets have changed the way that users see software. They now expect it to respond to their actions instantaneously and fluidly. For a developer to give the user the experience they want, they have to make sure that any operation that could prevent the application from responding is performed asynchronously.

Second, processor technology has evolved to put multiple processing cores on a single processor package. Machines now offer enormous processing power. However, because they have multiple cores rather than one incredibly fast core, we get no benefit unless our code performs multiple, concurrent, actions that can be mapped on to those multiple cores. Therefore, taking advantage of modern chip architecture inevitably requires asynchronous programming.

Last, the push to move processing to the cloud means applications need to access functionality that is potentially geographically remote. The resulting added latency can cause operations that previously might have provided adequate performance when processed sequentially to miss performance targets. Executing two or more of these remote operations concurrently may well bring the application back into acceptable performance. To do so, however, requires asynchronous programming.

Mechanisms for Asynchrony

There are typically three models that we can use to introduce asynchrony: multiple machines, multiple processes, and multiple threads. All of these have their place in complex systems, and different languages, platforms, and technologies tend to favor a particular model.

Multiple Machines

To use multiple machines, or *nodes,* to introduce asynchrony, we need to ensure that when we request the functionality to run remotely, we don't do this in a way that blocks the requester. There are a number of ways to achieve this, but commonly we pass a message to a queue, and the remote worker picks up the message and performs the requested action. Any results of the processing need to be made available to the requester, which again is commonly achieved via a queue. As can be seen from Figure 1-1, the queues break blocking behavior between the requester and worker machines and allow the worker machines to run independently of one another. Because the worker machines rarely contend for resources, there are potentially very high levels of scalability. However, dealing with node failure and internode synchronization becomes more complex.

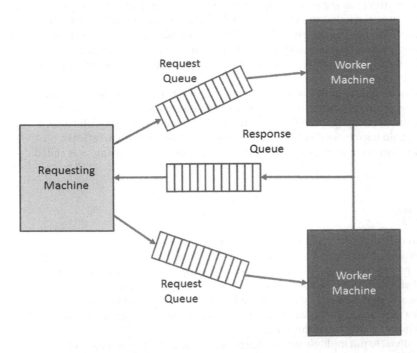

Figure 1-1. Using queues for cross-machine asynchrony

Multiple Processes

A *process* is a unit of isolation on a single machine. Multiple processes do have to share access to the processing cores, but do not share virtual memory address spaces and can run in different security contexts. It turns out we can use the same processing architecture as multiple machines on a single machine by using queues. In this case it is easier to some degree to deal with the failure of a worker process and to synchronize activity between processes.

There is another model for asynchrony with multiple processes where, to hand off long-running work to execute in the background, you spawn another process. This is the model that web servers have used in the past to process multiple requests. A CGI script is executed in a spawned process, having been passed any necessary data via command line arguments or environment variables.

Multiple Threads

Threads are independently schedulable sets of instructions with a package of nonshared resources. A thread is bounded within a process (a thread cannot migrate from one process to another), and all threads within a process share process-wide resources such as heap memory and operating system resources such as file handles and sockets. The queue-based approach shown in Figure 1-1 is also applicable to multiple threads, as it is in fact a general purpose asynchronous pattern. However, due to the heavy sharing of resources, using multiple threads benefits least from this approach. Resource sharing also introduces less complexity in coordinating multiple worker threads and handling thread failure.

Unlike Unix, Windows processes are relatively heavyweight constructs when compared with threads. This is due to the loading of the Win32 runtime libraries and the associated registry reads (along with a number of cross-process calls to system components for housekeeping). Therefore, by design on Windows, we tend to prefer using multiple threads to create asynchronous processing rather than multiple processes. However, there is an overhead to creating and destroying threads, so it is good practice to try to reuse them rather than destroy one thread and then create another.

Thread Scheduling

In Windows, the operating system component responsible for mapping thread execution on to cores is called the *Thread Scheduler*. As we shall see, sometimes threads are waiting for some event to occur before they can perform any work (in .NET this state is known as SleepWaitJoin). Any thread not in the SleepWaitJoin state should be allocated some time on a processing core and, all things being equal, the thread scheduler will round-robin processor time among all of the threads currently running across all of the processes. Each thread is allotted a time slice and, as long as the thread doesn't enter the SleepWaitJoin state, it will run until the end of its time slice.

Things, however, are not often equal. Different processes can run with different priorities (there are six priorities ranging from idle to real time). Within a process a thread also has a priority; there are seven ranging from idle to time critical. The resulting priority a thread runs with is a combination of these two priorities, and this effective priority is critical to thread scheduling. The Windows thread scheduler does preemptive multitasking. In other words, if a higher-priority thread wants to run, then a lower-priority thread is ejected from the processor (preempted) and replaced with the higher-priority thread. Threads of equal priority are, again, scheduled on a round-robin basis, each being allotted a time slice.

You may be thinking that lower-priority threads could be starved of processor time. However, in certain conditions, the priority of a thread will be boosted temporarily to try to ensure that it gets a chance to run on the processor. Priority boosting can happen for a number of reasons (e.g., user input). Once a boosted thread has had processor time, its priority gets degraded until it reaches its normal value.

Threads and Resources

Although two threads share some resources within a process, they also have resources that are specific to themselves. To understand the impact of executing our code asynchronously, it is important to understand when we will be dealing with shared resources and when a thread can guarantee it has exclusive access. This distinction becomes critical when we look at thread safety, which we do in depth in Chapter 4.

Thread-Specific Resources

There are a number of resources to which a thread has exclusive access. When the thread uses these resources it is guaranteed to not be in contention with other threads.

The Stack

Each thread gets its own stack. This means that local variables and parameters in methods, which are stored on the stack, are never shared between threads. The default stack size is 1MB, so a thread consumes a nontrivial amount of resource in just its allocated stack.

Thread Local Storage

On Windows we can define storage slots in an area called thread local storage (TLS). Each thread has an entry for each slot in which it can store a value. This value is specific to the thread and cannot be accessed by other threads. TLS slots are limited in number, which at the time of writing is guaranteed to be at least 64 per process but may be as high as 1,088.

Registers

A thread has its own copy of the register values. When a thread is scheduled on a processing core, its copy of the register value is restored on to the core's registers. This allows the thread to continue processing at the point when it was preempted (its instruction pointer is restored) with the register state identical to when it was last running.

Resources Shared by Threads

There is one critical resource that is shared by all threads in a process: heap memory. In .NET all reference types are allocated on the heap and therefore multiple threads can, if they have a reference to the same object, access the same heap memory at the same time. This can be very efficient but is also the source of potential bugs, as we shall see in Chapter 4.

For completeness we should also note that threads, in effect, share operating system handles. In other words, if a thread performs an operation that produces an operating system handle under the covers (e.g., accesses a file, creates a window, loads a DLL), then the thread ending will not automatically return that handle. If no other thread in the process takes action to close the handle, then it will not be returned until the process exits.

Summary

We've shown that asynchronous programming is increasingly important, and that on Windows we typically achieve asynchrony via the use of threads. We've also shown what threads are and how they get mapped on to cores so they can execute. You therefore have the groundwork to understand how Microsoft has built on top of this infrastructure to provide .NET programmers with the ability to run code asynchronously.

This book, however, is not intended as an API reference—the MSDN documentation exists for that purpose. Instead, we address why APIs have been designed the way they have and how they can be used effectively to solve real problems. We also show how we can use Visual Studio and other tools to debug multithreaded applications when they are not behaving as expected.

By the end of the book, you should have all the tools you need to introduce asynchronous programming to your world and understand the options available to you. You should also have the knowledge to select the most appropriate tool for the asynchronous job in hand.

■ ■ ■

CHAPTER 2

The Evolution of the .NET Asynchronous API

In February 2002, .NET version 1.0 was released. From this very first release it was possible to build parts of your application that ran asynchronously. The APIs, patterns, underlying infrastructure, or all three have changed, to some degree, with almost every subsequent release, each attempting to make life easier or richer for the .NET developer. To understand why the .NET async world looks the way it does, and why certain design decisions were made, it is necessary to take a tour through its history. We will then build on this in future chapters as we describe how to build async code today, and which pieces of the async legacy still merit a place in your new applications.

Some of the information here can be considered purely as background to show why the API has developed as it has. However, some sections have important use cases when building systems with .NET 4.0 and 4.5. In particular, using the Thread class to tune how COM Interop is performed is essential when using COM components in your application. Also, if you are using .NET 4.0, understanding how work can be placed on I/O threads in the thread pool using the Asynchronous Programming Model is critical for scalable server based code.

Asynchrony in the World of .NET 1.0

Even back in 2002, being able to run code asynchronously was important: UIs still had to remain responsive; background things still needed to be monitored; complex jobs needed to be split up and run concurrently. The release of the first version of .NET, therefore, had to support async from the start.

There were two models for asynchrony introduced with 1.0, and which you used depended on whether you needed a high degree of control over the execution. The Thread class gave you a dedicated thread on which to perform your work; the ThreadPool was a shared resource that potentially could run your work on already created threads. Each of these models had a different API, so let's look at each of them in turn.

System.Threading.Thread

The Thread class was, originally, a 1:1 mapping to an operating system thread. It is typically used for long-running or specialized work such as monitoring a device or executing code with a low priority. Using the Thread class leaves us with a lot of control over the thread, so let's see how the API works.

The Start Method

To run work using the Thread class you create an instance, passing a ThreadStart delegate and calling Start (see Listing 2-1).

Listing 2-1. Creating and Starting a Thread Using the Thread Class

```
static void Main(string[] args)
{
    Thread monitorThread = new Thread(new ThreadStart(MonitorNetwork));

    monitorThread.Start();
}

static void MonitorNetwork()
{
    // ...
}
```

Notice that the ThreadStart delegate takes no parameters and returns void. So that presents a question: how do we get data into the thread? This was before the days of anonymous delegates and lambda expressions, and so our only option was to encapsulate the necessary data and the thread function in its own class. It's not that this is a hugely complex undertaking; it just gives us more code to maintain, purely to satisfy the mechanics of getting data into a thread.

Stopping a Thread

The thread is now running, so how does it stop? The simplest way is that the method passed as a delegate ends. However, often dedicated threads are used for long-running or continuous work, and so the method, by design, will not end quickly. If that is the case, is there any way for the code that spawned the thread to get it to end? The short answer is not without the cooperation of the thread—at least, there is no *safe* way. The frustrating thing is that the Thread API would seem to present not one, but two ways: both the Interrupt and Abort method would appear to offer a way to get the thread to end without the thread function itself being involved.

The Abort Method

The Abort method would seem to be the most direct method of stopping the thread. After all, the documentation says the following:

> *Raises a ThreadAbortException in the thread on which it is invoked, to begin the process of terminating the thread. Calling this method usually terminates the thread.*

Well, that seems pretty straightforward. However, as the documentation goes on to indicate, this raises a completely asynchronous exception that can interrupt code during sensitive operations. The only time an exception isn't thrown is if the thread is in unmanaged code having gone through the interop layer. This issue was alleviated a little in .NET 2.0, but the fundamental issue of the exception being thrown at a nondeterministic point remains. So, in essence, this method should not be used to stop a thread.

The Interrupt Method

The Interrupt method appears to offer more hope. The documentation states that this will also throw an exception (a ThreadInterruptedException), but this exception will only happen when the thread is in a known state called WaitSleepJoin. In other words, the exception is thrown if the thread is in a known idle situation. The problem is that this wait state may not be in your code, but instead in some arbitrary framework or third-party code. Unless we can guarantee that all other code has been written with the possibility of thread interruption in mind, we cannot safely use it (Microsoft has acknowledged that not all framework code is robust in the face of interruption).

Solving Thread Teardown

We are therefore left with cooperation as a mechanism to halt an executing thread. It can be achieved fairly straightforwardly using a Boolean flag (although there are other ways as well). The thread must periodically check the flag to find out whether it has been requested to stop.

There are two issues with this approach, one fairly obvious and the other quite subtle. First, it assumes that the code is able to check the flag. If the code running in the thread is performing a long blocking operation, it cannot look at a flag. Second, the JIT compiler can perform optimizations that are perfectly valid for single-threaded code but will break with multithreaded code. Consider the code in Listing 2-2: if it is run in a release build, then the main thread will never end, as the JIT compiler can move the check outside of the loop. This change makes no difference in single-threaded code, but it can introduce bugs into multithreaded code.

Listing 2-2. *JIT Compiler Optimization Can Cause Issues*

```
class Program
{
    static void Main(string[] args)
    {
        AsyncSignal h = new AsyncSignal();

        while (!h.Terminate) ;
    }

    class AsyncSignal
    {
        public bool Terminate;

        public AsyncSignal()
        {
            Thread monitorThread = new Thread(new ThreadStart(MonitorNetwork));
            monitorThread.Start();
        }
        private void MonitorNetwork()
        {
            Thread.Sleep(3000);
            Terminate = true;
        }
    }
}
```

Once you are aware of the potential problem, there is a very simple fix: to mark the Terminate flag as volatile. This has two effects: first, to turn off thread-sensitive JIT compiler optimizations; second, to prevent reordering of write operations. The second of these was potentially an issue prior to version 2.0 of .NET, but in 2.0 the memory model (see sidebar) was strengthened to remove the problem.

MEMORY MODELS

A memory model defines rules for how memory reads and writes can be performed in multithreaded systems. They are necessary because on multicore hardware, memory access is heavily optimized using caches and write buffering. Therefore, a developer needs to understand what guarantees are given by the memory model of a platform and, therefore, to what they must pay attention.

The 1.x release of .NET defined its memory model in the accompanying ECMA specification. This was fairly relaxed in terms of the demands on compiler writers and left a lot of responsibility with developers to write code correctly. However, it turned out that x86 processors gave stronger guarantees than the ECMA specification and, as the only implementation of .NET at the time was on x86, in reality applications were not actually subject to some of the theoretical issues.

.NET 2.0 introduced a stronger memory model, and so even on non-x86 processor architectures, issues caused by read and write reordering will not affect .NET code.

Another Approach: Background Threads

.NET has the notion of foreground and background threads. A process is kept alive as long as at least one foreground thread is running. Once all foreground threads have finished, the process is terminated. Any background threads that are still running are simply torn down. In general this is safe, as resources being used by the background threads are freed by process termination. However, as you can probably tell, the thread gets no chance to perform a controlled cleanup.

If we model our asynchronous work as background threads, we no longer need to be responsible for controlling the termination of a thread. If the thread were simply waiting for a file to arrive in a directory and notifying the application when it did, then it doesn't matter if this thread is torn down with no warning. However, as an example of a potential issue, consider a system where the first byte of a file indicates that the file is currently locked for processing. If the processing of the file is performed on a background thread, then there is a chance that the thread will be torn down before it can reset the lock byte.

Threads created using the Thread class are, by default, foreground threads. If you want a background thread, then you must set the IsBackground property of the thread object to true.

Coordinating Threads (Join)

If code spawns a thread, it may well want to know when that thread finishes; for example, to process the results of the thread's work. The Thread class's Join method allows an observer to wait for the thread to end. There are two forms of the Join method: one that takes no parameters and returns void, the other that takes a timeout and returns a Boolean. The first form will block until the thread completes, regardless of how long that might be. The second form will return true if the thread completes before the timeout or false if the timeout is reached first. You should always prefer waiting with a timeout, as it allows you to proactively detect when operations are taking longer than they should. Listing 2-3 shows how to use Join to wait for a thread to complete with a timeout. You should remember that when Join times out, the thread is still running; it is simply the wait that has finished.

Listing 2-3. Using Join to Coordinate Threads

```
FileProcessor processor = new FileProcessor(file);
Thread t = new Thread(processor.Process);
t.Start();
```

```
PrepareReport();

if (t.Join(TimeSpan.FromSeconds(5)))
{
    RunReport(processor.Result);
}
else
{
    HandleError("Processing has timed out");
}
```

THREADING AND COM

The Component Object Model (COM) was Microsoft's previous technology for building components. Many organizations have legacy COM objects that they need to use in their applications. A goal of COM was to ensure that different technologies could use one another's components, and so a COM object written in VB 6 could be used from COM code written in C++—or at least that was the theory. The problem was that VB was not multithread aware and so internally made assumptions about which thread it was running on. C++ code could quite happily be multithreaded, and so by calling a VB component directly from a C++ one could potentially cause spectacular crashes. Therefore, thread-aware and thread-unaware code needed to be kept separate, and this was achieved by the notion of *apartments*.

Thread-unaware components lived in Single Threaded Apartments (STAs), which would ensure they were always called on the same thread. Other components could elect to live in the Multithreaded Apartment (MTA) or an STA (in fact there was a third option for these COM objects, but for brevity we'll omit that). In the MTA a COM object could be called by any MTA thread at any time so they had to be written with thread safety in mind.

Threads that did COM work had to declare whether they wanted to run their own STA or to join the MTA. The critical thing is that the overhead of calling from an MTA thread to an STA component, and vice versa, involved two thread switches and so was far less efficient that intra-apartment invocation.

Generally, then, you should always attempt to call a COM component from the same apartment that it lives in.

Controlling a Thread's Interaction with COM

One common use of the Thread class that is still important even in .NET 4.0 and 4.5 is to control how that thread behaves when it performs COM work (see the "Threading and COM" sidebar to understand the issues). If a thread is going to perform COM work, you should try to ensure it is in the same apartment as the COM objects it is going to be invoking. By default, .NET threads will always enter the MTA. To change this behavior, you must change the thread's ApartmentState. Originally, this was done by setting the ApartmentState property, but this was deprecated in .NET 2.0. From 2.0 onward you need to use the SetApartmentState method on the thread.

Issues with the Thread Class

The API for the Thread class is fairly simple, so why not use it for all asynchronous work? As discussed in Chapter 1, threads are not cheap resources: they are expensive to create; clean up; they consume memory for stack space and require attention from the thread scheduler. As a result, if you have regular asynchronous work to do, continuously creating and destroying the threads is wasteful. Also, uncontrolled creation of threads can end up consuming huge amounts of memory and causing the thread scheduler to thrash—neither of which is healthy for your application.

A more efficient model would be to reuse threads that have already been created, thus relieving the application code of control of thread creation. This would then allow thread management to be regulated. This is potentially highly complex code for you to maintain. Fortunately, .NET already comes with an implementation, out of the box, in the form of the system thread pool.

Using the System Thread Pool

The system thread pool is a process-wide resource providing more efficient use of threads for general asynchronous work. The idea is this:

- Application code passes work to the thread pool (known as a work item), which gets enqueued (see Figure 2-1).

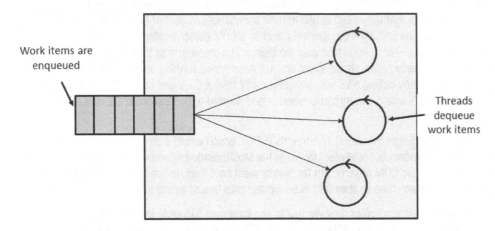

Figure 2-1. *The system thread pool*

- The thread pool manager adds threads into the pool to process the work.

- When a thread pool thread has completed its current work item, it goes back to the queue to get the next.

- If the rate of work arriving on the queue is greater than the current number of threads can keep up with, the thread pool manager uses heuristics to decide whether to add more threads into the pool.

- If threads are idle (there are no more work items to execute), then the thread pool manager will eventually degrade threads out of the thread pool.

As you can see, the thread pool manager attempts to balance the number of threads in the pool with the rate of work appearing on the queue. The thread pool is capped to ensure the maximum number of threads is constrained.

The heuristics used to decide whether to add new threads into the pool, and the default maximum number of threads in the pool, have changed with almost every version of .NET, as you will see over the course of this chapter. In .NET 1.0, however, they were as follows:

- The default maximum number of worker threads in the thread pool was 25. This could only be changed by writing a custom Common Language Runtime (CLR)-unmanaged host.

- The algorithm for adding new threads into the thread pool was based on allowing half a second for a work item to be on the queue unprocessed. If still waiting after this time, a new thread was added.

Worker and I/O Threads

It turns out there are two groups of threads in the thread pool: worker and I/O threads. Worker threads are targeted at work that is generally CPU based. If you perform I/O on these threads it is really a waste of resources, as the thread will sit idle while the I/O is performed. A more efficient model would be to kick off the I/O (which is basically a hardware operation) and commit a thread only when the I/O is complete. This is the concept of I/O completion ports, and this is how the I/O threads in the thread pool work.

Getting Work on to the Thread Pool

We have seen the basic mechanics of how the thread pool works but how does work get enqueued? There are three mechanisms you can use:

- ThreadPool.QueueUserWorkItem
- Timers
- The Asynchronous Programming Model (APM)

ThreadPool.QueueUserWorkItem

The most direct way to get work on to the thread pool is to use the API ThreadPool.QueueUserWorkItem. This method takes the passed WaitCallback delegate and, as the name suggests, wraps it in a work item and enqueues it. The work item is then picked up by a thread pool worker thread when one becomes available. The WaitCallback delegate takes an object as a parameter, which can be passed in an overload of ThreadPool.QueueUserWorkItem.

Timers

If you have work that needs to be done asynchronously but on a regular basis and at a specific interval, you can use a thread pool timer. This is represented by the class System.Threading.Timer. Creating one of these will run a delegate, on a thread pool worker thread, at the passed interval starting after the passed due time. The API takes a state object that is passed to the delegate on each invocation. The timer stops when you dispose it.

The APM

By far the most common way to run work on the thread pool, before .NET version 4.0, was to use APIs that use a pattern called the Asynchronous Programming Model (or APM for short). APM is modeled by a pair of methods and an object that binds the two together, known as a call object. To explain the pattern, let's take an API for obtaining search results that has a synchronous version that looks like this:

```
SearchResults GetResults(int page, int pageSize, out int itemsReturned);
```

The pattern has traditionally sat alongside a synchronous version, although this is not a requirement, so with APM you get two additional methods. These methods are the synchronous name prefixed with Begin and End, respectively. The signatures of these two methods are also very specific; for this example, here they are:

```
IAsyncResult BeginGetResults(int page,
                             int pageSize,
                             out int itemsReturned,
                             AsyncCallback callback,
                             object state);

SearchResults EndGetResults(out int itemsReturned, IAsyncResult iar);
```

BeginGetResults takes the same parameters as the synchronous version with an additional two (we'll come to these shortly) and always return an IAsyncResult. The object that implements IAsyncResult is known as the call object and is used to identify the asynchronous call in progress. The EndGetResults method takes the output (and any ref) parameters of the synchronous version, as well as the call object (in the form of IAsyncResult) and returns the same thing as the synchronous version. If the EndGetResults method is called before the work is completed, then the method blocks until the results are available.

The idea is that the BeginGetResults method enqueues the work and returns immediately, and the caller can now get on with other work. In most cases the work will occur asynchronously on the thread pool. The EndGetResults method is used to retrieve the results of the completed asynchronous operation.

WHY DOES THE BEGIN METHOD TAKE OUT PARAMETERS?

Something that might strike you as odd is that the Begin method takes out parameters as well as standard and ref ones. Normally out parameters come into play only when the operation is complete, so why are they on the Begin method? It turns out this is the abstraction leaking. The CLR has no notion of out parameters; it is a C# language idiom. At the CLR level, out parameters are simply ref parameters, and it is the C# compiler that enforces a specific usage pattern. Because APM is not a language-specific feature, it must conform to the needs of the CLR. Now ref parameters can be both inputs and outputs; therefore, the CLR does not know that these out parameters are only used for output and so they must be placed on the Begin method as well as the End method.

IAsyncResult

Why does the call object implement an interface at all? Why not just use it as an opaque token? It turns out that most of the members of the interface can be useful. There are four members on the interface, as described in Table 2-1.

Table 2-1. *The Members of IAsyncResult*

Name	Type	Description
IsCompleted	bool	States whether the asynchronous call has finished
AsyncWaitHandle	WaitHandle	Waitable object that signals when the asynchronous call completes
AsyncState	object	Can refer to a piece of context passed in the Begin method
CompletedSynchronously	bool	States whether the operation was performed on the thread that called the Begin method rather than asynchronously

As we shall see, IsCompleted, AsyncWaitHandle, and AsyncState all have their uses. CompletedSynchronously, on the other hand, turns out to be of little practical use and is there purely to indicate that the requested work was, in fact, performed on the thread that called the Begin method. An example where this might happen is on a socket where the data to be read has already arrived across the network.

Dealing with Errors

Things don't always go to plan. It is quite possible that the async operation might fail in some way. The question is, what happens then? In .NET 1.0 and 1.1 unhandled exceptions on background threads were silently swallowed. From .NET 2.0 onwards an unhandled exception, on any thread, will terminate the process. Because you are not necessarily in control of the code that is executing asynchronously (e.g., an asynchronous database query), the process arbitrarily terminating would be an impossible programming model to work with. Therefore, in APM, exceptions are handled internally and then rethrown when you call the End method. This means you should always be prepared for exceptions to calling the End method.

Accessing Results

One of the powerful things about APM, when compared with using the Thread API, is the simplicity of accessing results. To access results, for reasons we hope are obvious, the asynchronous call must have finished. There are three models you can use to check for completion, and which you use depends on your requirements:

1. Polling for completion

2. Waiting for completion

3. Completion notification

Polling for Completion

Imagine you are building a UI and need to perform some long-running task (we talk about async and UI in much more detail in Chapter 6). You should not perform this work on the UI thread, as its job is to keep the UI responsive. So you use APM via a delegate (more on this shortly) to put the task in the thread pool, and then you need to display the results once available. The question is how do you know when the results are available? You can't simply call the End method, as it will block (because the task isn't complete) and stop the UI; you need to call it once you *know* the task is finished. This is where the IsCompleted property on IAsyncResult comes in. You can call IsCompleted on, say, a timer and call the End method when it returns true. Listing 2-4 shows an example of polling for completion.

Listing 2-4. Polling for Completion

```csharp
private IAsyncResult asyncCall;
private Timer asyncTimer;

private void OnPerformSearch(object sender, RoutedEventArgs e)
{
    int dummy;

    asyncCall = BeginGetResults(1, 50, out dummy, null, null);

    asyncTimer = new Timer();
    asyncTimer.Interval = 200;
    asyncTimer.Tick += OnTimerTick;
    asyncTimer.Start();
}

private void OnTimerTick(object sender, ElapsedEventArgs e)
{
    if (asyncCall.IsCompleted)
    {
        int resultCount;

        try
        {
            SearchResults results = EndGetResults(out resultCount, asyncCall);

            DisplayResults(results,  resultCount);
        }
        catch(Exception x)
        {
            LogError(x);
        }

        asyncTimer.Dispose();
    }
}
```

Waiting for Completion

Although polling fits some use cases, it is not the most efficient model. If you can do no further useful work until
the results are available, and you are not running on a UI thread, it is better simply to wait for the async operation to
complete. You could just call the End method, which achieves that effect. However, if the async operation became
stuck in an infinite loop or deadlocked, then your waiting code would wait forever. It is rarely a good idea to perform
waits without timeouts in multithreaded code, so simply calling the End method should be avoided. Instead you can
use another feature of IAsyncResult: the AsyncWaitHandle. WaitHandles are synchronization objects that signal in
some specific circumstance (we'll talk more about them in Chapter 4). The AsyncWaitHandle of IAsyncResult signals
when the async operation has finished. The good thing about WaitHandles is that you can pass a timeout when you
wait for them to signal. Listing 2-5 shows an example of using AsyncWaitHandle.

Listing 2-5. Waiting for an Async Operation to Complete

```
int dummy;

IAsyncResult iar = BeginGetResults(1, 50, out dummy, null, null);

// The async operation is now in progress and we can get on with other work
ReportDefaults defaults = GetReportDefaults();

// We now can't proceed without the results so wait for the operation to complete
// we're prepared to wait for up to 5 seconds
if (iar.AsyncWaitHandle.WaitOne(5000))
{
    int resultCount;
    try
    {
        SearchResults results = EndGetResults(out resultCount, asyncCall);

        GenerateReport(defaults, results);
    }
    catch(Exception x)
    {
        LogError(x);
    }

}
else
{
    throw new TimeoutException("Async GetResults timed out");
}
```

HOUSEKEEPING IS IMPORTANT

The async operation may have to allocate resources to track completion; AsyncWaitHandle is an example of this. When is it safe for these resources to be freed up? They can only be safely cleaned up when it is known they are no longer required, and this is only known when the End method is called. It has always been an issue—though one that wasn't documented until .NET 1.1—that if you call the Begin method in APM, then you must call the End method to allow resources to be cleaned up, even if you don't care about the results. Failing to do so means resources may be leaked.

However, there is a problem in Listing 2-5. As explained in the "Housekeeping Is Important" sidebar, in APM you need to call the End method if you call the Begin method. Notice in the code in Listing 2-5 that in the event of a timeout, the End method isn't called. There is a fundamental problem: you've timed out, which suggests the async operation is somehow blocked, and so if we call the End method our code will block as well. There isn't really a solution to this issue, so although it appears to be an obvious use case, you should generally avoid AsyncWaitHandle.

Completion Notification

Probably the most flexible model for knowing when the operation is complete is to register a completion callback. One note of caution, however, is that this flexibility comes at a cost in terms of complexity, particularly when working in GUI frameworks, which have a high degree of thread affinity. Recall the signature of BeginGetResults; there were two additional parameters when compared to the synchronous version: an AsyncCallback delegate and an object. The first of these is the completion callback that gets invoked when the async operation completes. As you know the operation is complete, you can now safely call the EndGetResults, knowing that it will now not block.

AsyncCallback is defined as follows:

```
delegate void AsyncCallback(IAsyncResult iar);
```

Listing 2-6 shows the callback mechanism in action.

Listing 2-6. Using a Completion Callback

```
private void OnPerformSearch(object sender, RoutedEventArgs e)
{
    int dummy;

    BeginGetResults(1, 50, out dummy, new AsyncCallback(Callback), null);
}

private void Callback(IAsyncResult iar)
{
    try
    {
        int resultCount;
        SearchResults results = EndGetResults(out resultCount, asyncCall);

        DisplayResults(results, resultCount);
    }
    catch(Exception x)
    {
        LogError(x);
    }
}
```

This all seems very straightforward but, critically, you must remember that the callback will not be executing on the main thread; it will run on a thread pool thread. As a result, in GUI applications you will not be able to update the UI directly. GUI frameworks provide built-in mechanisms to move work back onto the UI thread. We will look at this very briefly, shortly and in much more detail in Chapter 6. The other issue to take note of is to remember that the End method may throw an exception if the async work didn't complete successfully. *If you do not put exception-handling code around this call, and an exception happens, then your process will terminate, as this is running on a background thread with no exception handlers higher up the stack.*

APM in the Framework

APM appears in many APIs in the .NET Framework. Typically, anywhere I/O takes place, there is an associated APM pair of methods. For example, on the WebRequest class we have the following three methods:

```
WebResponse GetResponse();
IAsyncResult BeginGetResponse(AsyncCallback callback, object state);
WebResponse EndGetResponse(IAsyncResult iar);
```

GetResponse is the synchronous version. This performs an HTTP or FTP request, which therefore may take some time. Blocking a thread while the network I/O is taking place is wasteful, and so an APM pair of methods is also provided that use I/O threads in the thread pool to perform the request. As we shall see in chapter 9, this idea is very important in building scalable server solutions.

Let's look at Listing 2-7, an example of using this API, as this will draw out some more important issues with APM.

Listing 2-7. Making an Async Web Request

```
private void Callback(IAsyncResult iar)
{
}


private void OnPerformSearch(object sender, RoutedEventArgs e)
{
    WebRequest req = WebRequest.Create("http://www.google.com/#q=weather");

    req.BeginGetResponse(new AsyncCallback(Callback), null);
}
```

As you can see in Listing 2-7, the API is quite straightforward. However, one important rule is that you must call the End method on the same object on which you call the Begin method. This presents a problem with the code in Listing 2-7 as the Callback method cannot see the WebRequest object. One obvious way around this is to make the WebRequest local variable into a member variable. This works fine in simple cases, but what if we wanted to fire off several of these async web requests at the same time? We would need separate fields for each request and some mechanism for the Callback method to call EndGetResponse on the correct one. This is obviously not a scalable solution.

Fortunately there is another parameter in APM that we have not yet discussed: the last one, of the type object, often named state. Whatever we pass as this parameter is available via the AsyncState property on IAsyncResult. Using the async state object to pass the WebRequest gives us a far more encapsulated solution for calling the EndGetResponse method on the right instance in Callback. Listing 2-8 shows this pattern in action.

Listing 2-8. Using AsyncState to Pass the WebRequest

```
private void Callback(IAsyncResult iar)
{
    WebRequest req = (WebRequest) iar.AsyncState;
    try
    {
        WebResponse resp = req.EndGetResponse(iar);

        ProcessResponse(resp);
    }
    catch(Exception x)
    {
        LogError(x);
    }
}

private void OnPerformSearch(object sender, RoutedEventArgs e)
{
    WebRequest req = WebRequest.Create("http://www.google.com/#q=weather");

    req.BeginGetResponse(new AsyncCallback(Callback), req);
}
```

Of course I/O isn't just about web requests. APM is implemented on all of the main I/O-based classes: Stream, Socket, SqlCommand, MessageQueue and more. Of course, not all long-running code is I/O based; what about sections of my code that you want to run asynchronously? Can APM help you there?

APM and Delegates

You can use APM with any arbitrary code by wrapping the operation in a delegate. Delegates have APM built in to execute the code on a worker thread in the thread pool. Let's have a look at what the compiler does with a delegate using the following declaration:

```
delegate bool CurrencyParser(string text, out decimal result);
```

Figure 2-2 shows the ILDASM output after the compiler has compiled this delegate. As you can see, the Invoke method has the same signature as the delegate and then the output has the corresponding pair of APM methods BeginInvoke and EndInvoke.

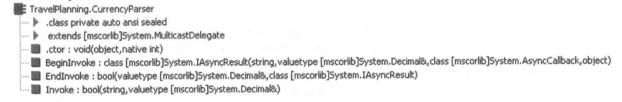

Figure 2-2. Compiler-generated code for delegate

Because delegates support APM, you can run any piece of arbitrary code asynchronously on the thread pool fairly easily. However, remember that your code becomes more complex as a result, because APM changes the structure of the synchronous code. Suppose you want to make the code in Listing 2-9 asynchronous:

Listing 2-9. Synchronous Version of Code

```
private void OnDecrypt(object sender, RoutedEventArgs e)
{
    ClearText = Decrypt(CipherText);
}
```

If you had a delegate that took a string and returned a string, then you could wrap the Decrypt method in a delegate instance and call BeginInvoke (see Listing 2-10).

Listing 2-10. Asynchronous Version of Code with APM

```
delegate string EncryptorDecryptor(string inputText);

private void DecryptCallback(IAsyncResult iar)
{
    EncryptorDecryptor del = (EncryptorDecryptor) iar.AsyncState;

    // remember we must protect the call to EndInvoke as an exception
    // would terminate the process as this is running on a worker thread
```

```
    try
    {
        // for a UI application this would potentially have to be marshalled on to
        // the UI thread if the setting of the ClearText property changed the UI
        ClearText = del.EndInvoke(iar);
    }
    catch(Exception x)
    {
        LogError(x);
    }
}

private void OnDecrypt(object sender, RoutedEventArgs e)
{
    EncryptorDecryptor del = new EncryptorDecryptor(Decrypt);

    del.BeginInvoke(CipherText, new AsyncCallback(DecryptCallback), del);
}
```

As you can see from Listing 2-10, the asynchronous version of the code is structured very differently from the synchronous version. Synchronous code is generally easier to understand than asynchronous code, so in an ideal world both versions would look very similar. However, to get to that point we have to continue our journey.

Changes to Async in .NET 1.1

The 1.1 release did not make any dramatic changes to the async world of .NET. One change, already mentioned, was the fact that the documentation changed to explicitly state that in APM, the End method must be called if the Begin method is. The other change was in the thread pool defaults. Remember that in 1.0 the default maximum size of the thread pool was 25 threads. In 1.1 this became 25 threads *per CPU*. So on a four-core machine the default maximum size was $4 \times 25 = 100$ threads.

Before .NET 2.0, then, we had two distinct mechanisms for performing asynchronous work: the Thread class and the thread pool. The Thread class gave you full control but forced you to manage the thread very explicitly. Also, the Thread class, if used for more general purposes, asynchrony could lead to large numbers of threads being created, consuming a lot of resources. The thread pool, on the other hand, allows you to use threads managed by a system component. These threads, with APM, give a good general-purpose programming model, but it is not without issues:

- APM makes your asynchronous code very different from the synchronous version, making it more complex to support.

- Care must be taken with GUI technologies when using callbacks because the callback will generally be running on the wrong thread to interact with the UI.

- You must remember to call the EndXXX method, even when you don't care about results, to allow the asynchronous code to clean up any resources it needs to allocate to perform the work.

Asynchrony in .NET 2.0

Version 2.0 of .NET introduced a number of important innovations in the Async API. One goal was to try to simplify common async tasks that were causing people issues. Another driver behind the changes was the ability of SQL Server to host CLR-based code.

Logical and Physical Separation

SQL Server had very specific requirements of the CLR to allow it to become a host for managed code. It needed to be able to take a lot of control over the CLR execution, such as memory allocation, controlling when and if garbage collection (GC) takes place, what code is and isn't allowed to do, how execution is mapped on to threads, and much more. For SQL Server to control the mapping of execution to threads, it has to control what the CLR views as a thread, which in theory might not be a thread in the unmanaged sense. To make this happen, the CLR team separated the notion of a managed thread from a physical thread. The method call that allowed you to get hold of the thread ID, (AppDomain.GetCurrentThreadId()), was deprecated and a new property of the thread class was created, called ManagedThreadId.

Although this separation is real in API terms, in reality, for all managed code, a managed thread still maps on to an unmanaged thread. However, in theory a hosting process could change that mapping, and so code should not rely on running on the same physical thread over the lifetime of a managed thread. If you call APIs that have native thread affinity (e.g., certain synchronization objects rely on being acquired and released on the same native thread), then the CLR needs to be forced to make the mapping from managed thread to native thread fixed. There are two methods on the Thread class that control this: BeginThreadAffinity and EndThreadAffinity. In normal circumstances you should never need to call these methods; however, the APIs that rely on thread affinity already wrap these calls up internally.

Passing Data into a Thread

We saw that previously, getting data into a thread in an encapsulated way involved creating a class to wrap the thread function. .NET 2.0 introduced a new constructor on the Thread class that took a ParameterizedThreadStart delegate instead of a ThreadStart delegate. The key difference is that the ParameterizedThreadStart delegate takes an object as a parameter:

```
delegate void ParameterizedThreadStart(object obj);
```

Now to get data into the thread you simply use a method with a matching signature (one that returns void and takes a single parameter of type object) and pass the data to the Thread's Start method. Listing 2-11 shows an example of this. Notice that, in the thread function, the code needs to cast the passed parameter to the type it actually needs. If the code is refactored and the code creating the thread changes the type of the parameter object, the compiler will not catch that there is a problem, and the failure will occur at runtime.

Listing 2-11. Using ParameterizedThreadStart

```
void ProcessResults(object obj)
{
    SearchResults results = (SearchResults) obj;

    // use results
    // ...
}

private void OnPerformSearch(object sender, RoutedEventArgs e)
{
    int itemCount;
    SearchResults results = GetResults(1, 50, out itemCount);
    ParameterizedThreadStart proc = ProcessResults;

    Thread t = new Thread(proc);
    t.Start(results);
}
```

Closures

For C# developers, .NET 2.0 saw the introduction of anonymous methods with their associated feature of closure (capturing the state of variables that are in scope). In many ways closures provided the most natural way for many async tasks. For example, the code in Listing 2-11 becomes much simpler with closures, as can be seen in Listing 2-12.

Listing 2-12. Using Closures with the Thread Class

```
private void OnPerformSearch(object sender, RoutedEventArgs e)
{
    int itemCount;
    SearchResults results = GetResults(1, 50, out itemCount);
    ParameterizedThreadStart proc = delegate
                                    {
                                        DisplayResults(results, itemCount);
                                    };

    Thread t = new Thread(proc);
    t.Start();
}
```

Closures also make life simpler when working with APM. As shown in Listing 2-13, it allows a simple model of accessing the right object to call the End method without having to smuggle it across in the async state.

Listing 2-13. Using Closures with APM

```
WebRequest req = WebRequest.Create("http://www.google.com/#q=weather");

AsyncCallback callback = delegate(IAsyncResult iar)
                         {
                             WebResponse resp = req.EndGetResponse(iar);

                             ProcessResponse(resp);
                         };

req.BeginGetResponse(callback, null);
```

SynchronizationContext

As we saw earlier, there are special considerations when using async and UI because UI objects have thread affinity (they must be manipulated on the thread that created them). Because of this, UI frameworks provide mechanisms to specify work that needs to be carried out on the UI thread: Windows Forms has the BeginInvoke method on the Control class; WPF and Silverlight have the dispatcher. The problem is that building a component that uses async internally becomes difficult because how marshalling code on to the UI thread is done is dependent on the framework under which the component is running. The solution to this is to provide a common abstraction over the different underlying mechanisms, and .NET 2.0 introduced one in the form of SynchronizationContext (see Listing 2-14).

Listing 2-14. The SynchronizationContext Class

```
public class SynchronizationContext
{
    public static SynchronizationContext Current { get; }
    public virtual void Post(SendOrPostCallback d, object state);
    public virtual void Send(SendOrPostCallback d, object state);

    // other members omitted for clarity
}
```

The programming model works as follows:

1. On the UI thread, get hold of the SynchronizationContext using the static `Current` property

2. On the background thread, use the SynchronizationContext `Send` or `Post` to perform the work wrapped in the SendOrPostCallback delegate on the UI thread (see Listing 2-15).

Listing 2-15. Using SynchronizationContext

```
private void OnPerformSearch(object sender, EventArgs e)
{
    WebRequest req = WebRequest.Create("http://www.google.com/#q=weather");

    // Must make this call on the UI thread
    uiCtx = SynchronizationContext.Current;

    AsyncCallback callback = delegate(IAsyncResult iar)
                               {
                                   WebResponse resp = req.EndGetResponse(iar);

                                   ProcessResponse(resp);
                               };
    req.BeginGetResponse(callback, null);
}

private SynchronizationContext uiCtx;

private void ProcessResponse(WebResponse resp)
{
    // This code is on the threadpool thread
    StreamReader reader = new StreamReader(resp.GetResponseStream());
    SendOrPostCallback callback = delegate
                                    {
                                        // this runs on the UI thread
                                        UpdateUI(reader.ReadToEnd());
                                        // must Dispose reader here as this code runs async
                                        reader.Dispose();
                                    };
    uiCtx.Post(callback, null);
}
```

Post is a "fire and forget" where the UI thread work is performed asynchronously; Send is synchronous in that the call blocks until the UI thread work has been performed. In general you should prefer Post as it is easier to end up in a deadlock with Send; however, occasionally Post can lead to race conditions if the background thread continues processing, having made assumptions about the state of the UI.

SynchronizationContext brings sanity to performing async work within different frameworks. This is especially important if you want to provide infrastructure that can automate some of the work.

Event-Based Asynchronous Pattern

APM has had some issues in terms of structure of code, UI interaction, and error handling, so in .NET 2.0 Microsoft introduced another async pattern called the Event-Based Asynchronous Pattern (EAP). The idea is that each operation has a pair of members: a method to start the async work and an event that fires when the operation is complete. This pattern was evident on the proxies generated with Add Web Reference in Visual Studio and also on the WebClient class. As an example, let's have a look at WebClient in Listing 2-16.

Listing 2-16. EAP in WebClient

```
private void OnPerformSearch(object sender, RoutedEventArgs e)
{
    WebClient client = new WebClient();

    client.DownloadStringCompleted += ClientOnDownloadDataCompleted;
    client.DownloadStringAsync(new Uri("http://www.google.com/#q=weather"));
}

private void ClientOnDownloadDataCompleted(object sender, DownloadStringCompletedEventArgs e)
{
    UpdateUI(e.Result);
}
```

As Listing 2-16 shows, with EAP, before calling the async method you wire up an event (if you wired up the event afterward, there would be a race condition between the completion and the event wire-up). When the async operation completes, the event is fired. Notice that we can update the UI directly from this event handler, as it uses SynchronizationContext under the covers to fire the event on the UI thread. The result of the async operation is available as the Result property on the event's event arguments.

Error Handling in EAP

Because completion is pushed in the form of an event rather than by making a call, error handling needs to work differently. EAP event arguments derive from AsyncCompletedEventArgs. One of the members of AsyncCompletedEventArgs is an Error property that contains any exception that occurred during the async processing. You should check that this is null before accessing the Result (an exception will be thrown if you access the Result and there was an error). Listing 2-17 shows EAP error handling in action. However, in some ways we've taken a step backwards. As developers, we have moved away from using return codes to signify error because they were so easy to ignore; instead we moved to using exception handling. EAP really takes us back to return codes, in that if the async operation doesn't produce any results, then it's very easy to ignore that an error has occurred.

Listing 2-17. Handling Errors in EAP

```
private void ClientOnDownloadDataCompleted(object sender, DownloadStringCompletedEventArgs e)
{
    if (e.Error == null)
    {
        UpdateUI(e.Result);
    }
    else
    {
        LogError(e.Error);
    }
}
```

EAP and Cancellation

In EAP, APIs are meant to support cancellation via a single `CancelAsync` method or a cancel method associated with each async operation. There is no magic here; however, it is purely a cooperative model in that the API is meant to respond to a request to cancel in the implementation of the async operation. If an operation was cancelled, then the event arguments of the completion event have the Boolean `Cancelled` property (another member of `AsyncCompletedEventArgs`) set to `true`.

Multiple Async Requests

There is a problem with EAP as so far described. What would happen if the async operation were called a second time before the first async operation completes? When the completion event fires, how do you know which operation the event relates to? If an EAP API supports multiple invocations, then it should have an overload of the async operation that takes an object that can be used for correlation (matching requests and their results). So, for example, WebClient has another version of `DownloadStringAsync` with the following signature:

```
void DownloadStrinAsync(Uri address, Object userToken);
```

Whatever gets passed as the `userToken` gets set on the event arguments as the `UserState` property when the associated completion event fires. This allows you to match the async operation to its completion.

If an EAP API does not support multiple concurrent invocations, then it should throw an exception if invoked again while an existing async operation is in progress.

EAP fixes one of the issues with APM by automatically marshalling the completion to the UI thread, and now gives us a standard model for cancellation. However, you still have very different code in async and synchronous invocations, and error handling is not ideal.

Minor Changes in .NET 3.5

.NET 3.0 was a release of libraries (WCF, WPF, and WF) with no changes to the async API or infrastructure, so the next change in the .NET async world was .NET 3.5. This shipped with a service pack for CLR 2.0 that, among other things, changed the thread pool heuristics. In terms of the framework class library, however, there were no significant changes to how the async API looked. There was one .NET 3.5 feature that has changed the way async code is now commonly written. Lambda expressions are very often used to define delegates used for async work. Also, the introduction of a rich set of generic delegate types generally removed the need to create your own delegate types to be invoked asynchronously.

Lambda Expressions

.NET 2.0 introduced anonymous delegates and closure. However, it turned out that we were commonly telling the compiler things it could already work out for itself. Consider the following anonymous delegate:

```
Predicate<Person> test = delegate(Person p)
                         {
                             return p.Age >= 18;
                         };
```

Let's start removing the things the compiler could work out. To begin with, the delegate keyword is superfluous as the compiler knows Predicate<T> is a delegate type:

```
Predicate<Person> test = (Person p)
                         {
                             return p.Age >= 18;
                         };
```

We don't need to specify the type of p as the compiler knows that the parameter for Predicate<Person> is a Person:

```
Predicate<Person> test = (p)
                         {
                             return p.Age >= 18;
                         };
```

Predicate<T> returns a Boolean and the return expression evaluates to a Boolean. There is just one statement in the body, so it must be the return. So let's omit the return keyword:

```
Predicate<Person> test = (p)
                         {
                             p.Age >= 18;
                         };
```

We only have one statement—we surely don't need braces:

```
Predicate<Person> test = (p) p.Age >= 18;
```

There is only one parameter, so we could omit the parentheses:

```
Predicate<Person> test = p p.Age >= 18;
```

Last, we do need to separate the parameter from the lambda body, so we use the symbol =>:

```
Predicate<Person> test = p => p.Age >= 18;
```

This is a lambda expression. There are other, more complex forms of lambda expression: multiple or no parameters require the use of parentheses and multiple statements in the body require the use of braces and an explicit return.

Why are lambda expressions often used to model asynchronous work? There are two main reasons: first, closure simplifies getting data into the asynchronous operation; and second, quite often the actual code that needs to run asynchronously is quite brief (in terms of syntax), so creating a whole new method for this clouds readability.

Thread Pool Heuristics in .NET 3.5

Remember from .NET 1.1 that the default maximum number of threads in the thread pool was 25 per core, and the algorithm for adding new threads was to pause for half a second, waiting for a thread to become idle, before adding a new thread into the pool. .NET 3.5 changed the maximum number of threads in the thread pool to 250 per core. On, say, an eight-core machine, this gives a maximum size to the thread pool of 2,000 threads. Each thread will consume 1MB of stack space, so simply creating these threads will consume 2GB of data. This seems to fly in the face of one of the purposes of using thread pools: namely, to constrain the number of threads—2,000 is not much of a constraint. However, the algorithm to add more threads to the thread pool was also changed to increase the wait time exponentially as the number of threads increases.

Why did the CLR team feel it necessary to increase the maximum number of threads tenfold? To understand this change, we need to look at what problem they were trying to solve. Consider the following code:

```
Func<SearchResults> resultRetriever = GetResults;

IAsyncResult iar = resultRetriever.BeginInvoke(null, null);

ReportDefaults defaults = GetReportDefaults();

SearchResults results = resultRetriever.EndInvoke(iar);
```

This code seems quite innocuous. However, what if this code were invoked from a thread pool thread? Remember that EndInvoke will block until the async method completes. Now, what if all threads in the thread pool were running this code? The async method would never start because no thread was available and no thread would ever become available, because they are all waiting for this code to finish. It has essentially deadlocked the thread pool. You might argue that this is a heavily contrived problem; that people generally don't spawn thread pool work from thread pool threads. And in many cases that is true—unless all of your code is running within a framework that always runs on thread pool threads like ASP.NET. Thread pool deadlock was an issue that people were experiencing in the field, so the .NET team decided to solve it by making sure another thread could always be added to break the deadlock—hence the tenfold increase in the maximum number of threads in the thread pool.

Big Changes in .NET 4.0

Part of the .NET 4.0 release was the Parallel Framework Extensions (PFx). The goal of this library was to provide support for parallelizing algorithms, but along the way it delivered an entirely new model for async processing in .NET. We are going to spend some time discussing the new API in the next few chapters. However, using this library potentially creates a lot of thread pool work to which the existing structure of the thread pool was poorly suited so let's take a look at what was changed behind the scenes to enable this new API to work efficiently.

Remodeling the Thread Pool Queue

Prior to .NET 4.0 the thread pool queue was a linked list of work items. Imagine lots of cores are generating lots of work items. There are two issues that are going to become apparent:

1. The thread pool will become a large data structure with a very large number of references. This is an expensive for the Garbage Collector to deal with during its mark phase.

2. A linked list is a terrible data structure for concurrent manipulation. Processing across the cores would have to be serialized as it updated the queue (see Figure 2-3).

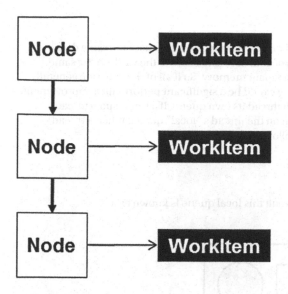

Figure 2-3. *Threadpool queue prior to .NET 4.0*

In .NET 4.0 the thread pool queue was redesigned with the new requirements of PFx in mind. Instead of using a simple linked list, the queue was built with arrays of work items with the arrays connected into a linked list. This means that there are a lot fewer references, and that adding and moving work items often will simply involve array index manipulation, which is a much cheaper way to make thread safe (see Figure 2-4).

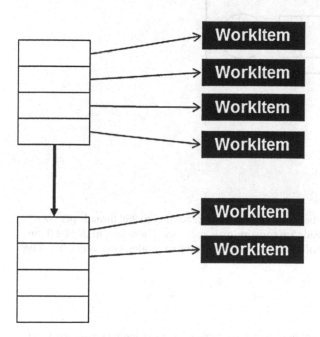

Figure 2-4. *The .NET 4.0 threadpool queue*

Work-Stealing Queues

As we explained in Chapter 1, processors have caches. If you need to spawn async work that uses the same data that you have been processing, it would be most efficient in terms of data access to execute the work on the same processor, as then the data may well be read from cache rather than main memory. So if all of the cores are generally busy, then trying to get related work on to the same core potentially would be a significant performance improvement. The internals of the thread pool have been remodeled to give each thread its own queue. If a thread pool thread creates async work using the new API, then by default it will be put on the thread's "local" queue. When a thread finishes its current work item, it looks for new work items in the following order:

1. It looks on its local queue.

2. It looks on the global queue.

3. It steals work from other threads' local queues. As a result this local queue is known as a work-stealing queue (see Figure 2-5).

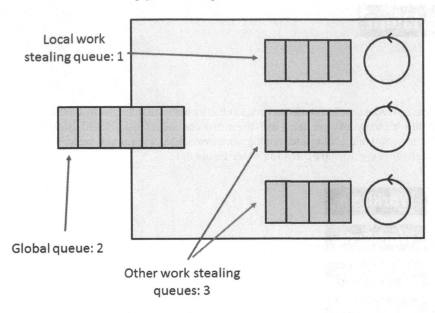

Figure 2-5. *Work-stealing queues in .NET 4.0*

Thread Pool Heuristics in .NET 4.0

As mentioned earlier, .NET 3.5 changed the maximum number of threads in the thread pool to 250 threads per core. However, we also noted that the main resource that the threads are consuming is memory. Therefore, in .NET 4.0 the maximum number of threads is determined by the amount of memory available (on most modern machines it will be 1,023 worker threads and 1,000 I/O threads).

Summary

As you have seen, the async API in .NET has seen quite a number of changes since version 1.0. Each change has tried either to make it simpler to write async code or address specific issues developers have experienced in the field. In the next few chapters you will see the full extent of the changes introduced in .NET 4.0 and 4.5. Along the way, you will also see that .NET has finally solved many of the issues in moving from synchronous to asynchronous code.

CHAPTER 3

Tasks

With the release of .NET 4.0, Microsoft introduced yet another API for building asynchronous applications: the Task Parallel Library (TPL). The key difference between TPL and previous APIs is that TPL attempts to unify the asynchronous programming model. It provides a single type called a Task to represent all asynchronous operations. In addition to Tasks, TPL introduces standardized cancellation and reporting of progress—traditionally something developers rolled for themselves. This chapter will examine these new constructs and how to take advantage of them to perform asynchronous operations.

What Is a Task?

A Task represents an asynchronous unit of work. This work could be, for example, to calculate a value based on some inputs, or it could represent a request to a network-based resource. It is important to recognize that this single item, called a Task, simply represents an activity that is ongoing while the main thread of execution continues. Tasks are not some new, magical way of performing asynchronous work; they are an abstraction over the underlying mechanics we discussed in Chapter 2. We can generally consider tasks to be either compute based, and thus bound to some kind of OS thread, or I/O based, and thus modeled around I/O completion ports. But as you will discover in later chapters, they really can represent anything running asynchronously.

Creating a Compute-Based Task

When learning any new language or technology, there is a style of program you just have to build as part of your journey to greater things—yes, you guessed it, asynchronous "Hello World."

The code in Listing 3-1 is very similar to the thread examples in Chapter 2. When creating the Task object, a method is supplied that matches the signature of the Action delegate. This delegate represents the work to run asynchronously. The asynchronous operation will be deemed to have completed when the Speak method completes. You may feel that this trivial example is not worth running; however, please do so as it may not do what you expect. For best effect, run it outside the debugger with CTRL+F5.

Listing 3-1. Asynchronous Hello World

```
class Program
{
  static void Main(string[] args){
    Task t = new Task(Speak);
    t.Start();
  }
```

```
  private static void Speak() {
     Console.WriteLine("Hello World");
   }
}
```

If it is your lucky day, "Hello World" will appear on your screen. But run the code a few times and you may well get different results; for most people absolutely nothing will be displayed. We hope you have figured out the reason: compute-based tasks run on background threads and, as explained in Chapter 2, background threads do not keep the process alive. By the time the task is about to run, the main thread has already terminated and, hence, the process will terminate as well. *This is an important point to remember, as when it comes to your own code, running tasks will simply be aborted if no foreground threads are executing.*

So how can you bring some determinism to this chaotic example? What you need to do is to keep the main thread alive until the asynchronous work has completed. A simple `Console.ReadLine();` would suffice, but a more elegant way would be to block the main thread, wait for the task to complete, and then exit (see Listing 3-2).

Listing 3-2. Asynchronous Guaranteed "Hello World"

```
static void Main(string[] args){
    Task t = new Task(Speak);
    t.Start();
    Console.WriteLine("Waiting for completion");
    t.Wait();
    Console.WriteLine("All Done");
  }
```

So far we have created and started tasks as two separate statements. It turns out this is not typical for compute-based tasks. We can actually create and start the task as a single statement, replacing

```
Task t = new Task(Speak);
t.Start();
```

with

```
Task t = Task.Factory.StartNew(Speak);
```

In .NET 4.5 it is made even simpler: if you just require a task configured using some predefined defaults, you can use `Task t = Task.Run(Speak)`. For the remainder of this chapter we will favor the factory-style approach as it will work in .NET 4.0 and 4.5. It also provides more flexibility to configure the task's behavior, something you will use in subsequent chapters.

As mentioned earlier, compute-based tasks run on OS threads, so where does this thread come from? There are two obvious possibilities: either a new thread is created, or you schedule the work to run on a reusable thread pool thread. As you will see in later chapters, to make your application fast and fluid and scalable, you may be creating lots of small, asynchronous units of work. It is therefore logical that, by default, compute-based tasks are assigned to thread pool threads. To confirm this, you can run the code in Listing 3-3.

Listing 3-3. Thread Pool Thread

```
static void Main(string[] args)
{
  Task.Factory.StartNew(WhatTypeOfThreadAmI).Wait();
}
private static void WhatTypeOfThreadAmI()
```

```
{
  Console.WriteLine("I'm a {0} thread" ,
                    Thread.CurrentThread.IsThreadPoolThread ? "Thread Pool" : "Custom");
}
```

So what if you want to have a long-running, asynchronous operation? As mentioned in Chapter 2, using a thread pool for this purpose would be considered an abuse of the thread pool. However, the creators of the TPL wanted to ensure that users have a uniform API irrespective of the type of asynchronous operation; you don't want to have to resort to old-style APIs.

When you create a task, in addition to supplying the Action delegate, hints can be supplied on how to create the task. These hints are known as task creation options and are represented as the enumeration type TaskCreationOptions. Listing 3-4 shows the creation of a long-running task. Long-running tasks will run on their own, newly created, dedicated thread, which is destroyed once the task has completed.

Listing 3-4. Long-Running Task

```
static void Main(string[] args)
{
  Task.Factory
      .StartNew(WhatTypeOfThreadAmI, TaskCreationOptions.LongRunning)
      .Wait();
}
```

There are many more creation options, and the options can be combined using the | operator. We will discuss the other options as required throughout this book.

Passing Data into a Task

So far you have simply created a task and assumed the method has all the necessary information to perform its function. Just as you generalize methods by adding parameters, you will want to do the same for tasks. You have seen that the StartNew method takes an Action delegate; this delegate takes no inputs and returns void. Consider the code in Listing 3-5.

Listing 3-5. Import Method: No Inputs, No Outputs

```
public class DataImporter
{
  public void Import()
  {
    // Import files from which directory ?
  }
}
```

The Import method takes no inputs and outputs and so, from what you have read so far, it could be executed as a Task body. But what if we want to pass the directory to import? It turns out there is another delegate type that the StartNew and Run method will take to represent the task body, Action<object>. This allows you to supply a method that takes a single parameter of type object (Listing 3-6).

Listing 3-6. Task Body with a Parameter

```
public class DataImporter
{
   public void Import(object o)
   {
     string directory = (string) o;
     . . .
   }
}

class Program
{
  private static void Main(string[] args)
  {
    var importer = new DataImporter();
    Task.Factory.StartNew(importer.Import,@"C:\data");
  }
}
```

This approach does seem rather restrictive and smelly, but is certainly one of the most efficient ways of passing data to a task body. Another possibility is to have the data for the Import method supplied via instance fields of the DataImporter class (Listing 3-7).

Listing 3-7. Task Inputs Supplied via Instance Fields

```
public class DataImporter
{
   private readonly string directory;
   public DataImporter(string directory)
   {
     this.directory = directory;
   }
   public void Import()
   {
     // Import files from this.directory
   }
 }
```

This would then allow use of the simple Task.Factory.StartNew(importer.Import) with an Action delegate. However, this is not always convenient, as a single DataImporter may want to allow different import sources over time. Fortunately, .NET 2.0 and later versions support closures via anonymous methods (and lambdas in .NET 3.5). This allows you to make use of the compiler to build a class that contains all the items you want to flow into the task, plus a small method that ultimately calls the asynchronous functionality (Listing 3-8).

Listing 3-8.

```
public class DataImporter
 {
   public void Import(string directory)
   {
     // Import files from this.directory
   }
```

```
}
class Program
{
  private static void Main(string[] args)
  {
    var importer = new DataImporter();
    string importDirectory = @"C:\data";

    Task.Factory.StartNew(() => importer.Import(importDirectory));    }
}
```

CLOSURES

During compilation, the compiler builds a class that contains an instance method containing the code used as part of the lambda, and public fields to hold any data the instance method requires from the outer scope. The following is an example of what the class may look like.

```
public class ImportClosure
{
  public string importDirectory;
  public DataImporter importer;

  public void ClosureMethod()
  {
    importer.Import(importDirectory);
  }
}
```

This class is instantiated when the first of the local variables used in the lambda is declared. The local variables are now no longer accessed directly via the stack, but instead via a stack-based reference to an instance of this generated class. The compiler then builds a delegate that matches the Action delegate pointing to the class instance method ClosureMethod. This method will obviously have access to the instance fields, and thus have access to the outer scope variables. The following code shows an example of how the C# compiler will rewrite Main to achieve the closure.

```
private static void Main(string[] args)
{
        var closure = new ImportClosure();
        closure.importer = new DataImporter();
        closure.importDirectory = @"C:\data";

        Task.Factory.StartNew(closure.ClosureMethod);
}
```

Closures make passing data into a task very simple, and they are therefore the norm for passing data into tasks. They are not as efficient as passing in a single object, but they keep the code simple and easy to understand.

Dangers of Closures

Closures provide a very convenient mechanism to flow local data into delegates. When the delegate is invoked synchronously there is no great need to understand what is going on under the covers; however, the same is not true for asynchronous invocation of the delegate. If you are not aware of the mechanics of closures, please do read the previous sidebar before proceeding. Let us first examine the following piece of code in Listing 3-9.

Listing 3-9.

```
for (int i = 0; i < 10; i++)
{
  Task.Factory.StartNew(() => Console.WriteLine(i));
}
Console.ReadLine();
```

The obvious intent of the code is to print out all the numbers from 0 to 9. They won't necessarily be in order, because you are simply issuing work to the thread pool infrastructure, and thus you have no control over the order in which the tasks will run. Run the code and you will perhaps find a much more unexpected result. You will most likely have seen ten 10s on the screen. This seems very strange, as you may well have expected only to see a set of unique values from 0 to 9; but instead you see the same value printed out, and not even one of the expected values. The cause lies with the closure; the compiler will have had to capture local variable i and place it into a compiler-generated object on the heap, so that it can be referenced inside each of the lambdas. The question is, when does it create this object? As the local variable i is declared outside the loop body, the capture point is, therefore, also outside the loop body. This results in a single object being created to hold the value of i, and this single object is used to store each increment of i. Because each task will share the same closure object, by the time the first task runs the main thread will have completed the loop, and hence i is now 10. Therefore, all 10 tasks that have been created will print out the same value of i, namely 10.

To fix this problem, you need to change the point of capture. The compiler only captures the variables used inside the closure, and it delays the capture based on the scope of the variable declaration. Therefore, instead of capturing I, which is defined once for the lifetime of the loop, you need to introduce a new local variable, defined inside the loop body, and use this variable inside the closure. As a result, the variable is captured separately for iteration of the loop.

Running the code in Listing 3-10 will now produce all values from 0 to 9; as for the order, well, that's unknown and part of the fun of asynchronous programming. As stated earlier, closures are the most natural way to flow information into a task, but just keep in mind the mechanics of how they work, as this is a common area for bugs and they are not always as obvious to spot as this example.

Listing 3-10. Working Capture

```
for (int i = 0; i < 10; i++)
{
    int toCaptureI = i;
    Task.Factory.StartNew(() => Console.WriteLine(toCaptureI));
}
Console.ReadLine();
```

```
C# 5 CHANGE OF BEHAVIOR
```

This classic gotcha with asynchronous delegates has been addressed to some degree with C# 5. The piece of code defined in this sidebar when compiled using the C# 4 compiler will result most likely in all 9s. However, compiling it under C# 5 will produce all values 0 to 9, although in an unknown order. The reason for this is that in the case of foreach, the compiler team has moved the point of capture to inside the loop automatically. Personally I don't like the fact that a foreach loop behaves differently than a for loop; also, it introduces inefficiency when we are not invoking the delegate asynchronously.

```
foreach( List<int> i in new List<int> {0,1,2,3,4,5,6,7,8,9} )
{
    Task.Factory.StartNew(() => Console.WriteLine(i));
}
Console.ReadLine();
```

Returning Data from a Task

Up to now we have just examined the notion of passing data into a task, but tasks can also be used to return results. Have you ever wondered what the chances are of winning a lottery that has 49,000 possible numbers of which you have to pick the 600 that are selected on the given night? You probably already know your chances of winning are slim, but Listing 3-11 contains partial implementation of the code necessary to calculate the odds.

Listing 3-11. ACME Lottery—The Odds Are with Us

```
BigInteger n = 49000;
BigInteger r = 600;

BigInteger part1 = Factorial(n);e
BigInteger part2 = Factorial(n - r);
BigInteger part3 = Factorial(r);

BigInteger chances = part1/(part2*part3);
Console.WriteLine(chances);
```

Executing this code sequentially will only use one core; however, since the calculation of part1, part2, and part3 are all independent of one another, you could potentially speed things up if you calculated those different parts as separate tasks. When all the results are in, do the simple divide-and-multiply operation—TPL is well suited for this kind of problem. Listing 3-12 shows the refactored code that takes advantage of TPL to potentially calculate all the parts at the same time.

Listing 3-12.

```
BigInteger n = 49000;
BigInteger r = 600;

Task<BigInteger> part1 = Task.Factory.StartNew<BigInteger>(() => Factorial(n));
Task<BigInteger> part2 = Task.Factory.StartNew<BigInteger>(() => Factorial(n-r));
Task<BigInteger> part3 = Task.Factory.StartNew<BigInteger>(() => Factorial(r));
```

```
BigInteger chances = part1.Result/(part2.Result*part3.Result);
Console.WriteLine(chances);
```

The code in Listing 3-12 is using a different form of StartNew. This form of StartNew has the following method signature:

```
public Task<TResult> StartNew<TResult>(Func<TResult> function);
```

The generic argument TResult identifies the type of result the task will return. For the task to be able to return a result of this type, the signature of the delegate used to represent the task body will also need an identical return type. So instead of supplying an Action delegate, now you use a Func<TResult>. Furthermore, StartNew<T> now returns not a Task but a Task<TResult>. This has an additional property called Result, which is used to obtain the result of the asynchronous operation. This property can only yield the result once the asynchronous operation has completed, so making a call to this property will block the calling thread until the asynchronous operation has completed. In Listing 3-12 three tasks will be created, each performing its part of the calculation in parallel. Meanwhile, the main thread moves forward to attempt to calculate the overall chance by combining the results from all the parts. As each part result is required by the main thread, it blocks until that result is available before evaluating the next part of the expression.

One key advantage TPL has over previous asynchronous APIs is that the asynchronous code in Listing 3-12 is not radically different in structure from the sequential code in Listing 3-11. This is in general contrast to asynchronous APIs of the past, which often required radical change to the structure of the algorithm, thus often overcomplicating the code. This was one of the key API guidelines.

FUTURES

In the very early days of the TPL Community Technology Preview (CTP), there was no Task<T>; it was called Future<T>. Personally I loved this as it added a certain elegance to your code. It allowed me to declare a variable here that would have a value at some point in the future. In the end, though, the design team rejected it in favor of general consistency.

Creating I/O-Based Tasks

So far we have only discussed compute-based asynchronous operations. When code executes, it clearly use CPU resources, but it often requires other resources too. These could take the form of I/O (e.g. disk); often code is written to utilize one of these resources and not proceed until the resource has completed the requested operation. Having user interface threads block for some I/O, even for just 250 milliseconds, can cause your application to feel annoyingly unresponsive. It therefore makes sense to request the resource asynchronously. Ask the resource for what you want, but don't wait for it to complete. While the resource is completing the request, use the CPU to keep the UI responsive. Once the resource has signaled it is done, use the CPU to obtain and process the response. It's not just in the world of UI applications where this is applicable. Consider an application wishing to make two independent web service calls; it makes sense to have it make the calls asynchronously rather than wait for the first call to complete before initiating the second. Once both results are in, then it can continue processing. In effect, you want to overlap as many requests as you can to take advantage of all resources available. Consider the code in Listing 3-13.

Listing 3-13.

```
static void Main(string[] args)
{
  string download = DownloadWebPage("http://www.rocksolidknowledge.com/5SecondPage.aspx");
  Console.WriteLine(download);
}

private static string DownloadWebPage(string url)
{
  WebRequest request = WebRequest.Create(url);
  WebResponse response = request.GetResponse();
  var reader = new StreamReader(response.GetResponseStream());
  {
    // this will return the content of the web page
    return reader.ReadToEnd();
  }
}
```

Executing the code produces a flashing cursor, leaving the user wondering if this is actually doing something or just hung. The main thread is blocking on the reader.ReadToEnd() until all the data arrives from the web site. What you would rather do is keep the main thread active and doing something to keep the user happy. With what you have learned so far you could easily fix this, with the creation of a DownloadPageAsync method (see Listing 3-14).

___

■ **Note**   The convention for .NET 4.5 is that asynchronous methods are identified with the suffix Async.

___

Listing 3-14.

```
private static Task<string> DownloadWebPageAsync(string url)
{
  return Task.Factory.StartNew(() => DownloadWebPage(url));
}
```

Now that you have an asynchronous version of DownloadWebPage, you can modify Main to take advantage of its asynchronous nature (Listing 3-15).

Listing 3-15.

```
Task<string> downloadTask = DownloadWebPageAsync("http://www.rocksolidknowledge.com/5SecondPage.aspx");

while (!downloadTask.IsCompleted)
{
  Console.Write(".");
  Thread.Sleep(250);
}
Console.WriteLine(downloadTask.Result);
```

The IsCompleted property on the task allows you to determine if the asynchronous operation has completed. While it is still completing, the task keeps the user happy by displaying dots; once it completes, you request the result of the task. Since you know the task has now completed, the result will immediately be displayed to the user.

This all looks good until you start to analyze the cost of achieving this asynchronous operation. In effect you now have two threads running for the duration of the download: the one running inside Main and the one attempting to get the response from the web site. The thread responsible for getting the content is spending most of its time blocked on the line reader.ReadToEnd(); you have taken a thread from the thread pool, denying others the chance to use it, only for it to spend most of the time idle.

A far more efficient approach would be to create a thread to request the data from the web server, give the thread back to the thread pool, and when the data arrives, obtain a thread from the pool to process the results. To achieve this prior to .NET 4.5, the I/O methods in the library use the APM idiom seen in Chapter 2:

```
public virtual IAsyncResult BeginGetResponse(AsyncCallback callback, object state);
public virtual WebResponse EndGetResponse(IAsyncResult asyncResult);
```

You could write your download code using this API, but you would actually like to continue to keep the DownloadAsync method returning a Task<string>—remember, the general goal of TPL is to represent every asynchronous operation as a task. To enable this, there is yet another way to create a task called Task.Factory. FromAsync. This method takes an IAsyncResult to represent the lifetime of the task and a callback method to call when the asynchronous operation has completed. In the case where the task being created is a Task<T>, this method has the role of producing the result for the task, so it will return a value of type T. The code in Listing 3-16 is making more efficient use of the thread pool by only consuming a thread when data arrives back from the web site. No threads are consumed from the pool while you are waiting for a response.

Listing 3-16.

```
private static Task<string> BetterDownloadWebPageAsync(string url)
{
    WebRequest request = WebRequest.Create(url);
    IAsyncResult ar = request.BeginGetResponse(null, null);

    Task<string> downloadTask =
        Task.Factory
        .FromAsync<string>(ar, iar =>
        {
            using (WebResponse response = request.EndGetResponse(iar))
            {
                using (var reader = new StreamReader(response.GetResponseStream()))
                {
                    return reader.ReadToEnd();
                }
            }
        });

        return downloadTask;
}
```

Although this approach feels far more complex than simply wrapping a piece of long-running code in a task, it is a far more efficient use of the thread pool, keeping the number of threads as small as possible for the same level of concurrency. This is advantageous because threads are not free to create and consume memory.

To simplify things further, in .NET 4.5 the I/O libraries have gotten some love and now offer asynchronous calls that return tasks, removing the need to wrap up old-style APIs with `FromAsync`:

```
public virtual Task<WebResponse> GetResponseAsync();
```

We will take advantage of this method later in the chapter, in the section "Chaining Tasks (Continuations)".

Error Handling

So far we haven't considered what happens if things don't go as expected. What should happen when you execute code in the context of a task that throws an unhandled exception? Having the process continue oblivious to this unhandled exception will, we hope, leave a bad taste in your mouth; after all you don't know what state the overall process is in (have any shared data structures been left in an inconsistent state?).

It is therefore hard to say if it is safe for the process to continue. In .NET 1.1 unhandled exceptions on a custom thread just caused the thread to die. This created a problem with regard to the finalizer thread, in that it could terminate because an objects finalizer threw an unhandled exception, resulting in no more finalization taking place, and causing a long-term memory leak. To fix this in .NET 2.0+, the behavior was changed so that an unhandled exception on any thread results in process termination. While this might initially feel bad—no one likes to see their process crash—it encourages programmers to fix the problem rather than crossing their fingers and hoping that the process limps on to better and greater things.

Regular .NET methods are synchronous calls, whereas tasks allow the calling of a method asynchronously. A method could produce a valid result or an exception, and so can be the case for a task. When a task completes, it can complete in one of the following states:

- Ran to Completion
- Canceled
- Faulted

Ran to Completion, as you would expect, means the root method of the task ended gracefully. Faulted implies that the task ended through an unhandled exception. We will discuss cancellation in the section of that name, later in this chapter.

The good news is that unlike raw threads, just because a task ends through an unhandled exception, it doesn't mean the process is terminated—you will get the opportunity to see and handle the error. The most natural way to handle exceptions is to use try/catch. Placing the try/catch just around the task creation is obviously not going to cut it, as any exception resulting from the task body won't happen until after the task has started. Delivering the exception on the thread that created the task at the point in time when the exception occurred is also not practical (or possible), as it would make it very hard to decide where to place the try/catch. The most logical place to deliver the exception is when another thread is waiting for the outcome of a given task—in other words, when a call is made to `Task.Wait`, `Task.WaitAll`, or `Task.Result` (see Listing 3-17).

Listing 3-17.

```
Task task = Task.Factory.StartNew(() => Import(@"C:\data\2.xml"));

 try
 {
    task.Wait();
 }
catch (Exception e)
```

```
{
  Console.WriteLine("Error : {0}",e);
}
private static void Import(string fullName)
{
  XElement doc = XElement.Load(fullName);
  // process xml document
}
```

In Listing 3-17, even if the Import method fails before we hit the Wait method call, the task object will hold onto the exception and re-throw it when the call to Wait is made. This all looks nice and simple—however, there is a twist. Let us say that the 2.xml file contains invalid XML. It would therefore seem logical that the type of exception being delivered would be an XML-based one. In fact what you will get is an AggregateException. This seems a little odd at first, since AggregateException implies many exceptions, and in this situation it looks like you could only get one exception. As you will see later in this chapter, tasks can be arranged in a parent/child relationship, whereby a parent won't be deemed completed until all its children have been. If one or many of those children complete in a faulted state, that information needs to propagated, and for that reason TPL will always wrap task-based exceptions with an AggregateException.

The role of an exception is twofold: first, to provide some error message that is normally understood by a developer; and second, to indicate the type of fault so that we construct the appropriate catch blocks to handle or recover from the error. Catching an AggregateException is probably not detailed enough to find the root cause of the error, so you need to crack open the aggregate exception and examine the underlying exceptions. The underlying exceptions are found via the InnerExceptions property on the AggregateException (Listing 3-18).

Listing 3-18.

```
try
{
  task.Wait();
}
catch (AggregateException errors)
{
  foreach (Exception error in errors.InnerExceptions)
  {
    Console.WriteLine("{0} : {1}" , error.GetType().Name,error.Message);
  }
}
```

This is somewhat cumbersome, made even more so in that it is possible that a given inner exception can also be an aggregate exception requiring another level of iteration. Thankfully the AggregateException type has a Flatten method that will provide a new AggregateException that contains a single, flat set of inner exceptions (Listing 3-19).

Listing 3-19.

```
catch (AggregateException errors)
{              {
  foreach (Exception error in errors.Flatten().InnerExceptions)
  {
    Console.WriteLine("{0} : {1}" , error.GetType().Name,error.Message);
  }
}
```

As explained earlier, the role of an exception handler is to look at the exception type and decide how to recover from the error. In the case of AggregateException errors, that would mean iterating through all the inner exceptions, examining each type in turn, deciding if it can be handled, and if not re-throw it and possibly any others that can't be handled.

This would be extremely tedious. So there is a method on the AggregateException called Handle, which reduces the amount of code you would need to write, and perhaps gets closer to the traditional try/catch block. The Handle method takes a predicate style delegate that is given each exception in turn from the AggregateException. The delegate should return true if the exception has been handled and false if the exception can't be handled. At the end of processing all the exceptions, any exceptions not handled will be re-thrown again as part of a new AggregateException containing just those exceptions deemed to have been unhandled.

Listing 3-20 shows code that catches an AggregateException and then only ignores the exception if it contains XML-based exceptions. Any other type of exception contained inside the AggregateException will be re-thrown as part of a new AggregateException. In essence the developer considers XML-based errors as not fatal, and is happy for the application to continue.

Listing 3-20.

```
catch (AggregateException errors)
{
    errors.Handle(IgnoreXmlErrors);
}
private static bool IgnoreXmlErrors(Exception arg)
{
    return (arg.GetType() == typeof (XmlException));
}
```

Ignoring Errors

There will be many scenarios where waiting on a task is not appropriate. The main purpose of asynchronous programming, after all, is to start asynchronous operations while letting the initiating thread move onto other things. This raises the question: What if I don't wait for a task? What if I simply want to fire and forget? For example, an application may launch a task at regular intervals to attempt to update a cache in the background. The application may not care if the task fails occasionally, as this will just result in a cache miss when a user attempts to fetch some data that failed to be loaded into the cache. So while the application developer may feel it's okay to just ignore any failures from the cache update task, is it really safe to do so? It turns out this will depend on the completion status of the task and the version of the .NET framework it is running under.

.NET 4.0

Under .NET 4.0, if a task ends in a faulted state you have an obligation to inspect the error, known as observing the error. Failure to do so can result in your application being forced to shut down at what appears to be some random time in the future. This behavior results from the fact that the TPL team decided it was bad practice simply to ignore errors (and I would agree). After all, exceptions are not thrown just for fun—they indicate some unexpected failure. The unexpected failure could result in your application being in an invalid state, and further execution could lead to further failures and corruption. The purpose of catching exceptions is to ensure, before processing continues, that the process remains in a valid state. Therefore, simply ignoring exceptions seems a very bad idea.

The question is, how does TPL know that you have decided to ignore the error? While you have a live reference to a task object, you have a chance to observe the error. But once you no longer have such a live reference, clearly you can't observe any error associated with the task. Once there are no more live references to the task object, it becomes a candidate for garbage collection. The task object contains a finalizer; when it is created, it is registered on the finalization queue. When the garbage collector decides to throw out the task, it sees it has a registration on the finalization queue and therefore can't remove it from memory just yet; instead it places the task on the reachable queue. The finalization thread eventually runs the finalizer for the task and, since no attempt has been made to observe the error, the error is rethrown on the finalization thread, thus ending the process.

The fact that this behavior is based on garbage-collection triggering means that there can be a long period of time between the task ending in a faulted state and the application terminating, making it very difficult to debug and sometimes not seen until the code hits production.

This isn't quite the full picture. There is one final opportunity available to handle the exception: by registering for the UnobservedTaskException event declared on the task scheduler class. Before a task's finalizer re-throws the exception, it fires this event, and any subscribers get a final chance to say they have observed the exception and it is safe to keep the process alive. This is indicated by calling the SetObserved method on the event arguments. Failure to do so will result in the exception being rethrown. Listing 3-21 shows code registering for the UnobservedTaskException event.

Listing 3-21.

```
TaskScheduler.UnobservedTaskException += HandleTaskExceptions;
. . .
static void HandleTaskExceptions(object sender, UnobservedTaskExceptionEventArgs e)
{
    Console.WriteLine(sender is Task);
    foreach (Exception error in e.Exception.InnerExceptions)
    {
        Console.WriteLine(error.Message);
    }
    e.SetObserved();
}
```

While this satisfies the need not to have to wait on a task, it still means that an error may or may not be seen until some random point in the future, or in some cases never. Additionally, in the meantime code has been executing against a possible invalid state. Exceptions are generally best handled as close to the source as possible. This event handler is really only useful for logging, and possibly for highlighting to a developer that they should be observing the task for errors.

.NET 4.5

There was a backlash in the developer community about this general "random error notification" mechanism. In response to this criticism, Microsoft thus decided to change the behavior in .NET 4.5. The fix was simple: don't re-throw the exception on the finalization thread. Offer it to any UnobservedTaskException subscriber, but don't ever re-throw it on the finalization thread. In other words, if the programmer doesn't take any action to handle errors, TPL will just simply swallow the error.

Run the code in Listing 3-22 under .NET 4.5 and the application will run forever; under 4.0 it will terminate at some point (for best results run under Release, using CTRL+F5). Try changing the infinite while loop to a simple Console.ReadLine() and you will see that it probably never crashes.

Listing 3-22.

```
Task t = Task.Factory.StartNew(() => { throw new Exception("Boom!"); });
t = null;
var objects = new object[10000];
int i=0;
```

```
while (true)
{
    objects[i++] = new object();
    i = i % objects.Length;
}
```

If you have .NET 4.5 installed, you can't run the application under 4.0. What you can do, though, is request that 4.5 use the 4.0 behavior by supplying an application configuration file that contains the following:

```
<configuration>
  <runtime>
    <ThrowUnobservedTaskExceptions enabled="true"/>
  </runtime>
</configuration>
```

When running Listing 3-22 in .NET 4.0 and 4.5, you will notice that the Boom exception is never delivered in 4.5 but is in 4.0. The question begs to be asked: is this progress? In the view of the present authors: far from it. This new approach allows the less well-informed developer to spin up tasks in blissful ignorance of the fact that some of them could be failing. At least with the .NET 4.0 approach, they would eventually be punished. My personal preference is to ensure that your application deals with the exception as soon as possible. One option is to ensure that all fire-and-forget–style tasks have a body that contains a top-level try/catch block. Any expected exceptions will be dealt with, unexpected exceptions logged, and the application safely recycled.

Designing Task-Based APIs

Designing a sequential API is pretty much the bread and butter of any seasoned .NET developer. Building an asynchronous API, however, can require a bit more thought. Let us first consider the synchronous API shown in Listing 3-23.

Listing 3-23.

```
public interface IImport
{
    void ImportXmlFiles(string dataDirectory);
}
```

Listing 3-24 shows the asynchronous version of this API. The differences are highlighted in bold. The most important difference is that the method now returns a Task as opposed to void, allowing the caller to determine when the asynchronous operation has completed. The other difference is that the name of the method has changed to include the suffix Async. Obviously this has no effect other than as an indicator to the programmer that this method executes asynchronously.

Listing 3-24.

```
public interface IImport
{
    Task ImportXmlFilesAsync(string dataDirectory);
}
```

If the method did not originally return void but some other type, then the method would return a Task<T>, allowing the caller the opportunity to obtain the result. This all looks relatively straightforward; however, the fact that we are now invoking a method asynchronously often means that we need to add additional requirements to the method. Perhaps we want to be able to cancel the asynchronous operation if it is taking too long, or we want to get some idea of progress to determine if it is worth waiting a bit longer. Historically it was left to the developer to create their own mechanisms to deliver this functionality. As of .NET 4.0 there was a standard way to deliver cancellation, and .NET 4.5 introduced a standard way to deliver progress.

Cancellation

As mentioned, asynchronous operations may need to be stopped, either when the user gets bored waiting, or the application simply doesn't require the result anymore. What isn't acceptable is simply aborting the task mid-flow, as it may be in the process of transitioning some process-wide state, and aborting it at that point could leave the process in an invalid state, causing future errors. Any method of cancellation requires cooperation from the asynchronous operation itself. The operation will define points in its execution where cancelling is safe. In effect the cancellation is politely requested, and the asynchronous operation will act on it when it can. It is therefore possible that an asynchronous operation can be requested to cancel but still complete successfully. To implement such a protocol, .NET 4.0 introduced two new types: CancellationTokenSource and CancellationToken. These two types coordinate the cancellation. The cancellation token source is used by the party wishing to request the cancellation; the cancellation token is given to each asynchronous operation you wish to be able to cancel. You can now evolve your interface as shown in Listing 3-25.

Listing 3-25.

```
public interface IImport
{
    Task ImportXmlFilesAsync(string dataDirectory);
    Task ImportXmlFilesAsync(string dataDirectory,CancellationToken ct);
}
```

Note you have not simply modified our original asynchronous method; you have added a new one, as not everyone will want the ability to cancel. To call the method with the cancellation token, you obviously need to have one. The cancellation token comes from a cancellation token source; as stated earlier, the cancellation token source is the object that is used by the part of the code wishing to initiate the cancellation process. Listing 3-26 shows some code taking advantage of this API, by first creating a cancellation token source, and then extracting the token from the source and passing the token to the asynchronous method—the same token can be passed to many asynchronous methods. If the user wishes to cancel all operations that have access to the token, the Cancel method on the cancellation token source is called. This simply changes the state of CancellationToken to cancelled.

Listing 3-26.

```
public static void DataImport(IImport import)
{
    var tcs = new CancellationTokenSource();
    CancellationToken ct = tcs.Token;

    Task importTask = import.ImportXmlFilesAsync(@"C:\data", ct);

    while (!importTask.IsCompleted)
    {
        Console.Write(".");
        if ( Console.KeyAvailable && Console.ReadKey(true).Key == ConsoleKey.Q)
```

```
    {
       tcs.Cancel();
    }
    Thread.Sleep(250);
  }
}
```

The second part to this protocol is responding to the polite request from the cancellation token source to cancel. There are two opportunities for this: before and during execution of the asynchronous operation. Remember that creating and starting a task doesn't mean immediate execution; it may be on the thread pool queue waiting to execute (more accurately, with a scheduler waiting to be run). Therefore, in order for the task infrastructure not to execute a task that has been requested to cancel, it also needs to have knowledge of the cancellation token. Listing 3-27 shows the cancellation token being passed to the StartNew method.

Listing 3-27.

```
public Task ImportXmlFilesAsync(string dataDirectory, CancellationToken ct)
{
  return Task.Factory.StartNew(() =>
  {
    foreach (FileInfo file in new DirectoryInfo(dataDirectory).GetFiles("*.xml"))
    {
      // convenient point to check for cancellation

      XElement doc = XElement.Load(file.FullName);

      InternalProcessXml(doc);

    }
  },ct);
}
```

Once the asynchronous operation is executing, it is the responsibility of the task to decide when it is safe to act on a cancellation request. The cancellation token object has a property called IsCancellationRequested. This is set to true if the Cancel method on its associated cancellation-token source object has been called. It would therefore seem intuitive to simply write some code as follows:

```
If ( ct.IsCancellationRequested) return;
```

This will appear to have the desired effect in that the asynchronous operation ends. The framework and ultimately the caller of the asynchronous method will care why the method ended. If it simply returns gracefully from the method, however, it will be impossible to tell if the method completed or was cancelled. We can't just assume that because the task was asked to cancel, it indeed honored the request, since at the very moment you ask it to cancel, it could have completed. If it has completed it would be nice to have the result, irrespective if cancellation was requested. By simply returning, TPL just considers the task as having finished in a RanToCompletion state. To inform TPL that the asynchronous operation has indeed responded to cancellation, the operation must terminate by throwing an OperationCancelledException.

```
if (ct.IsCancellationRequested) throw new OperationCanceledException("Cancelled",ct);
```

47

■ **Note** It is important that the cancellation token to which the code is responding is supplied as a parameter to the creation of the exception. Otherwise the task will have deemed to have completed in a Faulted state.

Fortunately there is a single method on the cancellation token that wraps this all up, called ThrowIfCancellationRequested:

```
ct.ThrowIfCancellationRequested();
```

■ **Note** It is in fact essential that when a task is created, the cancellation token be supplied to TPL. Failure to do so will mean the task is never deemed to be in a cancelled state even if OperationCanceledException is thrown, and will end up in a Faulted state. This can have even greater repercussions in .NET 4, as tasks that end in a Cancelled state don't need to be observed, whereas if we don't observe the outcome of a task that ends in the Faulted state, the exception will be re-thrown on the finalizer thread.

In addition to user-led cancellation, it is reasonable for asynchronous operations to be cancelled because they are taking too long to complete. Rather than supplying an additional time-out value, time-outs can be achieved via cancellation. When a CancellationTokenSource is created you can specify a time period after which cancellation will be trigged automatically. There is also a method, CancelAfter, that can be used on the CancellationTokenSource to set a time for when cancellation will be requested after creation. This feature is only available in .NET 4.5.

The API you have built contains two asynchronous methods, one that can provide cancellation and one that can't. We don't want to build two separate methods and just omit the cancellation logic; instead we can take advantage of a dummy cancellation token provided by TPL (in pattern-speak this is called the Null Pattern), which will never be signaled for cancellation. Listing 3-28 shows how we would implement a version of the asynchronous method that didn't take a cancellation token.

Listing 3-28.

```
public Task ImportXmlFilesAsync(string dataDirectory)
{
    return ImportXmlFilesAsync(dataDirectory, CancellationToken.None);
}
```

The techniques we have looked at so far work well when the code is in a position to keep polling the IsCancellationRequested flag. But what if your task is waiting on a handle, and it will not come out of the wait state until the handle is singled or a specified time out has elapsed? While it is in this wait state, you clearly can't be checking for cancellation. Let us say that before loading a specific XML document, a named mutex must be acquired so as to ensure only one process at a time processes the document (Listing 3-29).

Listing 3-29.

```
Mutex fileMutex = new Mutex(false,file.Name);
fileMutex.WaitOne();
```

The problem here is that while waiting for the mutex, you can't handle cancellation requests. However, the cancellation token also has a wait handle, which is signaled on cancellation. So instead of just waiting on the mutex handle, you can now wait on multiple handles (Listing 3-30).

Listing 3-30.

```
Mutex fileMutex = new Mutex(false,file.FullName);
WaitHandle.WaitAny(new WaitHandle[] {fileMutex, ct.WaitHandle});
ct.ThrowIfCancellationRequested();
```

WaitAny takes an array of wait handles. It will return when any of the handles are signaled, and the return value indicates which one.

Last, it is worth stating that a cancellation token source can only be used once—once signaled, it cannot be reset and used again.

Progress

The last addition to your asynchronous API is to add support for progress. Progress is typically represented by a percentage, but that isn't always appropriate; during an install it might be nice to see what component is being installed. .NET 4.5 introduces a standard way to represent progress, via an interface IProgress<T>.

```
public interface IProgress<in T>
{
    void Report(T value);
}
```

This is a very simple interface. The idea is that anyone wanting to view progress implements this interface, which then passes an instance of the object to an asynchronous method expecting an object of IProgress<T>. The asynchronous method then calls the Report method every time it wishes to report new progress. To add progress support to our asynchronous API, you could use the code in Listing 3-31.

Listing 3-31.

```
public interface IImport
{
  Task ImportXmlFilesAsync(string dataDirectory);
  Task ImportXmlFilesAsync(string dataDirectory,CancellationToken ct);
  Task ImportXmlFilesAsync(string dataDirectory, CancellationToken ct,
                           IProgress<ImportProgress> progressObserver);
}

public class ImportProgress
{
  public int OverallProgress { get; private set; }
  public string CurrentFile { get; private set; }

  public ImportProgress(int overallProgress, string currentFile)
  {
    OverallProgress = overallProgress;
    CurrentFile = currentFile;
  }
}
```

The asynchronous method now looks like Listing 3-32.

Listing 3-32.

```
public Task ImportXmlFilesAsync(string dataDirectory,
                                CancellationToken ct,IProgress<ImportProgress> progressObserver )
{
    return Task.Factory.StartNew(() =>
    {
        FileInfo[] files = new DirectoryInfo(dataDirectory).GetFiles("*.xml");
        int nFileProcessed = 0;
        foreach (FileInfo file in files)
        {
          XElement doc = XElement.Load(file.FullName);

          double progress = (double) nFileProcessed/(double) files.Length*100.0;
          progressObserver.Report(new ImportProgress((int)progress, file.FullName));

          InternalProcessXml(doc);
          nFileProcessed++;

          ct.ThrowIfCancellationRequested();
        }
    },ct);
}
```

To consume progress reports you need to supply an object that implements IProgress<T>. In a UI application this could easily be implemented by the ViewModel, but this can sometimes get tedious, especially if you are simply updating a value on a progress bar. To keep things simpler, TPL provides an implementation of IProgress<T> called Progress<T>. This type is an adapter for the IProgress<T> interface allowing you to consume the progress either via a simple delegate or a traditional event subscription.

```
Task importTask = import.ImportXmlFilesAsync(@"C:\data", ct ,
                                    new Progress<ImportProgress>(DisplayProgress));
. . .
private static void DisplayProgress(ImportProgress progress)
{
   Console.SetCursorPosition(0,0);
   Console.Write("Processing {0} {1}% Done", progress.CurrentFile,progress.OverallProgress);
}
```

Cancellation and Progress are by no means rocket science, but they are a welcome inclusion to TPL as they standardize this common requirement, simplifying the work of the developer, and allowing these concepts to flow into low-level APIs.

Task Relationships

Up until now we have generally considered each task to be its own island of activity. We will now look at how we can chain tasks together and arrange them in parent-child relationships as shown in Figure 3-1.

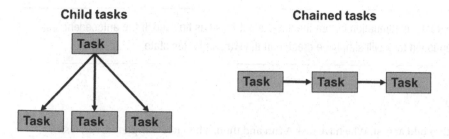

Figure 3-1. *Task relationships*

Chaining Tasks (Continuations)

In addition to creating tasks that are immediately ready to be run, TPL allows you to define a task that is not immediately scheduled to run, but is in a state of WaitingForActivation. The task moves into a WaitingToRun state once one or (in some cases) many antecedent tasks have completed. Listing 3-33 shows a piece of code that creates two such tasks, one with the normal StartNew method, the second with the ContinueWith method.

Listing 3-33. Simple Unconditional Continuation

```
Task<int> firstTask = Task.Factory
                        .StartNew<int>(() => { Console.WriteLine("First Task");return 42;});

Task secondTask = firstTask
    .ContinueWith(ft => Console.WriteLine("Second Task, First task returned {0}" , ft.Result));

secondTask.Wait();
```

The ContinueWith method creates the second task, which will be activated once the firstTask has completed. The delegate supplied to the ContinueWith method represents the secondTask body much in the same way as with StartNew, with one difference being that the method is passed a single parameter that represents the task from which this task is continuing. This allows results from one task to be flowed into another. The continuations defined thus far are unconditional—in other words, it doesn't matter what state the previous task completes in; the second task will be activated. It may be the case that we only wish to run a subsequent task if the previous task ran to successful completion. Conditional continuation is achieved by specifying one of the TaskContinuationOptions (an extended list of TaskCreationOptions used with StartNew) as part of the call to ContinueWith (Listing 3-34).

Listing 3-34. Two-Conditional Continuation

```
Task secondTask = firstTask.ContinueWith( ProcessResult ,
                            TaskContinuationOptions.OnlyOnRanToCompletion);
Task errorHandler = firstTask.ContinueWith(st => Console.WriteLine(st.Exception),
                            TaskContinuationOptions.OnlyOnFaulted);
```

The code in Listing 3-34 does pose an interesting question: what if another piece of code was continuing from the secondTask or just simply waiting on whether the secondTask does actually complete all well and good? If the secondTask does not complete successfully, then the task continuing from this will never run. How TPL handles this is by making the secondTask enter a cancelled state, and thus not producing a deadlock.

One common use for OnlyOnFaulted continuations is to use them to handle any unhandled exception from the antecedent task to prevent unobserved task exceptions. Obviously you have to make sure that this task can't throw an unhandled exception. I have seen code that just swallows the exception and so there is no risk of further exceptions. Personally I don't like the idea of having errors swallowed; at a minimum they should be logged.

■ **Note** It is not necessary to create the continuation before the antecedent task has finished. If the antecedent task has already finished, then the continuation task will simply be created in the Waiting to Run state.

Why Use Continuations?

Chaining tasks together seems rather odd at first. Why have task A run and then, when it is completed, run task B? After all, couldn't you just combine the functionality of tasks A and B into a single task. That can certainly be true for compute-based tasks, but what if task A were an I/O-based task, and task B were a compute-based task designed to process the data returned from the I/O based task. We can't simply combine this functionality into a single task, but what we can do is use a continuation. Listing 3-35 demonstrates this approach. It has the advantage that no thread pool thread is in use while waiting for a response from the web server, but once a response is received the continuation is now ready to run on a thread pool thread, and once running it proceeds to download the content.

Listing 3-35. Continuing from an I/O-Based Task

```
private static Task<string> DownloadWebPageAsync(string url)
{
    WebRequest request = WebRequest.Create(url);
    Task<WebResponse> response = request.GetResponseAsync();

    return response
        .ContinueWith<string>(grt =>
        {
            using (var reader = new StreamReader(grt.Result.GetResponseStream()))
            {
                return reader.ReadToEnd();
            }
        });
}
```

Earlier we alluded to the fact that continuations could be based on not just one task but many. Consider the following scenario: a large data set has an algorithm applied to it, and then once completed, a summary of the results is produced. Assuming the large data set can be broken down into isolated parts, we can create many tasks to run the algorithm against a small portion of the overall set, with a summary task defined as a continuation that will run upon completion of the all the algorithmic tasks (Listing 3-36).

Listing 3-36. Asynchronous Fork and Join

```
Task[] algorithmTasks = new Task[4];
for (int nTask = 0; nTask < algorithmTasks.Length; nTask++)
{
    int partToProcess = nTask;
    algorithmTasks[nTask] = Task.Factory.StartNew(() => ProcessPart(partToProcess));
}
Task.Factory.ContinueWhenAll(algorithmTasks, antecedentTasks => ProduceSummary());
```

Another continuation based on many tasks is ContinueWhenAny. As the name suggests, this can be used to continue when any *one* of the tasks in the array completes. This does sound very attractive for situations where, for example, you query three servers for a result and the first one back wins. However, this method is fraught with complexity. The continuation will fire irrespective of how a task completes, and you can't use the OnXXXX TaskContinuation options for the ContinueWhenAll/Any calls to remedy this. This obviously means that if the first task to complete does so in a Faulted state, then later successes will go unobserved. Even if the continuation fires successfully in .NET 4.0, you may still want to handle any errors from the remaining tasks, so as not to fall afoul of unobserved task exceptions. We will look at simpler techniques to get this behavior in Chapter 7; these use async and await.

Continuations are a very powerful technique to keep the number of active threads to a minimum and, most important, to allow asynchronous operations executing in different contexts to be chained together. We will make further use of continuations in Chapter 6 when we look at tasks and user interfaces.

Nested and Child Tasks

During the execution of a task, TPL allows for the task itself to create other tasks. These other tasks are called either nested or child tasks depending on how they are created. Nested tasks have no impact on the task that created them; the only thing of interest here is that the nested tasks will be entered onto the work-stealing queue of the thread that creates it, as opposed to the shared queue.

If you were to run just the code in Listing 3-37, there would be very little likelihood of the Nested message appearing, since the outer task will finish immediately after the nested task has been created.

Listing 3-37. Nested Task

```
Task.Factory.StartNew(() =>
{
  Task nested = Task.Factory.StartNew((() => Console.WriteLine("Nested..")));
}).Wait();
```

Modifying the code slightly to make the nested task a child task will result in the parent not being seen to have completed until its child has completed, and thus will guarantee the Nested message will be displayed. To make a nested task into a child task, supply a TaskCreationOption of AttachedToParent when the task is created, as shown in Listing 3-38.

Listing 3-38. Child Task

```
Task.Factory.StartNew(() =>
{
 Task child = Task.Factory.StartNew(() => Console.WriteLine("Nested.."),
TaskCreationOptions.AttachedToParent);
}).Wait();
```

The other effect of creating a child task as opposed to a nested task is around exception handling. Any unhandled exception originating from a child task is propagated to the parent. Any code acting on the result of the parent will see all the child-task exceptions as part of the aggregate exception.

In addition to being able to create a task as a child, it is also possible to prevent tasks from becoming children, by creating the parent task with the TaskCreationOptions of DenyChildAttach. If an attempt is made to create a child task, it is simply ignored and made a nested task. A possible use of this flag is to allow a library to expose tasks without fear that they will need to handle exceptions from code of which it has no knowledge.

■ **Caution** Creating the parent task using Task.Run will prevent the child task from attaching. This is because the implementation of Task.Run creates the task using the TaskCreationOptions of DenyChildAttach.

Why Use Child Tasks?

Let us revisit the asynchronous importer we presented earlier. Listing 3-39 is provided to save you skipping back.

Listing 3-39. Asynchronous XML File Importer

```
public Task ImportXmlFilesAsync(string dataDirectory, CancellationToken ct)
{
  return Task.Factory.StartNew(() =>
  {
    foreach (FileInfo file in new DirectoryInfo(dataDirectory).GetFiles("*.xml"))
    {
        XElement doc = XElement.Load(file.FullName);

        InternalProcessXml(doc);

    }
  },ct);
}
```

You could improve the performance of this piece of code by running the loading and processing as separate tasks. You don't really want to add complexity to the ImportXmlFilesAsync method by returning many tasks. You can simply make the body of the foreach loop create a child task. The complexity of using multiple, finer-grained tasks is then hidden from the consumer, and as such will continue to see a single task to represent the overall import process. Listing 3-40 shows the refactored code now using many finer-grained tasks to process many XML files at once.

Listing 3-40. Parallel XML File Import

```
public Task ImportXmlFilesAsync(string dataDirectory, CancellationToken ct)
{
          return Task.Factory.StartNew(() =>
          {
              foreach (FileInfo file in new DirectoryInfo(dataDirectory).GetFiles("*.xml"))
              {
                  string fileToProcess = file.FullName;
                  Task.Factory.StartNew(_ =>
                      {
                          // convenient point to check for cancellation

                          XElement doc = XElement.Load(fileToProcess);

                          InternalProcessXml(doc,ct);
                      }, ct, TaskCreationOptions.AttachedToParent);
              }
          }, ct);
}
```

Conclusion

The introduction of the TPL tasks for the first time in the .NET framework provides a consistent way to represent asynchronous activity, be it local compute, I/O, or even via third-party libraries for GPU-based computing. This drive for consistency is not limited just to tasks but also includes TPL as a whole with the creation of cancellation and progress primitives, resulting in consistent and familiar asynchronous APIs throughout the entire platform.

When designing and implementing your code from now on, consider how long each method may take to execute. Methods that use I/O-based resources should be written to be asynchronous, and all I/O operations inside the method should be asynchronous. Asynchronous methods are identified by the fact that they return a Task or Task<T> and have the suffix Async; follow this pattern to allow other developers to easily identify asynchronous methods. If possible, provide for progress and cancellation of asynchronous operations via the CancellationToken and IProgress<T> types. Leave methods that are pure compute synchronous, and allow the caller to decide to execute it asynchronously.

Last, remember that writing code that never blocks will most likely produce the most scalable solution.

It turns out creating tasks is the easiest part of asynchronous programming (it's stuff your granny could write). The hard part of asynchronous programming that requires skill is getting the tasks to cooperate with one another and scale—topics we will deal with in subsequent chapters.

CHAPTER 4

■ ■ ■

Basic Thread Safety

In the last two chapters, we looked at numerous ways of starting work that will run asynchronously. However, in all of the examples, that work has been relatively self-contained. Asynchrony opens up a whole new class of bugs that can infect your code: race conditions, deadlocks, and data corruption to name just three. We will look at how you debug asynchronous code in Chapters 13 and 14, but our starting point has to be how to prevent these issues in the first place. In this chapter, we will examine the need for thread safety and then introduce the primary tools used to achieve it. In Chapter 5, we will take this idea further and look at the constructs introduced in .NET 4.0 that take some of the work off our shoulders.

Asynchrony and Data

Data is where the trouble starts in asynchronous programming. Not all data is troublesome, of course; but data is at the heart of every asynchrony bug. So first you need to understand where the danger lies: what kinds of data will potentially cause us issues?

It's Not Always Good to Share

Children's author Brittany Hudson wrote a book called *It's Good to Share*. She is obviously not an asynchronous programmer. If two threads are working on completely independent states, then they are not going to interfere with each other and you will not have thread safety issues (however, what we mean by "completely independent" may be more far-reaching than you expect, as we shall see).

It is shared state that lies behind thread safety issues, so one common approach is to copy any data that needs to be used by two threads. Sometimes the amount of data you copy can be quite large, but the performance hit of copying the data is offset by the simplicity and efficiency of not sharing data. As an example, consider background printing in a word processor: the document is copied and the copy is printed. Why does this help? It means that the printing doesn't somehow have to be interleaved with the user typing into the document, and no special processing is required to ensure that the document is coherent (the print should represent the document as it existed at the point the print request was made).

If copying were always a viable solution to all data issues, then life would be very simple. What if you need to process terabytes of data? Copying it all would be impractical, so there must be other options.

Immutable State

If no one is changing the state, then it doesn't matter if it is shared. So if you have to analyze terabytes of data with a number of different algorithms, then, as long as those algorithms don't update the data, they can all be run concurrently on the same data without copying it.

You may argue that this is unrealistic for many situations, and you would be right, if this model only worked for total immutability. But if you can run most of the algorithm with immutable data, and isolate the areas that change the state, then you can run most of the algorithm concurrently and just worry about dealing with thread safety issues in a small part of the processing.

As an example, in 1995 an algorithm was discovered to calculate the nth hexadecimal digit of pi. This is a great opportunity for concurrency as you can calculate as many concurrent digits as you have cores available. Now, you could organize the processing so that each digit was concatenated on to a result as calculated, but this would present an issue: each core would be continuously fighting over the mutable combined result. Another way you could organize this processing is to give each core a range of values to calculate and only combine when the full range had been determined. This model allows the cores to run freely for most of their execution and only pay the cost of thread safety when they occasionally have to combine results.

But even this model doesn't fit with every scenario; sometimes there is a shared state that has to be written to by one or more of the parties—cache refreshes, for example. Whether you have to take any action over thread safety at such points depends on whether the state transition is atomic from the perspective of users of the state.

Atomic State Transition

First you need a definition of "atomic" when related to state transitions. For this discussion I'll define "atomic" as follows:

> *An atomic operation is one that, from the perspective of observers, transitions state from one valid value to another valid value without the state having a temporary invalid value.*

In general, without resorting to thread safety techniques, this means that a value can be changed in a single processor instruction. On 32-bit machines, state of length 32 bits or less can be written in a single processor instruction, and on 64-bit machines state of length 64 bits or less can be written in a single processor instruction. For example, a double can be written atomically on a 64-bit machine but not on some 32-bit machines. An important feature of the CLR is that a reference can always be written atomically, as a reference's size matches the "bit-ness" of the runtime.

With this definition in mind, you can see that as long as updates are atomic, readers will not see invalid states and writers will not collide as they change state. Therefore, in thread safety terms, mutable shared state is safe as long as all updates are atomic.

Nonatomic State Transition

With this definition of atomic state transition, it is quite easy to see what a nonatomic transition is: one that enters an observable invalid value during transition. For example, if you write a double on the 32-bit CLR, then each 32-bit word needs to be updated separately. If a thread reads the double when another thread has only written one of the two words, then it may see a corrupt state.

If only one thread ever writes to a piece of state, then a thread that reads may see an invalid value, but the state will always return to a valid value once the write is complete. So there is a chance of an observed temporary corruption. If you only care about the state at the end of all processing, then the fact that there is temporary corruption may be irrelevant to your processing.

As soon as we have more than one writer, state can get permanently corrupted, and this is always a problem. To illustrate this, consider the code in Listing 4-1. This code is currently performing a series of increments on an integer using a single task, and the increment is being performed using the postincrement operator (++). Now, as this code runs the increment on a single thread, it would hopefully be surprising if the actual value did not match the expected value.

Listing 4-1. Incrementing an int on a Single Thread

```
static void Main(string[] args)
{
    const int iterations = 100000000;
    const int numTasks = 1;
    List<Task> tasks = new List<Task>();
    int value = 0;

    for (int nTask = 0; nTask < numTasks; nTask++)
    {
        Task t = Task.Factory.StartNew(() =>
        {
            IncrementValue(ref value, iterations);
        });

        tasks.Add(t);
    }

    Task.WaitAll(tasks.ToArray());
    Console.WriteLine("Expected value: {0}, Actual value: {1}", numTasks * iterations, value);
}

private static void IncrementValue(ref int value, int iterations)
{
    for (int i = 0; i < iterations; i++)
    {
        value++;
    }
}
```

But what if you were to amend the code in Listing 4-1 so that you were using two tasks rather than one (by setting numTasks to 2). What would you expect to see then? Figure 4-1 shows the output; you are losing increments, so what is going on?

```
Expected value: 200000000, Actual value: 100405400
Press any key to continue . . . _
```

Figure 4-1. Output from incrementing on two threads

Remember that only atomic writes will work reliably. Here you have two threads that are both performing writes to the value variable, and it turns out that the ++ operator is not atomic. In fact, ++ is three operations because computation is performed in registers, not in main memory. The three steps are as follows:

1. Copy the value from the variable into a register

2. Increment the value in the register

3. Copy the new value to the variable

Imagine thread T0 starts the process and completes up to step 2. Now a second thread, T1, completes step 1 before thread T0 performs step 3. Thread T1 will have read the old value so it will also increment the old value. This results in both threads writing the same value back to the variable so, in effect, you lose one of the updates. This is why the actual value is lower than what is expected. Figure 4-2 shows this in action.

```
T0:  MOV  R0,count
T0:  ADD  R0,1          T1:  MOV  R0,count
T0:  MOV  count,R0      T1:  ADD  R0,1
                        T1:  MOV  count,R0
```

Figure 4-2. *Losing updates with simple increment*

Correctness Is Not the Only Problem

The code in Listing 4-1 shows threads updating a single piece of data. If you make the number of threads two or more, then on some processors the code will run slower on multiple cores than on a single core. To increase performance, processing cores use multiple levels of caching (see sidebar on processor caches). As far as the cores are concerned, they want to read data out of their cache and will only go to main memory (much slower) if a cached value is no longer valid. The problem is that when a thread running on a core writes a cached value, if another core is using the same value then its cached value will be invalidated, forcing it to go back to main memory for the next read. When only a single core is used, then all reads are from the cache. The performance difference can be significant in highly concurrent code.

Unfortunately, protecting the cached values is not as simple as making sure that different threads use different variables. Data is loaded into the cache in cache lines. These are generally 64 bytes (at least on Intel processors) and so will contain not just a single item of data, but also those adjacent to it in memory. This is normally a good thing as data that is close in memory is often used together, and so when the next item of data is needed, the processor finds it is already in the cache. In multithreaded processing, however, this can cause seemingly unrelated pieces of data to cause mutual cache invalidation because they are in the same cache line.

PROCESSOR CACHES

The processor is connected to main memory via the data bus. As processors have become faster, the speed of main memory and the data bus has become a limiting factor in execution speed when data is required. As a result, chip manufacturers started putting caches on their processors so the processor didn't have to keep going back to main memory if it had recently worked on the data. This initial cache was kept small to make it as fast as possible.

Over time, the manufacturers realized that they could back up this very fast cache with a slower, larger cache; even if the data wasn't in the fastest cache, the hope was that it would be in the slower cache, which was still significantly faster than going back to main memory. These caches became known as level 1 (L1) and level 2 (L2) caches. Some modern chips even have an L3 cache.

As multiple cores were placed on processors, additional decisions had to be made about whether any of the caches were going to be shared (L3 commonly is) and, if not, how to prevent stale values from being used. Different chips use different designs and these optimizations can mean that the same code runs very differently on different processors.

Thread Safety

Ensuring that data is not corrupted is known as thread safety and is often achieved by synchronizing threads to make sure that any updates are atomic. .NET provides a set of primitives to synchronize between threads, but it is up to developers to use the primitives correctly and thus achieve thread safety.

In fact, achieving thread safety can be quite straightforward: all you need to do is have one global synchronization construct, then every piece of code will be assured of gaining ownership of the construct before it does anything. The problem is we are doing asynchronous programming for a reason: we want different parts of our code to run concurrently. This global synchronization construct would cause all operations to happen serially. So there is a balancing act: we need just enough synchronization to ensure thread safety but not enough to kill concurrency. As a result we should always aim to use the cheapest construct that does the job that we can. The rest of this chapter will introduce the synchronization toolkit that .NET provides to get the job done.

The Interlocked Class

The Interlocked static class provides methods to turn nonatomic operations into atomic ones. It is fairly restricted in scope in that it generally only works on single pieces of data up to 64 bits in length (rather than more general data structures). However, as we shall see, there are special rules for using Interlocked with 64-bit values on 32-bit systems.

Basic Operations

Interlocked has three basic operations: Increment, Decrement, and Add (notice there is no Subtract, as you can simply Add a negative number). These methods turn their nonatomic counterparts into atomic operations. You can rewrite the IncrementValue method from Listing 4-1 to use Interlocked.Increment, and the resulting code (Listing 4-2) will always produce the expected value.

Listing 4-2. Using Interlocked.Increment

```
private static void IncrementValue(ref int value, int iterations)
{
    for (int i = 0; i < iterations; i++)
    {
        Interlocked.Increment(ref value);
    }
}
```

Now this functionality doesn't come for free; this code will run significantly slower than the original version (4 to 10 times slower depending on hardware). However, we are being quite unfair on Interlocked.Increment as people don't generally write code (or at least they shouldn't) where two threads continually battle to update a value. Interlocked.Increment is cheap if there is no contention with another thread, but becomes more expensive if there is.

As for the other two methods: we hope Interlocked.Decrement is now fairly obvious; and Interlocked.Add takes two values and adds the second to the first atomically.

We have already seen an example where Interlocked functionality has been taken advantage of: in chapter 2 we talked about how the thread pool queue had been remodeled from a linked list (which requires fairly heavy synchronization) to a linked list of arrays. While within an array segment, the "next item" pointer can be moved using Interlocked.Increment and Interlocked.Decrement.

■ **Caution**   Care should be taken if you are looking to see an `Interlocked` function change the data item to a specific value. If you check the data item after using an `Interlocked` function, you will have a race condition: another thread may have just called an `Interlocked` function to change the data item again. Instead you should use the return value from the call to the `Interlocked` function, as this will contain the new value for the data item.

Richer Functions

The `Interlocked` class has two other methods: `Exchange` and `CompareExchange`. Although they may seem quite innocuous, they can be used to build very lightweight synchronization primitives.

Interlocked.Exchange

`Interlocked.Exchange` assigns a value to a variable and returns the old value in an atomic operation. Simple assignment is normally atomic anyway, so why is this interesting? Because the old value is returned, which allows us to create richer constructs—for example, a `SpinLock`. A `SpinLock` is a mutual-exclusion synchronization primitive. If the `SpinLock` is already owned, another thread attempting to `Lock` will simply cause that thread to spin on the processor until the lock is available. For short-lived locking operations in highly concurrent systems, this is far better than, say, a `Monitor` (which we shall discuss shortly) because the thread doesn't lose its timeslice while waiting. Listing 4-3 shows a `SpinLock` implemented with `Interlocked.Exchange`. The interesting line is in the body of the `Lock` method: if already locked, then the `lock` field will have a value of 1. That means that when we use `Interlocked.Exchange` it will return 1 while the lock is already owned. As soon as the `locked` field is set to 0 (in the `Unlock` method), `Interlocked.Exchange` will return 0 as it sets the `locked` field back to 1. Now the `Lock` method returns and the `SpinLock` is locked again.

Listing 4-3. A SpinLock Using Interlocked.Exchange

```
public struct SpinLock
{
    private int locked;

    public void Lock()
    {
        while (Interlocked.Exchange(ref locked, 1) != 0) ;
    }

    public void Unlock()
    {
        locked = 0;
    }
}
```

As it happens, .NET already ships with a `SpinLock` class, but you can see how primitives such as this are built using fairly rudimentary building blocks.

Interlocked.CompareExchange

The semantics of `Interlocked.CompareExchange` are not obvious when first seen. Here is the method signature (there are other overloads for different value types):

```
public static T CompareExchange<T>(
                ref T location,
                T value,
                T comparand) where T : class
```

The method compares the `location` and `comparand` and, if they are the same, it assigns `value` to `location`, returning the original value of `location`. So how is this useful? One place you can use this is in building Singletons. If the crucial factor is that you don't mind more than one being created, but only one must be *used,* then `CompareExchange` can give you a lightweight tool for achieving this. Listing 4-4 shows how you can ensure that you only assign the new instance if the existing reference is `null`. Obviously you will create an instance each time we enter the `if` block, but only one will ever be used.

Listing 4-4. A Loose Form of Singleton with CompareExchange

```
public class Highlander
{
    private Highlander()
    {
        Console.WriteLine("created");
    }

    private static Highlander theInstance;

    public static Highlander GetInstance()
    {
        if (theInstance == null)
        {
            Interlocked.CompareExchange(ref theInstance, new Highlander(), null);
        }

        return theInstance;
    }
}
```

■ **Caution** Although the `Interlocked` class can manipulate 64-bit values safely, on a 32-bit system you are only guaranteed to see correct data if you also read the 64-bit value using `Interlocked.Read`.

So for quite a simple class, you can see that you can achieve some powerful lightweight synchronization. However, `Interlocked` is still limited to single items of data as a target; what if you need to manipulate state composed of multiple fields in a thread-safe way? For this you need something more flexible.

Monitor: The Workhorse of .NET Synchronization

Multistage transition means you need a way of protecting access to data that allows you to control access to arbitrary data. The SmallBusiness class in Listing 4-5 is an example of multistage transition. In this code you can see that when a payment comes in we have to change two separate items of data. Interlocked can't help us here: not only is decimal too large, but Interlocked only protects access to a single piece of data. The danger with the code in Listing 4-5 is that during ReceivePayment, the state of an instance is temporarily in an invalid state where we have increased the cash but not yet decreased the receivables. If another thread were to access the NetWorth property at that point they would see a value that is too high by the value of the amount parameter.

Listing 4-5. *Example of Multistage State Transition*

```
public class SmallBusiness
{
    private decimal cash;
    private decimal receivables;

    public SmallBusiness(decimal cash, decimal receivables)
    {
        this.cash = cash;
        this.receivables = receivables;
    }

    public void ReceivePayment(decimal amount)
    {
        cash += amount;
        receivables -= amount;
    }

    public decimal NetWorth
    {
        get { return cash + receivables; }
    }
}
```

To fix this, you have to somehow enforce a *protocol* that ensures that only one thread at a time has access to this composite state of cash and receivables. The CLR has a construct that can be used for just this purpose; it is known as a Sync Block. Sync Blocks are held in the Sync Block Table in the CLR internal data structures. Every instance of a reference type has an object header. One of the parts of this header is a reference to an entry in the Sync Block Table, which is empty by default. On demand, it will cause an entry in the Sync Block Table to be allocated. The object header will refer to this newly allocated Sync Block.

The Monitor class has a static method called Enter, which will try to take ownership of a Sync Block on behalf of the currently executing thread, potentially triggering allocation of the Sync Block. As a result, from now on we will use the shorthand term of a thread "owning the monitor" to refer to a thread having ownership of a specific Sync Block. A thread relinquishes ownership of a monitor by calling Monitor.Exit.

If a thread, A, calls Monitor.Enter and another thread, B, already owns the specified monitor, then Monitor.Enter blocks until thread B calls Monitor.Exit. When Monitor.Enter returns, thread A will now have ownership of the monitor (see Figure 4-3).

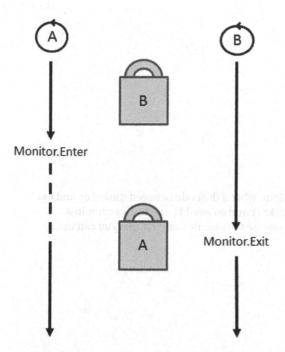

Monitor.Enter

Monitor.Exit

Figure 4-3. *Monitor.Enter blocks if another thread owns the monitor*

Monitor can therefore be used to prevent concurrent access to state *as long as everyone conforms to the protocol.* Listing 4-6 shows how we can apply the use of a Monitor to the SmallBusiness class we saw in Listing 4-5. Notice that both the ReceivePayment and NetWorth members need to use the Monitor to ensure no readers ever see the state midtransition.

Listing 4-6. Thread-Safe SmallBusiness

```
public class SmallBusiness
{
    private decimal cash;
    private decimal receivables;
    private readonly object stateGuard = new object();

    public SmallBusiness(decimal cash, decimal receivables)
    {
        this.cash = cash;
        this.receivables = receivables;
    }

    public void ReceivePayment(decimal amount)
    {
        Monitor.Enter(stateGuard);
        cash += amount;
        receivables -= amount;
        Monitor.Exit(stateGuard);
    }
```

```
    public decimal NetWorth
    {
        get
        {
            Monitor.Enter(stateGuard);
            decimal netWorth = cash + receivables;
            Monitor.Exit(stateGuard);
            return netWorth;
        }
    }
}
```

This seems quite straightforward but there is a potential problem: what if the code between the Enter and Exit throws an exception? In that case the owning thread would not call Exit and so would leave the monitor in a locked state forever. You therefore need to ensure that you always release the monitor, and for that you can use a try . . . finally block as the code in Listing 4-7 demonstrates.

Listing 4-7. Releasing the Monitor Using a Finally Block

```
public void ReceivePayment(decimal amount)
{
    Monitor.Enter(stateGuard);
    try
    {
        cash += amount;
        receivables -= amount;
    }
    finally
    {
        Monitor.Exit(stateGuard);
    }
}
```

Now, what if Monitor.Enter were to throw an exception? You really need to bring this call inside the try block. But then you need to cater for two possibilities: the exception happening before the monitor was acquired and the exception being thrown after the monitor was acquired. So you need to have some way of telling whether or not you should release the monitor. Fortunately, in version 4.0 of .NET a new overload was introduced that allows users to verify, one way or the other, whether the lock was taken. Listing 4-8 shows the code necessary to use this new overload.

Listing 4-8. Monitor.Enter Inside the try Block

```
public void ReceivePayment(decimal amount)
{
    bool lockTaken = false;
    try
    {
        Monitor.Enter(stateGuard, ref lockTaken);
        cash += amount;
        receivables -= amount;
    }
    finally
```

```
    {
        if (lockTaken)
        {
            Monitor.Exit(stateGuard);
        }
    }
}
```

If this is the code you should write to use monitors correctly, you have a problem: the chances of getting developers to write this every time and get it right every time are not great. And so the C# language has a keyword that makes the compiler emit the code in Listing 4-8.

The lock Keyword

The idea of the lock keyword is to allow you to concentrate on the work that needs to be protected rather than the semantics of using monitors correctly. Listing 4-9 shows how the lock keyword makes the code in Listing 4-8 much simpler. This is surely something you can expect developers to write.

Listing 4-9. Using the lock Keyword

```
public void ReceivePayment(decimal amount)
{
    lock(stateGuard)
    {
        cash += amount;
        receivables -= amount;
    }
}
```

WHAT SHOULD I LOCK?

In the early days of .NET it was very common to see people write code like the following:

```
lock(this)
{
    // change state here
}
```

In fact, this is also what the event keyword generated until .NET 4.0. The problem is that an object's this reference is really a public field, in that anyone with a reference to the object is looking at the same thing. This means that, although you are using this for your own internal synchronization, other code may also choose your object for synchronization. You then end up in needless contention at best and with hard-to-diagnose deadlocks at worst.

Objects are cheap to allocate, and so the simplest way to ensure you only have contention where necessary is to use private instance or static variables, depending on whether the state to be protected is instance or static data, respectively.

Even though the lock keyword appears to be a big improvement on manually manipulating the monitor, there is still a fundamental problem: when trying to acquire synchronization primitives it's a very good idea to be able to time out of a wait. Failing to do this can result in hard-to-identify deadlocks and other synchronization bugs (such as a thread failing to release a monitor). The problem is that neither Monitor.Enter nor lock supports the passing of a timeout.

Timing Out of Monitor Acquisition

Fortunately, the Monitor class supports another method, TryEnter, which can take a timeout. You can see how to use it in Listing 4-10.

Listing 4-10. Timeout out of Waits Using Monitor.TryEnter

```
public void ReceivePayment(decimal amount)
{
    bool lockTaken = false;

    try
    {
        Monitor.TryEnter(stateGuard, TimeSpan.FromSeconds(30), ref lockTaken);
        if (lockTaken)
        {
            cash += amount;
            receivables -= amount;
        }
        else
        {
            throw new TimeoutException("Failed to acquire stateGuard");
        }
    }
    finally
    {
        if (lockTaken)
        {
            Monitor.Exit(stateGuard);
        }
    }
}
```

■ **Note** Sometimes you hear it argued that timeouts introduce their own problems, as you don't know how long you should wait. In many cases the timeout is pretty clear: on the server side there is no point in waiting longer than a request timeout, as the caller already will have gone if you wait longer. But on the client side there are reasonable rules of thumb because the key is to timeout, not to wait for the exact optimal time. Take a figure for a reasonable time for the wait to be resolved, and then multiply it by 10. Of course you may end up waiting longer than necessary, but at least you are not waiting forever. The result is you will be able to proactively flag that there is a problem.

So we have a technical solution to acquiring monitors with timeouts, but unfortunately it's currently one that developers are unlikely to use in its raw form. However, we can package this very conveniently using IDisposable and using blocks, as Listing 4-11 demonstrates. Lock is an extension method on System.Object (not something generally encouraged as it pollutes the members of everything; however, it is probably justified in this occasion). The code pass Lock the timeout, which it forwards to Monitor.TryEnter. If the monitor is successfully acquired, then a LockHelper is used to provide the implementation of IDisposable so it can release the monitor in Dispose. The LockHelper is a struct to prevent another heap allocation (as it's a value type). Last, in Lock, if Monitor.TryEnter throws an exception, then the monitor is released (if it has been acquired) before rethrowing the exception.

Listing 4-11. Wrapping up Monitor.TryEnter

```
public static class LockExtensions
{
    public static LockHelper Lock(this object obj, TimeSpan timeout)
    {
        bool lockTaken = false;

        try
        {
            Monitor.TryEnter(obj, TimeSpan.FromSeconds(30), ref lockTaken);
            if (lockTaken)
            {
                return new LockHelper(obj);
            }
            else
            {
                throw new TimeoutException("Failed to acquire stateGuard");
            }
        }
        catch
        {
            if (lockTaken)
            {
                Monitor.Exit(obj);
            }
            throw;
        }
    }

    private struct LockHelper : IDisposable
    {
        private readonly object obj;

        public LockHelper(object obj)
        {
            this.obj = obj;
        }

        public void Dispose()
        {
            Monitor.Exit(obj);
        }
    }
}
```

Now, for developers, acquiring monitors with timeouts is almost as convenient as using the lock keyword, as Listing 4-12 shows quite clearly.

Listing 4-12. Acquiring Monitors with a using Block

```
public void ReceivePayment(decimal amount)
{
    using(stateGuard.Lock(TimeSpan.FromSeconds(30)))
    {
        cash += amount;
        receivables -= amount;
    }
}
```

RECURSIVE LOCKS

A synchronization construct or lock is said to be recursive, or re-entrant, if the same thread can acquire it when it already holds it. Generally a lock will hold a count to ensure that acquisition calls are balanced by relinquish calls to prevent premature release of the lock.

Monitors support recursion, and so a thread can call Monitor.Enter without blocking if it already holds the monitor. However, the thread must call Monitor.Exit the same number of times as it calls Enter/TryEnter before the monitor is released to another thread.

Signaling with Monitors

Controlling access to data is a primary concern with thread synchronization. However, another important aspect is the ability for threads to coordinate their actions by signaling to each other. So, in addition to providing a mechanism for mutually exclusive access to state, monitors also provide an API for signaling.

The goal of signaling is for one thread to be able to inform one or more other threads that a particular event has occurred. The Monitor class exposes three methods—Wait, Pulse, and PulseAll—for precisely this purpose. All three of these methods can only be invoked when the calling thread owns the monitor. Wait gives up the monitor but leaves the thread in a waiting, alertable state. Pulse wakes up one alertable thread. PulseAll wakes up all threads that have called Wait on the monitor in question.

To illustrate Wait and Pulse, let's look at an example by implementing the producer/consumer pattern: one thread produces work to be performed and enqueues it; another thread pulls the data off the queue and processes it. The key job that signaling will do is to ensure that the consumer thread consumes resources only when there is actually work available on the queue. Listing 4-13 shows the implementation with a monitor.

Listing 4-13. Producer/Consumer with Monitor

```
private static void Produce(object obj)
{
    var queue = (Queue<int>)obj;
    var rnd = new Random();

    while (true)
    {
        lock (queue)
```

```
            {
                queue.Enqueue(rnd.Next(100));

                Monitor.Pulse(queue);
            }

            Thread.Sleep(rnd.Next(2000));
        }
    }

    private static void Consume(object obj)
    {
        var queue = (Queue<int>)obj;

        while (true)
        {
            int val;
            lock (queue)
            {
                while (queue.Count == 0)
                {
                    Monitor.Wait(queue);
                }

                val = queue.Dequeue();
            }

            ProcessValue(val);
        }
    }
}
```

The Produce method generates the work and then acquires the queue's monitor so it can safely enqueue the work (Queue<T> is not internally thread safe). Once enqueued it calls Pulse on the monitor to wake up a waiting thread, in this case the consumer. Note that at this point the Producer still owns the monitor. Last, the producer releases the monitor and sleeps before enqueuing more work.

Meanwhile the Consume method starts its processing loop. The queue's Count and Dequeue must be bundled into an atomic operation to avoid a race condition (Count returning 1, then another thread dequeuing before we get to the call to Dequeue), so Consume first acquires the queue's monitor. However, if there is nothing on the queue then we need to give up the monitor so the producer can enqueue some work. If we simply called Monitor.Exit, then the only way we would know if there was work on the queue would be to poll, which would be inefficient. Therefore, you call Wait to give up the monitor but remain alertable by a Pulse. When Wait returns, the consumer once again owns the monitor and so can Dequeue safely. Once the data is dequeued, Consume releases the monitor so it can process the data without blocking the producer.

One possibly strange detail in Listing 4-13 is the use of a while loop around the Wait in the Consume method; what is that for? Well, there is another subtle race condition: sequencing of operations is nondeterministic, so in theory the producer could end up reacquiring the monitor before the consumer has been rescheduled. The effect of this is that Pulse would be called twice, waking more than one consumer thread. One of the threads could consume both items, so when the second consumer finally comes out of Wait, it will own the monitor but there will be nothing on the queue. Therefore, instead of immediately dequeuing it needs to check that there is still work to do on the queue by checking the Count.

Signaling As a Building Block

Now that you have a signaling mechanism, you can use it to build richer synchronization constructs. A semaphore is used to control access to data, but unlike a monitor it doesn't enforce mutual exclusion, but rather allows a constrained number of concurrent threads to own it. Semaphores are commonly used to control access to resource pools (whether those resources be threads, objects, or something else). Listing 4-14 shows an implementation of a rudimentary semaphore using a monitor with its signaling capability.

Listing 4-14. Implementing a Semaphore with Monitor

```csharp
public class MonitorSemaphore
{
    private int currentCount;
    private readonly int maxCount;
    private readonly object guard = new object();

    public MonitorSemaphore(int initialCount, int maxCount)
    {
        this.currentCount = initialCount;
        this.maxCount = maxCount;
    }

    public void Enter()
    {
        lock (guard)
        {
            while (currentCount == maxCount)
            {
                Monitor.Wait(guard);
            }
            currentCount++;
        }
    }

    public void Exit()
    {
        lock (guard)
        {
            currentCount--;
            Monitor.Pulse(guard);
        }
    }

    public int CurrentCount{get { return currentCount; }}
}
```

Optimizing for Read

So far we have been focusing on achieving thread safety via mutual exclusion: only one thread accessing thread sensitive code at a time. In situations of low contention, where it is unusual for two threads to want to access state at the same time, this is often the optimal approach, as you just use a lightweight guard to ensure those rare occasions are safe.

Sometimes, however, you will find yourself in a very different usage pattern, where many threads want to read a piece of state concurrently and occasionally a thread will need to perform an update. Because of this update you need to ensure thread safety via synchronization, but if you use mutual exclusion only one reader will be able to access the state at a time. We know that if every thread were reading, there would be no thread safety concerns, so the ideal situation would be if you could let lots of readers in at the same time, but then shut them out to allow a single writer access to the state. This is the role of a reader/writer lock.

There are two reader/writer locks in the .NET framework: ReaderWriterLock and ReaderWriterLockSlim. Why are there two? Well, let's look at their behavior.

ReaderWriterLock

The ReaderWriterLock class was introduced in .NET 2.0 to allow a synchronization strategy that was optimized for high read contention with occasional writes. Readers call AcquireReadLock and ReleaseReadLock; writers call AcquireWriteLock and ReleaseWriteLock. Listing 4-15 shows an example from a reader's perspective. One thing to notice in the listing is that the Acquire methods take a timeout but return void. The Acquire methods throw an ApplicationException if the timeout is exceeded before the lock is acquired. ReaderWriterLock supports re-entrancy so the same thread can acquire the same lock type multiple times without blocking. In addition, a writer can happily acquire a read lock without blocking. However, a thread holding a read lock may not be able to acquire a write lock without blocking as there may be other readers in progress.

Listing 4-15. Using a ReaderWriterLock

```
var rwLock = new ReaderWriterLock();

rwLock.AcquireReaderLock(TimeSpan.FromSeconds(3));
try
{
    ReadState();
}
finally
{
    rwLock.ReleaseReaderLock();
}
```

What if you already hold a read lock and you discover you also need to write? For example, you are accessing the cache and you find one of the items you need is not present and needs to be added to the cache. You could attempt to gain an additional write lock, but it would be convenient to be able to promote your read lock to a write lock. This is the concept of upgradable locks and is supported by the UpgradeToWriteLock method of ReaderWriterLock (this also takes a timeout, as the call may block due to other readers in progress).

Problems with ReaderWriterLock

ReaderWriterLock appears to have the necessary functionality, but there are two key issues with the implementation that are problematic. The first issue is that ReaderWriterLock is comparatively slow—four times slower than a monitor. However, the biggest problem is that ReaderWriterLock can be subject to *writer starvation*. What is writer starvation? Consider a ReaderWriterLock with active readers. Now, along comes a writer who gets blocked because of the readers. However, with ReaderWriterLock new readers are still allowed in, so if there is a sufficient flow of new readers, the writer will never obtain its lock.

ReaderWriterLockSlim

The deficiencies in ReaderWriterLock were such that with .NET 3.5, Microsoft introduced another reader/writer lock: ReaderWriterLockSlim. This is twice as fast as ReaderWriterLock and also does not suffer from writer starvation, as new readers get queued up behind a waiting writer. Listing 4-16 demonstrates its use.

Listing 4-16. Basic API for ReaderWriterLockSlim

```
var rwLock = new ReaderWriterLockSlim();

rwLock.EnterReadLock();
try
{
    ReadState();
}
finally
{
    rwLock.ExitReadLock();
}
```

Notice that we cannot pass a timeout to EnterReadLock. To use timeouts we need to use TryEnterReadLock, which takes a timeout and returns a Boolean that states whether or not the lock was acquired within the timeout. The usage is very similar to TryEnter on the Monitor class.

The priority for ReadWriterLockSlim's behavior is speed over functionality. By default, therefore, it does not support recursive acquisition. To enable recursion the constructor must be passed the LockRecursionPolicy. SupportsRecursion flag. Enabling recursion slows the lock down, but even then it is still significantly faster than ReaderWriterLock. Another area where the default behavior is less functional than ReaderWriterLock is in terms of upgradable locks. With ReaderWriterLockSlim, read locks are not automatically upgradable to write locks. To enable lock upgrade we need to call EnterUpgradableReadLock rather than EnterReadLock.

■ **Note** ReaderWriterLockSlim only supports one upgradable lock at a time (although it can be held at the same time as other read locks). In other words, if one thread already has an upgradable read lock, a second thread calling EnterUpgradableReadLock will block until the first thread exits its upgradable lock.

A more practical example of the use of a reader/writer lock is shown in Listing 4-17. Here we have a cache of news items that are tagged according to subject. Users can hit our site and ask for various kinds of news items (e.g., business news) via the GetNews method, and new NewsItems are added to the cache via the AddNewsItem method. The danger here is that a new NewsItem will arrive during the enumeration of the results of GetNews, causing an InvalidOperationException due to the collection being modified during iteration. So use a ReaderWriterLockSlim to guard the query using a read lock and the update to the cache with a write lock. This means you can have lots of users getting news from the cache concurrently, but when new NewsItems arrive they can be added in a thread-safe way.

Listing 4-17. ReaderWriterLockSlim in Action

```
public class Cache
{
    private readonly List<NewsItem> items = new List<NewsItem>();

    ReaderWriterLockSlim guard = new ReaderWriterLockSlim();

    public IEnumerable<NewsItem> GetNews(string tag)
    {
        guard.EnterReadLock();
        try
        {
            return items.Where(ni => ni.Tags.Contains(tag)).ToList();
        }
        finally
        {
            guard.ExitReadLock();
        }
    }

    public void AddNewsItem(NewsItem item)
    {
        guard.EnterWriteLock();
        try
        {
            items.Add(item);
        }
        finally
        {
            guard.ExitWriteLock();
        }
    }
}
```

One complication is that the GetNews method uses Linq to get the appropriate results. Linq's Where extension method will return an IEnumerable<NewsItem>, which is only processed when the consumer iterates the results. You therefore need to force immediate execution of the query within the confines of the lock by calling ToList on the result of Where.

A Semaphore Out of the Box

Earlier in this chapter you implemented a semaphore using the Wait and Pulse methods of the Monitor class. In .NET 4.0 the .NET framework team shipped a managed semaphore as part of the System.Threading namespace. There was already a Semaphore class (we'll come to this in a little while), so the new class was called SemaphoreSlim (you might be able to see a pattern emerging here). Internally, SemaphoreSlim uses the Wait and Pulse methods of the Monitor class, in a similar way to our version, so it is a very lightweight synchronization primitive. As explained earlier, semaphores are typically used to guard access to a limited resource such as a thread pool. Let's look at an example by implementing a Large Object Heap buffer pool.

WHY POOL LARGE OBJECT HEAP BUFFERS?

In interop scenarios it is not uncommon to pass unmanaged code a buffer for it to fill with data. When objects are passed across the interop barrier, the unmanaged code will see a raw memory address. This means we cannot allow the GC to move the object during a collection; this is known as pinning. Pinned objects make life a lot harder for the GC during the compact phase, so it would be good to allocate these pinned buffers somewhere that isn't compacted.

The Large Object Heap (LOH) is used for objects that are around 85,000 bytes and larger, and because the objects are large, it isn't compacted. Therefore, it can be a good idea to use buffers on the LOH for interop. However, it is expensive to allocate and collect LOH objects, so reusing the buffers can be an effective optimization. To reuse LOH buffers efficiently, you should pool them to make sure you constrain the number in use and centrally manage them.

To start with, we'll model the buffer by a pair of abstractions: one to model the actual buffer and the other to help us with resource management. You can see these in Listing 4-18. IBufferRegistration allows the user of the buffer to say they are finished with it, so it can be returned to the pool.

Listing 4-18. Abstractions for the Buffer Pool

```
public interface IBuffer
{
    byte[] Buffer { get; }
}
public interface  IBufferRegistration : IBuffer, IDisposable
{
}
```

Next you need an implementation of a buffer that will reside on the LOH. To ensure this, make sure the buffer is 85,000 bytes (the actual limit is slightly lower, but 85,000 is a nice round number). Listing 4-19 shows the implementation. Note the InUse flag: this allows you to locate pooled buffers that are not currently in use.

Listing 4-19. Wrapping a LOH Buffer

```
public class LOHBuffer : IBuffer
{
    private readonly byte[] buffer;
    private const int LOHBufferMin = 85000;
    internal bool InUse { get; set; }

    public LOHBuffer()
    {
        buffer = new byte[LOHBufferMin];
    }

    public byte[] Buffer { get { return buffer; } }
}
```

Last, you need the actual pool; this uses a semaphore to ensure that if we are using the maximum number of buffers, then the next attempt to obtain one will block until one becomes free. We wrap the LOHBuffer in a BufferRegistration class that returns the buffer to the pool when disposed. The code for the pool is shown in

Listing 4-20, and although the semaphore is only a small part of the code, it is critical to ensure that we constrain the pool and block requestors that exceed the maximum concurrent buffers.

Listing 4-20. The BufferPool Implementation

```
public class BufferPool
{
    private SemaphoreSlim guard;
    private List<LOHBuffer> buffers;

    public BufferPool(int maxSize)
    {
        guard = new SemaphoreSlim(maxSize);
        buffers = new List<LOHBuffer>(maxSize);
    }

    public IBufferRegistration GetBuffer()
    {
        // this blocks until a buffer is free
        guard.Wait();
        // can now get buffer so make sure we're the only thread manipulating
        // the list of buffers
        lock (buffers)
            {
                IBufferRegistration freeBuffer = null;

                // look for a free buffer
                foreach (LOHBuffer buffer in buffers)
                {
                    if (!buffer.InUse)
                    {
                        buffer.InUse = true;
                        freeBuffer = new BufferReservation(this, buffer);
                    }
                }

                // no free buffer so allocate a new one
                if (freeBuffer == null)
                {
                    var buffer = new LOHBuffer();
                    buffer.InUse = true;
                    buffers.Add(buffer);
                    freeBuffer = new BufferReservation(this, buffer);
                }

                return freeBuffer;
            }
    }
```

```csharp
        private void Release(LOHBuffer buffer)
        {
            // flag buffer as no longer in use and release the semaphore
            // to allow more requests into the pool
            buffer.InUse = false;
            guard.Release();
        }

        class BufferReservation : IBufferRegistration
        {
            private readonly BufferPool pool;
            private readonly LOHBuffer buffer;

            public BufferReservation(BufferPool pool, LOHBuffer buffer)
            {
                this.pool = pool;
                this.buffer = buffer;
            }

            public byte[] Buffer
            {
                get { return buffer.Buffer; }
            }

            public void Dispose()
            {
                pool.Release(buffer);
            }
        }
    }
```

■ **Note** SemaphoreSlim's Wait method can also take a timeout. The code in Listing 4-20 should really pass a timeout to the call to Wait to ensure that any waiting thread can recover should the pool somehow become deadlocked or unresponsive. However, to constrain the amount of code in the listing, the timeout processing has been omitted.

Raising the Starting Gate: ManualResetEventSlim

We saw how the Monitor class can be used to raise notifications with Pulse and PulseAll. These APIs are, however, fairly low level, requiring the thread wanting notification to take special actions. .NET 4.0 introduced the ManualResetEventSlim class that wraps up the low-level API into something easier to use.

A ManualResetEventSlim has two states: Set and Unset. If the event is Set, then a thread calling Wait will return immediately. If the event is Unset, then calling Wait will block until the event transitions to the Set state. The constructor takes the initial state (default to Unset) and the Set and Reset methods change the event's state to Set and Unset, respectively.

ManualResetEventSlim can be used for general purpose signaling between threads, but is also commonly used to ensure that a group of threads does not proceed beyond a certain point until some initialization work has been completed.

For example, imagine you have a set of threads that load data from various data sources for processing. The exact processing required is based on a configuration file that is generated from another system, so once the threads have loaded the initial data, they cannot proceed until the configuration file is available. A ManualResetEventSlim is the ideal synchronization primitive here, as the processing threads call Wait after the initial data load, which will block. Once the configuration file is available, Set is called, which wakes up the processing threads. They now read the file, obtain the processing parameters they need, and start processing. Listing 4-21 shows the controlling thread that sets the event, and Listing 4-22 shows the processing thread that performs its initial work and then waits for the control file by waiting on the event.

Listing 4-21. Processing Control Thread

```
static void Main(string[] args)
{
    var matchers = new[] {"dowjones", "ftse", "nasdaq", "dax"};
    var controlFileAvailable = new ManualResetEventSlim();
    var tasks = new List<Task>();

    foreach (string matcherName in matchers)
    {
        var matcher = new Matcher(matcherName, MatchesFound, controlFileAvailable);
        tasks.Add(matcher.Process());
    }

    Console.WriteLine("Press enter when control file ready");
    Console.ReadLine();

    controlFileAvailable.Set();

    Task.WaitAll(tasks.ToArray());
}
```

Listing 4-22. Processing Thread

```
private void InternalProcess()
{
    IEnumerable<TradeDay> days = Initialize();

    controlFileAvailable.Wait();

    ControlParameters parameters = GetControlParameters();
    IEnumerable<TradeDay> matchingDays = null;
    if (parameters != null)
    {
        matchingDays = from d in days
                       where d.Date >= parameters.FromDate &&
                            d.Date <= parameters.ToDate && d.Volume >= parameters.Volume
                       select d;
    }

    matchesFound(dataSource, matchingDays);
}
```

CountdownEvent: Simplifying Fork and Join

You saw in Chapter 3 that parent/child tasks can be used to model the fork-and-join pattern, where the parent splits up a complex task into a set of child tasks that can run concurrently. The parent task is then not deemed complete until all the child tasks have finished. This allows code interested in the completion of the entire process to simply wait for the parent to complete. However, what if it isn't completion that is of interest, but rather an intermediate state, or whether it's impractical for a single task to spawn the other tasks? In this case it would be useful to have another primitive that could keep a count of completions.

CountdownEvent was introduced in .NET 4.0 to give a flexible way for a "controller" to synchronize with a set of subordinate tasks. We could achieve a similar effect by associating each subordinate task with a ManualResetEventSlim and then have the controller wait on all of the events, but this becomes ungainly with many subordinate tasks. CountdownEvent provides a single primitive that keeps track of a count internally. When a controller calls Wait it blocks until this internal count reaches zero. The count is decreased by a subordinate task calling Signal on the CountdownEvent.

Returning to the data-matching example from Listings 4-21 and 4-22, if the requirement changes so the controller (Main in Listing 4-21) should not change the control file until all the matchers have finished their initialization, then we can use a CountdownEvent to provide this coordination. Main waits on the CountdownEvent before replacing the control file, and the matchers signal the CountdownEvent when they have finished their initialization. We can see the updated code in Listing 4-23 and 4-24.

Listing 4-23. Controller Waiting on CountdownEvent

```
static void Main(string[] args)
{
    var matchers = new[] {"dowjones", "ftse", "nasdaq", "dax"};
    var controlFileAvailable = new ManualResetEventSlim();
    var tasks = new List<Task>();

    var initializationComplete = new CountdownEvent(matchers.Length);

    foreach (string matcherName in matchers)
    {
        var matcher = new Matcher(matcherName,
                                  MatchesFound,
                                  controlFileAvailable,
                                  initializationComplete);
        tasks.Add(matcher.Process());
    }

    initializationComplete.Wait();

    Console.WriteLine("Press enter when control file ready");
    Console.ReadLine();

    controlFileAvailable.Set();

    Task.WaitAll(tasks.ToArray());
}
```

Listing 4-24. Worker Signalling CountdownEvent

```
private void InternalProcess()
{
    IEnumerable<TradeDay> days = Initialize();

    initializationComplete.Signal();

    controlFileAvailable.Wait();

    ControlParameters parameters = GetControlParameters();
    IEnumerable<TradeDay> matchingDays = null;
    if (parameters != null)
    {
        matchingDays = from d in days
                       where d.Date >= parameters.FromDate &&
                             d.Date <= parameters.ToDate &&
                             d.Volume >= parameters.Volume
                       select d;
    }
    matchesFound(dataSource, matchingDays);
}
```

As with all of the synchronization primitives introduced in .NET 4.0, the Wait method can take a timeout and a CancellationToken. The CountdownEvent's internal count can be manipulated by the AddCount and TryAddCount method, which increase it, and the Reset method, which returns it to the original, or a specific, value.

Barrier: Rendezvous-Based Synchronization

Both ManualResetEvent and CountdownEvent are used when an external controller or coordinator are involved with asynchronous work. However, for some kinds of work, we need the workers to coordinate their activity between themselves. A common situation where this is necessary is when using geometric decomposition to evaluate the state of a system over a series of time intervals (for example calculating the weather).

GEOMETRIC DECOMPOSITION

Geometric decomposition is a pattern for parallelizing execution of an algorithm over a set of data by splitting the data into chunks and concurrently applying the algorithm to each chunk. Commonly the calculation for a specific chunk will require data from other chunks (e.g., edge conditions). Geometric decomposition can be applied to a wide variety of problems such as heat diffusion, matrix multiplication, and weather calculation.

The issue is that, because of the edge conditions, each new time interval can only be calculated once all concurrent calculations for the current time interval have completed. The individual tasks, therefore, need a way to ensure that, once they have completed the current time interval, they wait until everyone has gotten to the same stage—essentially arranging a rendezvous point.

Listing 4-25 shows an example of calculating heat diffusion over a series of iterations using geometric decomposition. The Material class models the material over which heat is diffusing, and two Material buffers are alternatively used as the source data and new generated values. The Range class is used to break the material into the chunks on which to apply the diffusion algorithm. Last, the Barrier is used to ensure that each Task has finished its current iteration before any of the Tasks move on to the next iteration.

Listing 4-25. Geometric Decomposition Controlled with a Barrier

```
Material DiffuseHeat(Material material, int iterations)
{
    Material[] materials = new Material[2];
    materials[0] = material;
    materials[1] = new Material(materials[0].Width);
    materials[1][0] = material[0];
    materials[1][material.Width - 1] = material[material.Width - 1];

    double dx = 1.0 / (double)material.Width;
    double dt = 0.5 * dx * dx;

    int nCores = 4;
    Range range = new Range() { Start = 1, End = material.Width - 1 };

    Barrier barrier = new Barrier(nCores);

    Task[] tasks = new Task[nCores];
    int nTask = 0;

    foreach (Range subRange in range.CreateSubRanges(nCores))
    {
        Range localRange = subRange;
        tasks[nTask++] =
        Task.Factory.StartNew(() =>
        {
            for (int nIteration = 0; nIteration < iterations; nIteration++)
            {
                Material src = materials[nIteration%2];
                Material dest = materials[(nIteration + 1)%2];

                for (int x = localRange.Start; x <= localRange.End; x++)
                {
                    dest[x] = src[x] + (dt/(dx*dx))*(src[x + 1] - 2*src[x] + src[x - 1]);
                }

                barrier.SignalAndWait();
            }
        });
    }

    }
    Task.WaitAll(tasks);

    return material;
}
```

The Barrier can also be passed an Action<Barrier> delegate, which gets executed once all of the tasks have arrived at the rendezvous but before they are all released from their wait. This allows the delegate exclusive access to the data so it can retrieve any required interim results. The number of participants in the coordination (passed to the Barrier constructor) can vary over time via the AddParticipant and RemoveParticipant methods on the Barrier class. Last, as usual, the SignalAndWait method can take a timeout and a CancellationToken.

Crossing the AppDomain Boundary with WaitHandle

So far every synchronization construct that we have looked at is implemented fully in managed code. On that basis none of these primitives can be used to coordinate activity between AppDomains and separate processes. Sometimes you will need to be able to control access or signal beyond a single AppDomain. For example, if two applications both needed to update the same file then you would need to control access to the file between the processes. If the code was running in the same AppDomain, you could quite easily use a Monitor, but that isn't going to work cross-process. Another quite common requirement is to have only one instance of an application running, so that attempting to start another instance in fact just brings the existing instance to the fore. To achieve a single instance, you need some kind of signaling mechanism between the existing instance and the new instance.

The kernel has its own synchronization primitives: `Mutex`, `Semaphore`, `ManualResetEvent`, and `AutoResetEvent`. As these are kernel mode constructs they can be used for synchronization across the AppDomain and process boundaries. They all have the concept of being in a signaled and nonsignaled state.

Mutex

Mutex stands for Mutual Exclusion. It is conceptually very similar to a `Monitor`, though it does have some differences in functionality. Only one thread at a time can own a mutex, and the mutex is signaled when it has no owner and is nonsignaled when it is owned.

Unlike other synchronization primitives, mutexes support the concept of abandonment. A mutex is deemed abandoned if the thread that owns it terminates. An abandoned mutex is either a sign of abrupt termination of a process or a software bug where a code path does not release the mutex.

Semaphore

The kernel semaphore is very similar in functionality to `SemaphoreSlim`, but is not bound to a single AppDomain; it provides a counted lock for a pool of resources. Like mutexes, semaphores are shared between processes by naming them. A semaphore is deemed signaled while the current count is less than the maximum count and nonsignaled when the maximum count is reached.

Events

Kernel events provide a cross-AppDomain signaling mechanism. They are signaled when set and nonsignaled when reset. The idea is very similar to `ManualResetEventSlim`, although not limited to an AppDomain. However, there are actually two types of event in the kernel, Manual Reset Event and Auto Reset Event. Manual Reset Event is what `ManualResetEventSlim` was based on and so has the same behavior—that is, it moves between its set and reset states by explicit method calls. On the other hand, Auto Reset Event will, as the name suggests, automatically reset once one waiting thread has been woken up.

WaitHandle—The Kernel Synchronization Abstraction

The .NET framework models these kernel synchronization objects with an abstraction called `WaitHandle`. The key method on `WaitHandle` is the `WaitOne` method, which returns immediately if the kernel object is in a signaled state and blocks if in an unsignaled state. The `System.Threading` classes `Mutex`, `Semaphore`, `ManualResetEvent`, and `AutoResetEvent` all derive directly or indirectly from `WaitHandle`. You can see the inheritance model in Figure 4-4.

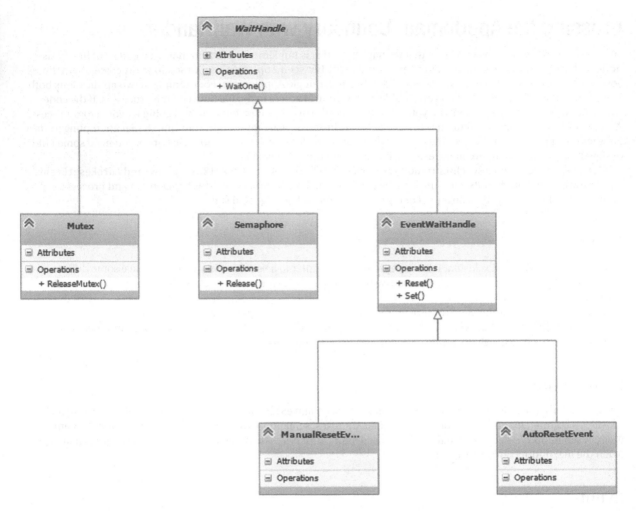

Figure 4-4. *WaitHandle-based class hierarchy*

To use a WaitHandle-based primitive across processes, you must give it a name when you create it. Both processes intending to access the same primitive must use the same name to ensure they both reference the same kernel object. The first process to attempt to create the primitive will create the kernel object; the second will just obtain a reference (a handle under the covers) to the existing one. If code needs to know whether or not it created the primitive, it can pass a Boolean out parameter to the constructor, which is set to true or false depending on whether the primitive was created or not, respectively. Also, if the process should always attach to an existing primitive, then it can call OpenExisting or TryOpenExisting on the named primitive.

EventWaitHandle is where all the real functionality of kernel events is based. ManualResetEvent and AutoResetEvent are only really façades that configure the EventWaitHandle in a specific way. In fact, if you want to create a named event, which is required for cross-process synchronization, you need to use EventWaitHandle directly rather than either ManualResetEvent or AutoResetEvent.

■ **Note** In general the behavior of these classes shouldn't be too surprising. However, it's worth calling out the potentially confusing behavior of the Mutex class when a mutex is abandoned. Because an abandoned mutex can indicate a coding bug, since version 2.0 of .NET the WaitOne method on a Mutex throws an AbandonedMutexException so you can record the fact that the mutex was abandoned. The waiting thread, though, does actually now have ownership of the mutex, and it must remember to release it. This is an unusual use of an exception, where the attempted function actually works even though the exception was thrown.

To see WaitHandles in action, let's look at an example of a single instance application. The idea is that we use a named auto reset event (via an EventWaitHandle). If the event is actually created, then the application knows it's the first instance, so it runs as normal but also asynchronously waits for the event to signal. A second instance will find that the kernel event already exists, so it simply sets the event and exits. Now the first instance wakes up and makes itself the active application, giving us the behavior we are looking for. An example of this, in Windows Presentation Foundation (WPF), is shown in Listing 4-26.

Listing 4-26. Single Instance Application Using an Auto Reset Event

```
public partial class App : Application
{
    private const string eventName = "84bb9974-fb13-4927-bf47-91f9fca1601c";
    private EventWaitHandle singleInstanceEvent;

    protected override void OnStartup(StartupEventArgs e)
    {
        bool created;
        singleInstanceEvent = new EventWaitHandle(false,
                                        EventResetMode.AutoReset,
                                        eventName,
                                        out created);

        if (!created)
        {
            singleInstanceEvent.Set();
            Shutdown();
        }
        else
        {
            SynchronizationContext ctx = SynchronizationContext.Current;
            Task.Factory.StartNew(() =>
                    {
                        while (true)
                        {
                            singleInstanceEvent.WaitOne();
                            ctx.Post(_ => MakeActiveApplication(), null);
                        }
                    });
        }

        base.OnStartup(e);
    }
```

```
    private void MakeActiveApplication()
    {
        MainWindow.Activate();
        MainWindow.Topmost = true;
        MainWindow.Topmost = false;
        MainWindow.Focus();
    }
}
```

Working with Multiple WaitHandles

Sometimes you need to be able to work with more than one WaitHandle at a time; for example, to gain ownership of two mutexes or take action if either of two events signals. For this purpose the WaitHandle class has three static methods: WaitAll, WaitAny, and SignalAndWait.

WaitHandle.WaitAll

The WaitAll method takes an array of WaitHandles and, optionally, a timeout. It blocks until all of the WaitHandles signal or the timeout elapses. The benefits of this over simply sequentially calling WaitOne on the individual WaitHandles are twofold. First, you can have an overall timeout for waiting for all of the kernel objects; but, probably more important in the case of mutexes and semaphores, the WaitAll method will obtain all or none of the synchronization objects—in other words, the lock acquisition is guaranteed deadlock free. The maximum number of items that can be passed in the array is 64.

WaitHandle.WaitAny

Similar to WaitAll, WaitAny takes an array of WaitHandles and an optional timeout. However, as the name suggests, WaitAny returns as soon as one of the WaitHandles signals. It returns the index of the signaled WaitHandle in the array or the discrete value defined by the constant WaitHandle.WaitTimeout if the timeout is reached before any of the WaitHandles signal. One common use of WaitAny is to spin up a set of asynchronous operations, all trying to achieve the same end but by different means. You can then use WaitAny to signal which one has achieved the goal first so the results can be retrieved. The other main use is to take a set of asynchronous operations and process their results as they finish by repeatedly calling WaitAny, removing the completed operation from the list and then calling WaitAny again.

WaitHandle.SignalAndWait

SignalAndWait takes two WaitHandles and an optional timeout as parameters. It signals the first WaitHandle and waits on the second up to the timeout. SignalAndWait is really a convenience wrapper rather than providing functionality that can't otherwise be achieved, as it does not guarantee atomicity between the signal and the wait.

■ **Caution** WaitHandles can seem the most flexible option for synchronization. However, be aware that, because they require a kernel transition, they are much more expensive than fully managed primitives—one to two orders of magnitude slower.

Integrating Standard Primitives and Kernel Objects

What if you needed to wait on a mutex and, say, a SemaphoreSlim? At first glance these seem to be two separate families of synchronization objects. However, nearly all of the primitives introduced in .NET 4.0 can provide a WaitHandle that can be used with WaitHandle.WaitAll and WaitHandle.WaitAny. ManulResetEventSlim and CountdownEvent have a WaitHandle property, and SemaphoreSlim has an AvailableWaitHandle property. Only Barrier is missing this facility. All three synchronization classes wrap up, directly or indirectly, a demand-allocated ManualResetEvent that provides the WaitHandle if required.

Synchronization Is Not the Only Answer

Cast your mind back to the start of this chapter. Remember, we only need synchronization when we have shared, mutable data with nonatomic update. Sometimes it is possible to restructure an algorithm to take advantage of this fact rather than having to introduce synchronization primitives.

In Listing 4-17 we reviewed using ReaderWriterLockSlim to optimize a news cache for high read and low write concurrency. This is obviously a huge improvement over using a Monitor that serializes all of the reads, but the reader is still paying a cost both in terms of having to take a read lock and, more importantly, having to create a copy of the matching news items using ToList. In an ideal world you could have the readers all free-running, even if we have to make the write operation much more expensive, as reads are far more frequent than writes.

The CLR gives you a very important guarantee: reference assignment is always atomic. On 32-bit CLR, references are 32 bit, and on 64-bit CLR, they are 64 bit. This means they can be assigned in a single processor instruction. You can therefore rewrite the AddNewsItem method to copy the existing news cache items (this is a read operation on the list), add the new item to the copy, and then assign the copy as the new items list. At this point the GetNews method is no longer affected by the AddNewsItem and so does not need synchronization. If you want to support multiple writers, you will still need synchronization in the AddNewsItem to ensure only one item is added at a time, but you can use a Monitor for this. You can see an implementation in Listing 4-27. Note that GetNews no longer needs to use ToList to copy the matching news items.

Listing 4-27. Lock-Free Implementation of the News Cache

```
public class LockFreeCache
{
    private List<NewsItem> items = new List<NewsItem>();

    readonly object writeGuard = new object();

    public IEnumerable<NewsItem> GetNews(string tag)
    {
        return items.Where(ni => ni.Tags.Contains(tag));
    }

    public void AddNewsItem(NewsItem item)
    {
        lock (writeGuard)
        {
            var copy = new List<NewsItem>(items);
            copy.Add(item);
            items = copy;
        }
    }
}
```

Before you get too excited and go and attempt to change all of your code to lock-free algorithms, some notes of caution.

- Not all algorithms can be written lock free; there are often inherent issues in the functionality that force synchronization.

- Writing lock-free algorithms is very often far more complex than the example in Listing 4-27. There can be many subtle race conditions and they commonly require the use of `Interlocked.Exchange` and `Interlocked.CompareAndExchange`.

- Most code won't benefit from being lock free, as the level of contention is, in reality, very small. Synchronization is needed to ensure correct behavior, but the code very rarely ends up waiting for a lock. In this case there is no real advantage in using a lock-free algorithm.

Conclusion

As soon as you create multithreaded code, you have to take thread safety into consideration. As you have seen, the .NET framework provides many tools, with different costs and approaches, to help you achieve thread safety, but it only provides the tools. It is up to us, as developers, to use the appropriate approach correctly to achieve safety at a minimum cost.

In some ways it would be good if the framework classes themselves were inherently thread safe, but in reality this would add a big overhead for code that often doesn't need that feature. However, from .NET 4.0 on there has been a set of data structures that are, in fact, designed for concurrency—but that is the subject of the next chapter.

■ ■ ■

CHAPTER 5

Concurrent Data Structures

In the previous chapter we introduced the need to consider thread safety when sharing state across multiple threads. The techniques demonstrated required the developer to understand the possible race conditions and select the cheapest synchronization technique to satisfy thread safety. These techniques, while essential, can often become tedious and make the simplest of algorithms seemingly overly complicated and hard to maintain. This chapter will explore the use of built-in concurrent data structures shipped with TPL that will simplify our multithreaded code while maximizing concurrency and efficiency.

Simplifying Thread Safety

Listing 5-1 defines a CsvRepository class that on construction loads all CSV files for a given directory into memory. When the client of the repository requires the contents of a given CSV file, a call is made to the generic Map method. The Map method is supplied a function that can turn a CSV row (string[ ]) into the supplied generic type argument. The Map method then returns an IEnumerable of the supplied generic type argument. Thus the repository returns each CSV row mapped to the more specific type.

Listing 5-1. Eager Loading CsvRepository

```
public class CsvRepository
{
  private readonly string directory;
  private Dictionary<string, List<string[]>> csvFiles;

  public CsvRepository(string directory)
  {
    this.directory = directory;
    csvFiles = new DirectoryInfo(directory)
              .GetFiles("*.csv")
             .ToDictionary(f => f.Name, f => LoadData(f.FullName).ToList());
  }
  public IEnumerable<string> Files { get { return csvFiles.Keys; }}

  public IEnumerable<T> Map<T>(string dataFile,Func<string[],T> map )
  {
    return csvFiles[dataFile].Skip(1).Select(map);
  }

  private IEnumerable<string[]> LoadData(string filename)
  {
```

```
    using (var reader = new StreamReader(filename))
    {
      while (!reader.EndOfStream)
      { yield return reader.ReadLine().Split(','); }
    }
  }
}
```

While the code in Listing 5-1 works, it may be inefficient, as all the CSV files are loaded immediately. This could affect startup time, and even result in a greater memory footprint than is ultimately required. An alternative approach would be to load each CSV when the Map method is called for the first time for each CSV file; this is known as Lazy Loading. Listing 5-2 shows the refactored code to implement Lazy Loading.

Listing 5-2. Lazy Loading CsvRepository

```
public class CsvRepository
{
  private readonly string directory;
  private Dictionary<string, List<string[]>> csvFiles;

  public CsvRepository(string directory)
  {
    this.directory = directory;
    csvFiles = new DirectoryInfo(directory)
              .GetFiles("*.csv")
              .ToDictionary<FileInfo,string,
                          List<string[]>>(f => f.Name, f => null);
  }
  public IEnumerable<string> Files { get { return csvFiles.Keys; }}

  public IEnumerable<T> Map<T>(string dataFile,Func<string[],T> map )
  {
      return LazyLoadData(dataFile).Skip(1).Select(map);
  }
  private IEnumerable<string[]> LoadData(string filename) { . . . }

  private IEnumerable<string[]> LazyLoadData(string filename)
  {
    List<string[]> csvFile = null;
    csvFile = csvFiles[filename];

    if (csvFile == null)
    {
        csvFile = LoadData(Path.Combine(directory, filename)).ToList();
        csvFiles[filename] = csvFile;
    }
     return csvFile;
  }
}
```

While Listing 5-2 achieves the goal of Lazy Loading, it does introduce a problem if this code is to be utilized in a multithreaded environment. When multiple threads access the repository at the same time, the following issues may arise.

1. The same CSV could be loaded multiple times, as checking for null and loading the CSV file is not an atomic operation.

2. The Dictionary class is not thread safe, and as such it may be possible that manipulating the Dictionary across multiple threads could put the Dictionary into an invalid state.

To resolve these issues, you could resort to a lock inside the LazyLoadData method to ensure that all access to the Dictionary is synchronized. Listing 5-3 shows the reworked LazyLoadData method. This new method fixes the preceding highlighted issues, but creates a new issue. The reason for the synchronization was to allow the repository to be shared by multiple threads; however, the locking strategy adopted potentially creates a bottleneck, if multiple threads require CSV access at the same time.

Listing 5-3. Thread-Safe Lazy Loading

```
private IEnumerable<string[]> LazyLoadData(string filename)
{
  lock (csvFiles)
  {
    List<string[]> csvFile = null;

    csvFile = csvFiles[filename];

    if (csvFile == null)
    {
      csvFile = LoadData(Path.Combine(directory, filename)).ToList();
      csvFiles[filename] = csvFile;
    }
    return csvFile;
  }
}
```

To reduce the number of possible bottlenecks, you could decide to synchronize only when you need to update the Dictionary. Listing 5-4 shows a refactored LazyLoadData method that now only acquires the lock on the Dictionary when accessing the Dictionary. This version will certainly have less contention, but there is now the possibility of two threads asking for the same unloaded CSV file and both threads loading it (although one of the two will ultimately become garbage).

Listing 5-4. Less Possibility for Contention

```
private IEnumerable<string[]> LazyLoadData(string filename)
{
  List<string[]> csvFile = null;
  lock (csvFiles)
  {
    csvFile = csvFiles[filename];
  }

  if (csvFile == null)
  {
    // Two threads could be loading the same csv
```

```
    csvFile = LoadData(Path.Combine(directory, filename)).ToList();
    lock (csvFiles)
    {
      csvFiles[filename] = csvFile;
    }
  }
  return csvFile;
}
```

To reduce contention and avoid loading the same CSV file repeatedly, you could introduce finer-grain locking. By having a lock for each CSV file you could allow multiple different CSV files to be accessed at the same time. When access is required to the same CSV file, the threads need to wait on the same lock. The aim of the lock is to protect the creation of the List<string> for a given CSV file, and as such you can't use the List<string> itself. You therefore need a stand-in, something similar to a virtual proxy. This stand-in will be very quick and inexpensive to create. The stand-in will provide the fine-grained lock, and in addition will contain a field that points to the loaded CSV file. Listing 5-5 shows the refactored code.

Listing 5-5. Finer-Grain Locking

```
 public class CsvRepository
{

    public class VirtualCsv
    {
        public List<string[]> Value;
    }

    private readonly string directory;
    private Dictionary<string, VirtualCsv> csvFiles;

    public CsvRepository(string directory)
    {
        this.directory = directory;
        csvFiles = new DirectoryInfo(directory)
            .GetFiles("*.csv")
            .ToDictionary<FileInfo,string,VirtualCsv>(f => f.Name, f => new VirtualCsv());
    }
    public IEnumerable<string> Files { get { return csvFiles.Keys; }}

    public IEnumerable<T> Map<T>(string dataFile,Func<string[],T> map )
    {
        return LazyLoadData(dataFile).Skip(1).Select(map);
    }


    private IEnumerable<string[]> LoadData(string filename){ . . . }

    private IEnumerable<string[]> LazyLoadData(string filename)
    {
        lock (csvFiles[filename])
        {
```

```
        List<string[]> csvFile = csvFiles[filename].Value;

        if (csvFile == null)
        {
            csvFile = LoadData(Path.Combine(directory, filename)).ToList();

            csvFiles[filename].Value = csvFile;

        }

        return csvFile;
    }
  }
}
```

With the modifications in Listing 5-5 you now have an implementation that guards access to each file separately, allowing multiple files to be accessed and loaded at the same time. This implementation ensures two things.

1. Each CSV file is only loaded once.

2. Multiple CSV files can be accessed concurrently, while preserving thread safety.

This latest version is therefore a vast improvement on previous versions in terms of thread safety and memory efficiency. If this was our homework assignment, the teacher might have written, "Good, but could do better." When each thread requests a given CSV file, LazyLoadData will be called. LazyLoadData obtains the lock for the given CSV file, and then proceeds to return the previously loaded file or loads it. The step of obtaining the lock is required only if you do need to load the CSV file and update the dictionary. It is perfectly safe to execute List<string[]> csvFile = csvFiles[filename].Value without the need to obtain the lock, as the reading and writing of this value is atomic. By removing the lock around this piece of code you only pay the cost of synchronization when you need it: when initially loading the CSV file (see Listing 5-6).

Listing 5-6. Less Synchronization

```
private IEnumerable<string[]> LazyLoadData(string filename)
{
    // Atomic operation, .NET 2.0+ Strong memory model means this is safe
    List<string[]> csvFile = csvFiles[filename].Value;

    if (csvFile == null)
    {
        lock (csvFiles[filename])
        {
            csvFile = LoadData(Path.Combine(directory, filename)).ToList();
            // Now the CSV file is fully loaded, use an atomic write to say it's available
            csvFiles[filename].Value = csvFile;
        }
    }
    return csvFile;
}
```

Listing 5-6 is more efficient in terms of synchronization, but it does create an opportunity for a race condition. If two threads attempt to access an unloaded CSV file, they will both end up loading the CSV file. Why?

Well, both threads will see that csvFile is null and proceed to the lock statement. The first one to arrive at the lock statement will enter the lock block and load the CSV file. The second thread will be waiting at the lock block, and once the first thread has completed it will then proceed to load the CSV file again. To resolve this problem, use a technique called double check locking. Listing 5-7 shows an implementation.

Listing 5-7. Double Check Locking

```
private IEnumerable<string[]> LazyLoadData(string filename)
{
    List<string[]> csvFile = csvFiles[filename].Value;

    if (csvFile == null)
    {
      lock (csvFiles[filename])
      {
         csvFile = csvFiles[filename].Value;
         if (csvFile == null)
         {
            csvFile = LoadData(Path.Combine(directory, filename)).ToList();
            csvFiles[filename].Value = csvFile;
         }
      }
    }

    return csvFile;
}
```

In the scenario where the CSV file has already been loaded, no synchronization is performed. If, however, the CSV file has not been loaded, then the lock is taken, which results in multiple threads requesting the same unloaded CSV file to be queued one behind another. As each thread gets the lock it checks again, since while waiting for the lock another thread may have loaded the CSV file. Therefore once the lock has been obtained, the null check is repeated and, if true, loads the CSV file. This technique means the creation path is a lot longer to execute; but accessing the resource, once created, is more efficient.

The code you have finally produced is now some way from its original state. The implementation of the CsvRepository is now organized along optimal concurrency principles, resulting in code that is harder to read and maintain. Further, the success of this code is reliant on the .NET 2.0 strong memory model; if that were to change, then the preceding code might become non-thread-safe. Alternatively you might think that having this level of complexity and coupling would be better encapsulated inside the platform, and to that end TPL exposes many concurrent data structures. This chapter will introduce these new types and demonstrate how greatly they simplify the implementation of thread-safe code, ensuring that you as a developer need to care a little less about the subtleties of the memory model.

Lazy<T>

The first of these data structures we will examine is Lazy<T>. The Lazy<T> type acts as a placeholder for an object that needs to be created not now, but sometime in the future. Why defer? The object could be expensive to create or use large amount of resources, so you don't want to create it until you need it, and for now you just need a placeholder. This is the use case in Listing 5-5, where you created your own type, VirtualCSV. Listing 5-8 shows a simple use of Lazy<T>.

Listing 5-8. Simple Use of Lazy<T>

```csharp
public class Person
{
  public Person()
  {
    Thread.Sleep(2000);
    Console.WriteLine("Created");
  }
  public string Name { get; set; }
  public int Age { get; set; }

  public override string ToString()
  {
    return string.Format("Name: {0}, Age: {1}", Name, Age);
  }
}
class Program
{
  static void Main(string[] args)
  {
    Lazy<Person> lazyPerson = new Lazy<Person>();

    Console.WriteLine("Lazy object created");
    Console.WriteLine("has person been created {0}", lazyPerson.IsValueCreated ? "Yes":"No");

    Console.WriteLine("Setting Name");
    lazyPerson.Value.Name = "Andy"; // Creates the person object on fetching Value
    Console.WriteLine("Setting Age");
    lazyPerson.Value.Age = 21; // Re-uses same object from first call to Value

    Person andy = lazyPerson.Value;
    Console.WriteLine(andy);
  }
}
```

Running the program from Visual Studio with Ctrl+F5 produces the results shown in Figure 5-1.

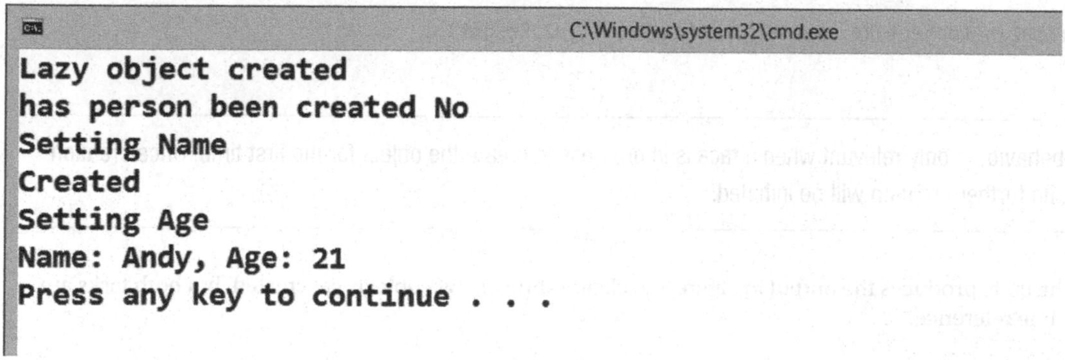

```
                          C:\Windows\system32\cmd.exe
Lazy object created
has person been created No
Setting Name
Created
Setting Age
Name: Andy, Age: 21
Press any key to continue . . .
```

Figure 5-1. Output from Listing 5-8

Figure 5-1 clearly demonstrates that the person object doesn't get created until the Value is requested, as shown by the "Created" message. The "Created" message only appears once, proving that subsequent calls made to lazyPerson.Value will result in the same object being returned. Lazy<T> is by default thread safe. If multiple threads share the same Lazy<T> object, the Lazy<T> object guarantees that only one object will ever be created. If, during the construction of the object, another thread requests the value, the second thread will block, waiting for the value to be fully constructed by the other thread. Once it has been constructed it is then shared with the second thread. If this level of thread safety is not required and you simply want lazy creation, an enumeration indicating thread safety is not required can be passed as a constructor parameter (see Listing 5-9).

Listing 5-9. Lazy<T>, No Thread Safety

```
static void Main(string[] args)
{
    Lazy<Person> lazyPerson = new Lazy<Person>(LazyThreadSafetyMode.None);

    Task<Person> p1 = Task.Run<Person>(() => lazyPerson.Value);
    Task<Person> p2 = Task.Run<Person>(() => lazyPerson.Value);

    Console.WriteLine(object.ReferenceEquals(p1.Result,p2.Result));
}
```

Since you have deliberately slowed down the construction of the Person object with a Thread.Sleep, running the code in Listing 5-9 will result in the constructor being called twice and both threads getting their own copies of Person. It turns out there is a halfway option that allows multiple objects to be created, but only the first one to be created will ever get exposed through the Value property. Listing 5-10 will cause two objects to be created, but the Person object returned from the Value property will be the same from both tasks. This technique can be useful if the creation logic is very cheap, and you only care about having one reference exposed. The thread safety logic for this approach is cheaper to implement inside the Lazy<T> object, as instead of using a full-blown lock an Interlocked.CompareExchange is used.

Listing 5-10. Possible Multiple Creation, but Only One Published

```
static void Main(string[] args)
{
    Lazy<Person> lazyPerson = new Lazy<Person>(LazyThreadSafetyMode.PublicationOnly);

    Task<Person> p1 = Task.Run<Person>(() => lazyPerson.Value);
    Task<Person> p2 = Task.Run<Person>(() => lazyPerson.Value);

    Console.WriteLine(object.ReferenceEquals(p1.Result,p2.Result));
}
```

■ **Note** This behavior is only relevant when a race is in progress to create the object for the first time. Once creation has completed, no further creation will be initiated.

Running the code produces the output in Figure 5-2, clearly showing two objects get created, but both tasks are returning the same reference.

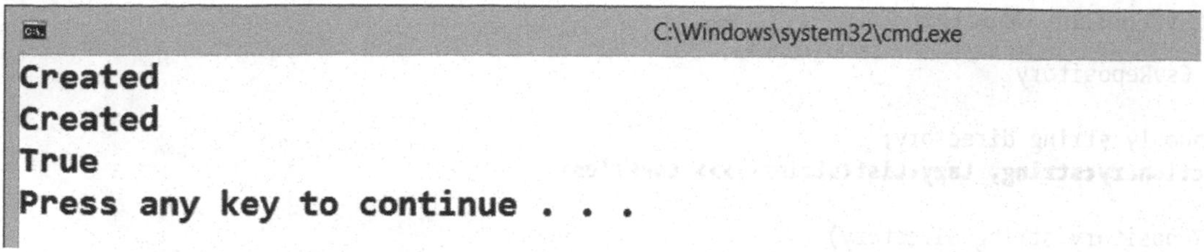

```
C:\Windows\system32\cmd.exe

Created
Created
True
Press any key to continue . . .
```

Figure 5-2. *Non-thread-safe creation*

Perhaps an obvious question is how does Lazy<T> create an instance of T? With the code you have developed so far it is relying on the fact that T has a public parameterless constructor. Lazy<T> is simply using reflection to create the instance. If you were to modify the Person class not to have one, then you would get not a compilation error but a runtime exception. To resolve this and thus support lazy construction scenarios where you need to supply construction parameters, Lazy<T> allows the supplying of a Func<T> that it will use to construct the object as opposed to using the constructor directly via reflection.

Listing 5-11 demonstrates a use of Lazy<T> that utilizes your supplied creation logic as opposed to a parameterless constructor. I find this the most common scenario for Lazy<T> as more often than not you need to supply constructor parameters; as an additional benefit it provides compile time checking for the creation logic.

Listing 5-11. Function to Create Object

```
public class Person
{
    public Person(string name)
    {
        Name = name;
    }
    public string Name { get; private set; }
    public int Age { get; set; }

    public override string ToString()
    {
        return string.Format("Name: {0}, Age: {1}", Name, Age);
    }
}
class Program
{
    static void Main(string[] args)
    {
        // Would cause a runtime exception, since Person now does not have
        // a parameterless constructor
        // var lazyPerson = new Lazy<Person>()

        var lazyPerson = new Lazy<Person>(() => new Person("Andy"));
    }
}
```

Armed with this new type you can now refactor your CsvRepository to use Lazy<T> as opposed to your own homegrown locking strategy. Listing 5-12 shows the refactored code.

Listing 5-12. CsvRepository Using Lazy<T>

```
public class CsvRepository
{
  private readonly string directory;
  private Dictionary<string, Lazy<List<string[]>>> csvFiles;

  public CsvRepository(string directory)
  {
    this.directory = directory;
    csvFiles = new DirectoryInfo(directory)
                .GetFiles("*.csv")
                .ToDictionary(f => f.Name,
                              f => new Lazy<List<string[]>>(() => LoadData(f.Name).ToList()));
  }
  public IEnumerable<string> Files { get { return csvFiles.Keys; } }

  public IEnumerable<T> Map<T>(string dataFile, Func<string[], T> map)
  {
    return csvFiles[dataFile].Value.Skip(1).Select(map);
  }

  private IEnumerable<string[]> LoadData(string filename)
  {
    using (var reader = new StreamReader(Path.Combine(directory, filename)))
    {
      while (!reader.EndOfStream)
      {
        yield return reader.ReadLine().Split(',');
      }
    }
  }
}
```

Listing 5-12 has all the same behavior as our final double check locking version in Listing 5-7 , but is almost identical to our initial eager-loading version, Listing 5-1. The only change you have made is to wrap our List<string[]> with a Lazy<List<string[]>>. Creating items ahead of time often simplifies concurrency issues, and Lazy<T> allows for this without having to pay the ultimate price of creating the actual thing until it is required.

Concurrent Collections

The standard .NET collection types Dictionary<K,V>, Queue<T>, Stack<T>, and the like form the bedrock of many applications. Unfortunately these collections are not thread safe, so having versions of them that work in a multithreaded environment would be a great asset. The remainder of this chapter will be spent examining a set of types that at first glance provide thread-safe versions of these standard collection types. It is important to understand that while these types have been implemented as a replacement for the non-thread-safe ones, they have at times a very different API.

The API has been designed with concurrency in mind; this is possibly best explained via the use of an example. Listing 5-13 shows the safe way of ensuring that a queue has at least one item before attempting to dequeue. If a check was not made and an attempt to dequeue was made against an empty queue, an exception would be thrown. Since you don't want to use exceptions for flow control, check if the operation is allowed before making the call. Now imagine you wanted to use a shared instance of the Queue<T> class with multiple threads. Unfortunately the Queue<T> type is not thread safe and so it would not be recommended to share this Queue<T> object between multiple threads. However, even if work was undertaken by Microsoft to ensure that the internal mechanics of the Queue<T> class were thread safe, this code would still not be fit for this purpose! Why?

Listing 5-13. Safe Use of Queue<T>

```
Queue<int> queue = new Queue<int>();
. . .

if (queue.Count > 0)
{
    int val = queue.Dequeue();
}
```

The internal thread safety of the object is just one issue. Assume for now that the Queue<T> class is thread safe. Assume also that the code in Listing 5-13 is being executed by multiple threads. As long as there are more items in the queue than threads attempting to dequeue, life is good. If there are two consumers and only one item in the queue, then you have a race condition. Both threads examine the Count; both move forward to dequeue; one dequeues successfully; and the second one throws an exception. While both the Count and Dequeue operations are thread safe, what you actually require is a method on the Queue<T> type that performs both these operations inside the Queue<T> type itself—in other words, make the check and dequeue operation a single atomic operation against the queue. It therefore does not make sense to have a simple dequeue operation on a concurrent queue working in the same way as the regular Queue<T> type, and so you will not find one. What you will find is a TryDequeue operation as shown in Listing 5-14. As its name suggests, TryDequeue attempts to dequeue, but if it fails due to no items it will return false, as opposed to throwing an exception.

Listing 5-14. ConcurrentQueue-Appropriate API

```
ConcurrentQueue<int> queue = new ConcurrentQueue<int>();

int val;
if (queue.TryDequeue(out val))
{
  Console.WriteLine(val);
}
```

There are many other examples where finer-grained operations on the original collection types have been replaced or augmented with larger atomic operations. The remainder of this chapter will explore how you can use these new types to simplify the process of writing thread-safe algorithms.

ConcurrentDictionary<K,V>

As stated earlier, the base class library type Dictionary<K,V> is not thread safe. Attempting to share such an object across multiple threads could result in unexpected behavior. Listing 5-1's implementation of the CsvRepository used Dictionary<string,List<string[]>>; the Map method could be safely used across multiple threads since the dictionary was completely built as part of the CsvRepository constructor and all further uses were read based. What if you changed CsvRepository to provide access not just to CSV files that were present at construction time, but also to whatever files are currently in the directory when the Map method is called? This would prevent you from prebuilding the dictionary in the constructor. Listing 5-15 shows a non-thread-safe version. Calling the Map method from multiple threads may very well work, but it may also fail.

Listing 5-15. Non-Thread-Safe Dynamic CsvRepository

```
public class DynamicLazyCsvRepository
{
  private readonly string directory;
  private Dictionary<string, List<string[]>> csvFiles;

  public DynamicLazyCsvRepository(string directory)
  {
    this.directory = directory;
    csvFiles = new Dictionary<string, List<string[]>>();
  }
  public IEnumerable<string> Files {
     get { return new DirectoryInfo(directory).GetFiles().Select(fi => fi.FullName); }
  }

  public IEnumerable<T> Map<T>(string dataFile, Func<string[], T> map)
  {
    List<string[]> csvFile;
    if (!csvFiles.TryGetValue(dataFile, out csvFile))
    {
      csvFile = LoadData(dataFile).ToList();
      csvFiles.Add(dataFile,csvFile);
    }
    return csvFile.Skip(1).Select(map);
  }

  private IEnumerable<string[]> LoadData(string filename)
  {
    using (var reader = new StreamReader(Path.Combine(directory, filename)))
    {
      while (!reader.EndOfStream)
      {
       yield return reader.ReadLine().Split(',');
      }
    }
  }
}
```

Failure may occur when two threads ask for the same unloaded CSV file, as both threads may well attempt to load it. Once each thread has loaded the CSV file, they then attempt to add it to the dictionary; the first will succeed but the second will receive an exception stating the item already exists (Figure 5-3). This would never have been a problem when running in a single-threaded environment.

```
C:\Windows\system32\cmd.exe                                      _  □  x

Unhandled Exception: System.AggregateException: One or more errors occurred. -
   at System.ThrowHelper.ThrowArgumentException(ExceptionResource resource)
   at System.Collections.Generic.Dictionary`2.Insert(TKey key, TValue value, B
   at ConcurrentDictionaryExample.ConcurrentDitionaryLazyCsvRepository.Map[T](
r5\ConcurrentDictionaryExample\ConcurrentDitionaryLazyCsvRepository.cs:line 33
   at ConcurrentDictionaryExample.Program.ProcessRandomFiles(ICSVRepository re
5\ConcurrentDictionaryExample\Program.cs:line 44
   at ConcurrentDictionaryExample.Program.<>c__DisplayClass2.<Main>b__0() in c
ogram.cs:line 27
   at System.Threading.Tasks.Task.InnerInvoke()
   at System.Threading.Tasks.Task.Execute()
   --- End of inner exception stack trace ---
   at System.Threading.Tasks.Task.WaitAll(Task[] tasks, Int32 millisecondsTime
   at ConcurrentDictionaryExample.Program.Main(String[] args) in c:\Repository
e 30
Press any key to continue . . .
```

Figure 5-3. Attempting to add same value to dictionary

The more fundamental issue with this code is that the Dictionary<K,V> type is not thread safe, so even if you never get an exception, you may still have harmed the internal state of the dictionary. The ConcurrentDictionary<K,V> on the other hand is thread safe, so using it avoids the risk of internal corruption. As we said earlier, just because this type is a thread-safe version of a dictionary, it does not therefore follow that the API will be identical. Also as discussed earlier, the Add method on the Dictionary<K,V> type throws an exception when an attempt is made to add a value with the same key. In a non-multithreaded environment this can be prevented by checking if the key exists before adding. In a multithreaded environment, however, you can't do that, since each call to the dictionary could be interlaced with another thread making similar calls. For that reason there is no Add method on the ConcurrentDictionary<K,V> only a TryAdd method, which will return false if the add fails due to the key already being present. Listing 5-16 shows an initial refactoring to ConcurrentDictionary<K,V>.

Listing 5-16. Initial Refactor to ConcurrentDictionary

```csharp
public class ConcurrentDictionaryLazyCsvRepository
{
    private readonly string directory;
    private ConcurrentDictionary<string, List<string[]>> csvFiles;

    public ConcurrentDictionaryLazyCsvRepository(string directory)
    {
        this.directory = directory;
        csvFiles = new ConcurrentDictionary<string, List<string[]>>();
    }

    public IEnumerable<string> Files {
        get { return new DirectoryInfo(directory).GetFiles().Select(fi => fi.FullName); }
    }
```

```
public IEnumerable<T> Map<T>(string dataFile, Func<string[], T> map)
{
  List<string[]> csvFile;
  if (!csvFiles.TryGetValue(dataFile, out csvFile))
  {
    csvFile = LoadData(dataFile).ToList();
    csvFiles.TryAdd(dataFile, csvFile);
  }
  return csvFile.Skip(1).Select(map);
}
    . . .
}
```

This initial refactoring satisfies the issue of thread safety, but masks a bigger issue. While you are only ever adding one dictionary entry per file, there is still the possibility of loading the CSV file many times. If two threads were to request the same unloaded CSV file, both would still load the file, which is clearly not what you want. What you want is for the CSV file to be loaded once only. The problem is that the process of checking if the item is in the dictionary, creating it, and adding it to the dictionary is not atomic. To resolve this you could perhaps use the AddOrGet method on the ConcurrentDictionary. This method takes the key and can either take the object to associate with the supplied key or a function that will create the object. The method returns the value associated with the supplied dictionary key. If a value is already associated with the key, the supplied value is ignored, and the associated value is returned. If the key is not present in the dictionary, the supplied value is inserted into the dictionary, and returned. Listing 5-17 shows a possible refactoring of the Map method. However this is not really much of an improvement, apart from being simpler code. The AddOrGet method on the ConcurrentDictionary will not prevent LoadData being called multiple times for the same key. It just removes the need to make two method calls for TryGetValue and then TryAdd. If only the object you wanted to place into the Dictionary were cheap to create this would not be an issue, as creating it many times would not matter as long as ultimately there is only one copy in the dictionary.

Listing 5-17. GetOrAdd

```
public IEnumerable<T> Map<T>(string dataFile, Func<string[], T> map)
{
  var csvFile = csvFiles.GetOrAdd(dataFile, df => LoadData(df).ToList());

  return csvFile.Skip(1).Select(map);
}
```

So while GetOrAdd doesn't solve our problem entirely, it does get you very close. To make it work you need to guarantee that the CSV data is loaded once only. You have already seen how to achieve this in a thread-safe way, Lazy<T>. By creating a Lazy<T> object that will ultimately load the data, you can safely create multiple lazy objects very cheaply, and rely on the fact that only one of them will ever reside in the dictionary. As long as you only ask for the value of the lazy object from a dictionary lookup, you can rely on the behavior of Lazy<T> to ensure you only get one copy of the CSV file loaded. Listing 5-18 shows an implementation utilizing ConcurrentDictionary with Lazy<T>

Listing 5-18. GetOrAdd with Lazy<T>

```
public class ConcurrentDictionaryLazyCsvRepository
{
  private readonly string directory;
  private ConcurrentDictionary<string, Lazy<List<string[]>>> csvFiles;
```

```
public ConcurrentDictionaryLazyCsvRepository(string directory)
{
    this.directory = directory;
    csvFiles = new ConcurrentDictionary<string, Lazy<List<string[]>>>();
}
public IEnumerable<string> Files {
    get { return new DirectoryInfo(directory).GetFiles().Select(fi => fi.FullName); }
}
public IEnumerable<T> Map<T>(string dataFile, Func<string[], T> map)
{
    var csvFile = new Lazy<List<string[]>>(() => LoadData(dataFile).ToList());
    csvFile = csvFiles.GetOrAdd(dataFile, csvFile);

    return csvFile.Value.Skip(1).Select(map);
}
```

I personally find the combination of ConcurrentDictionary<K,V> and Lazy<T> very useful. Other atomic operations on the ConcurrentDictionary<K,V> include AddOrUpdate and TryUpdate. AddOrUpdate method allows you to supply different values to use in the case that the Dictionary performs an Add or an Update. TryUpdate allows you to supply a comparison value, and if the value in the Dictionary is not the same as the comparison value, the value is not replaced.

Locking Mechanics

Last, it is worth mentioning that the implementation tries to keep contention low when accessing the dictionary. Figure 5-4 shows how ConcurrentDictionary<K,V> holds the key value pairs. It implements a chained hash table, in which each slot represents a set of possible values for a given hash value modulo the number of slots.

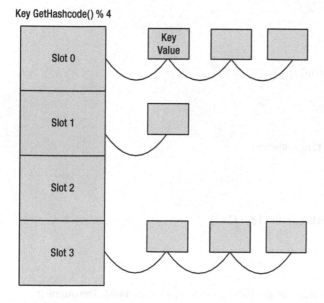

Figure 5-4. *Concurrent dictionary data structure*

Manipulating such a data structure by multiple threads will require synchronization. To do this it does not have a single lock to guard all access to the internals; rather it has a lock per slot. You can therefore add two values to the dictionary as long as their hashes don't end up in the same slot. If too many items end up inside one slot, the hash table is rebuilt with more slots to maintain access speed. Growing the dictionary will require all locks to be obtained by one thread; to limit this effect an initial size can be supplied as part of construction.

ConcurrentQueue<T> and ConcurrentStack<T>

ConcurrentQueue<T> and ConcurrentStack<T> provide thread-safe implementations of FIFO and LIFO, respectively. Having multiple threads consume items from one of these data structures lends itself to load-balancing the processing across a fixed number of threads. For example, suppose you have 20 files to process and four cores at your disposal. Giving each thread five files may seem logical, and would work assuming each file requires exactly the same amount of processing. Placing all work items into a queue and then letting each thread consume the next work item as it becomes free will result in fair distribution of the work when the work items could require differing amounts of processing. Listing 5-19 shows an example of a simple producer consumer implementation.

Listing 5-19. Simple Producer and Consumers

```
public class Program
{
  static void Main(string[] args)
  {
    var queue = new ConcurrentQueue<string>();

    foreach (FileInfo file in new DirectoryInfo(@"C:\Data")
                              .GetFiles("*.csv",SearchOption.AllDirectories))
    {
      queue.Enqueue(file.FullName);
    }

    var consumers = new Task[4];
    for (int i = 0; i < consumers.Length; i++)
    {
      consumers[i] = Task.Run(() => Consumer(queue));
    }
    Task.WaitAll(consumers);
  }

  public static void Consumer(ConcurrentQueue<string> queue)
  {
    string file;
    while (queue.TryDequeue(out file))
    {
      Console.WriteLine("{0}:Processing {1}",Task.CurrentId,file);
    }
  }
}
```

Listing 5-19 shows a simple example of a queue in which all the files to be processed are enqueued. The queue is then shared with four tasks, each of which will attempt to dequeue a filename and then process it. Notice that you are not calling a Dequeue method but TryDequeue. As mentioned earlier there is no Dequeue method as there is no thread-safe way to guarantee that there is an item to dequeue. You therefore have to use TryDequeue, which will return true if there is an item, the out parameter containing the dequeued item. If there are no items in the queue it will return false. There is, on the other hand, an Enqueue method, since this should only fail in exceptional circumstances, and therefore no need for a TryEnqueue method. Each of the consumer tasks will keep taking items from the queue until there are no more items to consume.

The consumers process the items in the order they were enqueued. Obviously if you used a ConcurrentStack<T> you would replace the Enqueue with a Push call and a TryDequeue with a TryPop. The items would then be processed in reverse order (LIFO).

ConcurrentBag<T>

You will often need to store a variable number of items for later consumption. A list is a standard data structure that achieves that goal and in addition preserves the order of insertion. So a list has items and order. A bag is another standard computer science data structure, which differs from a list in that a bag maintains all the items you add to it but doesn't guarantee the order. The base class library in .NET 4.0 provides a List<T> to implement a list, but this implementation is non-thread-safe. TPL does not provide a concurrent list but does offer a concurrent bag that you can use safely across threads without any application synchronization.

It is probably best to first describe what this type is not for. At first glance, you may be thinking, if I have multiple threads that wish to add and remove or fetch items from a shared bag, then this is the type for me. Unfortunately you would be wrong! A regular List<T> and a lock is more efficient. So what is it for? The ConcurrentBag<T> is useful for implementing a very specific form of the producer/consumer pattern. To implement the producer/consumer pattern the ConcurrentBag<T> has two key methods:

```
void Add(T item)

bool TryTake(T out item)
```

The ConcurrentBag<T> works best when the producer and consumer are running on the same thread. The reason for this is that each thread that adds items to the bag will have its own local linked list of items. A thread favors consuming items from its own local list before trying to steal items from another thread's list.

Algorithms that benefit from this take the following form: each thread takes items from the bag and decomposes them for further processing, ideally on the same thread. With multiple threads producing and consuming items from a shared bag, when a thread has no more items to process it will steal work from another thread. This provides a form of load balancing across the running threads. Listing 5-20 demonstrates this technique by walking the file system looking for files that match a given pattern. A task is created for each immediate directory under the initial directory, and supplied with the subdirectory it needs to explore, along with the file pattern match and a shared ConcurrentBag<DirectoryInfo>. Each task then walks its part of the directory structure by adding subdirectories to the bag and files that match to its own private result set. The task keeps looping, executing TryTake to obtain further subdirectories to explore. Once it has exhausted its part of the tree the TryTake will yield results from other tasks that have not completed their parts of the tree. Thus the tasks will run against their own highly concurrent internal list until they run out of work, then they will steal work from other threads' lists. When there are no more items in the bag all the tasks will have completed.

Listing 5-20. Directory Walker

```
public class ParallelFileFinderWithBag
{
  public static List<FileInfo> FindAllFiles(string path, string match)
  {
    var fileTasks = new List<Task<List<FileInfo>>>();
```

```
    var directories = new ConcurrentBag<DirectoryInfo>();

    foreach (DirectoryInfo dir in new DirectoryInfo(path).GetDirectories())
    {
        fileTasks.Add(Task.Run<List<FileInfo>>(() => Find(dir, directories, match)));
    }

    return (from fileTask in fileTasks
            from file in fileTask.Result
            select file).ToList();
}


private static List<FileInfo> Find(DirectoryInfo dir,
                                ConcurrentBag<DirectoryInfo> directories, string match)
{
    var files = new List<FileInfo>();

    directories.Add(dir);
    DirectoryInfo dirToExamine;
    while (directories.TryTake(out dirToExamine))
    {
        foreach (DirectoryInfo subDir in dirToExamine.GetDirectories())
        {
            directories.Add(subDir);
        }
        files.AddRange(dirToExamine.GetFiles(match));
    }
    return files;
}
}
```

In summary, ConcurrentBag<T> is not a general purpose thread-safe bag implementation. ConcurrentBag<T> is ideal when tasks need to further decompose work for future processing. Ideally the processing of decomposed work will be processed by the same thread that inserted the item into the bag; when a thread runs out of its own local items it is kept busy by stealing items from another thread for processing, which could result in the addition of more local work. Unlike a ConcurrentQueue<T> or ConcurrentStack<T>, the order the items to be processed is undefined.

Blocking Collections

Consider the producer/consumer implementation in Listing 5-21. The program creates a simple web server that delivers the current time when the following request is made from a browser: http://localhost:9000/Time. A single producer task is created, which has the role of listening for inbound HTTP requests, and then placing them on a concurrent queue. There are four consumer tasks, each of which is trying to obtain work from the concurrent queue.

Listing 5-21. Busy Producer Consumer

```
class Program
{
  static void Main(string[] args)
  {
```

```csharp
HttpListener listener = new HttpListener();
listener.Prefixes.Add("http://+:9000/Time/");

listener.Start();

var requestQueue = new ConcurrentQueue<HttpListenerContext>();
var producer = Task.Run(() => Producer(requestQueue, listener));

Task[] consumers = new Task[4];
for (int nConsumer = 0; nConsumer < consumers.Length; nConsumer++)
{
  consumers[nConsumer] = Task.Run(() => Consumer(requestQueue));
}

Console.WriteLine("Listening...");
Console.ReadLine();
}

public static void Producer(ConcurrentQueue<HttpListenerContext> queue, HttpListener listener)
{
  while (true)
  {
    queue.Enqueue(listener.GetContext());
  }
}


public static  void Consumer(ConcurrentQueue<HttpListenerContext> queue)
{
  while (true)
  {
    HttpListenerContext ctx;
    if (queue.TryDequeue(out ctx))
    {
      Console.WriteLine(ctx.Request.Url);
      Thread.Sleep(5000); // Simulate work
      using (StreamWriter writer = new StreamWriter(ctx.Response.OutputStream))
      {
        writer.WriteLine(DateTime.Now);
      }
    }
  }
}
}
```

While the application works, there is one major drawback in that when a consumer has no work to process, it executes a busy wait. The TryDequeue method returns immediately either with a value of true and an item to process, or most probably a return value of false, indicating nothing to process. In the case of no item, the code then simply tries again, hence the busy wait. In this situation it would be preferable if the thread simply went to sleep until an item of work becomes available, as in the producer/consumer pattern implemented in Chapter 4 with Pulse and Wait.

The Concurrent data structures are all about nonblocking, but as you can see there are times when you may desire blocking behavior. To that end TPL also includes a BlockingCollection<T>. BlockingCollection<T> adds blocking semantics to ConcurrentBag<T>,ConcurrentQueue<T>, and ConcurrentStack<T>. When creating the blocking collection you simply supply as a parameter an instance of the underlying collection type you wish to use; if you don't supply one it will use a ConcurrentQueue<T>. Since BlockingCollection<T> can wrap any of the collection types, it provides Add methods for adding and Take methods for removing. If the underlying collection is a ConcurrentQueue<T> the Add/Take will exhibit FIFO behavior; if it's a ConcurrentStack<T> they will exhibit LIFO behavior. The Take method is a blocking call so if no items are available from the underlying collection, the thread will be suspended until an item becomes available. The producer/consumer pattern has now been rewritten in Listing 5-22 to take advantage of BlockingCollection<T>. The consumer threads now peacefully sleep while waiting for items to process.

Listing 5-22. Blocking Producer/Consumer

```
public class Program
{
  static void Main(string[] args)
  {
    HttpListener listener = new HttpListener();
    listener.Prefixes.Add("http://+:9000/Time/");

    listener.Start();

    var requestQueue = new BlockingCollection<HttpListenerContext>(
                          new ConcurrentQueue<HttpListenerContext>());

    var producer = Task.Run(() => Producer(requestQueue, listener));

    Task[] consumers = new Task[4];
    for (int nConsumer = 0; nConsumer < consumers.Length; nConsumer++)
    {
      consumers[nConsumer] = Task.Run(() => Consumer(requestQueue));
    }
    Console.WriteLine("Listening..");
    Console.ReadLine();
    listener.Stop();
  }

  public static void Producer(BlockingCollection<HttpListenerContext> queue,
                          HttpListener listener)
  {
    while (true)
    {
      queue.Add(listener.GetContext());
    }
  }

  public static void Consumer(BlockingCollection<HttpListenerContext> queue)
  {
    while (true)
    {
      HttpListenerContext ctx = queue.Take();
      Thread.Sleep(5000); // Simulate work
      Console.WriteLine(ctx.Request.Url);
```

```
    using (var writer = new StreamWriter(ctx.Response.OutputStream))
    {
      writer.WriteLine(DateTime.Now);
    }
  }
 }
}
```

Listing 5-22 provides blocking behavior for the consumers. The Add operations, however, will not block, so currently all HTTP requests get enqueued. You may want to limit the size of the queue, and either timeout the client or return an appropriate response code. To enable this behavior, create the BlockingCollection<T> with a given capacity; once the collection reaches this level, Add operations will block. Alternatively you can call TryAdd, which will not block but instead return false if the addition fails, allowing you to inform the client that you are too busy (see Listing 5-23).

Listing 5-23. Bounded Collection

```
var requestQueue = new BlockingCollection<HttpListenerContext>(
                    new ConcurrentQueue<HttpListenerContext>(),2);
. . .

public static void Producer(BlockingCollection<HttpListenerContext> queue,
                            HttpListener listener)
{
  while (true)
  {
    HttpListenerContext ctx = listener.GetContext();
    if (!queue.TryAdd(ctx))
    {
      ctx.Response.StatusCode =(int) HttpStatusCode.ServiceUnavailable;
      ctx.Response.Close();
    }
  }
}
```

Listing 5-23 creates a blocking queue that has a capacity of two. Any attempt to grow the queue past a length of two will result in the TryAdd operation returning false, and the client being sent the busy status.

Graceful Shutdown

The web server is currently terminated by just ending the process, which is not exactly graceful. You can refactor the code to signal to the producer task that you wish to shut down by sending a URL in the form of http://localhost:9000/Time?stop=true. On the main thread, replace the Console.ReadLine() with a wait on the producer task. While this will result in graceful shutdown of the producer task, what about the consumers? You could use a cancellation token, which would be useful if you don't care about completing all the queued-up work. Alternatively you could make use of the CompleteAdding method on the blocking collection to signal that no more items will be enqueued, and any thread blocking on a call to Take will be awakened with an InvalidOperationException. If there are more work items, calls to Take will continue to return the next item until there are no more, and then the exception will be thrown. CompleteAdding therefore allows you to wake up threads waiting for items, but still allow all items inside the blocking collection to be processed. Listing 5-24 shows an example of graceful shutdown.

Listing 5-24. Graceful Shutdown

```
public class Program
{
  static void Main(string[] args)
  {
    HttpListener listener = new HttpListener();
    listener.Prefixes.Add("http://+:9000/Time/");

    listener.Start();

    var requestQueue = new BlockingCollection<HttpListenerContext>(
                          new ConcurrentQueue<HttpListenerContext>());

    var producer = Task.Run(() => Producer(requestQueue, listener));

    Task[] consumers = new Task[4];
    for (int nConsumer = 0; nConsumer < consumers.Length; nConsumer++)
    {
      consumers[nConsumer] = Task.Run(() => Consumer(requestQueue));
    }
    Console.WriteLine("Listening..");
    producer.Wait();
    Task.WaitAll(consumers);
  }

  public static void Producer(BlockingCollection<HttpListenerContext> queue,
                              HttpListener listener)
  {
    while (true)
    {
      HttpListenerContext ctx = listener.GetContext();
      if (ctx.Request.QueryString.AllKeys.Contains("stop")) break;

      if (!queue.TryAdd(ctx))
      {
        ctx.Response.StatusCode = (int) HttpStatusCode.ServiceUnavailable;
        ctx.Response.Close();
      }
    }
    queue.CompleteAdding();
    Console.WriteLine("Producer stopped");
  }

  public static void Consumer(BlockingCollection<HttpListenerContext> queue)
  {
    try
    {
      while (true)
      {
        HttpListenerContext ctx = queue.Take();
        Console.WriteLine(ctx.Request.Url);
```

```
            Thread.Sleep(5000);
            using (var writer = new StreamWriter(ctx.Response.OutputStream))
            {
                writer.WriteLine(DateTime.Now);
            }
        }
    }
    catch (InvalidOperationException error) {}

    Console.WriteLine("{0}:Stopped",Task.CurrentId);
    }
}
```

■ **Note**   Once CompleteAdding has been called, any attempt to add to the collection will cause an exception to be thrown.

Consuming Enumerable

It turns out Take is just one of the ways to consume items from a BlockingCollection<T>. An alternative and often far more convenient way is via foreach. One important thing to note is that while BlockingCollection<T> implements IEnumerable<T>, this is not the target for the consuming enumeration, since it will just deliver all items in the collection without consuming them. To consume the items as you enumerate them you need to use a consuming enumerable. To obtain this you call GetConsumingEnumerable against the BlockingCollection<T>; this will return an IEnumerable<T> but as you iterate through you remove the item from the collection, in the same way as you would with Take. When there are no more items to consume, the foreach is blocked, until either an item becomes available or CompleteAdding is called. Listing 5-25 shows an example of consuming the queue using a foreach.

Listing 5-25. Consuming Enumerable Consumer

```
public static void Consumer(BlockingCollection<HttpListenerContext> queue)
{
  foreach (HttpListenerContext ctx in queue.GetConsumingEnumerable())
  {
    Console.WriteLine(ctx.Request.Url);
    using (var writer = new StreamWriter(ctx.Response.OutputStream))
    {
        writer.WriteLine(DateTime.Now);
    }
  }
  Console.WriteLine("{0}:Stopped", Task.CurrentId);
}
```

BlockingCollection of X

Earlier we spoke about BlockingCollection<T> simply wrapping one of the underlying concurrent collections. It turns out that it is not bound to specific collection types, but rather to any type that implements IProducerConsumerCollection<T>. This interface provides all the necessary features that the BlockingCollection<T> needs to provide blocking behavior to a nonblocking collection. Essentially there are nonblocking TryAdd and TryTake methods. As long as all access to the underlying collection goes via the BlockingCollection<T>, it can determine if there are items in the collection and therefore build the blocking behavior.

Summary

In this chapter, we have shown that highly concurrent code doesn't need to be overly complex. The Concurrent Collections and Lazy<T> provided by TPL make the expression of the code clear and simple while delivering highly concurrent solutions. Writing multithreaded code utilizing concurrent data structures is often the key to making solutions scale.

CHAPTER 6

■ ■ ■

Asynchronous UI

Ever since the first graphical user interface, there has been a need to provide users with the feeling that while the computer is crunching numbers, the UI can still respond to input. This is perfectly reasonable: how many physical devices with buttons do you have that suddenly stop responding the moment they start doing any work?

With programming environments that didn't have threads, this was a challenge. Programmers had to build their own time slicing, do a bit of processing—oh, and now process any user input—and back to processing. Once programmers have threads the problem gets easier: simply have a thread dedicated to UI processing, and any compute task run on another thread, leaving the operating system's scheduler to handle time slicing automatically. This all sounds very easy, and it is; the complexity only starts to creep in when you want to update the UI from a non-UI thread.

In this chapter we will take a look at the UI threading model used by all Windows and Silverlight technologies including WinRT, and how you need to develop code to ensure your interfaces remain fast and fluid.

UI Mechanics

Before we dive into asynchronous UI, it is worth discussing the mechanics of how a click on the mouse eventually ends up causing something to happen inside an application. The two main players in achieving this goal are the OS and the application. The OS takes the underlying low-level event (mouse click) and then decides which application needs to respond to it. The OS determines the application by deciding which window has the focus for the event; the application that created that window is the target. Actually it is a little bit more complex than that, as it is not the application that is the target but the thread that created the window.

The OS has now established the target for the event, but how is the event delivered? The event is placed onto a queue accessible by the thread that created the window for the event (Figure 6-1).

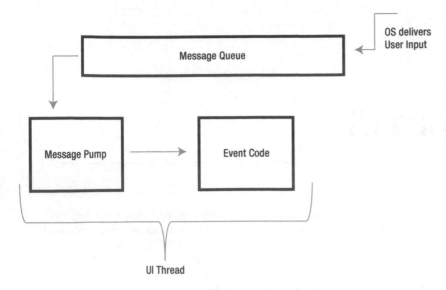

Figure 6-1. *How window events are delivered to the UI thread*

To process the event, the thread must remove the event from the queue, and then decide the appropriate action to handle the event and dispatch the event locally. What we have just described is the heart of nearly every UI platform—the message pump or message loop. Listing 6-1 shows an implementation of such a loop in .NET.

Listing 6-1. Example of a Windows Message Loop

```
MSG windowMsg;
while (User32.GetMessage(out windowMsg, IntPtr.Zero, 0, 0) != 0)
{
    User32.TranslateMessage(ref windowMsg);
    User32.DispatchMessage(ref windowMsg);
}
```

If the UI thread is not taking events out of the queue and dispatching them, the application can't respond to user input. So for a UI application to be responsive, the UI thread needs to be spending most of its time sitting in this loop consuming and dispatching events. You can spot applications that don't conform to this pattern when the OS turns the title of the window to "Not Responding."

One common misconception I frequently see amongst developers is that an application can have only one UI thread. While this is true for a lot of applications, it does not have to be the case. Any custom thread you create can be a UI thread, and as long as it pumps those messages, life is good. Internet Explorer does this for each top-level window, thus isolating each browser window from UI lockup issues in other windows.

UI Threading Model

Imagine the following scenario: a user hits a button, and the button event handler fires and runs a piece of code that takes about 2 seconds to complete. By default this code will run on the UI thread, and while it is running the UI becomes unresponsive as it is not processing UI events. Solution: make the "long-running code" run on a separate thread.

The code in Listing 6-2 shows a button handler starting a new task. Once the task has been created, the UI thread returns to processing UI events, thus keeping the application responsive. There is just one big problem with this code: the thread that is performing the long-running calculation is not allowed to update the ResultsTextBlock control. Why is this? Because all Windows controls have what is called thread affinity, meaning that they can only have their state manipulated on the same thread that created the control. This has always been the case in Microsoft Windows–based UIs and is still the case for modern frameworks such as WPF, WinRT, and Silverlight. To keep the UI responsive, we need to offload non-UI work onto another thread, but if that work needs to update the UI, we need to be back onto the UI thread.

Listing 6-2. Asynchronous Work Initated from the UI Thread

```
private void ButtonClick(object sender, RoutedEventArgs e)
{
  Task.Factory.StartNew(() =>
  {
    decimal result = CalculateMeaningOfLife();
    ResultTextBlock.Text = result.ToString();
  });

}
```

The technique to request execution of a piece of work on another thread is known as marshaling. Marshaling requires cooperation to make it happen. In other words, the non-UI thread needs to communicate with the UI thread and ask it to execute a specific piece of code. To marshal work back onto the UI thread, you will take advantage of the same message queue the OS uses to communicate user input. The marshaling will take the form of posting a Windows message onto the UI message queue for that UI thread. The UI thread will eventually see that message requesting that the said piece of code be run on this thread.

Fortunately you won't have to get involved at this low level, as there are a number of abstractions that simplify the process. Each of the various UI technologies has its own specific API. Having all these APIs leads to code being tightly coupled to a given UI technology, and in the world of unit testing and reusable components this is not ideal. Thankfully, in .NET 2.0 an abstraction was created called SynchronizationContext that provides a common way of marshaling onto the UI thread irrespective of UI technology.

Synchronization Context

Fundamentally, the role of SynchronizationContext is to run a delegate on a thread associated with the SynchronizationContext. Each UI technology will have its own native mechanism to marshal work back onto its UI thread, and as such each creates their own synchronization context type that derives from the SynchronizationContext base; consumers continue to use the base type (code to abstraction). When the UI framework is initialized, it creates an instance of its SynchronizationContext and then associates this instance with the current thread, by calling the method SynchronizationContext.SetSynchronizationContext. This method places the synchronization context instance into thread local storage, meaning it can only be retrieved by code executing on the same thread. To retrieve the synchronization context associated with the current thread applications, access the static property SynchronizationContext.Current.

■ **Caution** Calling SynchronizationContext.Current on a thread that has not had a call to SetSynchronizationContext will result in a null value. Therefore to have access to another thread's synchronization context, you must first read it while on that thread, and store it in a non–thread-scoped variable. SynchronizationContext does not flow across thread and task boundaries.

Send and Post

After capturing the synchronization context from the UI thread, you can use the captured synchronization context object on any other thread. The two key methods available to execute work are Send and Post. Send is a synchronous method that will block on the calling thread until work has been completed on the associated synchronization context thread, whereas Post executes asynchronously, allowing the calling thread to continue. Post is used most often; it is very rare to require the calling thread to block waiting for the UI to update. Listing 6-3 is a rewrite of Listing 6-2 taking advantage of synchronization context.

Listing 6-3. Using SynchronizationContext to Marshal Back onto the UI Thread

```
private void ButtonClick(object sender, RoutedEventArgs e)
{
    // Capture synchronization context while on the UI thread
    SynchronizationContext ctx = SynchronizationContext.Current;

    Task.Factory.StartNew(() =>
    {
        decimal result = CalculateMeaningOfLife();

        // request that the synchronization context object
        // runs ResultTextBlock.Text = result.ToString() on the UI thread asynchronsly

        ctx.Post(state => ResultTextBlock.Text = result.ToString(), null);
    });
}
```

The Send and Post methods both take a SendOrPostCallbackDelegate, which itself will match any method returning void and taking a single parameter of type object. This second parameter to the Send or Post call is the value that will be passed into the delegate when it executes on the correct thread. This is seldom used, instead favoring closures to flow data into the delegate body.

Favor using Post calls when, during the life of an asynchronous operation, you wish to modify the properties on a UI control, and you don't require the UI to remain 100 percent in step with the asynchronous operation. Use Send if it is imperative that the asynchronous processing and the UI processing be in lockstep. However, be careful when using Send as opposed to Post if the UI thread and the calling thread have shared locks, as this may result in a deadlock scenario (e.g., an asynchronous operation has lock; calls Send; UI thread attempts to acquire lock before performing the update).

Task Continuations

Examining the code in Listing 6-2, you can see that the asynchronous operation has two parts: perform the calculation and, when done, update the UI. Rather than placing all this in a single task, we could break it into two. The first task performs the long-running calculation, and the second task updates the UI. At first glance this seems pointless; however, remember what I said in chapter 3, that continuations are useful when you have a series of asynchronous operations that need to execute in a different context to one another. In this example, you want the first task to run on a thread pool thread, but the second task to run in a different context: on a UI thread. When a request is made to start a task it is given to a scheduler, and the default scheduler is the thread pool scheduler; hence tasks run on thread pools. The other out-of-the-box scheduler is a SynchronizationContextTaskScheduler; when this scheduler is given a task, it posts it onto the synchronization context associated with the scheduler. One of the overloads, Task.ContinueWith, takes the scheduler you would like to use. You can now rewrite Listing 6-2 to use a continuation (see Listing 6-4).

Listing 6-4. Background Thread Compute, with Continuation on UI Thread

```
private void ButtonClick(object sender, RoutedEventArgs e)
{
    Task.Factory
        .StartNew<decimal>(() => CalculateMeaningOfLife())
        .ContinueWith(t => ResultTextBlock.Text = t.Result.ToString(),
                    TaskScheduler.FromCurrentSynchronizationContext());
}
```

The UI thread creates the initial task object and sets up the continuation. Creating the continuation task on the UI thread results in having the TaskScheduler.FromCurrentSynchronizationContext return a scheduler that, when asked to start a task, will run it using the SynchronizationContext associated with this UI thread. Continuations are a convenient way to marshal asynchronous-result processing back onto the UI thread.

Event-Based Asynchronous Pattern (EAP)

In .NET 2.0, an effort was made to make the processing of asynchronous operations easier when running inside a UI environment. API developers were encouraged to provide asynchronous operations that signaled completion by firing an event using a captured synchronization context at the point when the asynchronous operation was requested. This effectively means UI developers need to care less about synchronization context; it all gets wrapped up inside the asynchronous API implementation. An example of this EAP pattern is shown in Listing 6-5. Note the event registration is only done once, not per asynchronous call, and the synchronization context is captured at the point when the asynchronous call is made. The one downside with this approach is error handling—instead of the conventional catch block, you have to resort to testing return values.

Listing 6-5. Example of EAP Pattern Client

```
public partial class MainWindow : Window
{
    private WebClient client = new WebClient();

    public MainWindow()
    {
        InitializeComponent();
        client.DownloadStringCompleted += ProcessResult;
    }

    private void ProcessResult(object sender, DownloadStringCompletedEventArgs e)
    {
        // event handler running on the UI thread
        if (e.Error != null)
            webPage.Text = e.Error.Message;
        else
            webPage.Text = e.Result;    }

    private void DownloadIt(object sender, RoutedEventArgs e)
    {
        // Captures Synchronization Context at this point
        client.DownloadStringAsync(new Uri("http://www.rocksolidknowledge.com/5SecondPage.aspx"));
    }
}
```

An example of building your own EAP component that encapsulates synchronization context is shown in Listing 6-6. On creation of the Clock, the synchronization context is captured. If there is no synchronization context present, it simply creates an instance of the base synchronization context. This keeps our programming model simple internally (not requiring null checks) and for nonthread affinity scenarios, allowing the asynchronous operation to continue processing while updating the consumer on another thread. When you wish to inform the client of a change of state, you simply post the event-firing code onto the captured synchronization context.

Listing 6-6. Example of EAP Implementation

```
public class Clock
{
    public int Hour { get { return DateTime.Now.Hour; } }
    public int Minutes { get { return DateTime.Now.Minute; } }
    public int Seconds { get { return DateTime.Now.Second; } }

    public event EventHandler<EventArgs> Tick = delegate { };

    private Timer timer;
    private SynchronizationContext uiCtx;

    public Clock()
    {
        uiCtx = SynchronizationContext.Current ?? new SynchronizationContext();
        timer = new Timer(OnTick,null,1000,1000);
    }

        private void OnTick(object state)
        {
            uiCtx.Post(_ => Tick(this, EventArgs.Empty), null);
        }
}
```

Background Worker

BackgroundWorker is a component that can be used in both Windows Forms and WPF that provides a solution to a common asynchronous UI scenario: user hits button; long-running activity on background thread; user wishes to receive progress, the final result, and the ability to cancel the long-running operation. Updating the user on progress of the operation and reporting a final outcome will need to be coordinated from the asynchronous operation, but almost certainly will require the ability to update UI controls. The background worker component has been developed to solve this very specific scenario.

The BackgroundWorker component follows the principles of the EAP pattern; it exposes a series of events to represent state changes during the life of the asynchronous operation. Apart from the event DoWork, all other events will fire on the UI thread. The work you wish to execute asynchronously is defined by subscribing to the DoWork event. When a call is made to RunWorkerAsync on the BackgroundWorker, it fires this event on a thread pool thread and thus starts the asynchronous operation. The code performing the asynchronous operation can then report progress and poll for cancellation (Listing 6-7).

Listing 6-7. BackgroundWorker for UI Marshaling

```
private BackgroundWorker backgroundWorker;

private void StartProcesing(object sender, RoutedEventArgs e)
{
    backgroundWorker = new BackgroundWorker();

    backgroundWorker.DoWork             += PerformCalculation;
    backgroundWorker.RunWorkerCompleted += CalculationDone;
    backgroundWorker.ProgressChanged    += UpdateProgress;

    // Define what behavior is supported by the background worker
    backgroundWorker.WorkerReportsProgress = true;
    backgroundWorker.WorkerSupportsCancellation = true;

    // On a background thread, fire the DoWork event
    backgroundWorker.RunWorkerAsync();
}

private void UpdateProgress(object sender, ProgressChangedEventArgs e)
{
    this.AsyncProgressBar.Value = e.ProgressPercentage;
}

private void CalculationDone(object sender, RunWorkerCompletedEventArgs e)
{
    // If the asynchronous operation completed by throwing an exception
    if (e.Error != null)
      this.ResultTextBlock.Text = e.Error.Message;
    else if (e.Cancelled)
      this.ResultTextBlock.Text = "CANCELLED";
    else
      this.ResultTextBlock.Text = e.Result.ToString();
}

private void PerformCalculation(object sender, DoWorkEventArgs e)
{
    // Dummy Loop to represent some idea of progress in
    // calculating the value
    for (int i = 0; i < 100; i++)
    {
        Thread.Sleep(50); // Simulating work
        backgroundWorker.ReportProgress(i);

        // Check if cancellation has been requested
        if (backgroundWorker.CancellationPending)
        {
          e.Cancel = true;  //Indicate the reason for completion is due to cancellation
          return;
        }
    }
}
```

```
  // set the result of the asynchronous operation
  e.Result = 42;
}

private void CancelProcessing(object sender, RoutedEventArgs e)
{
  // Politely ask for the background worker to cancel
  backgroundWorker.CancelAsync();
}
```

BackgroundWorker is a useful component that fits a very specific brief. If you need more flexibility than for what the BackgroundWorker is intended, don't be tempted to try and bend it—look to using more flexible techniques presented in this chapter. I have seen developers who for some reason see BackgroundWorker as the golden hammer for general purpose UI thread marshaling. This often takes the form of calling the ReportProgress method on the background thread to pass a known constant to indicate what UI update is required. The ProgressChanged event handler then typically switches on the value to decide how to update the UI. It would have been far simpler and more maintainable to have invoked the functionality directly via a post on a synchronization context from the asynchronous work.

■ **Note**   BackgroundWorker is not available in WinRT. The introduction of async and await keywords in the C#5 programming language means this component isn't required.

Data Binding

Modern smart-client UIs now rarely rely on directly updating visual controls. With the onset of architectures like MVVM (Model-View-View Model), developers use a technique called data binding to move data back and forth between application objects and visual objects. Data binding involves creating a relationship called a binding between the source (application object and Property) and the target (visual component and property), with the idea that updating the source object's property in code will cause the bound visual property to get updated. The trigger for updating comes from the fact that the source object must implement an interface called INotifyPropertyChanged. This interface exposes a single event called PropertyChanged, and it is further the responsibility of the source object to raise this event each time one of its bound properties is changed. The event arguments for the event specify which property has changed, or if a null value is used it signifies that all bound properties of this source object need to be refreshed. The UI framework registers for this event against the source object, and on receipt of this event causes the UI to update based on the new value from the source object (Listing 6-8).

Listing 6-8. Example View Model

```
public class ViewModel : INotifyPropertyChanged
{
    public ViewModel()
    {
        Task.Factory.StartNew(() =>
                {
                    while (true)
                    {
                        Result = CalculateNexResult();
                    }
                });
    }
```

```
        private decimal result;
        public decimal Result
        {
            get { return result; }
            private set { result = value; OnPropertyChanged("Result"); }
        }
```

```
    public event PropertyChangedEventHandler PropertyChanged = delegate { };
```

```
        protected virtual void OnPropertyChanged(string propertyName = null)
        {
            PropertyChanged(this, new PropertyChangedEventArgs(propertyName));
        }
}
```

All seems very straight forward until you ask which thread fires the event. It turns out it's the thread that modified the source property. If the source property is modified on the UI thread, there's no issue; but, as in Listing 6-8, what if it is modified on another thread? The answer to that question depends on what UI technology you are using. The following sections cover the specific technology differences.

Windows Forms

For data binding to work reliably in Windows Forms, all updates to source properties need to happen on the UI thread. Therefore the implementation in Listing 6-8 clearly shouldn't work. In the case of Windows Forms, if you run it outside the debugger it almost certainly will work, but run it inside the debugger and the framework will enforce the thread affinity rule, and simply refuse to update the UI—no exception, nothing. The fact that it works without the debugger attached is due to the fact that Microsoft did not enforce the thread affinity in .NET 1.1 and as such your program would be subject to just the possibility that the update would fail. To fix this issue, we need to ensure that the event fires on the UI thread, and for that we have used synchronization context (Listing 6-9). Notice, though, we have used Send and not Post.

Listing 6-9. Cross-Thread Data Binding in Windows Forms

```
private SynchronizationContext uiCtx;

public ViewModel()
{
  uiCtx = SynchronizationContext.Current;
    Task.Factory.StartNew(() =>
                {
                    while (true)
                    {
                        Result = CalculateNexResult();
                    }
                });
}
. . .
protected virtual void OnPropertyChanged(string propertyName = null)
{
  uiCtx.Send(_ => PropertyChanged(this, new PropertyChangedEventArgs(propertyName)),null);
}
```

We have used Send to ensure the result is read fully before calculating the next result; this is, after all, a multithreaded application, and having one thread update a value while another is reading could cause strange results to be displayed. This also makes you consider whether you might need to update a dozen or so data-bound values—having to marshal multiple times and block for each one may be too prohibiting. For those scenarios you could consider issuing a single PropertyChanged event with the affected property being null (assuming all bound properties are rooted through a single source), or alternatively you could wrap up all the properties updates in a SynchronizationContext.Send or Post, resulting again in just a single marshaling operation.

Windows Presentation Foundation (WPF)

The behavior of Windows Forms always seemed kind of strange to us; after all, you would have thought that the data-binding layer could automatically perform the marshaling for you. Fortunately, WPF does (well, almost; more later), so the changes you made to your ViewModel to make it work with Windows Forms are not necessary for WPF. WPF will marshal onto the UI thread, but for high-performance environments it may be also be prudent to update a set of properties on the UI thread to reduce the number of marshaling requests.

WPF data binding therefore does a pretty good job of hiding the need to perform marshaling. However, this is only true for single-value data bindings. WPF also supports data binding to collections, for visual controls like list views. Collections that wish to act as data-bound sources must implement INotifyCollectionChanged, and raise an event to say the content of the collection has changed. There is an out-of-the-box collection that implements this interface called ObservableCollection<T>. Listing 6-10 shows a view model that is utilizing the observable collection. The problem is once the Value property is data-bound, any attempt to Add to the collection will fail if the Add does not occur on the UI thread. The ObservableCollection<T> was not written to be thread safe; thus the only way to add items is to marshal onto the UI thread.

Listing 6-10. ObservableCollection<T>

```
public class ViewModel
{
  public ViewModel()
  {
    Values = new ObservableCollection<int>();
    Task.Factory.StartNew(GenerateValues);
  }

  public ObservableCollection<int> Values { get; private set; }

  private void GenerateValues()
  {
    var rnd= new Random();
    while (true)
    {
      Values.Add( rnd.Next(1,100));
      Thread.Sleep(1000);
    }
  }
}
```

To fix this, you can take advantage of synchronization context, and post the add operation onto the UI thread. You could wrap ObservableCollection<T> to do this for you, and if you do it may be worth supporting an AddMany method and performing a single marshaling operation for all the items you wish to add (Listing 6-11).

Listing 6-11. Updating ObservableCollection via SynchronizationContext

```
private SynchronizationContext uiCtx = SynchronizationContext.Current;

private void GenerateValues()
{
  var rnd = new Random();
  while (true)
  {
    uiCtx.Post( _ => Values.Add(rnd.Next(1, 100)),null);

    Thread.Sleep(1000);
  }
}
```

This obviously does mean introducing synchronization context back into the code, but as of .NET 4.5 you don't need to, as it is now possible to make ObservableCollection and any other data-bound collection work with multiple threads. To make this possible, we have to assist the data-binding layer so that it can ensure that, when it is accessing the collection, no other thread is modifying the data structure. To achieve this, some form of thread synchronization is obviously required. To request that the data binding performs synchronization prior to accessing the collection, make a call to the static method BindingOperations.EnableCollectionSynchronization. The first parameter represents the IEnumerable<T> object that contains the data binding source you wish to control access for, and the second parameter is the object to be used for thread synchronization. Before accessing the collection, the data-binding layer obtains the monitor for this object, and as long as your code abides to the contract by also obtaining the monitor before accessing the collection, all is good (see Listing 6-12).

Listing 6-12. Updating ObservableCollection Using Collection-Based Locking

```
public class ViewModel
{
  private object valuesLock = new object();
  public ObservableCollection<int> Values { get; private set; }

  public ViewModel()
  {
    Values = new ObservableCollection<int>();
    BindingOperations.EnableCollectionSynchronization(Values, valuesLock);
    Task.Factory.StartNew(GenerateValues);
  }

  private void GenerateValues()
  {
    var rnd = new Random();
    while (true)
    {
      lock (Values)
          Values.Add(rnd.Next(1, 100));
      Thread.Sleep(1000);
    }
  }
}
```

The synchronization strategy used here is mutual exclusion. If you want greater control over the locking strategy, this is also possible using an overloaded version of the BindingOperations.EnableCollectionSynchronization that takes a delegate that the data binding layer will invoke to obtain access to the collection. This allows you to use whatever synchronization method you feel appropriate. The code in Listing 6-13 shows an implementation that uses a reader-writer lock. The three parameters passed to EnableCollectionSynchronization are the collection, a user-defined context, and the delegate to be used to obtain access. The user-defined context is whatever you like and is passed into the delegate. The ControlAccessToValues method is called each time the data-binding layer wishes to access the collection. It indicates what type of access (read/write) and supplies an Action delegate that represents the code it wishes to have run while the thread synchronization is active.

Listing 6-13. Updating ObservableCollection Using ReaderWriterLockSlim

```
public class ViewModel
{

  ReaderWriterLockSlim valuesLock = new ReaderWriterLockSlim();
  public ViewModel()
  {
    Values = new ObservableCollection<int>();
    BindingOperations.EnableCollectionSynchronization(Values,valuesLock,ControlAccessToValues);
    Task.Factory.StartNew(GenerateValues);
  }

  public ObservableCollection<int> Values {get;private set;}

  private void ControlAccessToValues(IEnumerable collection, object context,
                                     Action accessmethod, bool writeaccess)
  {
   var collectionLock = (ReaderWriterLockSlim) context;
   Action enterLock = writeaccess  ? new Action(collectionLock.EnterWriteLock)
                                    : new Action(collectionLock.EnterReadLock);

   Action exitLock = writeaccess  ? new Action(collectionLock.ExitWriteLock)
                                   : new Action(collectionLock.ExitReadLock);

   enterLock();
   try { accessmethod(); }
   finally {exitLock();  }
  }
  private void GenerateValues()
  {
    var rnd = new Random();
    while (true)
    {
      valuesLock.EnterWriteLock();
      try{Values.Add(rnd.Next(1, 100));}
      finally{valuesLock.ExitWriteLock();}

      Thread.Sleep(1000);
    }
  }
}
```

So while the goal of data binding is to allow a simple, declarative way of moving data between a source and a target, you do still need to be aware of potential threading issues. WPF on the whole punishes you immediately, which results in UI threading issues being missed less often.

WinRT

WinRT has the same UI threading model for data binding as Windows Forms. When a data-bound source is updated from a thread not associated with the target, a COMException is raised. The message for this exception is as follows: "The application called an interface that was marshaled for a different thread. (Exception from HRESULT: 0x8001010E (RPC_E_WRONG_THREAD))." Unlike Windows Forms, this exception is raised with or without debugger attachment. The same techniques used with Windows Forms to marshal back onto the UI thread apply to WinRT. While this may appear to be cumbersome—especially considering this is, after all, the latest UI technology from Microsoft—you will see in Chapter 7 that the new features in C#5 actually make it all a lot simpler, and hence the extra efforts employed by WPF are not necessary.

WPF Dispatcher

So far in this chapter we have tried to be agnostic of UI technology by taking advantage of synchronization context and data binding. Both these abstractions for WPF are built using the WPF Dispatcher. The WPF Dispatcher is responsible for marshaling work from a background thread to the UI thread. In addition to providing support for Send- and Post-like behavior, it also offers support for UI timers, prioritizing work for the UI thread and the ability to cancel any pending work.

Obtaining the Dispatcher

There are multiple ways to obtain the dispatcher, if your code is not running on the UI thread itself, you can fetch the dispatcher of any UI element via the Dispatcher property, or you can call Application.Current.Dispatcher. If you are on the UI thread you can call Dispatcher.Current.

Executing Work Through the Dispatcher

Similar to synchronization context, we can execute work through the dispatcher synchronously (Invoke) or asynchronously using the APM pattern (BeginInvoke). Both these methods take an optional priority, allowing work to be scheduled on the UI thread at a lower priority than handling user-initiated interactions. In the case of the invoke method it returns void, but it does take an optional timeout so you don't end up blocking for too long. The BeginInvoke method returns a DispatcherOperation object; this object confers the ability to track and cancel the operation if it has not started. Most applications would typically use the Normal priority, which is what DispatcherSynchronizationContext uses for Post requests (Table 6-1).

Table 6-1. *WPF Dispatcher Priorities*

Priority	Description
Inactive	Work items are queued but not processed.
SystemIdle	Work items are only dispatched to the UI thread when the system is idle. This is the lowest priority of items that are actually processed.
ApplicationIdle	Work items are only dispatched to the UI thread when the application itself is idle.
ContextIdle	Work items are only dispatched to the UI thread after higher-priority work items are processed.
Background	Work items are dispatched after all layout, rendering, and input items are processed.
Input	Work items are dispatched to the UI thread at the same priority as user input.
Loaded	Work items are dispatched to the UI thread after all layout and rendering are complete.
Render	Work items are dispatched to the UI thread at the same priority as the rendering engine.
DataBind	Work items are dispatched to the UI thread at the same priority as data binding.
Normal	Work items are dispatched to the UI thread with normal priority. This is the priority at which most application work items should be dispatched.
Send	Work items are dispatched to the UI thread with the highest priority.

Listing 6-14. Marshaling onto UI thread Using WPF Dispatcher

```
private Dispatcher dispatcher = Dispatcher.CurrentDispatcher;

  private void GenerateValues()
  {
    var rnd = new Random();
    while (true)
    {
      int nextValue = rnd.Next(1,100);
      dispatcher.BeginInvoke(new Action(() => Values.Add(nextValue)));

      Thread.Sleep(1000);
    }
  }
```

Favor using the dispatcher over SynchronizationContext when you wish to take fine-grained control of dispatching work onto the UI thread, or you wish to have UI-based timers (see later).

WinRT Dispatcher

The WinRT dispatcher has a very similar API to that of WPF Dispatcher, with a couple of key differences: the way you obtain the dispatcher is slightly different, and the number of priorities is far smaller.

Obtaining the Dispatcher

There are multiple ways to obtain the dispatcher. If your code is not running on the UI thread itself, you can fetch the dispatcher of any UI element via the Dispatcher property. If you are on the UI thread, you can obtain the dispatcher via CoreWindow.GetForCurrentThread().Dispatcher; this property returns a type of CoreDispatcher. Once you have obtained the dispatcher you can share it with any other thread so, when required, they can request any UI updates to run on the UI thread.

Executing Work Through the Dispatcher

Unlike the WPF Dispatcher, the WinRT dispatcher can only execute work asynchronously. Asynchronicity is at the heart of WinRT: blocking is considered evil, and there are no means for you to block. To invoke work via the dispatcher, you can use the RunAsync method. The RunAsync allows you to pick a priority to determine when the code should run. This is similar to WPF Dispatcher, although the number of priorities is greatly reduced (Table 6-2).

Table 6-2. *WinRT Dispatcher Priorities*

Priority	Description
Low	Requested work is processed when the window's main thread is idle and there is no input pending in the queue.
Normal	Requested work is processed in the order it is requested.
High	Requested work is queued and processed before any other request type.

Excessive use of High priority can obviously result in a UI that is unresponsive to user input. Low priority provides the best way to schedule work to run, while keeping user interaction a top priority. Normal priority is equal priority with user interactions; this would be the same as utilizing SynchronizationContext. Listing 6-15 shows a UI thread executing a task asynchronously, which in turn runs the UI update logic asynchronously back on the UI thread.

Listing 6-15. WinRT Executing Work Back onto the UI Thread with the WinRT Dispatcher

```
private void DoIt(object sender, RoutedEventArgs e)
{
  // Button click handler running on UI thread, capture dispatcher
  CoreDispatcher dispatcher = CoreWindow.GetForCurrentThread().Dispatcher;

  Task.Run(() =>
        {
            int answer = CalculateMeaningOfLifeUniverseAndEverything();
            dispatcher.RunAsync(CoreDispatcherPriority.Low, () =>
                {
                    resultsTextBlock.Text = answer.ToString();
                });
        });
    }
```

UI Timers

In addition to updating the UI when an object's state changes, we can also update the UI at a given frequency. UI Timers provide a means of registering a piece of code to run a given interval. UI Timers are different from other forms of timers as they ensure that the timer fires on the UI thread. Because the timer fires on the UI thread, there is no need to consider synchronization context. It should go without saying that any UI timer executed must complete quickly in order to keep the UI responsive.

Windows Forms Timer

The Windows Forms timer takes the form of a component. Components are like controls but do not have any visual part. The System.Windows.Forms.Timer component is available on the Windows Forms Toolbox, and can be dragged and dropped onto a form just like a visual component. Once it has been dropped onto the form, it can be configured just like a control, setting properties and wiring up events. Listing 6-16 shows a form with the timer being created in the code behind. The frequency of the timer is defined via the Interval property, which takes a time period in milliseconds. The Tick event is used to identify the code you wish to run every time the timer fires. The timer by default is not started; it can be started either by setting the Enabled property to true or by calling the Start method. The Enabled property allows you to start the timer from the property sheet in the designer. The Start method provides a more code-readable form, to be used from code behind. The timer can be stopped by setting Enabled to false or calling the Stop method.

Listing 6-16. The Windows Forms Timer Updates Title of Form Every Second with Current Date and Time

```
public partial class ClockForm : Form
{
    private Timer timer = new Timer();
    public ClockForm()
    {
        InitializeComponent();

        timer.Interval = 1000; // 1000 ms == 1 second
        timer.Tick += UpdateFormTitleWithCurrentTime;

        //timer.Enabled = true; or
        timer.Start();

    }

    private void UpdateFormTitleWithCurrentTime(object sender, EventArgs e)
    {
        this.Text = DateTime.Now.ToString();
    }
}
```

WinRT and WPF Dispatch Timers

Listing 6-17 shows an example a partial piece of code to update a Values collection on the UI thread every second for both WinRT and WPF.

Listing 6-17. Example Use of a Dispatcher Time

```
// Created on the UI thread
timer = new DispatcherTimer {Interval = TimeSpan.FromSeconds(1)};
// Event handler will fire on the UI thread, making it
// safe to update UI elements
timer.Tick += (s, e) => Values.Add(rnd.Next(1, 100));
timer.Start();
```

WPF Freezable Components

Complex UI scenes may require the building of complex shapes and bitmaps. Building such items on the UI thread obviously will cause the UI thread to become nonresponsive. Building these UI objects on a background thread therefore makes sense; the rub comes when these components are referenced by components created on the UI thread. For example, an Image created on the UI thread refers to a BitmapSource to define the pixel data for the image. Not defining the BitmapSource on the UI thread causes an exception to be thrown when the image created on the UI thread is associated with the bitmap source. To solve this issue, WPF UI components that are not themselves visual but are used to define the data used by the visual component derive from a base class called Freezable. Freezable types can be created on a non-UI thread and then have the Freeze method applied to them, allowing them to be used (without change) by visual components on the UI thread. Listing 6-18 shows a partial example of creating a Bitmap on a non-UI thread; marked as Freezable, the bitmap can be used on the UI thread.

Listing 6-18. Creating UI Components on Background Threads

```
Task.Factory.StartNew<BitmapSource>(CreateImage)
            .ContinueWith(src => images.Children
                                    .Add( new Image() { Width = 100,Source=src.Result}),
                TaskScheduler.FromCurrentSynchronizationContext());

. . .

private BitmapSource CreateImage()
{
  var src = new WriteableBitmap(200,200,96,96,new PixelFormat(), BitmapPalettes.Gray256);

  // Calculate image
  src.Freeze();
  return src;
}
```

Too Much of a Good Thing

One of the main reasons to spin off separate threads from the UI is so that the UI thread is left to focus on pure UI and keep the user experience fast and fluid. Throughout this chapter we have reviewed the need for the asynchronous operations to keep the UI up to date by posting work back on to the UI, but it turns out this whole approach could end up creating the very environment we are trying to avoid. Consider the code in Listing 6-19. The CalculatePi method is going to be run on a background thread, and the synchronization context has already been captured on the UI thread. It should produce a nice progress bar for you as the calculation is being performed, but unfortunately the only thing that happens is the UI freezes. Why? Well, just think about how this whole marshaling thing works: it is about posting messages onto the UI thread, the same thread that is trying to handle user interactions. At the moment you have a background thread that is creating thousands of requests per second. The user events don't get looked into, and the UI thread spends most of its time trying to keep up and not repainting the screen. In fact, it is not uncommon for this application to run out of memory on a 32-bit machine, as the queue eats so much memory.

Listing 6-19. Windows Message Queue Overload

```
private SynchronizationContext uiCtx = SynchronizationContext.Current;

private void CalculatePi()
{
  const int iterations = 1000000000;
  double pi = 1;
  double multiplier = -1;
  int newProgress;

  for (int i = 3; i < iterations; i += 2)
  {
        pi += multiplier*(1.0/(double) i);
        multiplier *= -1;

        newProgress = (int) ((double) i/(double) iterations*100.0);
        uiCtx.Post(_ => progressBar.Value = newProgress, null);
    }

    uiCtx.Post(_ => this.result.Text = (pi*4.0).ToString(), null);
  }
}
```

The fix for this is not to marshal at this kind of rate—after all, the user can't possibly take all that information in, and really, will he or she want to see such a small change in progress? Listing 6-20, shows the refactored code.

Listing 6-20. Less Aggressive Update to Keep UI Thread Responsive

```
int nBlocks = 100;
int blockSize = iterations/nBlocks;

for (int nBlock = 0; nBlock < nBlocks; nBlock++)
{
   for (int i = 3 + nBlock*blockSize; i <  nBlock*blockSize + blockSize; i += 2)
   {
     pi += multiplier*(1.0/(double) i);
     multiplier *= -1;
   }
   uiCtx.Post(_ => progressBar.Value = nBlock, null);
}
```

Now we are only performing 100 post-backs during the lifetime of the calculation. This not only keeps the UI responsive but also reduces the time for the calculation. In WPF, if we had used data binding as opposed to updating the controls directly, then the UI would have remained responsive, as the data-binding engine uses a feature of the dispatcher that queues update operations with a low priority and ignores duplicate update requests, thus giving greater priority to user interactions. However, the overall calculation time would still be massively increased—not what we want. It is therefore very important to understand the inner workings and build your code to take this knowledge into account. In this example, it has been relatively easy to control the amount of marshaling onto the UI thread; for other algorithms it might be trickier, because triggering the need to update might itself be random in nature. In this situation it may be simpler to use a UI timer to regularly poll the current state and update the user.

Keeping the user abreast of state changes every 250ms is probably good enough, and won't kill the UI thread. We could also solve these kinds of problems by using the dispatcher with a low priority and only reissuing the update if the previous update has completed (Listing 6-21).

Listing 6-21. Dispatcher to Update UI Thread Only When UI Thread Is Idle

```
DispatcherOperation updateOp = null;

for . . .
{
    if (updateOp == null || updateOp.Status == DispatcherOperationStatus.Completed)
    {
        updateOp =Dispatcher.BeginInvoke(DispatcherPriority.ApplicationIdle,
            new Action(() => progressBar.Value = (int) ((double) i/(double) iterations*100.0)));
    }

}
```

An alternative approach is to sample and throttle. You don't have to build that yourself; the Reactive Framework gives you all the building blocks and is discussed in Chapter 14.

Summary

In this chapter, you have seen that Windows UI technology has thread affinity, requiring any UI updates initiated from the non-UI thread to be marshaled back onto the UI thread in order to update. You have also seen that the process of marshaling can take many forms, but they all boil down to sending a message to the UI thread. For WPF we often favor data binding to do the right thing; for the likes of Windows Forms and WinRT, you need to take control of the marshaling, and SynchronizationContext is our cross-technology preferred option. For finer-grained control in the case of WinRT and WPF, consider using its dispatcher directly. Keep in mind that the reason for performing asynchronous programming in UIs is to maintain responsiveness. Flooding the UI thread with update messages will reverse the effect, so you should consider batching updates.

While asynchronous UI processing isn't that hard, it does force you to structure your code differently from regular sequential code. In Chapter 7, we will look at the new features of C#5 that, to a large extent, remove this need and allow you to build fast and fluid UIs while maintaining the simple sequential structure that programmers are often most comfortable with.

CHAPTER 7

async and await

In view of Windows 8's mantra of "Fast and Fluid," it has never been more important to ensure that UIs don't stall. To ensure that UI developers have no excuses for not using asynchronous methods, the C# language introduces two new keywords: `async` and `await`. These two little gems make consuming and composing asynchronous methods as easy as their synchronous counterparts.

This chapter is a story of two parts. The first part explains how easy asynchronous programming can be in C# 5, while the second part is a deep dive into the compiler magic behind the keywords. The second part may not be for everyone, so feel free to skip it.

Making Asynchronous Programming Simpler

The code in Listing 7-1 represents a UI button handler that, when clicked, performs some calculation and updates the UI with the result. Assuming the `CalculateMeaningOfLife` method doesn't take too long to execute, life is good. If it were to take a noticeable amount of time, we would be encouraged to create an asynchronous form of the method for the UI developer. The UI developer would then combine this with a continuation on the UI thread to update the UI.

Listing 7-1. UI Event Handler Performing Some Processing

```
private void ButtonClick(object sender, RoutedEventArgs e)
{
  try
  {
      decimal result = CalculateMeaningOfLife();

      resultLabel.Text = result.ToString();
  }
  catch (MidlifeCrisisException error)
  {
      resultLabel.Text = error.Message;
  }
}
```

Listing 7-2 achieves the goal of keeping the UI responsive, but the style of programming has somewhat changed, becoming more complex. You now have to deal with a Task as opposed to just a simple decimal, and exception handling has changed to if/else checking.

Listing 7-2. Keeping the UI responsive using CalculateMeainigOfLifeAsync

```
private Task<decimal> CalculateMeaningOfLifeAsync() { . . . }

private void ButtonClick(object sender, RoutedEventArgs e)
{
  Task<decimal> calculation = CalculateMeaningOfLifeAsync();

  calculation.ContinueWith(calculationTask =>
  {
      var errors = calculationTask.Exception as AggregateException;

      if (errors == null)
      {
          resultLabel.Text = calculation.Result.ToString();
      }
      else
      {
          Exception actualException = errors.InnerExceptions.First();
          resultLabel.Text = actualException.Message;
      }
  }, TaskScheduler.FromCurrentSynchronizationContext());
}
```

If developers are to be encouraged to embrace the use of asynchronous methods, then the programming model needs to be as simple as the synchronous model; this is one goal of the async and await keywords introduced in C#5. Taking advantage of these two new keywords, rewrite the code as shown in Listing 7-3.

Listing 7-3. Utilising async/await to maintain synchronous structure

```
private Task<decimal> CalculateMeaningOfLifeAsync() { . . . }

private async void ButtonClick(object sender, RoutedEventArgs e)
{
  try
  {
    decimal result = await CalculateMeaningOfLifeAsync();
    resultLabel.Text = result.ToString();
  }
  catch (MidlifeCrisisException error)
  {
    resultLabel.Text = error.Message;
  }
}
```

Listing 7-3 does not block the UI; it continues to run CalculateMeaningOfLife asynchronously, but with the benefit of simplicity. It is identical in structure and type usage as the sequential version, and thus as easy to read as the original code laid out in Listing 7-1.

What Do async and await Actually Do?

Probably the most important thing to realize is that the async keyword does not make your code run asynchronously, and the await keyword doesn't make your code wait. Other than that the keywords are pretty straightforward.

Joking aside, the async keyword does not influence the code generated by the compiler; it simply enables the use of the await keyword in the method. If the await keyword had been conceived when the C# language keywords were first defined in Version 1, there would never have been the need for async, as await would always have been a reserved word in the language. The problem with creating new language keywords is that there could be code out there that is using any potential new keyword as an identifier and as such would now not compile under the C# 5 compiler. So the async keyword is necessary simply to inform the compiler that when it sees the word await, you do mean the new language keyword.

In contrast with async, the await keyword does quite a lot. As just mentioned, it does not perform a physical wait. In other words,

```
decimal result = await CalculateMeaningOfLifeAsync();
       !=
decimal result = CalculateMeaningOfLifeAsync().Result;
```

as this would result in the calling thread entering a wait state until the asynchronous task had completed. This would then lock up the UI—the very thing you are trying to avoid. On the other hand, the thread cannot proceed until the result from the asynchronous operation is known; in other words, it can't continue. What the compiler implements has the same intent as the code in Listing 7-2. It creates continuation (we will discuss the mechanics of this at the end of this chapter). In the current example all the code after the await statement forms a continuation, which runs when the asynchronous operation has completed, just like ContinuesWith. By having the compiler build the continuation for you, you have preserved the program structure.

The await statement consists of the await keyword and an asynchronous expression to wait upon. This expression is typically a Task; later, when we discuss the compiler mechanics in more detail, you will see it can potentially be other types as long as they follow certain conventions. Once the compiler has set up a continuation on the outcome of the asynchronous operation, it simply returns from the method. For the compiler to emit code that returns from the method without fully completing the method, the method must have a return type of one of the following:

- void

- Task

- Task<T>

For methods returning void there is no return value, and hence the caller is unaware if the call has fully completed or just started. (Is this good or bad? More later.) In the cases where a Task is being returned, the caller is fully aware that the operation may not have fully completed and can observe the returned task to obtain the final outcome.

Hopefully you will have noticed that, although the CalculateMeaningOfLifeAsync method returns a Task<decimal>, the code using the await keyword is simply written in terms of decimal, so a further behavior of the await keyword is to coerce the result from the asynchronous expression and present it in the same form you would have gotten from a synchronized method call. Listing 7-4 shows a two-step version of the code in Listing 7-3 for clarity.

Listing 7-4. Coercing the Task.Result

```
Task<decimal> calcTask = CalculateMeaningOfLifeAsync();
decimal result = await calcTask;
```

The await keyword therefore removes the need for having to deal with the Task directly.

For the UI to update successfully as part of your continuation, the continuation needs to run on the UI thread. At runtime the await behavior determines if SynchronizationContext.Current is non-null, and if so automatically ensures that the continuation runs on the same SynchronizationContext that was current prior to the await operation—again removing the need to write specific directives to continue running on the UI thread.

The final part of the story is error handling. Note that in Listing 7-3 you are now handling errors using a catch block, just as in the sequential code. The compiler, through the use of continuations, again ensures that the exception is caught and handled on the UI thread. However, you possibly may have thought that the new async/await code had a bug in it. After all if the CalculateMeaningOfLifeAsync() returns a task that ends in a faulted state, you would expect to receive an AggregateException. Just as the await coerces the return value from the task, it also coerces the underlying exception from the AggregateException. "Hold on," you might say. "There may be many exceptions; hence the reason why Task uses AggregateException: await just simply takes the first." Again, this is done to try and recreate the same programming model you would have with synchronized code.

To sum up: the async keyword just enables the use of await. The await keyword performs the following:

- Registers a continuation with the asynchronous operation.

- Gives up the current thread.

- If SynchronizationContext.Current is non-null, ensures the continuation is Posted onto that context.

- If SynchronizationContext.Current is null, the continuation is scheduled using the current task scheduler, which most likely will be the default scheduler, and thus schedules the continuation on a thread pool thread.

- Coerces the result of the asynchronous operation, be it a good return value or an exception.

Last, it is worth noting that although async/await are heavily used for UI programming, they are also an effective tool for non-UI-based scenarios. You will see in Chapter 7 that they provide a convenient programming model for building composite asynchronous operations. Further, as opposed to waiting for asynchronous operations to complete, you will utilize continuations, reducing the overall burden on the thread pool.

Returning Values from async Methods

Async methods are expected to have at least one await operation, in order to be able to return from them early when a noncompleted task is encountered. If the method has no return value, then returning early is not a problem. If, however, the method returns a value, the method of returning early is a problem. Consider the synchronous code in Listing 7-5. As the signature of the method stands, you can't simply add the async keyword—you need to change the method signature to return a Task<int> instead of just a simple int. This then informs the caller that the method will complete asynchronously, and hence to obtain the final outcome of the method they will need to observe the Task.

Listing 7-5. Synchronous web page word count

```
public static int CountWordsOnPage(string url)
{
  using (var client = new WebClient())
  {
    string page = client.DownloadString(url);

    return wordRegEx.Matches(page).Count;
  }
}
```

The asynchronous version of this method would therefore look as shown in Listing 7-6.

Listing 7-6. Asynchrnous web page word count

```
public static async Task<int> CountWordsOnPageAsync(string url)
{
  using (var client = new WebClient())
  {
    string page = await client.DownloadStringTaskAsync(url);

    return wordRegEx.Matches(page).Count;
  }
}
```

The return type has changed to a Task<int> allowing the compiler the possibility to return early. However, note the return statement didn't need to change; it still returns an int, not a Task<int>. The compiler takes care of that for you (as we will discuss later in the "async/await Mechanics" section). The client could utilize the method as follows:

```
CountWordsOnPageAsync("http://www.google.co.uk")
        .ContinueWith( wct => Console.WriteLine(wct.Result));
```

If all is good the caller will get their word count displayed on the screen. However, what if an exception fires inside the CountWordsOnPageAsync method? In the same way, the successful outcome of the method is communicated through the task, as are any unhandled exceptions. The Task returned from the method will now be in a completed state of faulted. When the caller observes the task result, the exception will be re-thrown and the caller will be aware of the error.

Now revisit the async method defined in Listing 7-3. It had a method signature of private async void ButtonClick(object sender, RoutedEventArgs e). Note that this method returns void, so there is no Task for the caller to observe. So what happens if the async method is terminated due to an unhandled exception? In this case the exception is simply re-thrown using the SynchronizationContext that was present at the point when the method was first called. This would then almost preserve the behavior of the synchronous version, delivering the exception on the UI thread. We say "almost" since wrapping the call to the method with a catch block won't see the exception if it originates after the first await. The only place left to handle the exception is a top-level UI exception handler. If there is no SynchronizationContext then it is simply re-thrown and allowed to bubble up in the normal way; if no exception handler is found, the process will terminate.

Therefore, if the async method returns a Task, normal task exception-handling behavior applies. If it returns void, then the exception is simply re-thrown and allowed to bubble up.

You could perhaps argue that the designers of async and await should not have supported void methods and insisted on all methods returning a Task, as this has two effects:

1. It makes the caller aware of the asynchronicity of the method.

2. It ensures the caller is always able to fully observe the outcome of a specific invocation. The distance a catch block is from the cause often makes it harder or impossible to produce the correct level of recovery. Global handlers lack the local information necessary to produce an effective recovery, and thus are often only able to log and bring down the application gracefully.

The need to support void stems from allowing async and await to be used in event handlers—this is, after all, one of the key places where this pair of keywords will be used. However, I personally feel that it is good practice for all non–event-handler-based code that uses async and await to return a Task, enabling the caller to see it is asynchronous and giving them maximum opportunity to handle the outcome as close to the source as possible.

Should You Always Continue on the UI Thread?

Examine the code in Listing 7-7; it is being invoked from a UI thread.

Listing 7-7. Synchronously load web page and remove adverts

```
private async void LoadContent(object sender, RoutedEventArgs e)
{
   var client = new WebClient();
   string url = "http://www.msdn.com";

   string pageContent = await client.DownloadStringTaskAsync(url);

    pageContent = RemoveAdverts(pageContent);
    pageText.Text = pageContent;
}
```

The page content is being downloaded asynchronously and thus not blocking the UI thread. When the asynchronous operation has completed, you will resume this method back on the UI thread to remove any adverts. Obviously if this remove method takes a long time it will block any UI processing. A bit of refactoring and you can do as shown in Listing 7-8.

Listing 7-8. Asynchronously load web page and remove adverts

```
private async void LoadContent(object sender, RoutedEventArgs e)
{
    var client = new WebClient();
    string url = "http://www.msdn.com";

    string pageContent = await client.DownloadStringTaskAsync(url);
    pageContent = await Task.Run<string>(() => RemoveAdverts(pageContent));

    pageText.Text = pageContent;
 }
```

Voilà—you now have a version that doesn't block up the UI. However, notice that you do end up back on the UI thread after the page has been downloaded, albeit for a short period of time to run a new task. Clearly you shouldn't need to do that. You could solve it with a `Task.ContinuesWith` method call instead of a `Task.Run` (Listing 7-9).

Listing 7-9. Continuing on a non UI thread using task continuations

```
private async void LoadContent(object sender, RoutedEventArgs e)
{
  var client = new WebClient();
  string url = "http://www.msdn.com";

  string pageContent = await client.DownloadStringTaskAsync(url)
                          .ContinueWith(dt => RemoveAdverts(dt.Result));
  pageText.Text = pageContent;
}
```

This now means it will continue processing the page on a thread pool thread, and the UI thread is not involved until both those operations are completed. This is an improvement, but at what cost? The cost of being easy to read and easy to write. Async and await allow you to structure code as you would sequentially; with the code in Listing 7-9 you have moved back to your old Task-based API ways. The answer to this problem is twofold. First, you can configure the await operation so that it does not always continue back on the UI thread, but on a thread pool thread. To make that happen, call the ConfigureAwait method on the task, supplying a value of false as shown in Listing 7-10. (Shame this wasn't an enum; lucky for you, you have named parameters.)

Listing 7-10. Continuing on a non UI thread using ConfigureAwait

```
private async void LoadContent(object sender, RoutedEventArgs e)
{
  var client = new WebClient();
  string url = "http://www.msdn.com";

  string pageContent = await client.DownloadStringTaskAsync(url)
                              .ConfigureAwait(continueOnCapturedContext: false);

  pageContent = RemoveAdverts(pageContent);

  pageText.Text = pageContent;
}
```

You have now removed the continuation, and the RemoveAdverts method is now running on a thread pool thread. So all is good . . . that is, until you come to the last line, which updates the UI. At this point, you obviously need to be back on the UI thread. This brings you to the second piece of refactoring to solve the problem. What you need to do is to turn the downloading and the removing of the adverts into a single task; then the LoadContent method can simply just await on that (Listing 7-11).

Listing 7-11. Composite tasks utilising async/await

```
private async void LoadContent(object sender, RoutedEventArgs e)
{
  var client = new WebClient();
  string url = "http://www.msdn.com";

  string pageContent = await LoadPageAndRemoveAdvertsAsync(url);

  pageText.Text = pageContent;
}

public async Task<string> LoadPageAndRemoveAdvertsAsync(string url)
{
  WebClient client = new WebClient();

  string pageContent = await client.DownloadStringTaskAsync(url)
                            .ConfigureAwait(continueOnCapturedContext: false);

  pageContent = RemoveAdverts(pageContent);
  return pageContent;
}
```

The LoadContent method now focuses on running 100 percent on the UI thread, delegating to the LoadPageAndRemoveAdvertsAsync method to run on whatever threads it needs to in order to get the job done. Once its job is done, the LoadContent method will resume on the UI thread. This latest refactoring has given you clean and efficient code.

Async and await *offer a convenient way to compose asynchronous operations, using simple conventional programming styles.*

Task.Delay

.NET 4.5 introduces a series of additional Task class methods to assist in writing code that works with the await keyword. We will now review some of them and show you how to use them to great effect with async and await.

I'm sure we are all used to seeing code that blocks for a period of time before attempting an operation. For example, the code in Listing 7-12 is attempting an operation; if it fails, it will back off and try again up to three times.

Listing 7-12. Synchronous back off and retry

```
for (int nTry = 0; nTry < 3; nTry++)
{
  try
  {
    AttemptOperation();
    break;
  }
  catch (OperationFailedException){}
  Thread.Sleep(2000);
}
```

While the code in Listing 7-12 works, when the execution hits Thread.Sleep it puts the thread to sleep for 2 seconds. This means the kernel will not schedule this thread to run for at least that period of time. While sleeping, the thread doesn't consume any CPU-based resources, but the fact that the thread is alive means that it is still consuming memory resources. On a desktop application this is probably no big deal, but on a server application, having lots of threads sleeping is not ideal because if more work arrives on the server, it may have to spin up more threads, increasing memory pressure and adding additional resources for the OS to manage. Ideally, instead of putting the thread to sleep, you would like to simply give it up, allowing the thread to be free to serve other requests. When you are ready to continue using CPU resources again, you can obtain a thread (not necessarily the same one) and continue processing. In a multithreaded application, you will want to perform maximum concurrency with the minimum number of threads. We will cover the topic of efficient server side async in a lot more detail in a later chapter. For now you can solve this problem by not putting the thread to sleep, but rather using await on a Task that is deemed to be completed in a given period. As stated in Chapter 3, a Task represents an asynchronous operation, not necessarily an asynchronous compute. To create such a task, use Task.Delay, supplying the time period as in Listing 7-13.

Listing 7-13. Thread efficient back off and retry

```
for (int nTry = 0; nTry < 3; nTry++)
{
  try
  {
    AttemptOperation();
    break;
  }
  catch (OperationFailedException){}
  await Task.Delay(2000);
}
```

The Task.Delay method produces the necessary task to await on, and thus you give up the thread. When the task enters the completed state, your loop can continue.

Task.WhenAll

Task.WhenAll creates a task that is deemed to have completed when all of a set of supplied tasks have completed. This allows you to await for a set of tasks to complete before proceeding, but without blocking the current thread. Examine the code in 7-14.

Listing 7-14. Downloading documents one by one

```
public static async Task DownloadDocuments(params Uri[] downloads)

{
  var client = new WebClient();
  foreach (Uri uri in downloads)
  {
     string content = await client.DownloadStringTaskAsync(uri);
     UpdateUI(content);
  }
}
```

Calling this code on the UI thread would not result in the UI thread locking up, which is good. However it is not the most efficient way to handle downloads from multiple sources, since you will only request one download at a time. Ideally you would like to download the documents simultaneously.

Taking advantage of Task.WhenAll, you could create all the tasks upfront and then wait on a single task; that way you would download the documents in parallel. Listing 7-15 shows a possible implementation.

Listing 7-15. Download many documents asynchronously

```
public static async Task DownloadDocuments(params Uri[] downloads)
{
 List<Task<string>> tasks = new List<Task<string>>();
 foreach (Uri uri in downloads)
 {
   var client = new WebClient();

   tasks.Add(client
             .DownloadStringTaskAsync(uri));
 }

 await Task.WhenAll(tasks);

 tasks.ForEach(t => UpdateUI(t.Result) );
}
```

The code in Listing 7-15 will produce the final result quicker but won't update the UI until all the downloads are complete. Another alternative would be to spin off all the tasks, keeping each task in a collection. Then, provide a loop that awaits on each one in turn. This would possibly update the UI as items are completed, assuming they completed in the order they are initiated.

Task.WhenAll, Error Handling

While it would be nice to ignore failures, you obviously shouldn't. The code in Listing 7-15 could possibly throw multiple exceptions as part of the downloading activity. As discussed earlier, if you just use a simple try/catch block, all you will get is the first exception of a possible set of exceptions contained inside the AggregateException. So while just simply calling await Task.WhenAll is convenient, it is often necessary to perform the statement as two steps: obtain the WhenAll task and then await on it (Listing 7-16).

Listing 7-16. Observing WhenAll task exceptions

```
Task allDownloads = Task.WhenAll(tasks);
try
{
   await allDownloads;
   tasks.ForEach(t => UpdateUI(t.Result));
}
catch (Exception e)
{
   allDownloads.Exception.Handle(exception =>
   {
     Console.WriteLine(exception.Message);
     return true;
   });
}
```

Alternatively, if you care about knowing which Task was responsible for a given exception, then you will have to iterate through the tasks you supplied to WhenAll, asking each task in turn if it faulted, and if so, what are the underlying exceptions. Listing 7-17 shows such an example.

Listing 7-17. Observing WhenAll specific task exceptions

```
catch (Exception e)
{
  for (int nTask = 0; nTask < tasks.Count; nTask++)
  {
    if (tasks[nTask].IsFaulted)
    {
       Console.WriteLine("Download {0} failed",downloads[nTask]);
                      tasks[nTask].Exception.Handle( exception =>
       {
         Console.WriteLine("\t{0}",exception.Message);
         return true;
       });
    }
  }
}
```

Task.WhenAny

Task.WhenAny takes a collection of tasks, and returns a task that is deemed to have completed when any one of tasks completes. You can therefore solve the lack of immediate UI update issue in Listing 7-16 using the code in Listing 7-18.

Listing 7-18. Download many documents and update UI they download

```
public static async Task DownloadDocumentsWhenAny(params Uri[] downloads)
{
  List<Task<string>> tasks = new List<Task<string>>();
  foreach (Uri uri in downloads)
  {
    var client = new WebClient();

    tasks.Add(client.DownloadStringTaskAsync(uri));
  }
  while (tasks.Count > 0)
  {
    Task<string> download =
                  await Task.WhenAny(tasks);

    UpdateUI(download.Result);

    int nDownloadCompleted = tasks.IndexOf(download);
    Console.WriteLine("Downloaded {0}",downloads[nDownloadCompleted]);
    tasks.RemoveAt(nDownloadCompleted);
  }
}
```

This now produces the desired result: UI updates as each asynchronous request completes. Notice that the await is not returning a string, but a Task<string>. This is a little strange as up to now you have seen await coercing the result of the task, and in fact it still does—it's just that the Task.WhenAny wraps the Task<string> with a Task, making the Task.WhenAny return type a Task<Task<string>>. This is to allow the caller to be told what task has completed. If you just got the string, you would not know which task had completed.

So, all good? Well, not really. Why so? Well, you can see that each iteration of the loop calls two tasks:

Task.WhenAny, which registers a continuation for all tasks in the list that are not in a completed state.

Tasks.IndexOf(downloaded), which performs a linear search of the entire list, looking for a match.

For both these pieces of code, the execution cost increases as the number of tasks increases. It is further compounded by the fact that the cost is repeated after each subsequent task completes, albeit with a lesser and lesser cost. In effect, using this technique for 10 tasks will result in one task having a possibility of 10 defined continuations, as opposed to just one with Task.WhenAll.

So Task.WhenAny is at first glance the obvious choice for this kind of usage, but beware: it doesn't scale. In Chapter 8 you will build a version that does scale. Use Task.WhenAny when you have a small number of tasks, or you only wish to take the result from the first completed tasks. For example, Listing 7-19 queries three web servers for a result and acts on the first response.

Listing 7-19. First task to complete wins

```
public static async Task<string> GetGooglePage(string relativeUrl)
{
  string[] hosts = {"google.co.uk","google.com","www.google.com.sg" };

  List<Task<string>> tasks =
                (from host in hosts
                 let urlBuilder = new UriBuilder("http", host, 80, relativeUrl)
```

```
            let webClient = new WebClient()
            select webClient
               .DownloadStringTaskAsync(urlBuilder.Uri)
               .ContinueWith<string>(dt =>
                          {
                             webClient.Dispose();
                             return dt.Result;
                          })
            ).ToList();
  return await Task.WhenAny(tasks).Result;
}
```

Wait—not so fast. The code in Listing 7-19 will return the result of the first task to complete. What if it fails? You obviously would be happy to wait to see if one of the other servers could respond. A more reliable version would replace the await Task.WhenAny with the code in Listing 7-20.

Listing 7-20. First task to run to completion wins

```
var errors = new List<Exception>();
do
{
   Task<string> completedTask = null;

   completedTask= await Task.WhenAny(tasks);
   if (completedTask.Status == TaskStatus.RanToCompletion)
   {
       return completedTask.Result;
   }

   tasks.Remove(completedTask);
   errors.Add(completedTask.Exception);

} while (tasks.Count > 0 );

throw new AggregateException(errors);
```

WhenAll and WhenAny are the built-in task combiners; they are very basic and we often need to add additional plumbing around them for use in our applications. In the next chapter you will develop more elaborate task combiners that will not require as much basic plumbing—for example, wait for all tasks to complete, but if any one fails cancel all outstanding tasks.

async/await Mechanics

Now that you have observed the magic, it is probably worth having a quick look at how this magic is achieved. In this final part of the chapter, you will examine how the compiler may rewrite your async method to achieve the continuations. To be very clear at the outset, we are not going to attempt to completely recreate everything, but just show you the bare bones so you get some idea of what is going on.

For this analysis, use the code in Listing 7-21.

Listing 7-21. Asynchronous tick/tock

```
private static async void TickTockAsync()
{
    Console.WriteLine("Starting Clock");
    while (true)
    {
        Console.Write("Tick ");

        await Task.Delay(500);

        Console.WriteLine("Tock");

        await Task.Delay(500);
    }
}
```

From what you have seen and learned so far, you know that the TickTockAsync method, when called, will continue executing on the calling thread up to the point when Task.Delay returns, at which point the method returns to the caller. When the delay task completes it will then "move" onto the next piece of code, and so the pattern repeats itself for each of the await calls. You could consider each of these pieces of code as a series of separate states, as in Figure 7-1. Now it turns out compilers are good at building state machines; all that is required now is a standard way for it to detect when a state transition should happen.

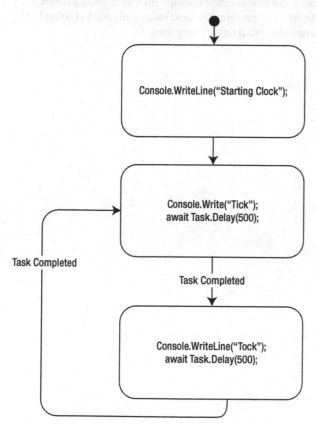

Figure 7-1. *Asynchronous tick/tock state machine*

It may be a reasonable assumption to assume that await only works with Tasks since they are the asynchronous building block for .NET 4.5, and the compiler could just utilize the Task.ContinueWith method. However, the compiler provides a more general approach. It turns out that the expression on the right side of the await keywords needs to yield an object that has a method on it called GetAwaiter. This method takes no parameters and can return any type it likes as long as this type.

- Contains a boolean property called IsCompleted;

- Contains a method called GetResult, takes no parameters, and the return type can be anything—this type will ultimately be the return type from the await statement; and

- Implements the interface INotifyCompletion (see Listing 7-22).

Listing 7-22. INotifyCompletion interface

```
namespace System.Runtime.CompilerServices
{
    public interface INotifyCompletion
    {
        void OnCompleted(Action continuation);
    }
}
```

It is therefore this awaiter object that provides the continuation functionality through the call to OnCompleted. The method is supplied with the delegate containing the code, which represents the next state. The code in Listing 7-23 shows a ridiculous awaiter implementation that represents something that never completes.

Listing 7-23. A ridiculous awaiter implementation

```
public struct WaitingForEverAwaiter : INotifyCompletion
{
  public bool IsCompleted { get { return false; } }
  public void OnCompleted(Action continuation)
  {
    return;
  }

  public int GetResult()
  {
    return 0;
  }
}

public class WaitingForEverAwaiterSource
{
  public  WaitingForEverAwaiter GetAwaiter()
  {
    return default(WaitingForEverAwaiter);
  }
}
```

```
. . .
private static async void WaitingForEverAsync()
{
    int result =  await new WaitingForEverAwaiterSource();
    // Never gets to here
}
```

The Task and Task<T> classes simply implement a GetAwaiter method that returns an awaiter, which utilizes the Task to provide the necessary functionality required of the awaiter object. The awaiter object is therefore to some degree simply an adapter. What you will be able to glean from this is that this awaiter object has all the necessary parts to build the continuations between the various states.

Now you have the necessary building blocks to register for completions, which will cause the state changes in your state machine. You can now look to rewriting your async method along similar lines to what the compiler will do for your initial TickTockAsyncMethod() (see Listing 7-24).

Listing 7-24. Asynchronous tick/tock as a state machine

```
private static void TickTockAsync()
{
    var stateMachine = new TickTockAsyncStateMachine();
    stateMachine.MoveNext();
}

public class TickTockAsyncStateMachine
    {
        private int state = 0;
        private TaskAwaiter awaiter;

        public void MoveNext()
        {

            switch (state)
            {
                case 0:
                    {
                        goto firstState;
                    }
                    break;
                case 1:
                    {
                        goto secondState;
                    }
                    break;
                case 2:
                    {
                        goto thirdState;
                    }
                    break;
            }
```

```
            firstState:
            Console.WriteLine("Starting clock");
            goto secondAndHalfState;
            secondState:
            awaiter.GetResult();

            secondAndHalfState:
            Console.Write("Tick");
            awaiter = Task.Delay(500).GetAwaiter();
            if (!awaiter.IsCompleted)
            {
                state = 2;
                awaiter.OnCompleted(MoveNext);
                return;
            }
            thirdState:
            awaiter.GetResult();
            Console.WriteLine("Tock");
            if (!awaiter.IsCompleted)
            {
                state = 1;
                awaiter.OnCompleted(MoveNext);
                return;
            }

            goto secondState;
        }
```

The code in Listing 7-24 should be fairly self-explanatory. The original async method is replaced by creating an instance of a state machine and initially kicking it off via a call to MoveNext. The MoveNext method is in effect the body of the original async method, albeit interleaved with a switch/case block. The state field is used to know what code to run when MoveNext is called again. When each piece of code reaches the point of the original await operation, it needs to orchestrate the transition to the next state. If the awaiter object is already marked as completed, it just transitions immediately to the next state; otherwise it registers a continuation to call itself back and returns from the method. When the awaiter object deems the operation to have completed, the OnCompleted action is called and the next piece of code dictated by the state field is executed. The process repeats until the state machine is deemed to have completed. (Note in this case that should never happen unless an unhandled exception is thrown).

Summary

That concludes your initial look at async and await. In this chapter you have seen how these keywords provide an effective way of consuming and composing asynchronous methods while still keeping the structure of the code as simple as their synchronous counterparts. These keywords will become common in all of your asynchronous code, be it UI development or streamlining server-side asynchronous processing to ensure no thread is left blocked.

CHAPTER 8

∎ ∎ ∎

Everything a Task

In Chapter 7 you discovered how the async and await keywords simplify the composing and consuming of Task-based asynchronous logic. Also, in Chapter 3 we mentioned that a Task represents a piece of asynchronous activity. This asynchronous activity could be compute but could as easily be I/O. An example of a noncompute Task is when you turned an IAsyncResult into a Task utilizing Task.Factory.FromAsyncResult. If you could literally represent anything as a Task, then you could have more areas of your code that could take advantage of the async and await keywords. In this chapter you will discover there is a very simple API to achieve just this. Taking advantage of this API, we will show you a series of common use cases, from an efficient version of WhenAny to stubbing out Task-based APIs for the purpose of unit testing.

Finally it is worth mentioning that this API works on .NET 4, and is extremely useful even without async/await.

TaskCompletionSource<T>

TaskCompletionSource<T> has two responsibilities, one of which is to produce a Task<T> object. The other is to provide a series of methods to control the outcome of the Task. As mentioned in Chapter 3, a Task can finish in one of three states (RanToCompletion, Cancelled, Faulted). Listing 8-1 shows a subset of the TaskCompletionSource class.

Listing 8-1. TaskCompletionSource<T>

```
public TaskCompletionSource<T>
{
    . . .

    public Task<TResult> Task { get; }

    public void SetCanceled();
    public void SetException(Exception exception);
    public void SetResult(TResult result);
}
```

You have seen a similar API to this before: CancellationTokenSource, for controlling the cancellation process. A TaskCompletionSource is used by code wishing to control the outcome of the Task under the control of a given TaskCompletionSource. The TaskCompletionSource object exposes a Task object via its Task property; this Task is passed to code wishing to observe the Task. The type argument used with the TaskCompletionSource<T> is used to indicate the result type for the Task. If you wish to produce a Task as opposed to a Task<T>, then Microsoft's advice is to use TaskCompletionSource<object>. Task<object> extends Task, so it can always be treated as just a Task.

Listing 8-2 shows a simple example of producing a Task<int> via a TaskCompletionSource<int>. The Task is not deemed to have completed until **Enter** is pressed and the Task's outcome is set by the call to SetResult.

Listing 8-2. Task<int> via TaskCompletionSource<int>

```
var tcs = new TaskCompletionSource<int>();

Task<int> syntheticTask = tcs.Task;

syntheticTask.ContinueWith(t => Console.WriteLine("Result {0}", t.Result));

Console.WriteLine("Press enter to complete the Task");
Console.ReadLine();

tcs.SetResult(42);
Console.ReadLine();
```

Worked Example: Creating a Foreground Task

There are two types of threads in .NET: foreground and background. For a process to remain alive there must be at least one foreground thread. If there are no foreground threads running, the process will exit even if there are still background threads in operation. A Task that will keep the process alive must be mapped to a foreground thread. Tasks produced by TPL are always mapped onto background threads, so that no running Task will keep the process alive. Since TaskCompletionSource<T> allows the lifetime of anything to be represented as a Task, you could use it to represent the lifetime of a foreground thread. Listing 8-3 shows a method that creates such a Task.

Listing 8-3. Foreground Task

```
static void Main(string[] args)
{
  Task fgTask = CreateForegroundTask<int>(() =>
                    {
                        Console.WriteLine("Running..");
                        Thread.Sleep(2000);
                        return 42;
                    })
                .ContinueWith(t => Console.WriteLine("Result is {0}",t.Result),
                            TaskContinuationOptions.ExecuteSynchronously);
            Console.WriteLine("Main Completed");
  }

    public static Task<T> CreateForegroundTask<T>(Func<T> taskBody)
    {
       return CreateForegroundTask(taskBody, CancellationToken.None);
    }

    public static Task<T> CreateForegroundTask<T>(Func<T> taskBody,CancellationToken ct)
    {
      var tcs = new TaskCompletionSource<T>();
      // Create a foreground thread, and start it
      var fgThread = new Thread(() => ExecuteForegroundTaskBody(taskBody, ct, tcs));
      fgThread.Start();
```

```
    // Return a task that is bound to the life time of the foreground thread body
    return tcs.Task;
}

private static void ExecuteForegroundTaskBody<T>(Func<T> taskBody, CancellationToken ct,
                                            TaskCompletionSource<T> tcs)
{
    try
    {
      T result = taskBody();
      tcs.SetResult(result);
    }
    catch (OperationCanceledException cancelledException)
    {
      // If the Task body ended in a OperationCancelledException
      // and the Cancellation is associated with the cancellation token
      // for this Task, mark the Task as cancelled, otherwise just set the exception
      // on the Task.
      if (ct == cancelledException.CancellationToken)
      {
          tcs.SetCanceled();
      }
      else
      {
          tcs.SetException(cancelledException);
      }
    }
    catch (Exception error)
    {
      // Set the Task status to Faulted, and re-throw as part of an AggregateException
      tcs.SetException(error);
    }
}
```

This same technique can be used for creating STA Tasks or Tasks bound to threads with high priority. TaskCompletionSource<T> is therefore a very powerful building block, allowing legacy code to be simply wrapped up and as exposed as a Task. Once wrapped up as a Task, it can be managed using modern constructs such async and await.

Unit Testing and Stubbing Asynchronous Methods

Writing unit tests for methods often requires us to stub out method calls to objects not under test. Consider writing a test for the WebPage class shown in Listing 8-4. The responsibility of this class is to load the document represented by the current Url property, and to make the content available via the Document property.

Listing 8-4. WebPage

```
public class WebPage
{
  private readonly Func<string, string> pageLoader;
  public WebPage()
```

```
  {
    pageLoader = uri =>
    {
      using (var c = new WebClient())
      {
        return c.DownloadString(uri);
      }
    };
  }

  public WebPage(Func<string, string> pageLoader)
  {
    this.pageLoader = pageLoader;
  }

  private string url;
  public string Url
  {
    get { return url; }
    set
    {
      Document = pageLoader(url);
      url = value;
    }
  }

  public string Document { get; private set; }

}
```

Listing 8-5 shows a possible unit test for the Url method. You will have noticed that the WebPage class allows the injection of a method responsible for loading the requested document. When unit testing, you will need to provide a non-web-based implementation of this method (stub).

Listing 8-5. Task.Run-Based Unit Test

```
[TestClass]
public class WebPageTests
{
  [TestMethod]
  public void Url_PropertyIsChanged_ShouldDownloadNewPageContent()
  {
    string expectedPageContent = "<html><i>Dummy content</i></html>";
    var sut = new WebPage(uri => expectedPageContent);
    sut.Url = "http://dummy.com";
    Assert.AreEqual(expectedPageContent, sut.Document);
  }
}
```

The test works perfectly well, but now say the developer of the WebPage class decides it would be better to load the page asynchronously. Listing 8-6 shows the refactored code.

Listing 8-6. Asynchronous WebPage

```
public class WebPage
{
  private readonly Func<string, Task<string>> pageLoader;

  public WebPage()
  {
    pageLoader = uri =>
    {
      using (var c = new WebClient())
      {
        return c.DownloadStringTaskAsync(uri);
      }
    };
  }

  public WebPage(Func<string, Task<string>> pageLoader)
  {
    this.pageLoader = pageLoader;
  }

  private string url;
  public string Url
  {
    get { return url; }
    set
    {
      Document = null;

      pageLoader(url)
              .ContinueWith(dt => Document = dt.Result);

       url = value;
    }
  }

  public string Document { get; private set; }
}
```

To test this version of the class, you now need to supply a stub that returns a Task<string> as opposed to just simply a string. Listing 8-7 shows a possible implementation of a test.

Listing 8-7. Task.Run-Based Test

```
[TestClass]
public class WebPageTests
{
  [TestMethod]
  public void Url_PropertyIsChanged_ShouldDownloadNewPageContent()
  {
    string expectedPageContent = "<html><i>Dummy content</i></html>";
```

```
    var sut = new WebPage(uri => Task.Run<string>(() => expectedPageContent));
    sut.Url = "http://dummy.com";

    Assert.AreEqual(expectedPageContent,sut.Document);
  }
}
```

The only difference between the two implementations of the tests is that in the second, you have wrapped the expected result with a Task.Run. This ensures you comply with the requirements of the page load delegate. Although all the code compiles, the test will fail. Why? Well, hopefully by now you are all Asynchronous Gurus and have spotted the race condition. With the synchronous version, the Document property gets set once the Url property setter has download the content. With the asynchronous version this is not guaranteed. For the test to run successfully the assertion phase can't happen until the Document property has been modified. One possible workaround is to add an additional property to the WebPage class to expose the Task responsible for updating the document. The test method could then wait for that Task to complete before performing the assertion. Listing 8-8 shows the modifications required to the WebPage class.

Listing 8-8. Exposing the DocumentLoadingTask

```
public Task DocumentLoadingTask { get; private set; }

private string url;
public string Url
{
  get { return url; }
  set
  {
    Document = null;
    DocumentLoadingTask =
                    pageLoader(url)
                        .ContinueWith(dt => Document = dt.Result);
    url = value;
  }
}
```

The test code is then modified to wait for the DocumentLoadingTask to complete before performing the assertion. This then allows the test to have deterministic behavior (Listing 8-9).

Listing 8-9. Waiting for DocumentLoadingTask

```
public void Url_PropertyIsChanged_ShouldDownloadNewPageContent()
{
  string expectedPageContent = "<html><i>Dummy content</i></html>";
  var sut = new WebPage(uri => Task.Run<string>(() => expectedPageContent));

  sut.Url = "http://dummy.com";
  sut.DocumentLoadingTask.Wait();

  Assert.AreEqual(expectedPageContent,sut.Document);
}
```

Rerunning the test now results in it passing. However, the use of Task.Run does seem wrong. As the goal of unit tests is to run as lightweight as possible, creating threads that return immediately seems overkill. A far lighter-weight approach would be to use TaskCompletionSource to generate the asynchronous value. Listing 8-10 contains a helper class that can be used with testing to create asynchronous stubbed results.

Listing 8-10. AsyncStubs

```
public static class AsyncStubs
{
    public static Task<T> FromResult<T>(T result)
    {
        var tcs = new TaskCompletionSource<T>();
            tcs.SetResult(result);

            return tcs.Task;
    }

    public static Task<T> FromException<T>(Exception e)
    {
        var tcs = new TaskCompletionSource<T>();
        tcs.SetException(e);
        return tcs.Task;
    }
}
```

Listing 8-11 shows the test method rewritten in terms of AsyncStubs.FromResult.

Listing 8-11. TaskCompletionSource-Based Stubs

```
[TestMethod]
public void Url_PropertyIsChanged_ShouldDownloadNewPageContent()
{
    string expectedPageContent = "<html><i>Dummy content</i></html>";
    var sut = new WebPage(uri => AsyncStubs.FromResult(expectedPageContent));
    sut.Url = "http://dummy.com";
    sut.DocumentLoadingTask.Wait();
    Assert.AreEqual(expectedPageContent, sut.Document);
}
```

This technique has now found its way into .NET 4.5 with the introduction of the Task.FromResult<T> method, but unfortunately no FromException. In effect, what you have done for testing is to make the asynchronous operation almost complete synchronously. The only bit that is still asynchronous is the ContinuesWith call, which sets the Document property. You could make it all complete synchronously if you modify the ContinuesWith to execute synchronously, which allows the removal of the property DocumentLoadingTask. Making a ContinuesWith execute synchronously results in either

- The continuation Tasks running on the same thread that causes the antecedent Task to transition into its final state, or

- Alternatively, if the antecedent is already complete when the continuation is created, the continuation will run on the thread creating the continuation.

Since all the continuation does is simply set a value of the property, then it is perfectly acceptable to execute synchronously. Listing 8-12 shows the modified WebPage class. The sut.DocumentDownloadTasking.Wait can now be removed from the test method as the Url set operation in the context of unit testing now executes synchronously, simplifying the test method.

Listing 8-12. ExecuteSynchronously

```
public string Url
{
  get { return url; }
  set
  {
    Document = null;
    pageLoader(url)
                   .ContinueWith(dt => Document = dt.Result,
                   TaskContinuationOptions.ExecuteSynchronously);

    url = value;
  }
}
```

Building Task-Based Combinators

In Chapter 7 we demonstrated the use of WhenAny and WhenAll as a means of awaiting on many Tasks. We highlighted the fact that making repetitive calls to WhenAny for a smaller and smaller subset of Tasks was not very efficient, due to the fact that it was repeatedly creating continuations. The out-of-the-box WhenAll also potentially has a failing in that when waiting for many Tasks to complete, it may be desirable for the wait to terminate early if any of the Tasks fail or get canceled. You can address both these issues by making use of TaskCompletionSource<T>.

Improved WhenAny

First, remind yourself of the code you developed in Chapter 7. Listing 8-13 shows repeated calls to Task.WhenAny setting up many continuations for an ever-decreasing set of Tasks. Ideally you would like to set up just one set of continuations.

Listing 8-13. Out of the Box WhenAny

```
public static async Task DownloadDocumentsWhenAny(params Uri[] downloads)
{
  List<Task<string>> tasks = new List<Task<string>>();
  foreach (Uri uri in downloads)
  {
    var client = new WebClient();

    tasks.Add(client.DownloadStringTaskAsync(uri));
  }
  while (tasks.Count > 0)
  {
    Task<string> download =
                await Task.WhenAny(tasks);
```

```
    UpdateUI(download.Result);
    int nDownloadCompleted = tasks.IndexOf(download);
    tasks.RemoveAt(nDownloadCompleted);
  }
}
```

Instead of returning a single Task from a Task.WhenAny style method, you could return an IEnumerable<Task<T>>, where each Task in the IEnumerable would complete in order. You could then simply loop over the set of Tasks, waiting on each of them in turn (Listing 8-14).

Listing 8-14. Simplified WhenAny, WhenNext

```
public static class TaskCombinators
{
  public static IEnumerable<Task<T>> OrderByCompletion<T>(this IEnumerable<Task<T>> tasks)
  { . . . }
}

public static async Task DownloadDocumentsWhenAny(params Uri[] downloads)
  {
    List<Task<string>> tasks = new List<Task<string>>();
    foreach (Uri uri in downloads)
    {
      var client = new WebClient();

      tasks.Add(client.DownloadStringTaskAsync(uri));
    }

    foreach(Task<string> downloadTask in tasks.OrderByCompletion() )
    {
      Task<string> download = await downloadTask;

      UpdateUI(download.Result);
    }
  }
}
```

The problem is that you don't know in what order the Tasks will complete; hence WhenAny. However if you were to return not the actual Tasks, but to a series of Tasks that represent the result of the first Task to complete, and then the second Task to complete, et cetera, that would suffice. To achieve this you will create as many TaskCompletionSources as there are Tasks. Each real Task would then have a single continuation registered; the responsibility of the first continuation to actually run is to set the result of the first TaskCompletionSource.Task to the outcome of the antecedent Task. Each subsequent continuation sets the next TaskCompletionSource result. Last, the method returns the Tasks for each of the TaskCompletionSources, to be consumed by the caller using a foreach. Listing 8-15 shows the implementation.

Listing 8-15. OrderByCompletion

```
public static class TaskCombinators
{
  public static IEnumerable<Task<T>> OrderByCompletion<T>(this IEnumerable<Task<T>> tasks)
  {
   if (tasks == null) throw new ArgumentNullException("tasks");
```

```
    List<Task<T>> allTasks = tasks.ToList();
    if ( allTasks.Count == 0 ) throw new ArgumentException("Must have at least one task");

    var taskCompletionsSources = new TaskCompletionSource<T>[allTasks.Count];

    int nextCompletedTask = -1;
    for (int nTask = 0; nTask < allTasks.Count; nTask++)
    {
      taskCompletionsSources[nTask] = new TaskCompletionSource<T>();
      allTasks[nTask].ContinueWith(t =>
        {
          int taskToComplete = Interlocked.Increment(ref nextCompletedTask);
          switch (t.Status)
          {
            case TaskStatus.RanToCompletion:
              taskCompletionsSources[taskToComplete].SetResult(t.Result);
              break;

            case TaskStatus.Faulted:
              taskCompletionsSources[taskToComplete]
                  .SetException(t.Exception.InnerExceptions);
              break;

            case TaskStatus.Canceled:
              taskCompletionsSources[taskToComplete].SetCanceled();
              break;
          }
      } ,TaskContinuationOptions.ExecuteSynchronously);
    }
  }
}
```

There are a couple of things to point out in the implementation. Notice it is using a form of SetException that takes a IEnumerable<Exception>. You could have simply called SetException(t.Exception), but this would have resulted in the final AggregateException wrapping the AggregateException returned from the antecedent Task. This way you have reduced the levels of exceptions. Last, you have ensured the continuation runs on the same thread as the antecedent Task completed on for efficiency.

Alternative WhenAll, WhenAllOrFail

The method Task.WhenAll returns a Task that is deemed to have completed when all the supplied Tasks have completed. As mentioned previously, "completed" could mean Faulted, Cancelled, or RanToCompletion. What if you want to stop waiting if any of the Tasks fail? The Task.WhenAll method will keep you unaware of the outcome of all the Tasks until the final one has completed. Listing 8-16 shows an implementation of WhenAllOrFail; the Task returned from this method will be signaled as complete when all the Tasks have RanToCompletion or any of them end in a Faulted or Cancelled state.

Listing 8-16. WhenAllOrFail

```
public static Task<T[]> WhenAllOrFail<T>(IEnumerable<Task<T>> tasks)
{
    List<Task<T>> allTasks = tasks.ToList();
    if ( allTasks.Count == 0) throw new ArgumentException("No tasks to wait on");

    var tcs = new TaskCompletionSource<T[]>();

    int tasksCompletedCount = 0;
    Action<Task<T>> completedAction = t =>
    {
     if (t.IsFaulted)
     {
       tcs.TrySetException(t.Exception);
       return;
     }
     if (t.IsCanceled)
     {
       tcs.TrySetCanceled();
       return;
     }
     if (Interlocked.Increment(ref tasksCompletedCount) == allTasks.Count)
     {
       tcs.SetResult(allTasks.Select(ct => ct.Result).ToArray());
     }
    };

    allTasks.ForEach(t => t.ContinueWith(completedAction));

    return tcs.Task;
}
```

You may have noticed the use of TrySetXX as opposed to just SetXX. The outcome of a Task can only be set once; if you attempt to call SetXX many times against a TaskCompletionSource, this will result in an InvalidOperationException. When calling SetResult you can be confident that no SetXX method has previously been called by virtue of the taskCompletedCount variable. The same cannot be said when wishing to complete early due to Task exception or cancellation. Rather than use further synchronization, you can simply use the TrySetXX methods, which will silently ignore the set if the Task is already in a completed state.

Summary

In this chapter, you have seen that virtually anything can be represented as a Task. TaskCompletionSource<T> lets you build adapters for old-style asynchronous operations, allowing old-style APIs to be integrated easily into the new TPL-based programming model. In addition to adapting conventional asynchronous operations to TPL, you have seen how to create synchronization primitives as tasks, dispensing with the need for threads to block and instead simply yielding the thread to perform other, more useful Tasks. We have just touched on a couple of examples of TaskCompletionSource in this chapter; we hope it has given you an appetite to create some of your own.

CHAPTER 9

■ ■ ■

Server-Side Async

In Chapter 6 we looked at asynchrony on the client side in some depth. Strong as the case is for using asynchronous execution on the client, it is even stronger on the server side. One could even say that the server side is fundamentally flawed unless request execution is handled, to some degree, asynchronously. In this chapter we will examine the reasons for implementing server-side asynchrony and the challenges it presents. Then we will analyze the asynchronous features in .NET 4.0 and 4.5 in the major server-side frameworks: ASP.NET (in a number of guises) and Windows Communication Foundation (WCF).

Natural Parallelism

The processing of requests from clients lends itself very naturally to parallel execution. Requests, by their nature, tend to be discrete and unrelated to other requests happening concurrently. So there should be no contention between clients when processing any given request (unless of course two clients try to update the same database record; but that's an issue for the database, not for the server). You can see this model in Figure 9-1 where the requests do not interact with one another as they are processed by the server on the way to the database.

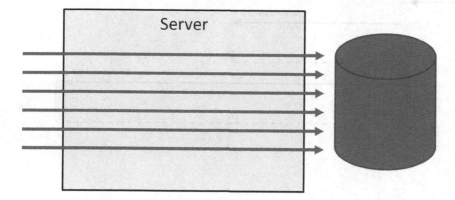

Figure 9-1. *Natural server request parallelism*

In general this isolation is achieved by dedicating a thread to the request over its whole lifetime. This means that any required request-specific state can be stored in thread- or call-specific constructs, such as thread local storage and CallContext, until the request is complete. ASP.NET makes request-specific state available via an HttpContext object, which is available to code running as part of the request through the HttpContext.Current static property. WCF makes request-specific state available in a similar way, but using a class called OperationContext and a static property OperationContext.Current.HttpContext is based on CallContext and OperationContext on thread local storage.

THREAD LOCAL STORAGE AND CALLCONTEXT

Thread Local Storage (TLS) is an operating system facility that allows data to be associated with a specific thread rather than on the heap or stack. The data is stored in "slots," which act as storage areas for data. The number of TLS slots is limited across the process (as all threads have all slots), but you are guaranteed to have at least 64 available. Data, once placed in a slot, will live for the lifetime of the thread unless overwritten or the slot itself is removed.

CallContext, on the other hand, is a .NET construct that allows state to be carried, out of band, along the logical thread of execution. In other words, if Method A calls Method B, which in turn calls Method C, then data set in the CallContext in A will be available in C without having to pass parameters down through the call chain.

The Problem of I/O

The natural parallelism model just described is ideal if the requests are CPU bound. However, if the requests perform I/O, then simply blocking a request thread while the I/O takes place means you have a thread that is consuming resources, but doing no useful work (see Figure 9-2). Inevitably, I/O-based work will, from the server's perspective, be performed by the hardware: disk heads moving to the data on disk, the network card waiting for packets to be received from the database server. In reality, it would be better to have the I/O running in the background and allow the request thread to get on with other work. This you can achieve using overlapped (asynchronous) I/O.

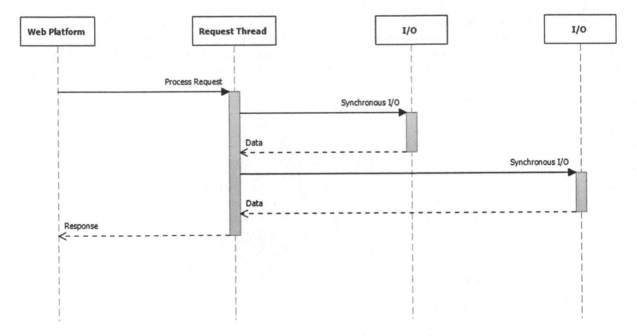

Figure 9-2. Request processing with synchronous I/O

By using overlapped I/O the request thread could perform many asynchronous pieces of I/O concurrently and then combine the results for the response message (see Figure 9-3). This is certainly one way to ensure that the thread can do more than simply block for multiple I/O requests sequentially. However, the majority of requests arguably do not need to perform multiple I/O operations to complete a single request. What you really need to do in this situation is to give up the request thread to allow it to get back to its primary job: servicing requests. You then only commit a thread once the I/O has completed and you have CPU-based work to perform once more. Windows has a feature called I/O Completion Ports (IOCP), and this is its core purpose.

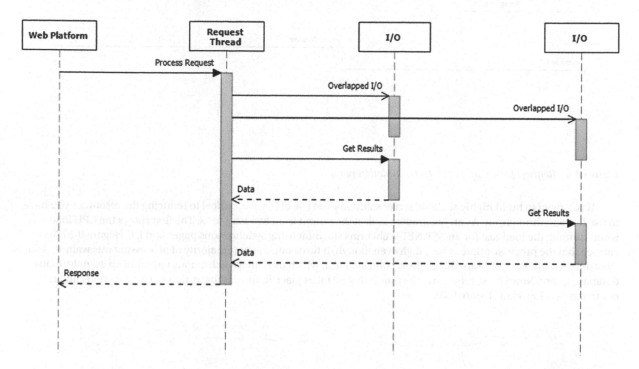

Figure 9-3. *Request Processing with Overlapped I/O*

The idea behind IOCP is that the I/O operations are performed overlapped but, rather than the request thread waiting for the completion, the completion gets enqueued, and then a thread from a thread pool is given the results of the I/O. This means, assuming you can correlate the completion of the I/O back to the request that caused it to be performed, the I/O thread pool can complete the request. This also means that the original request thread can get back to servicing new requests while the I/O takes place (see Figure 9-4).

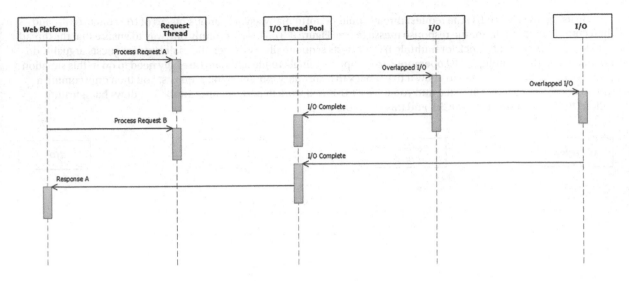

Figure 9-4. *Request processing with I/O completion ports*

If you need to build highly scalable server solutions, the use of IOCP is critical to reducing the resources you have to use for high throughput. As an illustration, look at the output from two load tests. The first shows the CPU load when running the load test for an ASP.NET WebForms site built using synchronous pages and I/O (Figure 9-5). You can see that the processor time is very high even though, it turns out, the vast majority of processing was waiting on a slow database query. Compare this to the second load test, which uses an asynchronous page and an asynchronous database query. Now you see, because the processing all takes place in the database, that the web server is under comparatively low load (Figure 9-6).

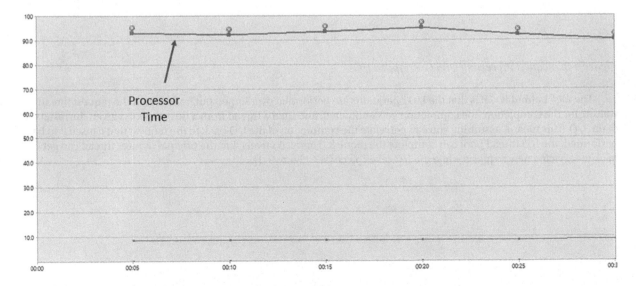

Figure 9-5. *Load test output for synchronous pages*

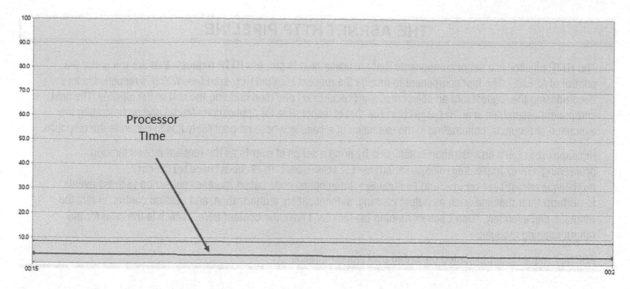

Figure 9-6. *Load test output for asynchronous pages*

Having seen that asynchrony can be very important on the server side, how do you go about implementing it in the four main .NET server-side technologies: ASP.NET WebForms, ASP.NET MVC, ASP.NET Web API, and WCF? If you look at the MSDN documentation for using IOCP you may suddenly feel quite daunted as it's not a simple API. Fortunately, however, you are on the .NET platform and the complexity in the IOCP model is wrapped up nicely by the .NET Framework class library.

How the IOCP functionality is exposed depends on which version of .NET you are using. .NET 4.0 introduced the TPL and so, as on other occasions in the past, the base class library (BCL) itself was not changed to take advantage of the new feature. Typically new patterns for building APIs don't come into heavy use until the version after the one that delivered the new functionality (generics are another example; although introduced in .NET 2.0, they didn't really appear heavily in the BCL until 3.5). Therefore, if you look at the BCL in 4.5 you see many new methods appearing on classes to take advantage of the power of TPL. As a result, how you build asynchronous code in 4.0 and 4.5 is quite different—especially with the introduction of the async and await keywords. We shall therefore examine how to build server-side asynchronous code in both .NET 4.0 and 4.5.

ASP.NET WebForms

ASP.NET WebForms) was the first .NET web technology, and it sits on top of a common HTTP processing pipeline. It is based on the concept of a page that contains a set of server-side controls. The controls have state and that state is used, by the control, to affect the rendering of the appropriate HTML to represent the UI for that control. A page is built from markup (in an ASPX file) and a code-behind file with .NET code in it. These files are compiled, as partial classes, into a single .NET type that derives, directly or indirectly, from System.Web.UI.Page, which is a handler.

THE ASP.NET HTTP PIPELINE

The HTTP pipeline is a set of components that are assembled to process HTTP requests that are run under the control of ASP.NET. The first component to receive the request is called `HttpRuntime`, which is responsible for decomposing the request into an object model (`HttpContext`) and then creating the rest of the pipeline. The next component assembled is an `HttpApplication` that is responsible for application lifetime and orchestrating the execution of requests, culminating in the execution of a *handler* whose responsibility it is to generate the response.

`HttpApplication`'s orchestration is achieved by firing a series of events as the request moves through processing. For example: `BeginRequest`, `AuthenticateRequest`, `PreRequestHandlerExecute`, `PostRequestHandlerExecute`, and `EndRequest`. Interception code called *modules* subscribe to these events to perform their function such as output caching, authentication, authorization, and session control. In fact the modules can even say, "Don't bother running the handler, I have the content here," which is the case for the output caching module.

ASP.NET requests are executed on thread pool worker threads.

There are a series of stages in building the page, and you can get involved in any stage by overriding the appropriate virtual member of the Page class. You can see the page lifecycle in Figure 9-7. Now if all actions within the page lifecycle are synchronous, the request thread is occupied by the same request for its entire duration. So if you perform, say, a synchronous long-running database query during OnLoad, then the request thread blocks.

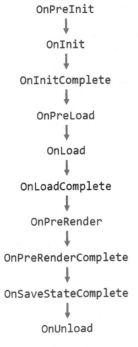

Figure 9-7. *The WebForms page lifecycle*

It is good practice to isolate the application code from the data access to allow yourself to make changes in the data access mechanism without forcing a cascading change throughout the application. Therefore, over the course of this chapter, you will be accessing the database via a repository. Take a look at the synchronous GetAuthors method of the repository (Listing 9-1). Notice that it calls the synchronous ExecuteReader method of SqlCommand to execute the GetAuthors stored procedure. It turns out that the GetAuthors stored procedure is long running.

Listing 9-1. Synchronous Implementation of the AuthorRepository

```
public class AuthorRepository
{
    private const string connStr = "Server=.;Database=pubs;Integrated Security=SSPI";

    public IEnumerable<Author> GetAuthors()
    {
        var authors = new List272103_1_En();
        using (var conn = new SqlConnection(connStr))
        {
            using (var cmd = new SqlCommand("GetAuthors", conn))
            {
                cmd.CommandType = CommandType.StoredProcedure;
                conn.Open();

                using (SqlDataReader reader = cmd.ExecuteReader())
                {
                    while (reader.Read())
                    {
                        authors.Add(new Author
                            {
                                FirstName = (string)reader["au_fname"],
                                LastName = (string)reader["au_lname"]
                            });
                    }
                }
            }
        }

        return authors;
    }
}
```

A Synchronous WebForms Implementation

Before we look at asynchronous pages, we should look at a synchronous page as a baseline. Listing 9-2 and Listing 9-3 show the code for a synchronous page where a Label called output is populated by the number of records returned from the synchronous GetAuthors method of the AuthorRepository.

Listing 9-2. ASPX File for a Synchronous Page

```
<%@ Page Language="C#" AutoEventWireup="true" CodeBehind="SyncPage.aspx.cs"
    Inherits="Dotnet40.SyncPage" %>

<!DOCTYPE html>

<html xmlns="http://www.w3.org/1999/xhtml">
<head runat="server">
    <title></title>
</head>
<body>
    <form id="form1" runat="server">
    <div>
        <asp:Label runat="server" ID="output"></asp:Label>
    </div>
    </form>
</body>
</html>
```

Listing 9-3. Code-Behind for a Synchronous Page

```
public partial class SyncPage : System.Web.UI.Page
{
    protected void Page_Load(object sender, EventArgs e)
    {
        var repo = new AuthorRepository();

        output.Text = repo.GetAuthors().Count().ToString();
    }
}
```

As stated earlier, however, the GetAuthors method of the AuthorRepository executes a very long-running stored procedure. Therefore, you could benefit greatly from using IOCP to manage the I/O and so you will make the page asynchronous. To do this you are going to need a repository that supports asynchronous execution. Initially you will need an APM version of GetAuthors (Listing 9-4). The BeginGetAuthors method now calls the APM version of ExecuteReader. Note that you need to add the Asynchronous Processing = true flag to the connection string to allow asynchronous queries to be executed on the connection.

Listing 9-4. APM Version of GetAuthors

```
private const string connStr =
            "Server=.;Database=pubs;Integrated Security=SSPI; Asynchronous Processing=true";
private SqlConnection apmConn;
private SqlCommand apmCmd;

public IAsyncResult BeginGetAuthors(AsyncCallback callback, object state)
{
    apmConn = new SqlConnection(connStr);
    apmCmd = new SqlCommand("GetAuthors", apmConn);

    apmConn.Open();
    return apmCmd.BeginExecuteReader(callback, state);
}
```

```
public IEnumerable<Author> EndGetAuthors(IAsyncResult iar)
{
    try
    {
        var authors = new List272103_1_En();
        using (SqlDataReader reader = apmCmd.EndExecuteReader(iar))
        {
            while (reader.Read())
            {
                authors.Add(new Author
                    {
                        FirstName = (string)reader["au_fname"],
                        LastName = (string)reader["au_lname"]
                    });
            }

            return authors;
        }
    }
    finally
    {
        apmCmd.Dispose();
        apmConn.Dispose();
    }
}
```

Asynchronous Pages in WebForms 4.0

Async pages in WebForms version 4.0 are based around APM. As such, you will break part of the processing into a method that starts the async I/O and returns an IAsyncResult, and another part that gets the results of the async I/O and uses the results. The asynchronous page lifecycle is shown in Figure 9-8.

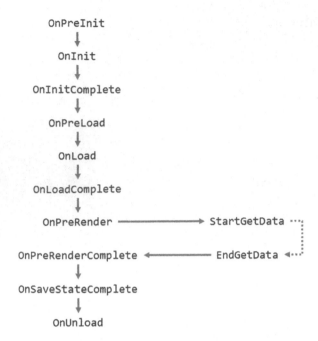

Figure 9-8. *Asynchronous page lifecycle*

You need to tell ASP.NET that there are asynchronous parts to the page execution, and you will do this in two parts: mark the page as asynchronous in the .ASPX file, and register the asynchronous methods early in the page lifecycle (Page_Load is a convenient hook). Let's step through the implementation.

Mark the Page As Asynchronous

Marking the page as asynchronous is very straightforward. Simply add the attribute Async="true" to the @page directive in the .ASPX file, as shown in Listing 9-5.

Listing 9-5. Marking a Page As Asynchronous

```
<%@ Page Async="true" Language="C#" AutoEventWireup="true"
        CodeBehind="AsyncPageThreading.aspx.cs" Inherits="Dotnet40.AsyncPageThreading" %>

<!DOCTYPE html>

<html xmlns="http://www.w3.org/1999/xhtml">
<head runat="server">
    <title></title>
</head>
<body>
    <form id="form1" runat="server">
    <div>
        <asp:Label runat="server" ID="outputT1"></asp:Label>
    </div>
```

```
    <div>
        <asp:Label runat="server" ID="outputT2"></asp:Label>
    </div>
    </form>
    <div>
        <asp:Label runat="server" ID="output"></asp:Label>
    </div>
</body>
</html>
```

Registering the Asynchronous Methods

You can register asynchronous methods using the AddOnPreRenderCompleteAsync API. This takes two delegate parameters of type BeginEventHandler and EndEventHandler, respectively, which both follow the APM pattern. BeginEventHandler, after the standard object and EventArgs parameters of events, takes an AsyncCallback delegate and object, and it returns an IAsyncResult. The EndEventHandler takes an IAsyncResult as a single parameter and returns void.

You can put the call to AddOnPreRenderCompleteAsync in your page load handling, but you should make sure that it is only processed the first time the page is rendered. You do not want to be going to the database if the user has submitted a form or pressed a button on the page, so you should only register the async methods if you are not in a post-back (see Listing 9-6).

Listing 9-6. Registering the Asynchronous Methods

```
protected void Page_Load(object sender, EventArgs e)
{
    if (!IsPostBack)
    {
        AddOnPreRenderCompleteAsync(StartGetData, EndGetData);
    }
}

private void EndGetData(IAsyncResult ar)
{
    // details omitted for clarity
}

private IAsyncResult StartGetData(object sender, EventArgs e,
                                  AsyncCallback cb, object extradata)
{
    // details omitted for clarity
}
```

Implementing the "Begin" Method

The key responsibility of the StartGetData method in Listing 9-6 is to initiate the asynchronous I/O. It must also return an object that signals when the I/O has completed and the results can be processed; this signaling object must implement IAsyncResult. If there is only one asynchronous I/O operation to be performed, the implementation is very straightforward. The method simply hands off to the I/O operation and returns the IAsyncResult that it returns. Listing 9-7 shows an example of this.

Listing 9-7. Implementing a Simple Initiating Async Method

```
AuthorRepository repo = new AuthorRepository();

private IAsyncResult StartGetData(object sender, EventArgs e,
                                  AsyncCallback cb, object extradata)
{
    return repo.BeginGetAuthors(cb, extradata);
}
```

Implementing the "End" Method

The EndGetData method from Listing 9-6 must pick up the results of the async I/O operation and process them in some way. Bear in mind with APM that the EndXXX method of the async I/O may throw an exception, and so any specific error handling you want to be performed must be placed around that call. The EndGetData method will also be responsible for any cleanup of resources committed in the StartGetData method. You can see the implementation of the EndGetData method in Listing 9-8.

Listing 9-8. Implementing a Simple Completing Async Method

```
private void EndGetData(IAsyncResult ar)
{
    IEnumerable<Author> authors = repo.EndGetAuthors(ar);
    output.Text = authors.Count().ToString();
}
```

Dealing with Multiple Asynchronous I/O Requests

We've looked at the simple case of a single async I/O operation, but what if you have to perform more than one in the rendering of the page? The solution shown in Listing 9-7 will not work because the IAsyncResult returned does not represent all of the async work in progress. For this more complex case you need an implementation of IAsyncResult that represents all of the async I/O work—that means you need a custom implementation.

There are a number of ways in which you can create a general purpose IAsyncResult implementation. If the number of asynchronous operations being managed is fixed, then you can use an implementation that keeps a count internally of the outstanding operations; if you need more flexibility, then you could have an implementation that is explicitly set to complete by the consuming code. Listing 9-9 shows an implementation of an internally counting version of IAsyncResult.

Listing 9-9. Implementation of a CountingAsyncResult

```
public class CountingAsyncResult : IAsyncResult
{
    private readonly object state;
    private readonly AsyncCallback callback;

    // For the implementation of IAsyncResult.AsyncCallback
    private readonly ManualResetEventSlim asyncEvent = new ManualResetEventSlim();

    private int outstandingAsyncOperations;
```

```csharp
    // Store the callback and state passed
    public CountingAsyncResult(AsyncCallback callback, object state, int asyncOperationCount)
    {
        this.state = state;
        this.callback = callback ?? delegate { };
        outstandingAsyncOperations = asyncOperationCount;
    }

    // Called by consumer to state an async operation has completed
    public void OperationComplete()
    {
        if (outstandingAsyncOperations == 0)
        {
          throw new InvalidOperationException("All expected operations have already completed");
        }

        // signal the event object
        int currentOutstanding = Interlocked.Decrement(ref outstandingAsyncOperations);
        if (currentOutstanding == 0)
        {
            asyncEvent.Set();
            callback(this);
        }
    }

    public object AsyncState
    {
        get { return state; }
    }

    public WaitHandle AsyncWaitHandle
    {
        get { return asyncEvent.WaitHandle; }
    }

    public bool CompletedSynchronously
    {
        get { return false; }
    }

    public bool IsCompleted
    {
        get { return outstandingAsyncOperations == 0; }
    }

    // Clean up the event as it may have allocated a WaitHandle
    public void Dispose()
    {
        asyncEvent.Dispose();
    }
}
```

WHY NOT JUST WRAP THE I/O IN A DELEGATE?

Creating custom implementations of IAsyncResult seems like a lot of work when you could simply create a delegate, execute the I/O synchronously inside the delegate, and then invoke the delegate asynchronously. This would give you an IAsyncResult that modeled all of the I/O work. So why not take this approach? After all, it still runs asynchronously to the page.

The critical issue is where asynchronous delegate runs. Asynchronous delegate invocation runs on worker threads in the thread pool, which means the thread is blocked while the I/O takes place (something you're trying to avoid), but more importantly you are handing the async I/O work to the same group of threads that are trying to process ASP.NET requests, which means you might as well have left the processing on the request thread in the first place.

Now you can use a counting IAsyncResult version in a more complex asynchronous page that performs two async I/O operations during its rendering. Listing 9-10 shows the implementation of the page; notice that the CountingAsyncResult is initialized in the StartGetData method. As the async I/O operations complete (inside the AsyncCallback passed to the Begin operations on the repositories), asyncResult is signaled to say that one of the operations has completed.

Listing 9-10. Complex Async Page Using a CountingAsyncResult

```
public partial class ComplexAsyncPage : System.Web.UI.Page
{
    private AuthorRepository authorRepo = new AuthorRepository();
    private TitleRepository titleRepo = new TitleRepository();

    private IAsyncResult authorIar;
    private IAsyncResult titleIar;

    private CountingAsyncResult asyncResult;

    protected void Page_Load(object sender, EventArgs e)
    {
        AddOnPreRenderCompleteAsync(StartGetData, EndGetData);
    }

    private void EndGetData(IAsyncResult ar)
    {
        try
        {
            int authorCount = authorRepo.EndGetAuthors(authorIar).Count();
            int titleCount = titleRepo.EndGetTitles(titleIar).Count();

            output.Text = (authorCount + titleCount).ToString();
        }
        finally
        {
            asyncResult.Dispose();
        }
    }
}
```

```
private IAsyncResult StartGetData(object sender, EventArgs e,
                                  AsyncCallback cb, object extradata)
{
    asyncResult = new CountingAsyncResult(cb, extradata, 2);

    authorIar = authorRepo.BeginGetAuthors(iar =>
                {
                    asyncResult.OperationComplete();
                }, null);

    titleIar = titleRepo.BeginGetTitles(iar =>
                {
                    asyncResult.OperationComplete();
                }, null);

    return asyncResult;
}
}
```

■ **Caution** In the "End" method `HttpContext.Current` will be null. If you are using APIs or components that rely on this value being set (as it is in synchronous page processing throughout the page life cycle), then you will either have to change the code so it is not reliant on `HttpContext.Current` (which will also make the code easier to unit test) or put the following line of code before any of these API calls in your "End" method:

```
HttpContext.Current = Context;
```

Handling Errors in Asynchronous Pages Using APM

There is a nasty gotcha lurking in the code in Listing 9-10: what happens if an exception is thrown during processing? For most of the code the normal ASP.NET error handling will be invoked and the browser will see an error page. However, if the exception is thrown during the `AsyncCallback` of one of the async I/O methods, then the page processing will hang (as there is no signal that that operation has completed) and the browser will get a timeout. This is because ASP.NET is completely unaware of the thread on which the exception occurs. The problem is, how can you use exception handling to make sure an error ends up on the request thread?

ASP.NET has its own `SynchronizationContext`, which allows you to marshal processing on to the right request thread. If you can push the exception on to the request thread, then ASP.NET will handle it normally. You could use `SynchronizationContext.Post` to run all of the `AsyncCallback` code on the request thread. This works, although you have to be very careful to ensure that, whether or not an exception occurs, the operation gets marked as completed (see Listing 9-11).

Listing 9-11. Error Handling Using SynchronizationContext.Post

```
SynchronizationContext ctx = SynchronizationContext.Current;

authorIar = authorRepo.BeginGetAuthors(iar =>
               {
                    ctx.Post(_ =>
                      {
                          try
                          {
                              OperationThatCouldThrowException();
                          }
                          finally
                          {
                              asyncResult.OperationComplete();
                          }
                      }, null);
               }, null);
```

What if you need to make sure the standard code execution stays on the background thread? In that case you need to do something more subtle. You will have to put a try/catch block around the code that could throw the exception and then do something more inventive in the catch block. The problem is you don't want to lose the stack trace from the original exception, so you have to package the original exception as an inner exception to a wrapper and throw the wrapper using SynchronizationContext.Send (you don't want the operation marked as complete before you have pushed the error to the request thread). You can see an example in Listing 9-12.

Listing 9-12. Fine-Grained Error Handling with SynchronizationContext.Send

```
SynchronizationContext ctx = SynchronizationContext.Current;

authorIar = authorRepo.BeginGetAuthors(iar =>
               {
                   try
                   {
                       OperationThatCouldThrowException();
                   }
                   catch (Exception x)
                   {
                       ctx.Send(_ =>
                          {
                              throw new
                                  WrapperException("An error occurred during processing", x);
                          }, null);
                   }
                   finally
                   {
                       asyncResult.OperationComplete();
                   }
               }, null);
```

WebForms 4.0, then, has asynchronous functionality built in, although it does require some effort to do anything beyond the simplest case. Fortunately WebForms 4.5 addresses this issue.

Asynchronous Pages in WebForms 4.5

The introduction of TPL in .NET 4.0 and the resulting BCL changes in .NET 4.5—along with async and await in C#5—have hugely simplified creating async pages in WebForms. However, now you will need a TPL-friendly version of GetAuthors that returns a Task<IEnumerable272103_1_En> rather than IEnumerable272103_1_En (Listing 9-13).

Listing 9-13. TPL-Friendly Version of GetAuthors

```
private const string connStr = "Server=.;Database=pubs;Integrated Security=SSPI";

public async Task<IEnumerable<Author>> GetAuthorsAsync()
{
    var authors = new List<Author>();
    using (var conn = new SqlConnection(connStr))
    {
        using (var cmd = new SqlCommand("GetAuthors", conn))
        {
            cmd.CommandType = CommandType.StoredProcedure;
            conn.Open();

            using (SqlDataReader reader = await cmd.ExecuteReaderAsync())
            {
                while (reader.Read())
                {
                    authors.Add(new Author
                    {
                        FirstName = (string)reader["au_fname"],
                        LastName = (string)reader["au_lname"]
                    });
                }
            }
        }
    }

    return authors;
}
```

■ **Note** From .NET 4.5 onward, you no longer need to specify the Asynchronous Processing = true flag on a SqlConnection connection string to be able to execute asynchronous queries.

To create an asynchronous page, instead of implementing APM, all you now need to do is to model the code that performs the async I/O operation as a method or lambda that returns a Task. You now tell ASP.NET about the Task using the RegisterAsyncTask method on the Page class. With async and await this becomes very easy, as Listing 9-14 demonstrates.

Listing 9-14. Simple Asynchronous Page Using async and await

```
public partial class AsyncPage : System.Web.UI.Page
{
    protected void Page_Load(object sender, EventArgs e)
    {
        RegisterAsyncTask(new PageAsyncTask(GetDataAsync));
    }

    async Task GetDataAsync()
    {
        var repo = new AuthorRepository();

        IEnumerable<Author> authors = await repo.GetAuthorsAsync();

        output.Text = authors.Count().ToString();
    }
}
```

WHY NOT MAKE PAGE_LOAD ASYNC?

In this simple case you could have simply marked Page_Load as async and put the asynchronous I/O code directly in there. This would have worked, but is generally discouraged by the ASP.NET team. They have had to jump through a lot of hoops to try to ensure that the request does not finish before the async work completes. This is complex because Page_Load does not return a Task so the ASP.NET team has to infer what is happening in an async event handler.

For anything complex you should use RegisterAsyncTask. As code has a tendency to evolve over time, it is safer always to use this method rather than rely on making Page_Load asynchronous.

In fact, even with more complex pages that perform multiple async operations, the code is straightforward as you can use Task.WhenAll to generate a Task that models the completion of all of the asynchronous I/O. You can see how simple the code is in Listing 9-15, compared to the equivalent code in 4.0, shown in Listing 9-10.

Listing 9-15. Complex Async Page Using Task.WhenAll

```
public partial class ComplexAsyncPage : System.Web.UI.Page
{
    protected void Page_Load(object sender, EventArgs e)
    {
        RegisterAsyncTask(new PageAsyncTask(GetDataAsync));
    }

    async Task GetDataAsync()
    {
        var authorRepo = new AuthorRepository();
        var titleRepo = new TitleRepository();

        Task<IEnumerable<Author>> authorsTask = authorRepo.GetAuthorsAsync();
        Task<IEnumerable<Title>> titlesTask = titleRepo.GetTitlesAsync();
```

```
    await Task.WhenAll(authorsTask, titlesTask);

        int authorCount = authorsTask.Result.Count();
        int titleCount = titlesTask.Result.Count();

        output.Text = (authorCount + titleCount).ToString();
    }
}
```

■ **Note**   Unlike WebForms 4.0, in the 4.5 `Task`-based pattern `HttpContext.Current` will be set correctly for all code in the page life cycle.

You do not need to do anything special with error handling. Just use try/catch blocks as you normally would. The awaiter makes sure that any errors end up on the correct thread.

With WebForms you have seen that, whether using 4.0 or 4.5, you can make your page processing more efficient and scalable in the face of async I/O. However, in 4.5 life gets much simpler and the required code is far closer to the synchronous version than in 4.0.

ASP.NET MVC

MVC takes a very different approach to web programming than WebForms. Rather than trying to provide a similar model to smart client control-based UI, it embraces the Web and HTTP to provide an API that gives you direct control over HTML, CSS, and JavaScript. To understand the separation of concerns, let's look at a simple synchronous example, and then how you can turn a synchronous MVC application into an asynchronous one.

Remember that the original GetAuthors method is synchronous and long running. Listing 9-16 shows this synchronous operation being used from inside a controller, the HomeController. The MVC routing infrastructure maps requests to the appropriate controller method, known as an *action* based on pattern matching of the URI and HTTP verb. In this case the Index action will be invoked. The Index action gets the authors from the repository and selects the Index view, passing the authors as the data that the view will display.

Listing 9-16. Synchronous Controller Using Synchronous Repository Operation

```
public class HomeController : Controller
{
    public ActionResult Index()
    {
        var repo = new AuthorRepository();

        IEnumerable<Author> authors = repo.GetAuthors();

        return View("Index", authors);
    }
}
```

WHAT DOES MVC MEAN?

MVC stands for Model, View, Controller. These are the three concepts into which code is separated in an MVC application, and each has a distinct responsibility. One of the core goals of MVC is to make as much of the application code easily unit testable as possible, and as such we try to keep as much of the code as simple classes rather than using ASP.NET functionality directly.

The Model is the business logic. This is how data is accessed and business rules applied.

The View is the rendering of the UI. The only logic in here is what is necessary for rendering the view correctly

The Controller's job is orchestration. Its role is to interact with the Model, select the View, and present the data from the Model to the View. It does not contain business logic, nor does it determine the appearance of the UI.

Both the Model and the Controller should be unit testable as normal classes. It is only the View that will require manual or specialized UI/HTML-based test frameworks.

Listing 9-17 shows the view code, using a markup language called *Razor* that allows you to embed C# inside the HTML to inject the view logic. You can see that each author is displayed as a list item in an unordered list. The interaction of the routing infrastructure, controller action, repository, and view turns the HTTP request into an HTML page to display.

Listing 9-17. Index View to Display the Authors

```
@{
    ViewBag.Title = "Index";
}


<h2>Authors</h2>
<ul>
    @foreach (Dotnet40MVC.Models.Author author in Model)
    {
        <li>
            <span>@author.FirstName</span>
            <span>@author.LastName</span>
        </li>
    }
</ul>
```

Again, the underlying GetAuthors stored procedure is very slow, so now let's look at what you need to do to make this processing asynchronous with respect to the request thread. It turns out that two things are needed: the repository needs to use asynchronous I/O, and the controller needs to be able to release the request thread during the async I/O.

Asynchronous MVC Processing in .NET 4.0

MVC is generally released to the Web, although a version is packaged with the .NET framework each time it ships. A version commonly used with .NET 4.0 is MVC 3, and so we will look at how to build asynchronous functionality with that version of MVC. MVC 4 does work with .NET 4.0 and does take advantage of TPL, but the real benefit doesn't really appear until you have the I/O classes that use TPL and the async and await keywords in .NET 4.5. We will look at MVC 4 shortly, but for the time being we will stay with MVC 3. Like most of .NET 4.0, MVC 3 does not take advantage of TPL, and so let's model our asynchronous repository functionality using EAP (Listing 9-18).

Listing 9-18. Asynchronous GetAuthors Using EAP

```
public void GetAuthorsEAP()
{
    var syncCtx = SynchronizationContext.Current;

    var conn = new SqlConnection(connStr);
    var cmd = new SqlCommand("GetAuthors", conn);
    cmd.CommandType = CommandType.StoredProcedure;
    conn.Open();

    cmd.BeginExecuteReader(iar =>
        {
            try
            {
                using (SqlDataReader reader = cmd.EndExecuteReader(iar))
                {
                    var authors = new List<Author>();
                    while (reader.Read())
                    {
                        authors.Add(new Author
                            {
                                FirstName = (string) reader["au_fname"],
                                LastName = (string) reader["au_lname"]
                            });
                    }

                    var args = new GetAuthorsCompletedEventArgs(authors);

                    syncCtx.Post(_ =>
                    {
                        GetAuthorsCompleted(this, args);
                    }, null);
                }
            }
            finally
            {
                cmd.Dispose();
                conn.Dispose();
            }
        }, null);
}

public event EventHandler<GetAuthorsCompletedEventArgs> GetAuthorsCompleted = delegate { };
```

Asynchrony is implemented within MVC at the controller level. To be able to make actions asynchronous, you need to derive your controller not from Controller directly but rather from the AsyncController class. AsyncController itself derives from Controller, so you can still have synchronous actions on the controller as well as asynchronous ones—AsyncController simply makes it *possible* to have asynchronous actions. To make an action asynchronous, you must split its functionality into two methods: one that starts the processing and one that returns the ActionResult. These two methods have specific names: <action name>Async and <action name>Completed, so for our Index action they would be IndexAsync and IndexCompleted.

Implementing IndexAsync

IndexAsync has three responsibilities:

1. Set up the constructs that will tell MVC that the async I/O has completed

2. Execute the asynchronous I/O-based operations

3. Put the results of the asynchronous I/O somewhere that allows them to be passed to the IndexCompleted method

IndexAsync can take any route- and request-based parameters, such as IDs. However, in this case there are no specific inputs into the action, so it will take no parameters. It interacts with the asynchronous controller via the AsyncManager property on AsyncController. AsyncManager allows you to specify how many asynchronous operations are going to be executed within the action; to say when an asynchronous operation has completed and to store the results of that operation (see Listing 9-19). The name given as the index into the AsyncManager's Parameters dictionary is important as this will be mapped to a corresponding parameter name in IndexCompleted. Note that both Increment and Decrement on the OutstandingOperations count can take integers if the count needs to be adjusted by more than 1. When the OutstandingOperations count goes to zero, then the IndexCompleted method will be called.

Listing 9-19. The Implementation of IndexAsync

```
public void IndexAsync()
{
    AsyncManager.OutstandingOperations.Increment();

    var repo = new AuthorRepository();

    repo.GetAuthorsCompleted += (s, e) =>
        {
            AsyncManager.Parameters["authors"] = e.Authors;
            AsyncManager.OutstandingOperations.Decrement();
        };

    repo.GetAuthorsEAP();
}
```

■ **Caution** If the calls to Increment and Decrement on the OutstandingOperations count become unbalanced, then the IndexCompleted method will never execute—even if the count goes negative. The IndexCompleted method is called only when the count goes to exactly zero.

Implementing the IndexCompleted Method

The IndexCompleted method looks very much like a normal action, as it typically returns an ActionResult. The parameters that get passed to it are the named items from the AsyncManager.Parameters dictionary, so in this case it will take an IEnumerable272103_1_En parameter called authors (Listing 9-20). Matching the names is important, as otherwise the parameter will be the default for that type (null, 0, false, etc.).

Listing 9-20. The Implementation of IndexCompleted

```
public ActionResult IndexCompleted(IEnumerable<Author> authors)
{
    return View("Index", authors);
}
```

Take Care with APM

The code in IndexAsync is straightforward, partly because EAP uses an available SynchronizationContext to marshal the completed event onto a known thread. In the case of ASP.NET this thread is a thread with the right HttpContext. With APM you get no such guarantee, so in an AsyncCallback you cannot use the controller instance safely and HttpContext.Current is null. This also means you cannot safely add results to AsyncManager.Parameters, as this is simply a Dictionary<string,object> and is not thread safe—if two AsyncCallbacks were to run at the same time, they could corrupt the dictionary.

To solve this problem, you could use the SynchronizationContext yourself and do a Post or Send (remember—if using Post you must Decrement the OutstandingOperations count in your SendOrPostCallback, as it runs asynchronously and would otherwise cause a race condition). Alternatively, you can use the AsyncManager Sync method, which takes an Action that it will execute using SynchronizationContext.Send.

Performing Multiple Async I/O Operations Within an Asynchronous Action

You saw that with WebForms 4.0, performing multiple async I/O operations within a page was relatively complex. Fortunately, with MVC 3 the world is a lot simpler—especially if your async I/O operations are modeled with EAP. You can see an implementation in Listing 9-21 that simply states the number of async operations and then, as the results come in, stores the results and decrements the count of the OutstandingOperations property of AsyncManager.

Listing 9-21. Asynchronous Action with Two Async I/O Operations

```
public void FullAsync()
{
    AsyncManager.OutstandingOperations.Increment(2);

    var authorRepo = new AuthorRepository();
    authorRepo.GetAuthorsCompleted += (s, e) =>
        {
            AsyncManager.Parameters["authors"] = e.Authors;
            AsyncManager.OutstandingOperations.Decrement();
        };
    authorRepo.GetAuthorsEAP();

    var titleRepo = new TitleRepository();
    titleRepo.GetTitlesCompleted += (s, e) =>
        {
            AsyncManager.Parameters["titles"] = e.Titles;
            AsyncManager.OutstandingOperations.Decrement();
        };
    titleRepo.GetTitlesEAP();
}
```

```
public ActionResult FullCompleted(IEnumerable<Author> authors, IEnumerable<Title> titles )
{
    return View("Full", new FullViewModel{Authors = authors, Titles = titles});
}
```

MVC 3 has reasonably succinct infrastructure for asynchronous processing. However, one of our goals is to try to make the asynchronous code as easy to understand as the synchronous code. In MVC 3's async pattern, the asynchronous code looks very different from the synchronous code with the action being separated into two methods. MVC 4 has TPL at its disposal so hopefully it can do even better.

Asynchronous MVC Processing in .NET 4.5

MVC 4 ships with .NET 4.5 and leverages the availability of TPL. In fact, the asynchronous code in MVC 4 is almost identical to the synchronous code—the action method just returns Task<ActionResult>, is marked as async, and uses await on the async I/O operation.

You can see the similarity between the synchronous and asynchronous code when you compare the MVC 4 asynchronous code in Listing 9-22 and the synchronous code in Listing 9-16. Note that there is no need to derive from AsyncController in MVC 4.

Listing 9-22. An Asynchronous Action in MVC 4

```
public class HomeController : Controller
{
    public async Task<ActionResult> Index()
    {
        var repo = new AuthorRepository();

        IEnumerable<Author> authors = await repo.GetAuthorsAsync();
        return View("Index", authors);
    }
}
```

It's very straightforward to deal with one async I/O operation; what about more than one? You've seen that this can bring extra complexity, so how does this work in MVC 4? Again, Task.WhenAll comes to your rescue as it allows you to take a set of async operations and wait for all of them to finish in an async/await-friendly way (Listing 9-23).

Listing 9-23. An Action with Multiple Async I/O Operations in MVC 4

```
public async Task<ActionResult> Full()
{
    var authorRepo = new AuthorRepository();
    var titleRepo = new TitleRepository();

    var authorsTask = authorRepo.GetAuthorsAsync();
    var titlesTask = titleRepo.GetTitlesAsync();

    await Task.WhenAll(authorsTask, titlesTask);

    IEnumerable<Author> authors = authorsTask.Result;
    IEnumerable<Title> titles = titlesTask.Result;

    return View("Full", new FullViewModel {Authors = authors, Titles = titles});
}
```

Once more you see that although .NET 4.0 supports asynchronous invocation via IOCP, the programming model is much simpler under .NET 4.5.

ASP.NET Web API

We have now looked at the two UI web technologies in the .NET framework. There is, however, a new API on the block: one for building server-side code to be consumed by other code. This is ASP.NET Web API, a framework for building HTTP-based services that use the REST model for exposing functionality. Web API uses HTTP verbs and URIs to define the functionality that will be invoked, and as such fits in very well with the ASP.NET MVC view of the world. As a result, Web API leverages part of the MVC infrastructure to expose its functionality. Web API ships as part of MVC 4 and so is available on both .NET 4.0 and 4.5. We will look at the asynchronous programming model in both; but first, as previously, we will start with a synchronous version.

WHAT IS REST?

REST, or REpresentational State Transfer, is an architectural style for building web-accessible services. Roy Fielding proposed this model in his doctoral thesis in 2000, and it has gained a lot of traction in recent times, particularly for public-facing APIs.

REST has a very different approach to SOAP-based models. SOAP uses self-describing messages that can be sent over arbitrary transports. REST embraces HTTP as an application protocol rather than purely as a transport, thus mirroring the model of the World Wide Web. In REST, functionality is partitioned into resources that have a Uniform Resource Identifier (URI). You then state how you want to manipulate that resource via the HTTP verb you use—for example, a GET is a read of the resource, whereas a DELETE deletes the resource.

Like all architectural models, there is a lot of debate about implementation details. However, REST has become one of the key architectures for building scalable web-facing services.

Web API uses a controller to model the HTTP verbs for the URI that maps to that controller. Mapping to the controller uses the same kind of pattern matching that ASP.NET MVC uses. So for a simple controller that gets the authors, use the code in Listing 9-24.

Listing 9-24. Synchronous Web API Request

```
public class AuthorsController : ApiController
{
    // GET api/authors
    public IEnumerable<Author> Get()
    {
        var repo = new AuthorRepository();

        return repo.GetAuthors();
    }
}
```

Asynchronous Web API Operations in .NET 4.0

As you are using MVC 4, you have the same simplified Task-based asynchronous model. However, the APIs you will typically have to deal with will be APM or EAP based. To combine APM and Tasks you need to use an adapter to change the APM code into a Task. Fortunately, as you saw in Chapter 3, you have the FromAsync method of the TaskFactory for just this purpose. You can see the resulting async version of the Web API method in Listing 9-25.

Listing 9-25. Asynchronous Web API Operation in .NET 4.0

```
public class AuthorsController : ApiController
{
    // GET api/authors
    public Task<IEnumerable<Author>> Get()
    {
        var repo = new AuthorRepository();

        return Task.Factory.FromAsync<IEnumerable<Author>>(repo.BeginGetAuthors,
                                                            repo.EndGetAuthors,
                                                            null);
    }
}
```

In the simple case, then, Web API with .NET 4.0 is very straightforward but, as always, composing multiple operations brings more complexity. .NET 4.0 doesn't have Task.WhenAll, which is the ideal way to combine two tasks, but you can achieve the same end, with a little more work, with TaskCompletionSource. You can see the implementation in Listing 9-26.

Listing 9-26. Composing Multiple Operations with Web API and TaskCompletionSource

```
public Task<FullResponse> Get()
{
    var authorRepo = new AuthorRepository();
    var titleRepo = new TitleRepository();

    var tcs = new TaskCompletionSource<FullResponse>();

    var response = new FullResponse();

    int outstandingOperations = 2;

    Task.Factory.FromAsync(authorRepo.BeginGetAuthors(null, null), iar =>
        {
            response.Authors = authorRepo.EndGetAuthors(iar);
            int currentCount = Interlocked.Decrement(ref outstandingOperations);
            if (currentCount == 0)
            {
                tcs.SetResult(response);
            }
        });
```

```
Task.Factory.FromAsync(titleRepo.BeginGetTitles(null, null), iar =>
    {
        response.Titles = titleRepo.EndGetTitles(iar);
        int currentCount = Interlocked.Decrement(ref outstandingOperations);
        if (currentCount == 0)
        {
            tcs.SetResult(response);
        }
    });

    return tcs.Task;
}
```

You can see that, as a result of MVC 4 having a Task-based approach to asynchrony, creating asynchronous Web API operations, even in .NET 4.0, is not too complex. But as you have seen previously, with Task becoming ubiquitous in the framework API and asynchrony being supported in languages, life gets even easier.

Asynchronous Web API Operations in .NET 4.5

You have already seen a Task-friendly version of the AuthorsRepository (Listing 9-13), so plugging this into Web API is very straightforward; you can see the result in Listing 9-27.

Listing 9-27. Asynchronous Web API Operation in .NET 4.5

```
public class AuthorsController : ApiController
{
    // GET api/authors
    public Task<IEnumerable<Author>> Get()
    {
        var repo = new AuthorRepository();

        return repo.GetAuthorsAsync();
    }
}
```

You have also seen that even when you have multiple async I/O operations, with Task.WhenAll that scenario is also very simple. If you compare Listing 9-26 and Listing 9-28, you can see this simplicity in action.

Listing 9-28. Composing Multiple Operations with Web API and Task.WhenAll

```
public class FullController : ApiController
{
    // GET api/Full/
    public async Task<FullResponse> Get()
    {
        var authorRepo = new AuthorRepository();
        var titleRepo = new TitleRepository();

        var authorTask = authorRepo.GetAuthorsAsync();
        var titleTask = titleRepo.GetTitlesAsync();

        await Task.WhenAll(authorTask, titleTask);
```

```
        var response = new FullResponse
            {
                Authors = authorTask.Result,
                Titles = titleTask.Result
            };

        return response;
    }
}
```

You have looked at three different ASP.NET technologies and how, whether using .NET 4.0 or 4.5, you can take advantage of IOCP to create efficient and scalable server-side code. You have also seen that the integration of TPL into the BCL and `async` and `await` into C# simplifies implementation—even in quite complex scenarios. However, ASP.NET is not the only server-side infrastructure in .NET; we will now move on to look at Windows Communication Foundation.

Windows Communication Foundation

Windows Communication Foundation (WCF) provides a framework for building service-based code, principally using SOAP as the basis of an architectural style. Service functionality is exposed via endpoints, which are composed of three parts:

1. Address—where the service is listening

2. Binding—how communication takes place on the wire: transport protocol, wire format, security, et cetera

3. Contract—what operations are exposed, what data they need, and what they might return

WCF contracts are .NET types (commonly interfaces) annotated with the [ServiceContract] attribute. Operations are methods on the type that are annotated with the [OperationContract] attribute. .NET types can be used in the operation definition and are serialized to an XML Infoset when messages are sent over the wire. The [DataContract] and [DataMember] attributes are used to control that serialization.

Asynchrony in WCF is controlled by the contract and the service implementation, so let's look at the synchronous model as a starting point. Listing 9-29 shows the contract and implementation of the synchronous version of a service. We will now examine how the code changes to make this service asynchronous in both .NET 4.0 and 4.5.

Listing 9-29. Contract and Implementation of Synchronous Service

```
[DataContract(Name="Author", Namespace = "")]
public class AuthorDTO
{
    [DataMember]
    public string FirstName { get; set; }
    [DataMember]
    public string LastName { get; set; }
}


[ServiceContract]
interface IGetPubs
{
    [OperationContract]
    List<AuthorDTO> GetAuthors();
}
```

```
public class Service : IGetPubs
{
    AuthorRepository authorRepo = new AuthorRepository();
    TitleRepository titleRepo = new TitleRepository();

    public List<AuthorDTO> GetAuthors()
    {
        return authorRepo.GetAuthors()
                        .Select(a => new AuthorDTO
                        {
                            FirstName = a.FirstName,
                            LastName = a.LastName
                        })
                        .ToList();
    }
}
```

Asynchronous WCF Services in .NET 4.0

From the release of WCF in .NET 3.0 to .NET 4.0, the asynchronous model for service operations was based on APM. Rather than the interface specifying the contract having a single method, it has a pair of methods that, together, define the operation. To make sure WCF understands they are a pair of methods for one operation, the begin method has the [OperationContract] attribute with the AsyncPattern property set to true.

■ **Caution**   The naming of the async pattern methods is very important. The methods must be called Begin<Operation Name> and End<Operation Name>. If the methods do not follow this model, the service will compile but will fail to start.

■ **Note**   It is important to differentiate here between the interface and the contract. The interface is a means to model the contract; it is not the contract itself. So while the interface has two methods, the contract only has a single operation that matches the synchronous version of the method. The asynchrony is not a function of the contract but rather an implementation detail.

A Simple Asynchronous Server Operation

As you have seen before, the simple case of a single async I/O operation is fairly straightforward. You can see an example of an async contract definition in Listing 9-30.

Listing 9-30. Asynchronous Version of the Contract Using APM

```
[ServiceContract]
interface IGetPubs
{
    [OperationContract(AsyncPattern = true)]
    IAsyncResult BeginGetAuthors(AsyncCallback callback, object state);
    List<AuthorDTO> EndGetAuthors(IAsyncResult iar);
}
```

As usual with APM, the Begin method must return a call object that signals when the async I/O work is complete, and the End method retrieves the results. Because the AuthorRepository supports APM, the implementation of these methods is very straightforward—simply return the IAsyncResult you get from the repository as in Listing 9-31.

Listing 9-31. Implmentation of the Async Contract Using APM

```
public IAsyncResult BeginGetAuthors(AsyncCallback callback, object state)
{
    return authorRepo.BeginGetAuthors(callback, state);
}

public List<AuthorDTO> EndGetAuthors(IAsyncResult iar)
{
    return authorRepo.EndGetAuthors(iar)
                    .Select(a => new AuthorDTO
                        {
                            FirstName = a.FirstName,
                            LastName = a.LastName
                        })
                    .ToList();
}
```

Complex Asynchronous Service Operations

You have already seen that the real complexity with service-side APM is when you need to perform multiple async I/O operations within a service request. You have also seen that you can achieve a fairly concise implementation if you use a custom IAsyncResult implementation. However, as you are using .NET 4.0, there is another approach you can take—one that takes advantage of the fact that Task implements IAsyncResult. You can use TaskCompletionSource as an adapter to turn multiple APM operations into a Task and, therefore, an implementation of IAsyncResult (see Listing 9-32). Notice that for this to work you need to pass the state parameter to the TaskCompletionSource constructor so it ends up as the AsyncState of the IAsyncResult implementation.

Listing 9-32. Complex Service Operation Using TaskCompletionSource

```
FullDetails response = new FullDetails();

public IAsyncResult BeginGetAuthorsAndTitles(AsyncCallback callback, object state)
{
    var tcs = new TaskCompletionSource<FullDetails>(state);
    int outstandingOperations = 2;

    authorRepo.BeginGetAuthors(iar =>
        {
            response.Authors = authorRepo.EndGetAuthors(iar)
                                    .Select(a => new AuthorDTO
                                        {
                                            FirstName = a.FirstName,
                                            LastName = a.LastName
                                        })
                                    .ToList();
```

```
                    int currentOutstanding = Interlocked.Decrement(ref outstandingOperations);
                    if (currentOutstanding == 0)
                    {
                        tcs.SetResult(response);
                        callback(tcs.Task);
                    }
                }, null);

        titleRepo.BeginGetTitles(iar =>
            {
                response.Titles = titleRepo.EndGetTitles(iar)
                                    .Select(a => new TitleDTO()
                                        {
                                            Name = a.Name,
                                            Price = a.Price == 0.0m ?
                                                        (decimal?)null : a.Price
                                        })
                                    .ToList();
                int currentOutstanding = Interlocked.Decrement(ref outstandingOperations);
                if (currentOutstanding == 0)
                {
                    tcs.SetResult(response);
                    callback(tcs.Task);
                }
            }, null);

    return tcs.Task;
}

public FullDetails EndGetAuthorsAndTitles(IAsyncResult iar)
{
    return response;
}
```

■ **Note** In Listing 9-32 we are assuming an `InstanceContextMode` of `PerCall` or at least a `ConcurrencyMode` of `Single`. If multiple requests enter one instance, then there will be contention of the response member variable, and one of the requests will likely receive the wrong response.

However, as you saw with WebForms, things can start to get interesting when you try to weave error handling into the implementation.

Error Handling in APM-Based Services

In WCF, errors are expressed by throwing a special exception type called a `FaultException`. This gets translated by the WCF infrastructure into a SOAP fault message, which is a platform-independent way of stating something has gone wrong in processing. This is the familiar problem of how to throw this `FaultException` on the right thread, so WCF is aware of the issue.

Unfortunately, in WCF you do not have access to an implementation of SynchronizationContext, so you cannot use the same techniques that you saw in WebForms. However, one advantage you do have is, by design, fault messages should not contain things like stack traces, as they can expose security-sensitive information to remote callers. So as long as you can capture the fact that a FaultException needs to be thrown, you can simply store the fault message information you need to send (see Listing 9-33).

Listing 9-33. Error Handling in APM-Based Service

```
FullDetails response = new FullDetails();
private string faultMessage = null;

public IAsyncResult BeginGetAuthorsAndTitles(AsyncCallback callback, object state)
{
    var tcs = new TaskCompletionSource<FullDetails>(state);
    int outstandingOperations = 2;

    authorRepo.BeginGetAuthors(iar =>
        {
            try
            {
                response.Authors = authorRepo.EndGetAuthors(iar)
                                        .Select(a => new AuthorDTO
                                            {
                                                FirstName = a.FirstName,
                                                LastName = a.LastName
                                            })
                                        .ToList();
            }
            catch (Exception x)
            {
                faultMessage = "Error retrieving authors";
            }
            finally
            {
                int currentOutstanding = Interlocked.Decrement(ref outstandingOperations);
                if (currentOutstanding == 0)
                {
                    tcs.SetResult(response);
                    callback(tcs.Task);
                }
            }
        }, null);

    // rest of method omitted for clarity

    return tcs.Task;
}
```

```
        public FullDetails EndGetAuthorsAndTitles(IAsyncResult iar)
        {
            if (faultMessage != null)
            {
                throw new FaultException(faultMessage);
            }

            return response;
        }
```

This, then, is the asynchronous model on the service side of WCF prior to .NET 4.5. It involves modifying the contract interface to use APM and then providing an implementation of that interface that hands off to the required async I/O methods. This ensures that the request thread is free to process further requests while the I/O takes place. However, you can see that there are a number of places where the code becomes complex to maintain, as the service performs more asynchronous work.

Asynchronous WCF Services in .NET 4.5

As with other server-side frameworks, asynchronous WCF has had an overhaul in .NET 4.5 to take advantage of TPL. Instead of modeling an asynchronous implementation of a contract operation using APM, now you can simply use Task as a return type, as you can see in Listing 9-34.

Listing 9-34. TPL-Based WCF Contract

```
[ServiceContract]
interface IGetPubs
{
    [OperationContract]
    Task<List<AuthorDTO>> GetAuthors();

    [OperationContract]
    Task<FullDetails> GetAuthorsAndTitles();
}
```

You have seen, in the previous examples of TPL-based server-side APIs, that using Tasks also removes a lot of the complexity in the implementation code, as shown by the GetAuthors implementation in Listing 9-35.

Listing 9-35. TPL-Based Implementation of GetAuthors Operation

```
public async Task<List<AuthorDTO>> GetAuthors()
{
    IEnumerable<Author> authors = await authorRepo.GetAuthorsAsync();

    return authors.Select(a => new AuthorDTO
            {
                FirstName = a.FirstName,
                LastName = a.LastName
            }).ToList();
}
```

Last, as you have seen, even complex asynchronous operations are heavily simplified by the use of Task.WhenAll to combine the wait for multiple async I/O operations into a single Task. Listing 9-36 shows the elegance of this approach, which leaves you with asynchronous code that has the same structure and error-handling approach as a synchronous version of the operation.

Listing 9-36. Implementation of Complex Operation Using TPL

```
public async Task<FullDetails> GetAuthorsAndTitles()
{
    var authorTask = authorRepo.GetAuthorsAsync();
    var titleTask = titleRepo.GetTitlesAsync();

    await Task.WhenAll(authorTask, titleTask);

    var response = new FullDetails
    {
        Authors = authorTask.Result.Select(a => new AuthorDTO
            {
                FirstName = a.FirstName,
                LastName = a.LastName
            }).ToList(),

        Titles = titleTask.Result.Select(t => new TitleDTO()
            {
                Name = t.Name,
                Price = t.Price == 0.0m ? (decimal?)null : t.Price
            }).ToList(),
    };

    return response;
}
```

Summary

To really scale with the minimum hardware, server code requires the use of asynchronous I/O and IOCP to allow the freeing of the request thread while the I/O takes place. Because of this, the main server-side technologies have been given the ability to run requests asynchronously.

Prior to .NET 4.5 the server-side frameworks used a variety of techniques to achieve asynchrony. Although these techniques work, they can lead to complex solutions, particularly when error handling is laid in. For .NET 4.5 the frameworks have been standardized on a common model using TPL. With async and await these new asynchronous models provide a very clean and simple asynchronous API that manages to retain the simplicity of the synchronous model, while giving you the asynchronous functionality you require.

CHAPTER 10

■ ■ ■

TPL Dataflow

Classic concurrent programming simply took synchronous programming and said, "Let us have lots of synchronous execution running at the same time, through the use of threads." To this end we have used the Task abstraction to describe concurrency; all is good until we introduce mutable shared state. Once mutable shared state is involved, we have to consider synchronization strategies. Adding the correct and most efficient form of synchronization adds complexity to our code. The one glimmer of hope is that we can retain some degree of elegance through the use of concurrent data structures and more complex synchronization primitives; but the fact remains that we still have to care about mutable shared state.

But let us dream of a world where we don't have to think about synchronization; where we just write the code, and the way we structure it results in no synchronization issues. In this world each object has its own private thread of execution, and only ever manipulates its own internal state. Instead of one single thread executing through many objects by calling object methods, objects send asynchronous messages to each other. If the object is busy processing a previous message, the message is queued. When the object is no longer busy it then processes the next message. Fundamentally, if each object only has one thread of execution, then updating its own internal state is perfectly safe. To alter another object's state, it needs to send a message, which again will only get acted upon by that object's private thread. It is this style of programming that TPL Dataflow is looking to promote, not a single lock or semaphore insight.

The Building Blocks

TPL Dataflow comprises a series of blocks (an odd word, we realize, when discussing concurrency). Blocks are essentially a message source, target, or both. In addition to receiving and sending messages, a block represents an element of concurrency for processing the messages it receives. Multiple blocks are linked together to produce networks of blocks. Messages are then posted asynchronously into the network for processing. Each block can perform processing on the message prior to offering a message to another block. So while by default each block only processes one message at a time, if multiple messages are active in different blocks we have concurrency.

Consider the following use case. At periodic times in the day, a report is run against a database and the results from the report uploaded to a web service. The data contained in each database row need to be transformed into a data object ready to be sent to the web service. For network efficiency the web service receives multiple data objects as part of a single request, up to a defined maximum. The following process could be broken down into a series of blocks, where each block is responsible for doing some part of the overall processing. Figure 10-1 shows what that might look like.

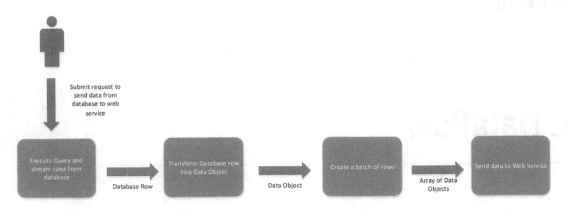

Figure 10-1. *Process pipeline*

Each block has its own thread of execution, so in the case just described, while one thread is fetching the next row from the database another thread is transforming the previous row. When we have sufficient rows, another thread will send the data to the web server, while the other blocks continue to fetch and transform database rows. This is akin to Henry Ford's car production line, where each worker was autonomous in performing his specific job. This concurrency works beautifully as long as each block takes the same time to process; otherwise we end up with bottlenecks.

Obviously we can't always guarantee that each block will take the same time, so blocks have buffers, allowing the previous block to reliably deliver its result and move on to its next piece of processing. Buffers are useful to iron out bursts of activity, but they don't solve the fundamental problem of a bottleneck. If this were a car production line, we could solve the problem either by breaking down the bottleneck block into smaller blocks or, alternatively, by introducing multiple workers for that particular block with each worker still working autonomously. The equivalent of workers in our domain is threads, so we could introduce the idea of multiple threads inside a given block. Assuming each thread in a given block does not share mutable state with another thread, all will remain good. Figure 10-2 shows how the application could be reconfigured to use multiple threads inside some of the blocks. This new configuration allows three database rows to be processed concurrently and allows two concurrent batches to be delivered to the web server.

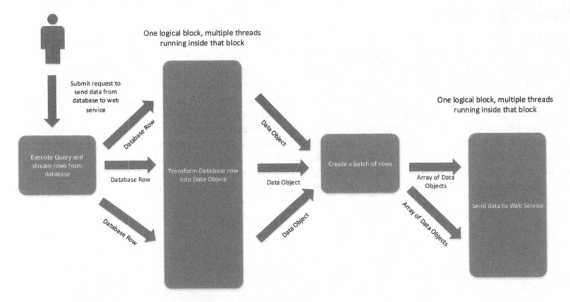

Figure 10-2. *Improved pipeline, multiple threads per block*

This is essentially what TPL Dataflow is: the ability to describe algorithms using a network of asynchronous message-passing autonomous blocks.

GETTING TPL DATAFLOW

TPL Dataflow, unlike TPL itself, is not distributed as part of the .NET framework. It is available as a package installed via NuGet. See `www.nuget.org/packages/Microsoft.Tpl.Dataflow` for more details of how to install it. To use TPL Dataflow you will also need to be using at least .NET 4.5.

Producer and Consumer Revisited

I can hear you groaning, so I promise this will be the last time we revisit this pattern. In chapter 5 you built a producer consumer implementation using `BlockingCollection<T>`; for that particular implementation you spun up a fixed number of consumer threads. When these threads had no items to process they slept peacefully. As discussed in Chapter 9, having a thread sleeping is often better than having it spinning, but ideally you would like the thread to retire back to the thread pool. Implementing such a scheme is nontrivial using basic TPL; however, TPL Dataflow makes it a breeze. Listing 10-1 shows a very simple Dataflow application that achieves our goal. Here we have a single `ActionBlock<int>`. `ActionBlock<T>` can receive input of type T, executing the supplied logic (`Action<T>`) to act on the value of T. `ActionBlocks` are leaf nodes in a Dataflow network, and therefore cannot be used as sources to other blocks. One way of supplying values of T to a `ActionBlock<T>` is to call the `Post` method on the `ActionBlock<T>` itself. The `Post` method will attempt to deliver the value to the `ActionBlock<T>`; if it is unable to accept it immediately the post will fail and the `Post` method will return `false`.

Listing 10-1. Lazy Producer Consumer

```
using System;
using System.Threading;
using System.Threading.Tasks;
// You will need to get the TPL bits from NuGet, as per start of chapter
using System.Threading.Tasks.Dataflow;

namespace ProducerConsumerDataFlow
{
    class Program
    {
        static void Main(string[] args)
        {
            var consumerBlock = new ActionBlock<int>(new Action<int>(Consume));
            PrintThreadPoolUsage("Main");

            for (int i = 0; i < 5; i++)
            {
                consumerBlock.Post(i);
                Thread.Sleep(1000);
                PrintThreadPoolUsage("loop");
            }

            // Tell the block no more items will be coming
            consumerBlock.Complete();
```

```
        // wait for the block to shutdown
        consumerBlock.Completion.Wait();
    }
    private static void Consume(int val)
    {
        PrintThreadPoolUsage("Consume");
        Console.WriteLine("{0}:{1} is thread pool thread {2}",Task.CurrentId,val,
        Thread.CurrentThread.IsThreadPoolThread);
    }
    private static void PrintThreadPoolUsage(string label)
    {
        int cpu;
        int io;
        ThreadPool.GetAvailableThreads(out cpu,out io);
        Console.WriteLine("{0}:CPU:{1},IO:{2}",label,cpu,io);
    }
  }
}
```

Running the code in Listing 10-1 produces the output shown in Figure 10-3. This shows that the items are being consumed on a thread pool thread, and as a consequence there are fewer threads available in the thread pool. When no items are available for consumption, the number of available threads in the thread pool returns to the recorded initial level of 1,023. This therefore shows that while there are no items to consume, you are not simply sleeping on a thread pool thread.

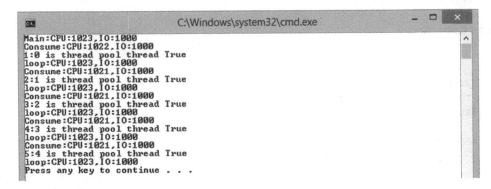

Figure 10-3. *Lazy producer consumer*

ActionBlock<T> *therefore consumes thread resources when it has items to process, but retires the thread when it has no work to do, thus fulfilling our initial requirement.*

Let us examine what happens if we supply more work than can be immediately dealt with by the ActionBlock<T>. Listing 10-2 shows an eager producer and a slow consumer.

Listing 10-2. Slow Consumer

```
class Program
{
  static void Main(string[] args)
  {
    var consumerBlock = new ActionBlock<int>(new Action<int>(SlowConsumer));

    for (int i = 0; i < 5; i++)
    {
      consumerBlock.Post(i);
    }

    consumerBlock.Complete();
    consumerBlock.Completion.Wait();
  }

  private static void SlowConsumer(int val)
  {
    Console.WriteLine("{0}: Consuming {1}", Task.CurrentId,val);
    Thread.Sleep(1000);
  }
}
```

The SlowConsume method in Listing 10-2 takes approximately 1 second to process each item. You are posting items at a far greater frequency than that, so you may have therefore expected the Post to fail. While the ActionBlock<T> by default can only process one item at a time, it also has by default an unbounded buffer so it can keep receiving items while processing. This is known as a greedy block (see Figure 10-4).

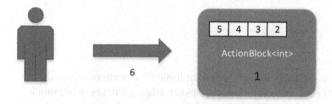

Figure 10-4. *Greedy ActionBlock<int>*

By default ActionBlock<T> only has a single thread of execution; this and many other options can be changed by supplying a configured instance of ExecutionDataflowBlockOptions when creating the ActionBlock<T> (see Figure 10-5). The fragment of code in Listing 10-3 creates a block that can process two messages concurrently. Needless to say, if there is only one item to process only one thread will be active.

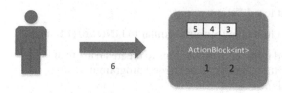

Figure 10-5. *ActionBlock<int> with MaxDegreeOfParallelism = 2*

Listing 10-3. Two-Thread Action Block

```
. . .
var blockConfiguration = new ExecutionDataflowBlockOptions()
{
    NameFormat="Type:{0},Id:{1}", // Effects ToString() on block (useful for debugging/logging)
    MaxDegreeOfParallelism = 2, // Up to two tasks will be used to process items
};

var consumerBlock = new ActionBlock<int>(new Action<int>(SlowConsumer) ,
                                         blockConfiguration);
Console.WriteLine(consumerBlock.ToString());
```

Modifying Listing 10-2 to use the preceding block configuration would result in the output shown in Figure 10-6. Now you can see two tasks are being used to process the items concurrently (Tasks 2 and 3).

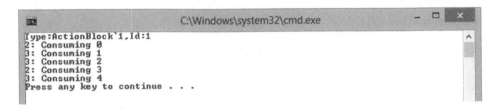

Figure 10-6. *Multiple tasks executing inside a block*

While the examples so far are very simple, they set you off on a new approach to writing concurrent applications. Rather than having to deal with the mechanics of creating tasks, simply define blocks of code and associated levels of concurrency.

Linking Blocks

Isolated blocks aren't really that interesting. What is far more interesting is when multiple blocks are connected together to form a network of concurrent activity. An `ActionBlock<T>` acts as a network edge, there are other block types that can be used to form the start or body of a network. These blocks are linked together to form a network, so that as data are posted into one block and processed, they can then flow into the input of a connected block. Table 10-1 contains details of the block types that come out of the box.

Table 10-1. *Types of Dataflow Blocks*

Block Type	Description
BufferBlock<T>	Buffers input, useful for load balancing non greedy consumers
TransformBlock<TInput,TOutput>	Transforms an input to a different output
TransformManyBlock<TInput,TOutput>	Transforms an input into many outputs, similar to LINQ SelectMany
BatchBlock<T>	Collects a configured number of input items to create an array of output items. In addition, batch can be trigged programmatically (e.g., every n seconds).

(continued)

Table 10-1. (*continued*)

Block Type	Description
BroadcastBlock<T>	Makes the last value posted to the block available for any connected block. Useful for when you just want to know the latest value, and old values are meaningless.
WriteOnceBlock<T>	Same as broadcast but only makes available first posted value.
JoinBlock<T1,T2> JoinBlock<T1,T2,T3>	Takes input from two or three blocks, only consumes value when there is sufficient inputs. Produces an output of Tuple<T1,T2> or Tuple<T1,T2,T3>. Useful for Fork/Join scenarios
BatchedJoinBlock<T1,T2> BatchedJoinBlock<T1,T2,T3>	A batched version of the JoinBlock

Transform Block

Let us first consider the piece of code in Listing 10-4. The purpose of this code is to turn a color-based image into a grayscale image. The code is expected to initially run on the UI thread; so as to not block the UI thread, it creates a task to run the image processing and, once completed, fires an event on the UI thread to indicate it is done.

Listing 10-4. Asynchronously Converts Images to WPF Grayscale Bitmap Images

```
public class ImageProcessor
{
  public event EventHandler<ProcessedImageEventArgs> ProducedGrayScaleImage = delegate { };

  public void ProcessFile(string filename)
  {
    Task.Run(() =>LoadAndToGrayScale(filename))
        .ContinueWith(toGrayTask =>ProducedGrayScaleImage(this,
                          new ProcessedImageEventArgs(toGrayTask.Result)),
                TaskScheduler.FromCurrentSynchronizationContext());



  }
  private static  BitmapSource LoadAndToGrayScale(string path)
  {
      var img = new BitmapImage(new Uri(path));
      return ToGrayScale(img);
  }

  private static  BitmapSource ToGrayScale(BitmapSource bitmapSource)
  {
      . . .
  }
}
```

Instead of explicitly using tasks, you could refactor to use two dataflow blocks, as per Figure 10-7.

Figure 10-7. *Convert image to grayscale using dataflow blocks*

Items can be posted to the transform block in the same way as you previously posted work to an action block. Unlike the action block, the transform block has a responsibility not just to consume but to produce. For the transform block to work, you need to supply the transformation logic. This is achieved by supplying a Func<TInput,TOuput> to the block. When data are posted to the block, the supplied function is invoked to produce the output. As with the action block, the transform block will have by default only a single task executing at any one time to perform the transformation logic.

By default ActionBlock<T> tasks will use the default task scheduler, which is not what we want, since this block's responsibility is to fire the event on the UI thread. To solve this, create the ActionBlock<T> specifying that you want it to use the task scheduler associated with the current synchronization context.

Once both the blocks have been created, you need to link them up. To do this, there is a LinkTo method on the TransformBlock<TInput,TOutput>. This LinkTo method takes as an argument any block that has an input type of TOutput. The LinkTo method is actually defined on the ISourceBlock<TOutput> interface, which is implemented by any block that can be a source (i.e., has an output). In a similar fashion, any block that has input, implements ITargetBlock<T>. The LinkTo method returns an IDisposable object, which when disposed removes the link between the blocks.

Last, modify the ProcessFile method simply to post the requested file to the transform block, and return in the hope that someday an event will fire with the converted image (see Listing 10-5).

Listing 10-5. Dataflow for Converting Image to Grayscale

```
public class ImageProcessor
{
  public event EventHandler<ProcessedImageEventArgs> ProducedGrayScaleImage = delegate { };

  private TransformBlock<string, BitmapSource> loadAndToGrayBlock;
  private ActionBlock<BitmapSource> publishImageBlock;

  public ImageProcessor()
  {
    loadAndToGrayBlock = new TransformBlock<string, BitmapSource>(
                        (Func<string, BitmapSource>)LoadAndToGrayScale);
    publishImageBlock = new ActionBlock<BitmapSource>((Action<BitmapSource>) PublishImage,
                new ExecutionDataflowBlockOptions()
                {
                    TaskScheduler = TaskScheduler.FromCurrentSynchronizationContext()
                });
    loadAndToGrayBlock.LinkTo(publishImageBlock);
  }

  public void ProcessFile(string filename)
  {
    loadAndToGrayBlock.Post(filename);
  }
```

```
private void PublishImage(BitmapSource img)
{
    ProducedGrayScaleImage(this,new ProcessedImageEventArgs(img));
}

private static  BitmapSource LoadAndToGrayScale(string path)
{
  var img = new BitmapImage(new Uri(path));
  return ToGrayScale(img);
}
private static  BitmapSource ToGrayScale(BitmapSource bitmapSource)
{
  . . .
}
}
```

Listing 10-5 contains the refactored code that now utilizes blocks to provide concurrency as opposed to using tasks explicitly. Instead of thinking about threads of execution, think about blocks of concurrent execution, stimulated by asynchronous messages.

Transform Many Block

The ImageProcessor class currently allows you to process individual files, but what if you wanted to process an entire directory? Simple enough—just iterate through all the image files from a directory search and post the file, as per Listing 10-6. While this will obviously work, you are in fact missing an opportunity to keep things fast and fluid: rather than performing the directory search on the UI thread, you could encapsulate the directory search functionality inside a new block. The UI thread will then just simply post the directory start point to that block, and return to UI processing.

Listing 10-6. Process Multiple Files

```
public void ProcessDirectory(string dir)
{
    DirectoryInfo directory = new DirectoryInfo(dir);
    foreach (FileInfo file in directory.GetFiles("*.jpg"))
    {
    loadAndToGrayBlock.Post(file.FullName);
    }
}
```

The TransformBlock<TInput,TOuput> block produces as many outputs as it receives inputs. You now need a block that takes a directory path as an input and potentially can produce many image files, thus producing an imbalance of inputs to outputs. You could make the directory block produce, say, a List<string>, but that would batch as opposed to stream. A more scalable approach would be to use a TransformManyBlock<TInput,TOutput>; this block does not simply take a Func<TInput,TOutput> but a Func<TInput,IEnumerable<TOutput>>. The code for the block produces an IEnumerable<TOutput>, potentially offering many results that can then be passed onto a linked block. The Dataflow framework consumes the IEnumerable<TOutput>, making the output as it becomes available to any linked blocks. Figure 10-8 shows the new block topology, allowing directories and files to be processed concurrently.

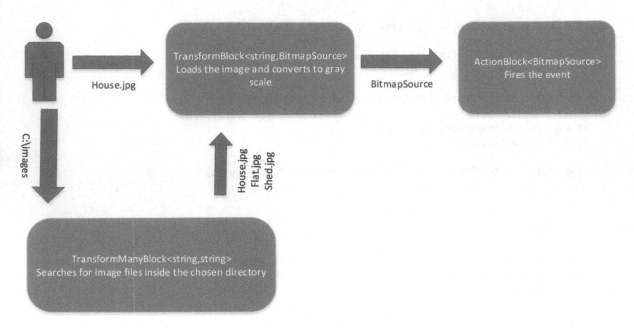

Figure 10-8. *Transform many images*

To implement this new topology, you need to create an instance of a `TransformManyBlock` and provide a method on the `ImageProcessor` class to take a directory and post it to the block (Listing 10-7).

Listing 10-7. `TransformMany`

```
public class ImageProcessor
{
  public event EventHandler<ProcessedImageEventArgs> ProducedGrayScaleImage = delegate { };

  private TransformManyBlock<string, string> imageCollectionBlock;
  private TransformBlock<string, BitmapSource> loadAndToGrayBlock;
  private ActionBlock<BitmapSource> publishImageBlock;

  public ImageProcessor()
  {
    imageCollectionBlock = new TransformManyBlock<string, string>(
                (Func<string, IEnumerable<string>>) FindImagesInDirectory);

    loadAndToGrayBlock = new TransformBlock<string, BitmapSource>(
                           (Func<string, BitmapSource>)LoadAndToGrayScale);

    publishImageBlock = new ActionBlock<BitmapSource>((Action<BitmapSource>) PublishImage,
              new ExecutionDataflowBlockOptions()
              {
                  TaskScheduler = TaskScheduler.FromCurrentSynchronizationContext()
              });
```

```
    imageCollectionBlock.LinkTo(loadAndToGrayBlock);
    loadAndToGrayBlock.LinkTo(publishImageBlock);
}

public void ProcessFile(string filename)
{
    loadAndToGrayBlock.Post(filename);
}

public void ProcessDirectory(string dir)
{
    imageCollectionBlock.Post(dir);
}

private IEnumerable<string> FindImagesInDirectory(string dir)
{
    var directory = new System.IO.DirectoryInfo(dir);
    return directory
            .GetFiles("*.jpg")
            .Select(file => file.FullName);
}
private void PublishImage(BitmapSource img)
{
    ProducedGrayScaleImage(this, new ProcessedImageEventArgs(img));
}
private static  BitmapSource LoadAndToGrayScale(string path)
{
    var img = new BitmapImage(new Uri(path));
    return ToGrayScale(img);
}
private static  BitmapSource ToGrayScale(BitmapSource bitmapSource)
{
    . . .
}
}
```

Now that you have a working network of blocks, you can start to consider further concurrency. At present you are only using a single task to turn images into grayscale; of all the blocks this is the one that will take the time. The grayscale processing of each image is isolated—you don't need to care about the order in which the images appear, and therefore it seems logical that you should assign multiple tasks to this block. Listing 10-8 shows the necessary change to the ImageProcessor class to enable concurrent processing of images.

Listing 10-8. Many Tasks Performing Image Conversion

```
loadAndToGrayBlock = new TransformBlock<string, BitmapSource>(
                            (Func<string, BitmapSource>)LoadAndToGrayScale,
                new ExecutionDataflowBlockOptions()
                {
                    MaxDegreeOfParallelism = 4,
                });
```

While you easily could have written the image processor using tasks, one advantage to using TPL Dataflow is being able to control the number of threads for a given role. In a large application you may very well want to take finer control over how compute resources are being shared across the entire application, and not just have them be shared evenly, as would be the case if everything were throttled exclusively by the thread pool.

RELINQUISHING TASKS

A very strange option on the `ExecutionDataflowBlockOptions` is the ability to set the maximum number of requests handled by a given task, by setting the `MaxMessagesPerTask` property. Unlike humans, tasks don't degrade over time, so why would you do this? If a dataflow block is constantly fed work, the task will never end, and if the thread pool is inclined not to create more threads, there may be a buildup of work waiting to run. Ending the task after it has processed n pieces of work could help short-lived tasks run without having to grow the thread pool.

Preservation of Order

Increasing the concurrency for a given block allows a block to process multiple messages at the same time. If the processing of each message takes the same time, then you might expect the order of the output messages to be in the same order as their corresponding input messages: I1,I2,I3 => O1,O2,O3. If, however, it took a lot longer to process I1 compared to I2,I3, then perhaps O2,O3,O1 would be an expected outcome. TPL Dataflow blocks preserve order; if I1 did take longer to process than I2,I3, then O2,O3 will be not be published until I1 had completed and O1 published. This preservation of order can be advantageous for solving problems concurrently that still require order, something that is often hard to solve with conventional parallel programming techniques.

If order is not a requirement, then don't increase the degree of parallelism for a given block; instead allow a single source block to link to multiple consumer blocks.

Linking to Multiple Targets

So far we have only considered linking a source block to a single target block. Consider the situation where, based on a given input, data are fetched from a database, and for performance reasons the database is mirrored, allowing data to be fetched from either database. You should therefore consider building a dataflow as described in Figure 10-9. Assuming that if Server A is busy, Server B will be offered the query, then if both blocks are busy the previous block will wait until either becomes available. Just simply linking up multiple targets in this way, unfortunately, will not give you this effect. Most blocks by default have associated with them an unbounded queue that allows them to receive messages even if they are busy. This is known as greedy behavior, and the level of greediness can be controlled by setting the capacity of the queue. To make a block non-greedy, simply set the queue length to 1. Greedy blocks can therefore accept messages even if they are busy processing a previous message. Non-greedy blocks will refuse messages while they are busy processing message(s). If a message is refused by one block, the next linked block will be offered the message. If all blocks refuse the message, the first block to become available to process the message will do so (see Listing 10-9).

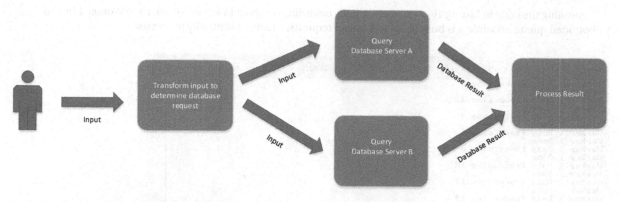

Figure 10-9. *Load-balanced mirrored databases*

Listing 10-9. Greedy and Non-greedy Blocks

```
class Program
{
    static void Main(string[] args)
    {
        var greedy = new ExecutionDataflowBlockOptions();

        var nonGreedy = new ExecutionDataflowBlockOptions()
        {
            BoundedCapacity = 1
        };

        ExecutionDataflowBlockOptions options = greedy;

        var firstBlock = new ActionBlock<int>(i => Do(i,1,2),options);
        var secondBlock = new ActionBlock<int>(i => Do(i,2,1), options);
        var thirdBlock = new ActionBlock<int>(i => Do(i,3,2), options);

        var transform = new TransformBlock<int,int>(i=>i*2);

        transform.LinkTo(firstBlock);
        transform.LinkTo(secondBlock);
        transform.LinkTo(thirdBlock);

        for (int i = 0; i <= 10; i++)
        {
            transform.Post(i);
        }
        Console.ReadLine();
    }
    private static void Do(int workItem , int nWorker, int busyTimeInSeconds)
    {
        Console.WriteLine("Worker {0} Busy Processing {1}",nWorker,workItem);
        Thread.Sleep(busyTimeInSeconds * 1000 );
        Console.WriteLine("Worker {0} Done",nWorker);
    }
}
```

Running the code in Listing 10-9 will show greedy behavior, as shown in Figure 10-10. Here Worker 1 has an unbounded queue, so while it is busy it can still accept requests, which it eventually processes.

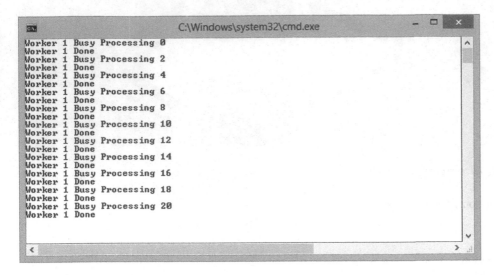

Figure 10-10. *Greedy worker*

Modifying the code in Listing 10-9 to use the nonGreedy configuration will produce the output shown in Figure 10-11. With a capacity of 1, each worker refuses any more work until it is idle, resulting in messages being acted upon by the first available worker.

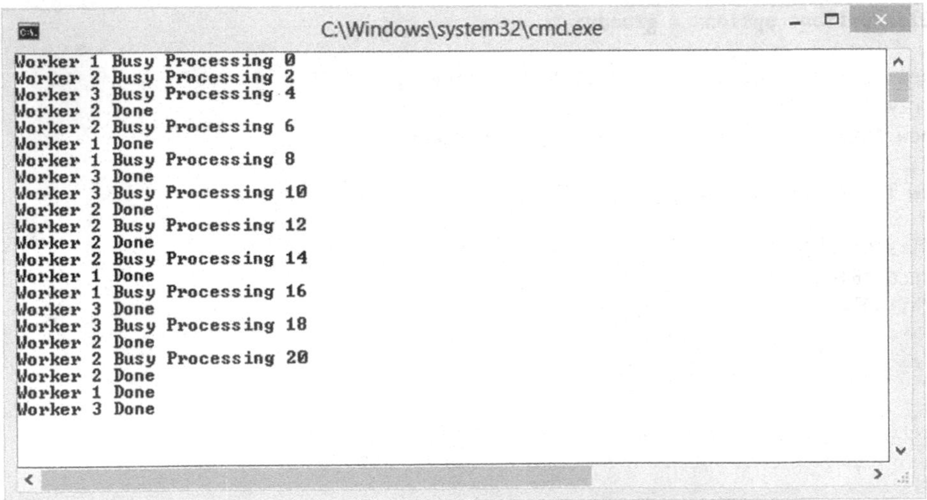

Figure 10-11. *Non-greedy blocks*

Conditional Linking

All the linking discussed so far has been unconditional; all the output of the source block has flowed to the input of one of the linked target blocks. Dataflow blocks can be linked on a conditional basis, too, allowing data to be filtered. This allows the programming constructs of if/else, switch/case, and recursion to be modeled in a dataflow network.

If/else and switch/case

Consider the following use case. A report needs to be run against an accountancy ledger. In the ledger there will be credit entries and debit entries. The purpose of the code is to generate two CSV files: one to contain credit entries, the other debit. Utilizing TPL Dataflow, one possible topology is shown in Figure 10-12. The last block examines the data and decides which CSV file to write the data to, a simple if/else in this case.

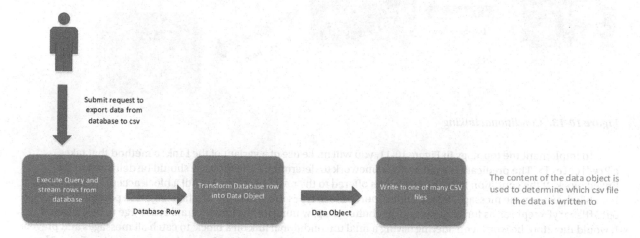

***Figure 10-12.** Accountancy ledger to CSV files*

The topology in Figure 10-12 will undoubtedly work and provide some degree of concurrency, but you could do better. After all, it should be possible to write a debit row at the same time as a credit row, since different resources are being consumed (Credit.csv or Debit.csv). You can't simply increase the concurrency of the block, since you clearly can't have multiple credit rows being written at the same time, as this would potentially lead to corruption of the file on disk. What you need to do is create two blocks: one for writing credit rows and the other for writing debit rows. The credit row block should only receive data objects that contain credit information, and the debit row block should receive only data objects that contain debit information. This new topology is shown in Figure 10-13.

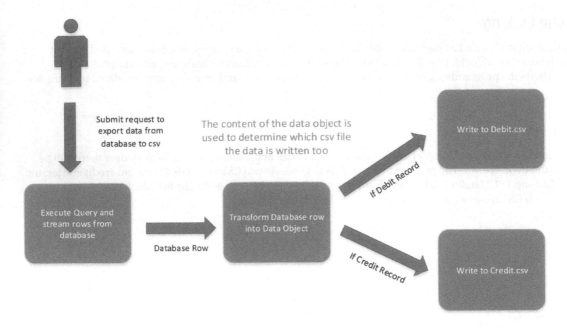

Figure 10-13. *Conditional linking*

To implement the topology in Figure 10-11, you will make use of a variant of the LinkTo method that takes a Predicate<T>. The predicate is used by the framework to determine if the message should be delivered to the linked block. If the condition fails, the message is offered to the next linked block, until a block accepts the message. If no block accepts the message, then for most source block types this will result in a blockage and potentially an OutOfMemoryException as further messages get buffered up, waiting for the undeliverable message to be delivered. It would therefore be worth considering having a final unconditional link on a block, to catch all messages and prevent a blockage. Listing 10-10 provides a skeleton implementation of Figure 10-13. Having the unknownLedgerEntryBlock means you will have a point in the application where you can gracefully handle unexpected behavior.

Listing 10-10. Skeleton Code for Concurrent CSV Processing

```
public interface ILedgerEntry
{
   bool IsCredit { get; }
   bool IsDebit { get; }
};

public class CsvImporter
{
  private TransformManyBlock<string, object[]> databaseQueryBlock;
  private TransformManyBlock<object[], ILedgerEntry> rowTGoLedgerBlock;
  private ActionBlock<ILedgerEntry> debitBlock;
  private ActionBlock<ILedgerEntry> creditBlock;
  private ActionBlock<ILedgerEntry> unknownLedgerEntryBlock;
```

```csharp
public CsvImporter()
{
    databaseQueryBlock = new TransformManyBlock<string, object[]>(
                    (Func<string, IEnumerable<object[]>>) ExecuteQuery);
    rowTGoLedgerBlock = new TransformManyBlock<object[], ILedgerEntry>(
                    (Func<object[], IEnumerable<ILedgerEntry>>) MapDatabaseRowToObject);
    debitBlock = new ActionBlock<ILedgerEntry>((Action<ILedgerEntry>) WriteDebitEntry);
    creditBlock = new ActionBlock<ILedgerEntry>((Action<ILedgerEntry>) WriteCreditEntry);

    unknownLedgerEntryBlock = new ActionBlock<ILedgerEntry>(
                            (Action<ILedgerEntry>)LogUnknownLedgerEntryType);

    databaseQueryBlock.LinkTo(rowTGoLedgerBlock);
    rowTGoLedgerBlock.LinkTo(debitBlock, le => le.IsDebit); //if IsDebit
    rowTGoLedgerBlock.LinkTo(creditBlock, le => le.IsCredit); // else if IsCredit
    rowTGoLedgerBlock.LinkTo(unknownLedgerEntryBlock); // else
}

public void Export(string connectionString)
{
    databaseQueryBlock.Post(connectionString);
}

private IEnumerable<object[]> ExecuteQuery(string arg){ yield break; }
private IEnumerable<ILedgerEntry> MapDatabaseRowToObject(object[] arg) { yield break;}
private void WriteDebitEntry(ILedgerEntry debitEntry) { }
private void WriteCreditEntry(ILedgerEntry creditEntry) { }
private void LogUnknownLedgerEntryType(ILedgerEntry obj){}
}
```

■ **Note**   We are not stating that all traditional if/else should be turned into dataflow blocks. What we are suggesting is that when the bodies of the if/else blocks are not mutating shared resources, we have an opportunity to introduce greater concurrency.

Recursion

Another interesting use of conditional linking is in implementing recursion. It is not unusual to see algorithms that use call stack–based recursion to walk a tree. Listing 10-11 shows an example of classic recursive programming technique to obtain a list of all files under a supplied directory.

Listing 10-11. Call Stack–Based Recursion

```csharp
private static IEnumerable<string> GetFiles(string path)
{
    DirectoryInfo dir = new DirectoryInfo(path);
    foreach (FileInfo file in dir.GetFiles())
    {
        yield return dir.FullName;
    }
```

```
    foreach (DirectoryInfo subDir in dir.GetDirectories())
    {
      foreach (string file in GetFiles(subDir.FullName))
      {
        yield return file;
      }
    }
  }
}
```

Recursive programming can be expressed with dataflow blocks by conditionally linking blocks back to themselves, as shown in Figure 10-14 and implemented in Listing 10-12.

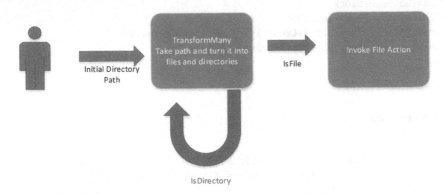

Figure 10-14. *Recursive directory walk using TransformMany block*

Listing 10-12. Recursion Using Dataflow Blocks

```
public class DirectoryWalker
{
    private ActionBlock<string> fileActionBlock;
    private TransformManyBlock<string, string> directoryBrowseBlock;

    public DirectoryWalker(Action<string> fileAction)
    {
      directoryBrowseBlock = new TransformManyBlock<string, string>(
                            (Func<string, IEnumerable<string>>)(GetFilesInDirectory));
      fileActionBlock = new ActionBlock<string>(fileAction);

      directoryBrowseBlock.LinkTo(directoryBrowseBlock, Directory.Exists);
      directoryBrowseBlock.LinkTo(fileActionBlock);
    }

    public void Walk(string path)
    {
      directoryBrowseBlock.Post(path);
    }
```

```
private IEnumerable<string> GetFilesInDirectory(string path)
{
  var dir = new DirectoryInfo(path);
  return dir.EnumerateFileSystemInfos().Select(fi => fi.FullName);
}
}
. . .
var walker = new DirectoryWalker(Console.WriteLine);
walker.Walk(@"C:\temp");
Console.ReadLine();
```

Shutting Down Gracefully

Graceful termination of dataflow networks can be just as important as initiating them. It may be important to know when a given dataflow network has processed all the inputs. Running Listing 10-13 will not display numbers 0 to 9, since the main thread will terminate and hence the process before the block's task will process any items.

Listing 10-13. Early Termination

```
class Program
{
    static void Main(string[] args)
    {
      var actionBlock = new ActionBlock<int>( (Action<int>)Console.WriteLine );

      for (int i = 0; i < 10; i++)
      {
        actionBlock.Post(i);
      }
    }
}
```

To remedy the situation, you need to refactor the code to wait for the action block to complete all posted items. Each block has associated with it a property called Completion of type Task. The status of this task reflects the status of the block. While the block is still processing or waiting for more items, it is in a state of WaitingForActivation. Once it knows there are no more items to process, it will end in a state of RanToCompletion. This means therefore that to wait for a block to complete, you can use Task.Wait or await on the Completion property. Obviously the block isn't psychic; you need to inform it that no more items will be sent to the block. To signal no more items will be sent, a call is made to the block's Complete method. Any further posts to the block will now fail; once all the queued-up items on the block have been processed, the Completion task will end in a state of RanToCompletion. Listing 10-14 shows the refactored code now in a form that will post all 10 items and then declare no more items will be coming by calling Complete, and then waiting for the block to process all 10 items by calling Completion.Wait. Running the code will now produce the output shown in Figure 10-15.

Listing 10-14. Graceful Termination

```
class Program
{
  static void Main(string[] args)
  {
    var actionBlock = new ActionBlock<int>((Action<int>) Console.WriteLine);
```

```
    for (int i = 0; i < 10; i++)
    {
      actionBlock.Post(i);
    }
    Console.WriteLine("Completing..");
    actionBlock.Complete();
    Console.WriteLine("Waiting..");
    actionBlock.Completion.Wait();
    Console.WriteLine(actionBlock.Completion.Status);
  }
}
```

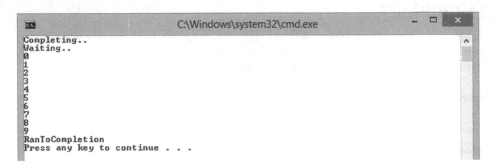

Figure 10-15. *Waiting for block to complete*

Propagating Completion

As already discussed, dataflow blocks are often not used as islands but as part of a larger network of blocks. Listing 10-15 shows some example code that contains two linked blocks. Ten items are posted to the first block; then the block is told there will be no more, and the main thread then waits for the first block to complete. Once the block is completed, the application terminates. Since the second block takes 0.5 seconds to process each block, the main thread will terminate before the second block completes processing its first item.

Listing 10-15. Premature Completion

```
class Program
{
  static void Main(string[] args)
  {
    var firstBlock = new TransformBlock<int, int>(i => i*2);
    var secondBlock = new ActionBlock<int>( i =>
    {
      Thread.Sleep(500);
      Console.WriteLine(i);
    });

    firstBlock.LinkTo(secondBlock);
```

```
    for (int i = 0; i < 10; i++)
    {
      firstBlock.Post(i);
    }
    firstBlock.Complete();
    firstBlock.Completion.Wait();
  }
}
```

To resolve this premature termination issue, you could add two additional lines after the completion logic for the first block:

```
secondBlock.Complete();
secondBlock.Completion.Wait();
```

It is important to ensure that you don't complete the second block until the first block has completed, since the second block will not accept any further input once it has been told to complete. As you can probably imagine this would get tedious as you increased the number of blocks. An alternative is to allow completion to automatically flow to each of its linked blocks as a block completes. Listing 10-16 shows refactored code that now utilizes completion propagation. Automatic propagation is requested as part of linking one block to another. Once the source block has been marked as complete and it has processed all queued items, it informs the linked block that it is now complete. This now greatly simplifies the logic necessary to determine when all inputs have been fully processed by the dataflow network.

Listing 10-16. Automatic Completion Propagation

```
class Program
{
  static void Main(string[] args)
  {
    var firstBlock = new TransformBlock<int, int>(i => i*2);
    var secondBlock = new ActionBlock<int>( i =>
    {
      Thread.Sleep(500);
      Console.WriteLine(i);
    });

    firstBlock.LinkTo(secondBlock , new DataflowLinkOptions(){PropagateCompletion = true});

    for (int i = 0; i < 10; i++)
    {
      firstBlock.Post(i);
    }

    firstBlock.Complete();
    secondBlock.Completion.Wait();
  }
}
```

215

Error Handling

So far we have only considered the happy side of programming, when everything just works. In the real world we have to consider error handling, and in .NET this takes the form of exceptions. Dataflow blocks are fundamentally blocks of code, and as such they can throw exceptions. Consider the code in Listing 10-17. The first two work items should work fine. The third item will cause a divide by zero exception and hence will not produce any output. But what about the fourth item? There are two possibilities: the block swallows the exception and processes the fourth item, or it refuses to process any more items. The actual behavior is the latter; once a block experiences an unhandled exception, it places the block into a faulted state and refuses to process or receive any more messages.

Listing 10-17. Unhandled Divide by Zero Exception

```
private static void Main(string[] args)
{
  var divideBlock = new ActionBlock<Tuple<int, int>>(
          (Action<Tuple<int, int>>) (input => Console.WriteLine(input.Item1/input.Item2)));

  divideBlock.Post(Tuple.Create(10, 5));
  divideBlock.Post(Tuple.Create(20, 4));
  divideBlock.Post(Tuple.Create(10, 0));
  divideBlock.Post(Tuple.Create(10, 2));

  Console.ReadLine();
}
```

Catching the exception and dealing with it inside the block is obviously one remedy, and makes perfect sense if the exception doesn't indicate that the overall dataflow network is now effectively broken, as shown in Listing 10-18.

Listing 10-18. Handling Nonfatal Exceptions Inside the Block

```
private static void Main(string[] args)
{
  var divideBlock = new ActionBlock<Tuple<int, int>>((Action<Tuple<int, int>>)
        delegate(Tuple<int, int> pair)
        {
          try
          {
            Console.WriteLine(pair.Item1/pair.Item2);
          }
          catch (DivideByZeroException)
          {
            Console.WriteLine("Dude, can't divide by zero");
          }
        });
  divideBlock.Post(Tuple.Create(10, 5));
  divideBlock.Post(Tuple.Create(20, 4));
  divideBlock.Post(Tuple.Create(10, 0));
  divideBlock.Post(Tuple.Create(10, 2));

  Console.ReadLine();
}
```

In cases where the underlying exception implies that it is not safe or desirable to proceed with any more messages, then the recovery logic is probably best suited outside the dataflow network. The Completion task discussed earlier provides a means for externally observing if a block has received an unhandled exception. If the status of the Completion task is in a state of Faulted, then this indicates the block is in a faulted state and will perform no further processing. Listing 10-19 demonstrates the wiring up of a continuation in the case of the block ending in a faulted state.

Listing 10-19. Externally Handling a Block Exception

```
private static void Main(string[] args)
{
    var divideBlock = new ActionBlock<Tuple<int, int>>(
            (Action<Tuple<int, int>>) (input => Console.WriteLine(input.Item1/input.Item2)));

    divideBlock.Post(Tuple.Create(10, 5));
    divideBlock.Post(Tuple.Create(20, 4));
    divideBlock.Post(Tuple.Create(10, 0));
    divideBlock.Post(Tuple.Create(10, 2));

    divideBlock
      .Completion
      .ContinueWith(dbt =>
      {
          Console.WriteLine("Divide block failed Reason:{0}",
                              dbt.Exception.InnerExceptions.First().Message);
      }, TaskContinuationOptions.OnlyOnFaulted);

    Console.ReadLine();
}
```

■ **Note** The Exception exposed by the Completion task will be an AggregateException. This allows for the fact that a block may have multiple active tasks (MaxDegreeOfParallelism > 1), all of which may have ended in a faulted state.

So far we have examined error handling at the individual block level. Externally handling errors at the block level can become tedious. A more convenient approach may be to just handle the final outcome of the dataflow network, in the same way we often put a try/catch around a block of sequential processing. When linking blocks together, the setting of the PropagateCompletion flag as part of the DataflowLinkOptions will not only propagate successful completion but also propagate errors. Listing 10-20 implements a two-block network, where the error originates in the first block but it is the Wait on the second block that receives the error.

Listing 10-20. Propagating Errors

```
private static void Main(string[] args)
{
    var divideBlock = new TransformBlock<Tuple<int, int>, int>(
                            input => input.Item1 / input.Item2);
    var printingBlock = new ActionBlock<int>((Action<int>)Console.WriteLine);

    divideBlock.LinkTo(printingBlock, new DataflowLinkOptions() { PropagateCompletion = true });
```

```
divideBlock.Post(Tuple.Create(10, 5));
divideBlock.Post(Tuple.Create(20, 4));
divideBlock.Post(Tuple.Create(10, 0));
divideBlock.Post(Tuple.Create(10, 2));

divideBlock.Complete();

try
{
    printingBlock.Completion.Wait();
}
catch (AggregateException errors)
{
  foreach (Exception error in errors.Flatten().InnerExceptions)
  {
    Console.WriteLine("Divide block failed Reason:{0}", error.Message);
  }
}
}
```

Error handling is a fundamental part of any application, and dataflow networks are no exception to this rule. When building a dataflow network, consider where to place the error handling.

- If the exception can be handled internally, keeping the dataflow network integrity intact, do so.

- If the exception implies the dataflow network integrity is now compromised, consider handling the exception externally, via a continuation.

- Propagating completion often simplifies exception handling, allowing a single piece of error-handling logic.

Ignoring error handling can easily result in a dataflow network that sits idle, not receiving any new messages—a nightmare to debug.

Cancellation

You have seen that dataflow networks can be asked to complete by stating no further inputs will be supplied to the block. The block will still continue running while it has more queued work to process and has not entered a Faulted state. If you then wait on the block, you can be confident that all requests have been successfully acted upon. Waiting for the network to fully process all outstanding items may not be completely desirable. A quicker form of termination may be required; obviously simply ending the process would be one such technique, potentially leaving external resources in an inconsistent state (e.g., an XML file not closed off correctly). A halfway point between fully completing all requests and ending abruptly is to make use of TPL's CancellationTokenSource and CancellationToken.

When a block is created, it can be supplied with a CancellationToken. This token is observed by the block to determine if the block should cease receiving, acting on, or producing values. Listing 10-21 creates a block and associates a CancellationToken with the block. The block is then posted three items; the processing of each item takes 1 second. If at any time the Enter key is pressed while these items are being processed, the main thread calls cts.Cancel(), thus requesting the block to cancel. If the block has not already completed all the enqueued requests, the block will end in a canceled state.

Listing 10-21. Cancelling a Block

```
private static void Main(string[] args)
{
    CancellationTokenSource cts = new CancellationTokenSource();

    var slowAction = new ActionBlock<int>( (Action<int>) (
        i =>
            {
                Console.WriteLine("{0}:Started",i);
                Thread.Sleep(1000);
                Console.WriteLine("{0}:Done", i);
        }),
            new ExecutionDataflowBlockOptions() { CancellationToken = cts.Token} );

    slowAction.Post(1);
    slowAction.Post(2);
    slowAction.Post(3);

    slowAction.Complete();

    slowAction
            .Completion
            .ContinueWith(sab => Console.WriteLine("Blocked finished in state of {0}",
                                                sab.Status));

    Console.ReadLine();
    cts.Cancel();

    Console.ReadLine();
}
```

Running the code in Listing 10-21 and pressing Enter while it is processing the second item produces the output shown in Figure 10-16. Once called, the block does not attempt to process Item 3, but it does complete the processing of Item 2. Thus far the cancellation token is only being observed by the block and not the code running inside the block.

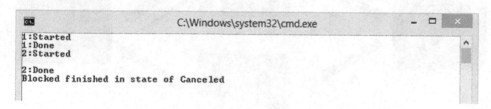

Figure 10-16. *Cancelling while processing Item 2*

The framework can't just simply decide to abort the code, and so the code inside the block also needs to observe the cancellation token when it is safe to abort. Listing 10-22 shows the necessary changes to the block to make it respond to the cancellation, too.

Listing 10-22. Cancelling Block and Code

```
var slowAction = new ActionBlock<int>(
            (Action<int>) (i =>
            {
                Console.WriteLine("{0}:Started",i);
                cts.Token.WaitHandle.WaitOne(1000);
                cts.Token.ThrowIfCancellationRequested();
                Console.WriteLine("{0}:Done", i);
            }),
            new ExecutionDataflowBlockOptions() { CancellationToken = cts.Token} );
```

When multiple blocks are linked together with the PropagateCompletion property set to true, canceling a block will then mark the linked blocks as complete and in a state of RanToCompletion, potentially starting a completion chain reaction through the remaining linked blocks. To cause a more rapid shutdown, each block must share the cancellation token.

Glue Blocks

All the blocks we have looked at so far have required some additional code to fulfill the main purpose of the block. These blocks are sometimes referred to as execution blocks. In addition to these blocks, there are some general-purpose glue blocks that help in connecting various execution blocks together.

Buffer Block

Execution blocks have the possibility to buffer items internally. Earlier you saw that you can control the size of that buffer to create non-greedy blocks, blocks that would not consume items unless they could process them immediately. You can use this technique to provide a form of load balancing as shown in Figure 10-17, in which the Server A block will only accept requests if it is not busy, and likewise Server B.

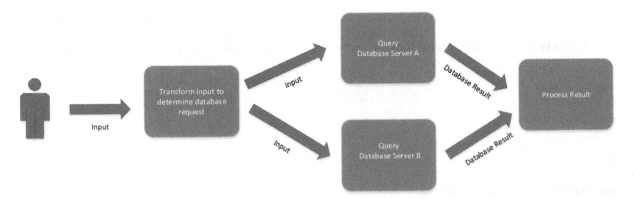

Figure 10-17. *Nonbuffered load balancing*

The problem with the approach in Figure 10-17 is that if both Server A and Server B are busy, the transform feeding these two blocks becomes blocked and cannot process any more inputs. So ideally you want to buffer any output from the transform block and then have either Server A or Server B process the output when they are free.

Listing 10-23 shows a simplified example using the topology shown in Figure 10-18. Running the code will demonstrate that the transfer block completes all its processing very quickly and that the two load-balanced processor blocks eventually consume everything in the buffer.

Listing 10-23. Buffered Load Balanced

```
static void Main(string[] args)
{
    var nonGreedy = new ExecutionDataflowBlockOptions() {BoundedCapacity = 1};
    var flowComplete = new DataflowLinkOptions() {PropagateCompletion = true};

    var processorA = new ActionBlock<int>((Action<int>)( i => Processor("A",i)),nonGreedy);
    var processorB = new ActionBlock<int>((Action<int>)( i => Processor("B",i)),nonGreedy);
    var transform = new TransformBlock<int, int>(i => i*2);
    var buffer = new BufferBlock<int>();

    buffer.LinkTo(processorA,flowComplete);
    buffer.LinkTo(processorB,flowComplete);

    transform.LinkTo(buffer);

    // transform.LinkTo(processorA);
    // transform.LinkTo(processorB);

    for (int i = 0; i < 5; i++)
    {
        transform.Post(i);
    }
    transform.Complete();
    transform.Completion.Wait();
    Console.WriteLine("All work buffered ");

    Console.ReadLine();
}
private static void Processor( string name , int value)
{
    Console.WriteLine("Processor {0}, starting : {1}",name,value);
    Thread.Sleep(1000);
    Console.WriteLine("Processor {0}, done : {1}",name,value);
}
```

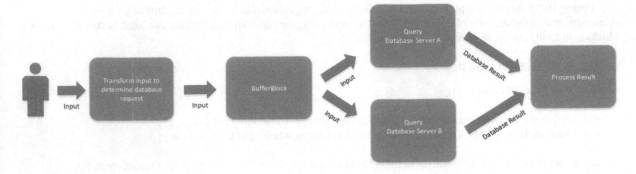

Figure 10-18. *Buffered load balancing*

Modifying Listing 10-23 by uncommenting the `transform.LinkTo(processorA)` or `transform.LinkTo(processorB)` and commenting out `transform.LinkTo(buffer)` will show the effect of load balancing without the buffer. The effect you will observe is that the transform block takes longer to produce all the items as it is waiting for a consumer before publishing the next value.

Buffer blocks are therefore useful when you need a shared buffer across multiple consumers, and each consumer has its own internal constrained buffer. The internal constrained buffer should be set to the same value as the `MaxDegreeOfParallelism` property for the block in order to ensure a non-greedy block.

Batch Block

Thus far you have seen that transform blocks for a given input can produce one to many outputs. The consumer of these outputs needs to receive the output before the transform block can produce a new item. There will be times when for efficiency or convenience the consumer would rather not deal with each individual output, but would prefer a batch of outputs. Classic use cases for this may be to upload results to a web service or update a database; a round trip per result is inefficient, and batching them means paying the latency cost once for all the items in the batch. Another possible use case would be a dataflow network producing values that need to be used to update the UI, but marshaling back onto the UI thread per request may cause the UI to become sluggish. Marshaling less frequently and performing many updates may result in a more fluid UI. Listing 10-24 shows an example of using buffer blocks to provide sampling of a dense dataflow. The main thread is producing a new value every 10 milliseconds, the `averager` action block receives the generated values in batches of 100, and then outputs a sample result by simply averaging all the values. If the batch block was marked as complete, a partial batch is propagated.

Listing 10-24. *Sampling by Averaging 100 Items*

```
public static void Main()
{
  int batchSize = 100;
  var batcher = new BatchBlock<int>(batchSize);

  var averager = new ActionBlock<int[]>(values => Console.WriteLine(values.Average()));

  batcher.LinkTo(averager);
  var rnd = new Random();
  while (true)
```

```
{
    Thread.Sleep(10);
    batcher.Post(rnd.Next(1, 100));
  }
}
```

Listing 10-24 demonstrates batching based on quantity; it may be more desirable to batch on a time interval basis (e.g., for UI update). This can be achieved with the BatchBlock, too, by setting the batch size to int.MaxValue and then calling TriggerBatch method at a given time interval (see Listing 10-25).

Listing 10-25. Sampling by Interval

```
public static void Main()
{
    var batcher = new BatchBlock<int>(int.MaxValue);
    var averager = new ActionBlock<int[]>(values => Console.WriteLine(values.Average()));

    batcher.LinkTo(averager);

    var timer = new Timer(_ => batcher.TriggerBatch(), null,
                          TimeSpan.FromSeconds(1),
                          TimeSpan.FromSeconds(1));

    var rnd = new Random();
    while (true)
    {
      batcher.Post(rnd.Next(1, 100));
    }
}
```

BatchBlocks are useful when processing of individual results is too costly, or there is a need to perform a Many-1 transformation.

Broadcast Block

Broadcast blocks differ from all the other blocks in that they can deliver the same message to multiple targets. This allows the building of networks where many blocks receive the same message, and thus can act on it in parallel. Consider the network in Figure 10-19; here data arrive via some external input and are posted to a BroadcastBlock<T>. The broadcast block can then propagate the input to all the linked blocks. If the block is not busy or it has sufficient buffer (greedy), then the input will be propagated. If the block is busy or has insufficient buffer, the input is not propagated. The two consumers in Figure 10-19 both get to see all the messages. Processing the data inside the Process Data block is very quick compared to writing to disk, and therefore it may be that the disk can't keep up with the input stream. Buffering could be used, but this could easily result in an out of memory exception if the input rate is relentless. Configuring the write data block to be non-greedy means that it writes as much data as it can, and any items that occur while it is busy it will never see. The process data block, on the other hand, is configured to be greedy, so any slight bumps in processing will still result in it receiving all the input. BroadcastBlock<T> therefore doesn't guarantee delivery.

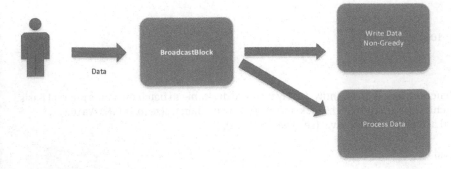

Figure 10-19. *Broadcast block with greedy and non-greedy consumers*

Listing 10-26 shows a simplified code example of Figure 10-19. The key point of interest is around the constructor of the BroadcastBlock<T>. As stated earlier, BroadcastBlock<T> can propagate the same input to many receivers. It may be important to ensure that each receiver, while getting the same data, receives them as a cloned copy. With each receiver getting their own copy this removes any potential mutable shared state issues. The BroadcastBlock<T> takes a function responsible for cloning the value to propagate; in this case you are simply using an identity function, as with a value type the value is always cloned.

Listing 10-26. Greedy and Non-greedy Broadcast Consumers

```
private static void Main(string[] args)
{
    var nonGreedy = new ExecutionDataflowBlockOptions() {BoundedCapacity = 1};
    var greedy = new ExecutionDataflowBlockOptions();

    var source = new BroadcastBlock<int>(i => i);

    var consumeOne = new ActionBlock<int>((Action<int>) ConsumerOne, nonGreedy);
    var consumeTwo = new ActionBlock<int>((Action<int>) ConsumerTwo, greedy);

    source.LinkTo(consumeOne);
    source.LinkTo(consumeTwo);

    for (int j = 0; j < 10; j++)
    {
        source.Post(j);
        Thread.Sleep(50);
    }
    Console.ReadLine();
}

private static void ConsumerTwo(int obj)
{
    Console.WriteLine("Consumer two {0}",obj);
    Thread.Sleep(60);
}
```

```
private static void ConsumerOne(int obj)
{
  Console.WriteLine("Consumer one {0}",obj);
  Thread.Sleep(100);
}
```

Running the code in Listing 10-26 produces the output shown in Figure 10-20. With "Consumer one" taking longer than "Consumer two" to process each request, and configured to be non-greedy, it does not see all requests. "Consumer two" is configured to be greedy and as such will always see all requests. Consider using a BroadcastBlock<T> when many blocks need to act upon a single message, or when live processing is more relevant than historical processing.

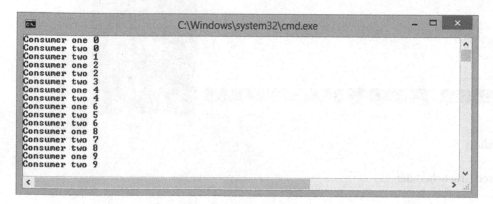

Figure 10-20. Output of greedy and non-greedy broadcast consumers

Joining

In situations where a block requires multiple inputs in order to perform its processing, you can utilize the JoinBlock<T1,T2> or JoinBlock<T1,T2,T3>. Consider the network described in Figure 10-21. Here we have two buffers: one that contains work items, the other network nodes capable of acting on work items. The scheduler's job is to pair up a work item with an available node. Once it has paired up, it passes the paired value as a Tuple<T1,T2> onto the dispatcher who acts on the pair by sending the work item to the node. Once the dispatcher is aware that the node has completed the work item, the node is placed back into the work buffer. Listing 10-27 shows an implementation of such a scheduler using WCF. The key part to note is that when linking up to a JoinBlock<T1,T2>, you don't link up directly to the block but to one of its targets. The JoinBlock then outputs a form of tuple depending on the number of blocks it has been asked to join. The implementation of the dispatcher block that actually invokes the work item is invoking the remote node asynchronously, allowing the dispatcher to immediately process any more work item node pairs. Thus there is very little need to increase the level of parallelism at this point.

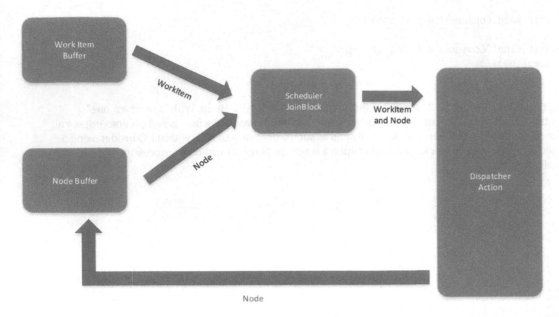

Figure 10-21. *Grid scheduler*

Listing 10-27. WCF-Based Grid Scheduler

```
[ServiceContract]
public interface IGridNode<in T>
{
  [OperationContract]
  Task InvokeAsync(T workItem);
}

public class GridDispatcher<T>
{
  private BufferBlock<T> workItems = new BufferBlock<T>();
  private BufferBlock<Uri> nodes = new BufferBlock<Uri>();
  private JoinBlock<Uri, T> scheduler = new JoinBlock<Uri, T>();

  private ActionBlock<Tuple<Uri, T>> dispatcher;

  public GridDispatcher(IGridNode<T> localService )
  {
    dispatcher  = new ActionBlock<Tuple<Uri, T>>((Action<Tuple<Uri, T>>) Dispatch);

    workItems.LinkTo(scheduler.Target2);
    nodes.LinkTo(scheduler.Target1);

    scheduler.LinkTo(dispatcher);
  }
```

```
public void RegisterNode(Uri uri)
{
    nodes.Post(uri);
}

public void SubmitWork(T workItem)
{
    workItems.Post(workItem);
}

private void Dispatch(Tuple<Uri, T> nodeAndWorkItemPair)
{
    var cf = new ChannelFactory<IGridNode<T>>(new NetTcpBinding(),
                        new EndpointAddress(nodeAndWorkItemPair.Item1));

    IGridNode<T> proxy = cf.CreateChannel();
    proxy.InvokeAsync(nodeAndWorkItemPair.Item2)
        .ContinueWith(t =>
            {
                ((IClientChannel)proxy).Close();
                nodes.Post(nodeAndWorkItemPair.Item1);
            });
}
}
```

Greedy and Non-greedy Joining

The code in Listing 10-27 will only send a work item to a node when it is not busy and there are work items to act upon. Let us now modify the network to allow the scheduler node to also act upon work locally. Figure 10-22 shows what this new network looks like; you now have two blocks feeding off the work items buffer. The local dispatcher executes the work item on the local node; this does not need to go via WCF. The local dispatcher can have MaxDegreeOfParallelism configured based on the number of cores you wish to utilize. Simply implementing a new ActionBlock<T> would by default be greedy, so this would not be desirable behavior. The new ActionBlock<T> needs to be configured so that it only concurrently consumes as many work items as it has MaxDegreeOfParallelism. Unfortunately that is not the only change that will be required—the JoinBlock<T1,T2> also has to have its greediness configured. By default the join block will consume each of its sources one by one, and when it has a request from all sources it propagates the tuple. This therefore creates a problem with the network in Figure 10-22, because in the case where there are no nodes available the JoinBlock<T1,T2> will still consume work items, preventing the local dispatcher of consuming when it is available. To prevent this behavior you need to configure the JoinBlock<T1,T2> so that it only consumes items when all the sources have an item available.

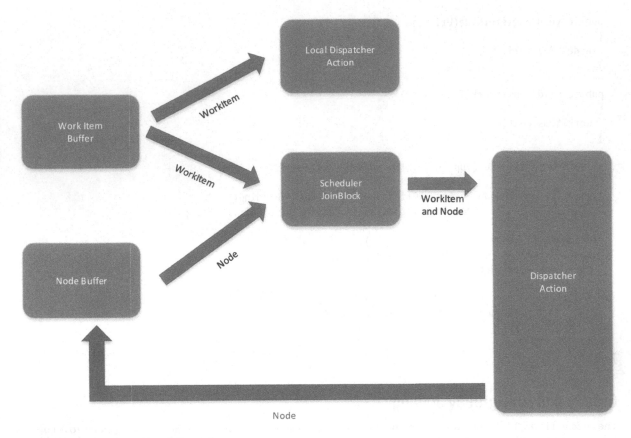

Figure 10-22. *Node and local dispatcher*

The code in Listing 10-28 contains a partial rework of the GridDispatcher<T> class presented in Listing 10-27, but now with the local dispatcher and the JoinBlock<T,T2> configured to be non-greedy.

Listing 10-28. Node and Local Dispatcher

```
public class GridDispatcher<T>
{
    private BufferBlock<T> workItems = new BufferBlock<T>();
    private BufferBlock<Uri> nodes = new BufferBlock<Uri>();
    private JoinBlock<Uri, T> scheduler = new JoinBlock<Uri, T>(
                new GroupingDataflowBlockOptions() { Greedy = false});

    private ActionBlock<Tuple<Uri, T>> dispatcher;
    private ActionBlock<T> localDispatcher;

    public GridDispatcher(IGridNode<T> localService )
    {
        localDispatcher = new ActionBlock<T>(wi =>
            {
                Console.WriteLine("Executing Locally");
                return localService.InvokeAsync(wi);
            },
```

```
new ExecutionDataflowBlockOptions()
        { BoundedCapacity = 2,MaxDegreeOfParallelism = 2});

dispatcher  = new ActionBlock<Tuple<Uri, T>>((Action<Tuple<Uri, T>>) Dispatch);

workItems.LinkTo(localDispatcher);

nodes.LinkTo(scheduler.Target1);
workItems.LinkTo(scheduler.Target2);


scheduler.LinkTo(dispatcher);
    }
    . . .
}
```

While this solution could have been built with two blocking concurrent queues and some long-running tasks, the dataflow solution is far more elegant, removing the need to concern yourself with having idle threads, or considering which queue to consume first. Consider using join blocks when multiple resources are required in order to perform the next process step. By configuring the blocks to be non-greedy, resources can be efficiently shared by multiple consumers.

Asynchronous Blocks

ActionBlock, TransformBlock, and TransformManyBlock all require additional code to perform the core function of the block. The code for the block is executed inside one or many tasks, and during its execution the code may very well need to execute long-running operations such as database queries or web service calls. If these interactions take the form of blocking calls it could be considered an abuse of the thread. An example of such an abuse is Listing 10-29. The code attempts to determine which web sites from a set of known web sites contain the word *happy* on their home page. Multiple web sites can be accessed in parallel, so MaxDegreesOfParallelism is set to 4. The abuse in this code comes in the form of blocking while trying to download the web page content. While the code is blocked waiting for the web server to respond, the thread is sitting idle, when it potentially could have been put to other uses inside the process.

Listing 10-29. Blocking Block

```
public static void Main()
{
   string[] urls = new string[] {
     "http://www.bbc.co.uk",
     "http://www.cia.gov",
     "http://www.theregister.co.uk"
   };

  var happySites = new List<string>();
  var isHappySiteBlock = new TransformBlock<string, Tuple<string, bool>>(
              (Func<string, Tuple<string, bool>>) IsHappy,
              new ExecutionDataflowBlockOptions() { MaxDegreeOfParallelism = 4 }
              );
```

```
var addToHappySitesBlock = new ActionBlock<Tuple<string, bool>>(
              (Action<Tuple<string, bool>>) (tuple => happySites.Add(tuple.Item1)));

isHappySiteBlock.LinkTo(addToHappySitesBlock,
                       new DataflowLinkOptions() {PropagateCompletion = true},
                       tuple => tuple.Item2);

// non happy sites just ignored
isHappySiteBlock.LinkTo(DataflowBlock.NullTarget<Tuple<string, bool>>());

foreach (string url in urls)
{
    isHappySiteBlock.Post(url);
}
isHappySiteBlock.Complete();

addToHappySitesBlock.Completion.Wait();
happySites.ForEach(Console.WriteLine);
}

private static Tuple<string,bool> IsHappy(string url)
{
  using(var client = new WebClient())
  {
   // Blocking call, thread idle waiting for response
   string content = client.DownloadString(url);
   return Tuple.Create(url,content.ToLower().Contains("happy"));
  }
}
```

Ideally you would like the isHappyBlock to execute code up to the point of performing the I/O and then yield, executing again once the I/O has completed. To this end the executing code blocks can accept code that returns a Task or Task<T> in the case of a transform blocks. The code in Listing 10-30 shows a refactored version that now returns a Task<T>, allowing the method thread to be reused.

Listing 10-30. Asynchronous Code Block

```
var isHappySiteBlock = new TransformBlock<string, Tuple<string, bool>>(
                       (Func<string, Task<Tuple<string, bool>>>) IsHappyAsync,
                         new ExecutionDataflowBlockOptions() {MaxDegreeOfParallelism = 4});
. . .
private static  Task<Tuple<string, bool>> IsHappyAsync(string url)
{
   var client = new WebClient();

   // Execute asynchronous IO with a continuation
   return client.DownloadStringTaskAsync(url)
              .ContinueWith(dt =>
              {
                  string content = dt.Result;
                  return Tuple.Create(url, content.ToLower().Contains("happy"));
              });
}
```

■ **Note**   Just as with a synchronous code block, the block does not consider an asynchronous code block to have completed until the task it returns has completed, preserving the behavior of processing only `MaxDegreeOfParallelism` requests at a time per block.

This gets a load easier in C# 5 with `async` and `await`. Listing 10-31 shows the refactored code utilizing `async` and `await`.

Listing 10-31. Simpler Asynchronous Code Block Using `async` and `await`

```
private static async  Task<Tuple<string, bool>> IsHappyAsync(string url)
{
  using (var client = new WebClient())
  {
    string content = await client.DownloadStringTaskAsync(url);
    return Tuple.Create(url, content.ToLower().Contains("happy"));
  }
}
```

Asynchronous code blocks allow dataflow execution blocks to utilize threads efficiently using the simple programming model of `async` and `await`.

Summary

Dataflow blocks present an alternative approach to classical multithreaded programming. In lots of ways the structure of the code is closer to the real world, where component parts of an overall system are generally autonomous. The fact that each piece of autonomous execution can maintain its own state greatly simplifies the complexity of thread safety, keeping the code simple and elegant. The declarative nature of how the networks are put together further enhances the ability to visualize and maintain the code. Chapter 15 will utilize a debugger visualizer to visualize the topology and state of a live dataflow network. Also, in Chapter 14 we will introduce the Reactive Framework, which makes it a breeze to turn the output of a TPL Dataflow network into an observable event stream.

CHAPTER 11

■ ■ ■

Parallel Programming

No book on asynchronous programming would be complete without discussing how to improve the performance of your computationally intensive algorithms. Back in March 2005, Herb Sutter, who works for Microsoft, coined the phrase "The free lunch is over," and he wasn't referring to the Microsoft canteen. He was referring to the fact that prior to that date, when engineers were faced with the need to make their code run faster, they had two choices. They could profile and optimize the code to squeeze a bit more out of the CPU, or just wait a few months and Intel would produce a new, faster CPU. The latter was known as the "free lunch," as it didn't require engineering effort. Around March 2005, the computer industry, faced with the need to keep delivering faster and faster computational units, and the fact that clock speeds couldn't keep growing at historical rates, made the design decision to add more cores. While more cores offer the possibility of greater throughput, single-threaded applications won't run any faster on multicore systems, unlike CPUs of the past. Making the code run faster now requires engineering effort. Algorithms have to be rewritten to spread the work across multiple cores; hence "the free lunch is over."

Traditionally, targeting multicore meant taking readable code and transforming it into a far more complex and hard-to-maintain version utilizing the traditional threading APIs. In an effort to restore the free lunch, there has been a long-term goal of allowing parallelism to be expressed more naturally through the use of constructs like ParallelFor. This was the original goal behind TPL: if parallel programming is to be adopted, it needs to be as easy as conventional programming.

Consider the following piece of code:

```
int total = SumX() + SumY() + SumZ();
```

This single line of code currently executes synchronously, computing each individual sum in turn, combining each result as it goes. If the sum methods don't interfere with each other in any way—in other words they are completely independent of each other—then you could execute them at the same time. Listing 11-1 shows an asynchronous implementation using pre-TPL-like code. This implementation is a far cry from the original synchronous code.

Listing 11-1. Pre-TPL Asynchronous Compute

```
Func<int> sumX = SumX;
Func<int> sumY = SumY;
Func<int> sumZ = SumZ;

IAsyncResult sumXAsyncResult = sumX.BeginInvoke(null, null);
IAsyncResult sumYAsyncResult = sumY.BeginInvoke(null, null);
IAsyncResult sumZAsyncResult = sumZ.BeginInvoke(null, null);

int total = sumX.EndInvoke(sumXAsyncResult) +
            sumY.EndInvoke(sumYAsyncResult) +
            sumZ.EndInvoke(sumZAsyncResult);
```

One of the goals of TPL was to remove this complexity, allowing parallelism to be expressed while keeping the overall structure of the code the same as the synchronous version. For this example it can be achieved just by using the Task API that we have already discussed, as shown in Listing 11-2. In this example, while the code has changed to take advantage of TPL, it has not changed completely—the general structure is retained and arguably has similar levels of readability to that of the synchronous code.

Listing 11-2. TPL-Based Asynchronous Compute

```
Task<int> sumX = Task.Factory.StartNew<int>(SumX);
Task<int> sumY = Task.Factory.StartNew<int>(SumY);
Task<int> sumZ = Task.Factory.StartNew<int>(SumZ);

int total = sumX.Result + sumY.Result + sumZ.Result;
```

While this summing algorithm is extremely simple, it does demonstrate that the old-style APIs are not ideal for expressing even this most simple form of parallelism, known as Fork and Join. In this chapter we will examine the features of TPL that enable the parallelization of algorithms while keeping the algorithm as close as possible to its simple synchronous origins—after all, who doesn't enjoy a free lunch? These features are commonly known as Parallel Framework Extensions (Pfx).

What Is Driving the Need for Parallelism?

Since the start of the computer age we have strived to get solutions to our problems with faster and faster response times. Real-time problems require an answer in a given period of time from when the question is posed, otherwise the answer is useless. Airplane flight control would be one obvious example; another may be voice recognition. A voice recognition system in a car that takes 5 minutes to 100 percent accurately interpret the command is far worse than one that gets it 90 percent right in 2 seconds. Throwing multiple cores at the perfect algorithm will one day result in a 2-second response with 100% accuracy.

Achieving better and better results often requires processing larger and larger datasets. After all, we can produce photorealistic graphics given sufficient rendering time. One day there may be enough parallel computing power inside a games console to do just that. So in all these cases it is not that we can't solve the problems; we just need to do it faster and with better results, which often requires larger volumes of data.

Coarse- and Fine-Grained Parallelism

There are various ways to distinguish types of parallel programs. One is to describe them as coarse grained or fine grained. Coarse-grained parallelism refers to problems where a single thread handles a request from start to finish, and that parallelism is achieved by the fact that many independent requests are being processed in parallel, thus consuming multiple threads. Examples of coarse-grained parallelism would be a web server or a payroll application. This type of parallelism is relatively easy to implement by mapping each request onto a thread. Each thread then provides a programming model, the same as synchronous programming of old. Coarse-grained parallelism is often found on the server, since servers have plenty of opportunity to handle multiple independent requests. On the client side, things are a little different—there is after all just one user and there are only so many independent things a single user will wish to do at any moment in time.

Consider Microsoft Word. While it is running it is performing multiple tasks:

- UI interaction
- layout
- spell checking

- grammar checking
- autosaving
- printing

We could assign each of these activities its own thread, and if we have six or more cores, maybe the single-user-based task of word processing could utilize all our cores, keeping the application responsive and delivering spelling and grammar suggestions in real time. Six to eight cores on a desktop around the year 2008 would have seemed a powerful machine; the future suggests we will more likely have 200+ cores per desktop. Even if Microsoft reinstated Clippy, it is hard to see how even MS Word could consume that many cores with each core focused on an independent task such as spell checking. To cope with the ever-increasing number of cores on the client, a different approach needs to be considered. One such approach is fine-grained parallelism.

Fine-grained parallelism requires taking each coarse-grained activity and further dividing it into many smaller tasks. Each of these smaller tasks executes in parallel, collaborating with one another where necessary to perform the overall task. It is this form of parallelism that often requires more effort and leads to algorithms becoming extremely complex. The TPL constructs that we will investigate throughout this chapter will attempt to keep the structure of the algorithm intact while supporting fine-grained parallelism.

Task and Data-Based Parallelism

A further way to categorize parallelism is by Task and Data. Task-based parallelism is where an algorithm is broken down into a series of discrete tasks, with each task running a logically different part of the algorithm. Our initial example of calculating a total in Listing 11-2 would be one such example. A car production line would be another example of Task-based parallelism; each stage of the line is performing a different role. Data parallelism, on the other hand, is the same logical code executing in parallel but with a different data set. Weather forecasting algorithms often use such techniques to break down the globe into a series of regions, and each processing element works on its own piece for a given interval.

Is It Worth Trying to Parallelize Everything?

First you have to decide: can something be parallelized? Consider the algorithm to calculate Fibonacci numbers (1, 1, 2, 3, 5, 8, 13, 21, etc.). The next number in the sequence is the sum of the previous two numbers; therefore, in order to calculate the next number you must have already calculated the previous two. This algorithm is inherently sequential, and therefore as much as you may try, it can't be parallelized. There are many other algorithms or parts of algorithms that have this characteristic. Consider the process of making a cup of tea:

1. Fetch the cups
2. Fetch the milk
3. Put the tea in the pot
4. Fill the kettle and switch it on
5. Wait for kettle to boil, then pour water into pot
6. Wait for tea to brew
7. Pour tea into cups, and add milk if required

Clearly we can't parallelize all these steps, since pouring the water while fetching the milk and cups is clearly not going to work. But we can certainly improve on these steps. The boiling of the kettle is one of the longest parts of the process and has no dependency on anything else, so we should do that first. Assuming that takes longer than fetching the cups and milk and putting tea in the pot, we will have reduced the time taken to brew the cup of tea:

1. Fill the kettle and switch it on

2. Fetch the cups

3. Fetch the milk

4. Put tea in pot

5. Wait for kettle to boil

6. Wait for tea to brew

7. Pour tea into cups, and add milk if required

My mother-in-law is a tea-aholic and is always looking for new ways to brew her tea even faster without sacrificing the taste—can we help? We have identified that the boiling the water is one of the most costly parts of the process and we will undoubtedly be blocked in waiting for it to complete. Focusing on parallelizing this part of the process may well yield the best return on effort. Understanding how much of an algorithm can be parallelized is important, since it will dictate what is the maximum potential speedup. This was formalized by Amdahl as follows:

The speedup of a program using multiple processors in parallel computing is limited by the sequential fraction of the program. For example, if 95% of the program can be parallelized, the theoretical maximum speedup using parallel computing would be 20×, no matter how many processors are used.

Source Wikipedia `http://en.wikipedia.org/wiki/Amdahl's_law`

This is known as Amdahl's law. Even after considering Amdahl's law, focusing on boiling the water seems like a good plan. If we were to use two kettles, then we should be able to halve the boil time. In fact, what about having 50 kettles—will that make it even faster? In theory, yes; in practice, possibly not. Imagine the scene: fetching and filling 50 kettles, plugging them in, taking them in turns to fill each one up, switching it on, and, once boiling, fetching each one in turn to pour on the tea. The use of 50 kettles is adding a lot more extra work above and beyond our original single-kettle solution—this is going to consume additional time that may outweigh the benefit of boiling in parallel. Perhaps if we had 50 extra pairs of hands and 50 extra taps it might help, but we would still need to coordinate boiling the water for the tea. The bottom line is that the coordination of running code in parallel has a cost; thus the parallel version of any algorithm is going to require more code to run in order to complete the task. Therefore, when throwing two CPUs at a problem, don't expect it to become twice as quick.

You now have a good understanding of the need to parallelize and what can and can't be parallelized. All that is left now is how to parallelize.

Before You Parallelize

One reason for parallelizing an algorithm is to produce a faster result than would be possible if you just used one core. If the parallel version is slower than a single core, other than heating up the room on a cold day this would be regarded as a failure. Unless you have implemented the best single-core implementation of the algorithm first, you will have no idea when you run the code if it is indeed worth that extra energy and complexity. The very nature of parallel programming is that it is asynchronous in nature, and as such every time you run the algorithm there is the possibility for race conditions, affecting the integrity of the overall result. So in the same way that having parallel code that takes longer than a single core is wrong, it is just as wrong to have a faster parallel version that produces wrong results. *Therefore, before you parallelize any algorithm, write the best single-threaded version you can first—this will act as a benchmark for your parallel implementations.*

Parallel Class

One of the main entry points to implementing parallel functionality using TPL is the System.Threading.Tasks. Parallel class. There are three static methods on this class, with the main focus on loops:

- Parallel.Invoke
- Parallel.For
- Parallel.ForEach

These methods provide a high-level abstraction of the world of parallel programming, allowing algorithms to continue to resemble a familiar synchronous structure. All these methods implement the Fork/Join pattern: when one of these methods is invoked, it will farm out work to multiple TPL tasks and then only complete on the calling thread once all tasks have completed.

A small amount of influence and control is possible with all these methods via a class called ParallelOptions. ParallelOptions allows you to set the following:

- Max number of tasks to be used
- Cancellation token
- Task Scheduler to use

Max number of tasks is useful if you wish to limit the number of tasks that can be used by the framework for a given parallel invocation, and thus most likely influence the number of cores that will be used. With all the Parallel methods, the runtime needs to make a guess at the number of tasks to use for a given parallel invocation. Often this guess is refined if the parallel invocation executes for a reasonable amount of time, as is often the case of parallel loops. If you are aware of the *exact* hardware you are running on, then in some situations it can be beneficial to set the MaxNumberOfTasks.

CancellationToken allows for external control over early termination of the parallel invocation. Once the supplied cancellation token is signaled, the parallel invocation will not create any more tasks. Once all created tasks have completed, the parallel invocation will return; if it did not successfully complete the parallel invocation due to the effect of cancellation, it will throw an OperationCancelledException.

The Task Scheduler option allows you to define the task scheduler to use for each of the tasks created by the parallel invocation. This allows you to provide your own scheduler and thus influence where and when each task produced by the parallel invocation will run. Otherwise the default scheduler will be used.

Parallel.Invoke

The Invoke method on the parallel class provides the ability to launch multiple blocks of code to run in parallel and, once all are done continue the classic Fork and Join. Listing 11-3 shows a reworked version of our SumX, SumY, and SumZ example. The Invoke method takes an array of the Action delegate (or a variable number of Action delegates, which the compiler turns into an array of Action delegates).

Listing 11-3. Parallel.Invoke

```
int sumX = 0;
int sumY = 0;
int sumZ = 0;
```

```
// Executes SumX, SumY and SumZ in parallel
Parallel.Invoke(
    () => sumX = SumX(),
    () => sumY = SumY(),
    () => sumZ = SumZ()
);

// SumX,SumY and SumZ all complete

 int total = sumX + sumY + sumZ;
```

Is this approach radically different than just explicitly creating the tasks and then combing the results? Probably not, but it does feel a little closer to how the sequential might have originally looked.

One concern regarding Parallel.Invoke is that it only returns when all its supplied actions have completed. If any one of those actions somehow enters an infinite wait, then the Parallel.Invoke will wait forever, something you would wish to avoid. There is no option to pass a timeout to Parallel.Invoke but you could use a CancellationToken instead. A first attempt might look something like the code in Listing 11-4.

Listing 11-4. First Attmept at Canceling a Parallel.Invoke

```
int sumX = 0;
int sumY = 0;
int sumZ = 0;

CancellationTokenSource cts = new CancellationTokenSource();
cts.CancelAfter(2000);

Parallel.Invoke ( new ParallelOptions() { CancellationToken = cts.Token},
    () => sumX = SumX(),
    () => sumY = SumY(),
    () => sumZ = SumZ()
);

  int total = sumX + sumY + sumZ;
```

This approach will almost certainly not work if one of those methods ends up waiting forever. The only part of the code that is cancellation aware is the Parallel.Invoke method. Once the cancellation has been signaled, it knows not to create any new tasks, but it can't abort the already spawned tasks. All it can do is wait for the already spawned tasks to complete and, being the patient soul it is, that could be forever. To make this work you need to flow the cancellation token into the various actions and ensure that they are proactive in polling the cancellation token, too, as shown in Listing 11-5.

Listing 11-5. Parallel.Invoke with More Reliable Cancellation

```
{
    Parallel.Invoke(new ParallelOptions() {CancellationToken = cts.Token},
        () => sumX = SumX(cts.Token),
        () => sumY = SumY(cts.Token),
        () => sumZ = SumZ(cts.Token)
    );

    int total = sumX + sumY + sumZ;


}
```

```
catch (OperationCanceledException operationCanceled)
{
    Console.WriteLine("Cancelled");
}
```

If any unhandled exception propagates from any of the actions it is caught and held until all the other actions have completed, and the exception is re-thrown along with any other exceptions from other actions as part of an AggregateException. Since you don't get access to the underlying Task objects for a given action, there is no way to know which action produced which exception (see Listing 11-6).

Listing 11-6. Parallel.Invoke Error Handling

```
try
{
    Parallel.Invoke( new ParallelOptions() { CancellationToken = cts.Token },
        () => { throw new Exception("Boom!"); },
        () => sumY = SumY(cts.Token),
        () => sumZ = SumZ(cts.Token)
        );

    int total = sumX + sumY + sumZ;
}
catch (OperationCanceledException operationCanceled)
{
    Console.WriteLine("Cancelled");
}
catch (AggregateException errors)
{
    foreach (Exception error in errors.Flatten().InnerExceptions)
    {
        Console.WriteLine(error.Message);
    }
}
```

Parallel.Invoke is therefore a relatively easy way to spawn off multiple parallel actions, wait for them all to complete, and then proceed. But be aware that methods that can wait forever, and have a tendency to one day do just that. By abstracting away the underlying Task API, your code is simpler, but you do lose the ability to easily identify which action failed.

Parallel Loops

As mentioned earlier, when wishing to parallelize an algorithm you should consider Amdahl's law and decide which parts of the algorithm justify the effort of parallelism. When examining algorithms, we often find that loops typically offer the best opportunity for parallelism, since they can execute a relatively small body of code tens of thousands of times, thus creating a lot of computation—something worth speeding up. Just because a loop has a lot of computation doesn't necessary mean it is a candidate for parallelizing. A single threaded loop executes in a set order, while a parallel loop works by farming out ranges of the loop to different cores, with each core executing its range in parallel with the other cores. This has the effect of processing the loop out of order. Does that matter? For some algorithms, no, but for others the order does matters. Listing 11-7 is an example of one such loop. This algorithm for producing Fibonacci numbers (as discussed earlier) cannot be parallelized. If the order does matter, the loop is not a candidate for parallelization.

Listing 11-7. Example of Order-Sensitive Loop

```
long prev = 0;
long prevPrev = 0;
long current = 1;

for (int nFib = 0; nFib < 200; nFib++)
{
    Console.WriteLine(current);

    prevPrev = prev;
    prev = current;

    current = prev + prevPrev;
}
```

If the loop you do wish to parallelize is not order sensitive, then TPL provides two forms of loop parallelization: Parallel.For and Parallel.ForEach, the parallel versions of the C# for and foreach keywords, respectively.

Parallel.For

Listing 11-8 shows a normal C# loop, which when executed prints out all values from 0 to 19 inclusive. If the goal of this loop is to simply output all values from 0 to 19 inclusive and you don't care about the order, then you can parallelize it.

Listing 11-8. Regular C# Loop

```
for( int i = 0 ; i < 20 ; i++ )
{
  Console.WriteLine(i);
}
```

To parallelize this loop, remove the use of the C# for statement and replace it with a call to Parallel.For. In this example Parallel.For takes the start and end values for the loop along with an Action<int> delegate representing the body of the loop. The code in Listing 11-9 shows such an implementation; when executed it will display all the values between 0 and 19 inclusive, but each time you run it you may well see varying orders. Even a program as simple as this exposes chaotic behavior, as shown in Figure 11-1.

Listing 11-9. Simple Parallel.For Loop

```
Parallel.For(0,20,i =>
{
  Console.WriteLine(i);
} );
```

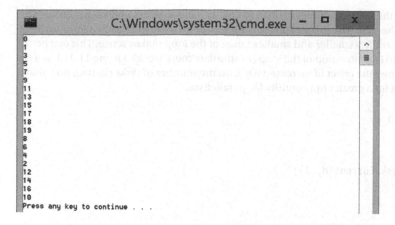

Figure 11-1. *One possible outcome of Listing 11-9*

The refactored code still resembles the original single-core implementation. The use of lambdas/anonymous methods has allowed you to express the loop body inline, thus resembling the original structure, and hopefully maintaining its readability.

All of the `Parallel.XXX` methods utilize TPL tasks to execute pieces of work in parallel. One obvious mapping in the case of loops would be to create as many tasks as there are loop iterations, so in the case of Listing 11-9, it would create 20 tasks. If you have at least 20 cores this may well be a good idea, but if you only have 4, not a great idea. The effort required to create a task is not free—it adds additional workload above and beyond the single-core implementation. Therefore it makes sense to create many tasks but to allow many tasks to do many iterations. Listing 11-10 has a modified parallel loop that is printing out the loop index and also the task ID associated with that loop iteration. As you can see from Figure 11-2, many tasks are involved in producing the final result, but not 20.

Listing 11-10. `Parallel.For` and Associated Tasks

```
Parallel.For(0, 20, i =>
{
    Console.WriteLine("{0} : {1}",Task.CurrentId,i);
});
```

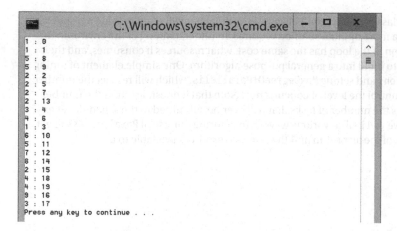

Figure 11-2. *Parallel loop showing task ID and iteration association*

241

The Parallel.For method can't know the perfect number of tasks to create; it has to guess and keep adjusting its guess based on observed throughput of the loop. The longer and longer a task takes to process each iteration, the more likely it is that creating more tasks to handle a smaller and smaller range of the loop makes sense. This can be illustrated by adding a Thread.SpinWait into each iteration of the loop (to simulate more work). Listing 11-11 has a bit more work per iteration, and Figure 11-3 shows the effect of increased work on the number of tasks created, now that a lot more tasks have been created, allowing for a greater opportunity for parallelism.

Listing 11-11. A Bit More Work per Iteration

```
Parallel.For(0, 20, i =>
{
    Console.WriteLine("{0} : {1}", Task.CurrentId, i);
    Thread.SpinWait(100000000);
});
```

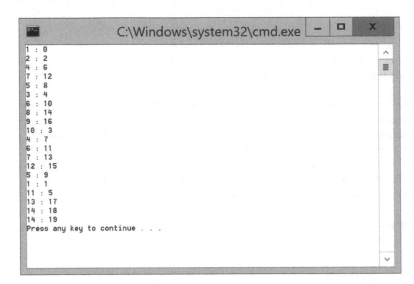

Figure 11-3. *The effect of increased work on the number of tasks created*

This approach taken by the Parallel class certainly won't always be optimal but will often provide a respectable speedup (a moderate free lunch). To reach a more optimal solution requires an understanding of the environment the code is running in, whether each iteration of the loop has the same cost, what resources it consumes, and their availability. This level of knowledge is hard to build into a general purpose algorithm. One simple element of tuning you can provide is stating via ParallelOptions and setting MaxDegreeOfParallelis, which will restrict the number of tasks active at any one time, and hence control the level of concurrency. Note that it doesn't restrict the number of tasks that will be created, but rather limits the number of tasks that will ever be submitted to the scheduler at any moment of time. Throughout this chapter we will look at various ways of refactoring our use of Parallel.XXX to get better performance through our knowledge of the algorithm and the process resources available to us.

Beyond the Trade Show Demos

The code we have looked at so far reassembles the typical trade show demos of Pfx. These examples give you a feeling that parallelization is now really easy and being a threading guru is not essential. Unfortunately the reality of parallelization is somewhat removed from these simple Thread.Sleep or Thread.SpinWait examples, and in this part of the chapter we will look at the more typical issues involved with parallel loops.

For now let us play along with the hope that parallelization is easy. Consider the code in Listing 11-12, which calculates the value of pi (we know, not a typical example for your average workplace, but it is simple enough to highlight a lot of the issues). The algorithm used to calculate pi is a series of summations, and since summing a series in any order produces the same result, this loop does not depend on order and therefore is a candidate for parallelization. Before we start parallelizing this piece of code, we must first benchmark it to obtain the time taken to run on a single core and obtain the expected result. Calling CalculatePi(1000000000) in Listing 11-12 on a single core produce the following result:-

```
Time Taken: 01.9607748 seconds Result: 3.14159265158926
```

Listing 11-12. Calculating Pi

```
// 4 * ( -1.0 / 3.0 + 1.0/5.0 - 1.0/7.0 + 1.0/9.0 - 1.0/11.0 ... )
private static double CalculatePi(int iterations)
{
    double pi = 1;
    double multiplier = -1;
    for (int i = 3; i < iterations; i+=2)
    {
        pi += 1.0/(double) i*multiplier;
        multiplier *= -1;
    }

    return pi*4.0;
}
```

An initial first cut at parallelizing Listing 11-12 could be to simply replace the use of a regular for with a Parallel.For. There is, however, one initial obstacle in your way: the Parallel.For loop counter can only be a long or an int and can only be incremented by 1. For this loop you need it to increment by 2, but this is software so you can work around this hiccup. Listing 11-13 represents an initial attempt. On running this code you will receive the following results:

```
Time Taken: 05.1148 seconds Result: 3.13983501709191
```

Listing 11-13. First Cut Parallel Pi

```
private static double ParallelCalculatePi(int iterations)
{
    double pi = 1;
    double multiplier = -1;
    Parallel.For(0, (iterations - 3)/2, loopIndex =>
```

```
    {
        int i = 3 + loopIndex*2;
        pi += 1.0/(double) i*multiplier;
        multiplier *= -1;
    });

    return pi * 4.0;
}
```

This is hardly the result we had hoped for—perhaps the cores weren't working hard enough—but as you can see from Figure 11-4, the cores were pegged at 100 percent CPU.

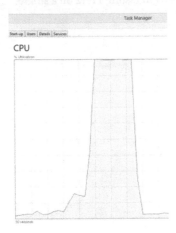

Figure 11-4. *CPU utilization when running* `Parallel.For`

Of a greater concern is that you have the wrong result, and multicore sucks. So why the wrong result? Well, `Parallel.For` isn't magic. Sure, it is providing an abstraction over the Task API, but fundamentally it is multithreaded programming. In the case of `Parallel.For` it is executing the body of the loop in parallel by utilizing multiple tasks. The loop body is reading and updating shared variables non-atomically (`multiplier` and `pi`), and therefore this is a problem. In the past we have resorted to synchronization primitives in order to update safely; this will further increase the time taken, which is already slower than the single-threaded version.

The use of shared variables is also having an impact on the performance. Each core has its own L1 cache, and in an ideal world, when a method executes it likes to have all its variables already inside that cache. The cache memory is far faster than main memory. If multiple cores are updating the same variable, then clearly they will invalidate one another's private caches. There is cache coherency logic on the machine to ensure that the other cores get told to eject their cached value, resulting in their having to rebuild the cached entry. Having to rebuild your cache slows things down; by contrast, the single-core version can potentially run 100 percent of the time inside the cache.

CACHE LINES

The CPU caches don't simply cache discrete values; they cache blocks of memory, typically 256-byte chunks. If any one value inside that 256-byte chunk gets modified, the whole line needs to be rebuilt. Therefore two threads incrementing two different variables could have the same effect on performance as incrementing the same variable—although they won't suffer from corruption.

To solve this problem we need each task involved in the calculation of pi to just calculate its portion of pi (feeling hungry?), and once it has completed combine it with the other portions of PI to produce the final result. When calculating its portion it does not need to share any variables with any other tasks, thus requiring no synchronization and hopefully not thrashing the cache.

When Parallel.For wishes to use a new task for a portion of the loop, it needs to initialize the local value for the task. To enable this, supply a Func<T> delegate that is responsible for returning the initial value. Note that it's of type T so your method can return whatever it likes.

Parallel.For then flows this new local value into the loop body in addition to the loop index. During the iteration the task can modify this value, and on completion of an iteration of the loop body, return the value back to Parallel.For. If the Parallel.For wishes to reuse the task for another iteration, the returned value is passed into the task again.

The final part is when a task is no longer required. Parallel.For needs to take its last local value and allow it be combined with local values from other tasks to produce the final result. The combining logic is going to vary, so Parallel.For needs another delegate to provide that functionality. In addition to the initialize delegate, supply an Action<T> with responsibility to receive the last local value for a task and combine it with a global result. Listing 11-14 shows the version of Parallel.For you need to use to make your parallel computation of pi work.

Listing 11-14. Signature of Parallel.For with Per-Task Local State

```
public static ParallelLoopResult For<TLocal>(int fromInclusive, int toExclusive,
                                             Func<TLocal> localInit,
                                             Func<int,ParallelLoopState, TLocal, TLocal> body,
                                             Action<TLocal> localFinally);
```

The code in Listing 11-15 has been refactored to use this form of Parallel.For. The loop body now does not use any method-scoped local variables; rather, it is relying purely on variables local to it or ones passed in.

Listing 11-15. Parallel.For Using a Per-Task Value of Pi

```
private static double ParallelCalculatePi(int iterations)
{
    double pi = 1;

    Parallel.For(0, (iterations - 3) / 2,
        InitialiseLocalPi,
        (int loopIndex, ParallelLoopState loopState, double localPi) =>
        {
            double multiplier = loopIndex%2 == 0 ? -1 : 1;
            int i = 3 + loopIndex*2;
            localPi += 1.0/(double) i*multiplier;

            return localPi;
        },
    (double localPi) =>
    {
        pi += localPi;
    });

    return pi * 4.0;
}

private static double InitialiseLocalPi()
{ return 0.0;}
```

Running the code produced the following result:

```
Time Taken: 01.05 seconds Result: 4.00000021446738
```

From a time perspective, not bad, but from a results perspective it sucks. In fact, running it a few more times produced the following results:

```
Time Taken: 01.09 seconds Result: 3.14159265247552
Time Taken: 01.0571 seconds Result: 3.14159266368947
Time Taken: 01.0283 seconds Result: 3.14159265565936
```

Welcome to the chaotic world of parallel programming. We could just as easily have gotten a good value of pi the first time we ran the code and thus thought our implementation was therefore a good one. Calculating such a well-known value makes it easy to see that producing a value of PI as 4.0 is clearly wrong. When parallelizing algorithms that don't have such obvious return values it is a lot harder to spot when things go wrong. This is why it is so important to have a simpler single-threaded version of the algorithm to validate results against. The reason for this error is the fact that while the loop body is completely thread safe, the combining logic is not. If multiple tasks complete at the same time, multiple tasks will be executing the line pi += localPi concurrently, and as you know from previous chapters this is not thread safe. To remedy the situation you will need to introduce synchronization; as this is a double you can't use Interlocked.Add, and thus you will have to use a monitor. Listing 11-16 shows the refactored code.

Listing 11-16. Parallel Pi with Thread-Safe Combiner

```
private static double ParallelCalculatePi(int iterations)
{
    double pi = 1;
    object combineLock = new object();

    Parallel.For(0, (iterations - 3) / 2,
        InitialiseLocalPi,
        (int loopIndex, ParallelLoopState loopState, double localPi) =>
        {
            double multiplier = loopIndex%2 == 0 ? -1 : 1;
            int i = 3 + loopIndex*2;
            localPi += 1.0/(double) i*multiplier;

            return localPi;
        },
    (double localPi) =>
    {
        lock (combineLock)
        {
            pi += localPi;
        }
    });
    return pi * 4.0;
}
```

Running the code in Listing 11-16 produced the following results over multiple runs.

```
Time Taken: 01.02 seconds Result: 3.14159265558957
Time Taken: 01.04 seconds Result: 3.1415926555895
Time Taken: 01.07 seconds Result: 3.14159265558942
```

And so forth.

Note however that the values of pi are all slightly different. While with integer mathematics order doesn't matter, unfortunately it can make a difference with doubles due to their floating point nature. There are various approaches to get around this but they are beyond the scope of this chapter (see Shewchuk's algorithm or Sterbenz's theorem).

Putting the floating issue to one side, you have improved the performance of the pi calculation and produced consistently good approximation values of pi. The speedup isn't earth-shattering—these numbers were produced on an Intel i7 with four real cores. Expecting a fourfold speedup would be insane, as stated earlier; with the parallel version you need to execute more code to orchestrate the parallelism. Over time more and more cores will appear inside the average machine, thus reducing this effect, with tens of iterations of the loop executing in parallel as opposed to just four in this case. The one big factor affecting performance is the difference in how the loop is being expressed. The synchronous version is using a regular C# for loop, and the parallel version is using a delegate to represent the body of the loop, meaning for each iteration of the loop it has to perform a delegate invocation passing in and returning values. This is far more expensive than just jumping back to the start of the loop. This additional cost is most noticeable when the amount of computation per iteration of the loop is small, as in this case. Therefore to reduce the effect, you need to increase the work undertaken in the loop body. We will explain how this is achieved later in the section titled Nested Loops.

So far you have seen that you can take a for loop and parallelize it if you don't care about order. Parallel.For requires the loop index to be either an int or a long and can only be incremented by 1. To get the best possible speedup, you need to ensure the loop iterations have no shared state. Parallel.For provides the necessary overloads to allow for this, but the resulting code certainly looks far more complex than our original for loop—not a totally free lunch.

Parallel.ForEach

As you can probably guess, Parallel.ForEach provides the parallel equivalent of the C# foreach loop. Parallel.ForEach works by consuming an IEnumerable<T> and farming out elements consumed through the enumerator to multiple tasks, thus processing the elements in parallel. Listing 11-17 shows the equivalent Parallel.ForEach of the initial Parallel.For example in Listing 11-9.

Listing 11-17. Simple Parallel.ForEach

```
IEnumerable<int> items = Enumerable.Range(0, 20);

Parallel.ForEach(items, i =>
{
    Console.WriteLine(i);
});
```

Parallel.ForEach can therefore be applied to anything that implements IEnumerable (Lists, Arrays, Collections, etc.). One limiting factor with Parallel.For was that you were constrained to int or long and had to increment by 1s. This can be worked around by using an iterator method and Parallel.ForEach instead of Parallel.For as shown in Listing 11-18.

Listing 11-18. Parallel Loop from 1 to 2 in Steps of 0.1

```
Parallel.ForEach(FromTo(1, 2, 0.1), Console.WriteLine);

. . .
private static IEnumerable<double> FromTo(double start, double end,double step)
{
    for (double current = start; current < end; current += step)
    {
        yield return current;
    }
}
```

Parallel.ForEach has similar overloads to that of Parallel.For, allowing for the use of local loop state and combining logic in the same way they were used for Parallel.For. What makes life harder for Parallel.ForEach compared to Parallel.For is that it potentially won't know how many items there are to process, since a pure IEnumerable object has no way of yielding how many items there are to consume. Therefore Parallel.ForEach has to start off consuming a few items per task so as to allow many tasks to work on a small data set. As it learns that the IEnumerable stream keeps yielding an initial block size, it asks for larger and larger block sizes. This process is known as partitioning. If Parallel.ForEach could know the size of the IEnumerable stream, it could do a better job of partitioning. Therefore, to give itself the best possible chance internally, it attempts to discover at runtime if the IEnumerable<T> is in fact an array or an IList<T>. Once it knows it is a list or an array, it can use the Count and Length properties respectively to determine the size, and hence do a better job of initial partitioning. Parallel.ForEach therefore works best with arrays or lists.

ParallelLoopState

With a regular loop in C#, you can leave the loop early through the use of a break statement. Since the body of a parallel loop is represented by a delegate, you can't use the break keyword. To allow this style of behavior for parallel loops, both Parallel.For and Parallel.ForEach provide an overload that allows the loop body delegate to take, in addition to the loop index, a ParallelLoopState object. This loop state object is used to both signal and observe if the loop is to terminate early. Listing 11-19 shows an example of a loop that for each iteration has a 1 in 50 chance of terminating.

Listing 11-19. Early Termination using ParallelLoopState.Break

```
Random rnd = new Random();
Parallel.For(0, 100, (i, loopState) =>
{
    if (rnd.Next(1, 50) == 1)
    {
        Console.WriteLine("{0} : Breaking on {1}",Task.CurrentId, i);
        loopState.Break();
        return;
    }
    Console.WriteLine("{0} : {1}", Task.CurrentId, i);
});
```

The big difference between break in a regular loop to a parallel loop is that the break can be acted upon immediately and no further iterations will occur. With a parallel loop other iterations could be in progress when a particular iteration requests the break, in which case these iterations can't be stopped without some cooperation of the iteration. Figure 11-5 shows an example of an early loop termination with break.

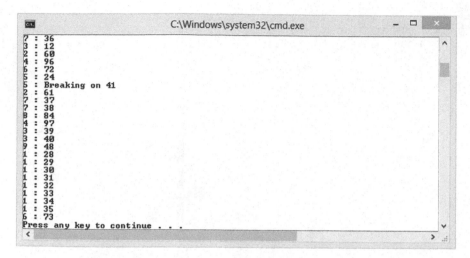

```
7 : 36
3 : 12
2 : 60
4 : 96
6 : 72
5 : 24
5 : Breaking on 41
2 : 61
7 : 37
7 : 38
8 : 84
4 : 97
3 : 39
3 : 40
9 : 48
1 : 28
1 : 29
1 : 30
1 : 31
1 : 32
1 : 33
1 : 34
1 : 35
6 : 73
Press any key to continue . . .
```

Figure 11-5. *Early terminaton of parallel loop using* `ParallelLoopState.Break()`

Although Task 5 has requested termination, Tasks 7, 3, and 1 continue to execute many more iterations. The reason for this is that `ParallelLoopState.Break` is trying to recreate the semantics of a regular loop break. With a regular loop break, if you break on Iteration 20 you know that all iterations prior to that will have executed. When you issue a `ParallelLoopState.Break()` the parallel loop ensures that all lower-value iterations will be executed before the loop ends. Studying the output shown in Figure 11-5, we can see that once Task 5 has issued the break apart from Tasks 7, 3, and 1, all other tasks complete their current iteration and end. Tasks 7, 3, and 1 keep running to complete all iterations less than 41. Obviously if iterations have already completed that represent values greater than 41, then there will be no way of rolling back. The behavior is thus not an exact match to the regular break, but it is as close as you can get considering the loop is being executed out of order.

If you do want to terminate the loop as soon as possible and don't care about guaranteeing that all prior iterations have completed, then `ParallelLoopState` has another method called `Stop`. The `Stop` method attempts to end the loop as soon as possible—once issued, no loop task will start a new iteration. Listing 11-20 shows the same example using `Stop` instead of a `Break`. Figure 11-6 shows an example of a run where `Stop` is issued by Task 9: all remaining tasks finish their current iteration and don't process any more.

Listing 11-20. Early Loop Termination with `ParallelLoopState.Stop()`

```
Random rnd = new Random();
Parallel.For(0, 100, (i, loopState) =>
{
    if (rnd.Next(1, 50) == 1)
    {
        Console.WriteLine("{0} : Stopping on {1}", Task.CurrentId, i);
        loopState.Stop();
        return;
    }

    Console.WriteLine("{0} : {1}", Task.CurrentId, i);
});
```

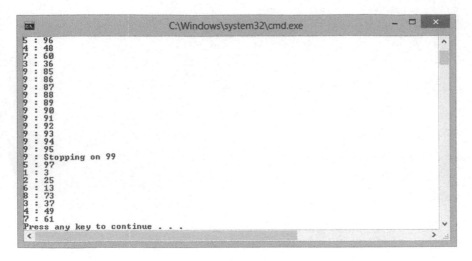

Figure 11-6. Early loop termination using `ParallelLoopState.Stop()`

In addition to initiating termination of the loop, `ParallelLoopState` can also be used to determine if another iteration of the loop has initiated termination, or has thrown an unhandled exception. In situations where the loop body takes a considerable amount of time, it may be desirable for the loop body to observe the fact that the loop should end, and assist in shutting down the loop early. Table 11-1 lists the properties available on `ParallelLoopState` to assist in detection of the need to terminate early.

Table 11-1. Observing Loop State

Property	Description
IsExceptional	Returns `true` if another iteration has thrown an unhandled exception, preventing the loop from fully completing
IsStopped	Returns `true` if another iteration has requested the loop be stopped as soon as possible
ShouldExitCurrentIteration	Returns `true` if the current iteration is no longer required to complete. In the case of a `Stop` or `Break` has been issued by a lower iteration.
LowestBreakIteration	Returns a `long?` representing the iteration in which a `Break` was issued, null if no `Break` has been issued.

Listing 11-21 shows an example of a loop body detecting a stop request and ending the loop body prematurely. Early termination can also be observed outside the loop body by examining the return value from `Parallel.For` or `Parallel.ForEach`. The return value is of type `ParallelLoopResult` and it provides a property called `IsCompleted`. If the loop did not complete all intended iterations due to a `Stop` or `Break` being issued, this will be set to `false`. Figure 11-7 shows an example run where early termination is being observed.

Listing 11-21. Observing Stop Requests

```
Random rnd = new Random();

ParallelLoopResult loopResult = Parallel.For(0, 100, (i, loopState) =>
{
    if (rnd.Next(1,50) == 1)
    {
        Console.WriteLine("{0} : Stopping on {1}", Task.CurrentId, i);
        loopState.Stop();
        return;
    }

    Thread.Sleep(10);

    if (loopState.IsStopped)
    {
        Console.WriteLine("{0}:STOPPED",Task.CurrentId);
        return;
    }

    Console.WriteLine("{0} : {1}", Task.CurrentId, i);
});

Console.WriteLine("Loop ran to completion {0}",loopResult.IsCompleted);
```

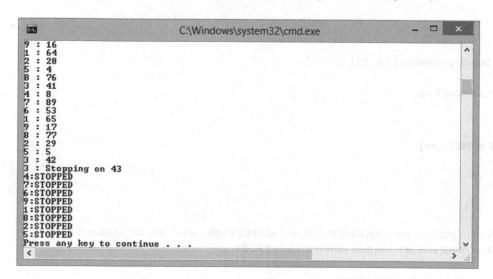

Figure 11-7. Observing Stop requests

If a loop body were to throw an unhandled exception, this would be similar to issuing a Stop request. The exception would be caught by Parallel.For or Parallel.ForEach and then be re-thrown as part of an AggregateException, in order to inform the caller that the loop failed to complete due to exceptions.

Parallel loops are not the same as synchronous loops but, where possible, similar constructs are provided to allow for early termination of a loop. If a loop has completed its said purpose early, use Break and Stop for early graceful termination of the loop. If the loop fails to complete its purpose, then throw an exception, making the caller fully aware that the loop failed to complete its task.

Nested Loops

Earlier in Listing 11-16 we parallelized an algorithm to approximate the value of pi. While it was faster than the single-threaded version, the gain wasn't earth shattering. The reason suggested for the lack of boost was the additional overhead introduced through the use of Parallel.For. The fact that the loop body is now represented by a delegate, and as such each iteration of the loop now involves a delegate invocation this will drastically increase the amount of work for each iteration of the loop. With the amount of work per delegate invocation being so small the effect of parallelization is further lessened. This is a common problem with lots of loops, and as such we often find that one of the better structures to parallelize is not a single loop but nested loops. The code in Listing 11-22 has two loops; each iteration of the outer loop results in 100 iterations of the inner loop. The inner loop could therefore represent a reasonable amount of work. If the outer loop were to be parallelized, leaving the inner loop as the body, this could then represent a reasonable amount of work to compensate for the overhead of delegate invocation.

Listing 11-22. Simple Nested Loop

```
for (int i = 0; i < 500; i++)
{
    for (int j = 0; j < 100; j++)
    {
        // Do Stuff
    }
}
```

Listing 11-23 shows how to parallelize Listing 11-22.

Listing 11-23. Parallelized nested loop

```
Parallel.For(0, 500, i =>
{
    for (int j = 0; j < 100; j++)
    {
        // Do Stuff
    }
});
```

"All well and good," you might say, "but what if my algorithm just has a single loop?" Any single loop can always be turned into an equivalent outer and inner loop as shown in Listing 11-24.

Listing 11-24. Single Loop and Equivalent Nested Loop

```
for (int i = 0; i < 50000; i++)
{
    // Do Stuff
}
```

```
for (int i = 0; i < 500; i++)
{
    for (int j = 0; j < 100; j++)
    {
        // Do Stuff
    }
}
```

So the first task is to turn the single loop into two loops. Before we dive into how to produce the parallel version, see Listing 11-25, which shows a refactored nonparallel version of CalculatePI that now uses two loops. The outer loop is a foreach iterating over a stream of Tuple<int,int>. Each Tuple<int,int> represents a range of values for the inner loop to iterate over.

Listing 11-25. CalculatePi Turned into Two Loops

```
public static double CalculatePi(int iterations)
{
  IEnumerable<Tuple<int, int>> ranges = Range(3, iterations, 10000);
  double pi = 1;

  foreach (var range in ranges)
  {
    double multiplier = range.Item1 % 2 == 0 ? 1 : -1;

    for (int i = range.Item1; i < range.Item2; i+=2)
    {
        pi += 1.0/(double) i*multiplier;
        multiplier *= -1;
    }
  }
  pi *= 4.0;
  return pi;
}

private static IEnumerable<Tuple<int, int>> Range(int start, int end, int size)
{
    for (int i = start; i < end; i+=size)
    {
        yield return Tuple.Create(i, Math.Min(i + size,end));
    }
}
```

Now that the algorithm has been refactored into two loops, you can parallelize the outer loop, leaving the inner loop to run synchronously and thus generate sufficient work to justify the overhead of delegate invocation, as shown in Listing 11-26.

Listing 11-26. ParallelCalculatePi with Nested Loops

```
private static double TwoLoopsParallelCalculatePi(int iterations)
{
    IEnumerable<Tuple<int, int>> ranges = Range(3, iterations, 10000);
    double pi = 1;
    object combineLock = new object();
```

```
Parallel.ForEach(ranges.ToList(),
    () => 0.0,
    (range, loopState, localPi) =>
    {
        double multiplier = range.Item1%2 == 0 ? 1 : -1;

        for (int i = range.Item1; i < range.Item2; i += 2)
        {
            localPi += 1.0/(double) i*multiplier;
            multiplier *= -1;
        }

        return localPi;
    },
    localPi =>
    {
        lock (combineLock)
        {
            pi += localPi;
        }
    });
    pi *= 4.0;

    return pi;
}
```

As explained earlier, when Parallel.ForEach executes it has to partition the IEnumerable stream, and it does this by combination of guessing and inspecting the actual source type of the stream. It is very hard to write a partitioner that is perfect for every scenario. Rather than Parallel.ForEach consuming an IEnumerable and also creating and using the default partitioner, you can supply it with a partitioner (see Listing 11-27). You can create your own partitioner that has explicit knowledge of how to partition your data source, but we won't discuss that in this book. TPL ships with some out-of-the-box partitioners that you can take advantage of, made available through Create methods on the System.Collections.Concurrent.Partitioner class.

Listing 11-27. Using Parallel.ForEach Using Partitioner Directly

```
private static double OptimizedParallelCalculatePiWithPartitioner(int iterations)
{
    //IEnumerable<Tuple<int, int>> ranges = Range(3, iterations, 10000);
    var ranges = Partitioner.Create(3, iterations, 10000);

    double pi = 1;
    object combineLock = new object();
    Parallel.ForEach(ranges, () => 0.0,
        (range, loopState, localPi) =>
        {
            double multiplier = range.Item1 % 2 == 0 ? 1 : -1;

            for (int i = range.Item1; i < range.Item2; i += 2)
            {
                localPi += 1.0 / (double)i * multiplier;
                multiplier *= -1;
            }
```

```
            return localPi;
        },
        localPi =>
        {
            lock (combineLock)
            {
                pi += localPi;
            }
        });
    pi *= 4.0;

    return pi;
}
```

Table 11-2 presents all the times from running the implementations of `CalculatePi`. The two-loops implementation gets us very close to linear scaling, albeit with some refactoring of the algorithm, so it's not exactly a free lunch.

Table 11-2. *Times for Pi Calculations, Running on an i7 with Four Real Cores and Four Hyper-threaded Cores*

Method	Time Taken (Seconds)
CalculatePi	1.89
ParallelCalculatePi	0.88
TwoLoopsParallelCalculatePi	0.5
OptimizedParallelCalculatePiWithPartitioner	0.48

PLINQ

PLINQ is the parallel form of LINQ over `IEnumerable<T>`. PLINQ is not a general parallel framework for all forms of LINQ such as LINQ to Entities. Conventional LINQ is built along the lines of functional programming and typically immutable data. These two characteristics alone make it a great candidate for parallelism as it means multiple tasks can run concurrently, producing and consuming nonshared values. The other key characteristic of LINQ that makes it applicable for parallelism is that LINQ is all about intent, not mechanics. Expecting the compiler to parallelize an arbitrary piece of code is hard. With LINQ we chain together a series of high-level primitives (`Where`, `Select`, `OrderBy`) where each is well understood, and therefore we could have parallel versions of them instead.

■ **Note**   It is assumed that the reader understands LINQ, and how LINQ utilizes extension methods to provide a declarative mechanism to define queries.

Listing 11-28 shows a simple LINQ query that produces a list of all the even numbers and prints the length of the list.

Listing 11-28. LINQ Query to Find Even Numbers

```
using System.Linq;
. . .
IEnumerable<int> numbers = Enumerable.Range(0, 100000000);

var evenNumbers = from number in numbers
    where number%2 == 0
    select number;

Console.WriteLine(evenNumbers.ToList().Count());
```

At compile time, the compiler turns the language keywords into extension methods, as per Listing 11-29. It does this by looking for extension methods that extend the source of the query. In this case, since the numbers variable is of type IEnumerable<int>, it selects extension methods that extend IEnumerable<int>, and as such we pick up the single-threaded Where method implementation for LINQ to objects.

Listing 11-29. Extension Method Form of the LINQ Query in Listing 11-28

```
var evenNumbers = numbers
                  .Where(number => number%2 == 0);
```

If numbers were not of type IEnumerable<T>, then the compiler would be looking for another extension method in scope called Where that extends whatever type numbers is. The fact that the compiler is not bound to a specific implementation of Where means that by changing the type of numbers from IEnumerable<T> to a different type, you can bring into scope other implementations of Where—perhaps a parallel version. Listing 11-30 shows how to enable the use of a parallel version of Where. The AsParallel extension method on IEnumerable<T> returns a ParallelQuery<T>; from then on the compiler will have to look for the Where extension method not on IEnumerable<T> but on ParallelQuery<T>. The System.LINQ.ParallelEnumerable class defines all the extension methods for ParallelQuery<T>, so as long as you are using System.Linq you are good to go.

By being able to simply add an AsParallel call to an already easy-to-understand LINQ query and then have it run in parallel makes for a perfect free lunch: code that is not only readable but scales as you add more cores.

Listing 11-30. Parallel Form of LINQ query

```
IEnumerable<int> numbers = Enumerable.Range(0, 100000000);

 var evenNumbers = from number in numbers.AsParallel()
     where number%2 == 0
     select number;

 var evenNumbers2 = numbers.AsParallel()
     .Where(number => number%2 == 0);
```

Moving from Sequential LINQ to PLINQ

Moving from sequential LINQ to Parallel LINQ therefore looks a breeze; however, like all things, there are plenty of issues to consider. In the case of Parallel.For we discussed the issue of having a small loop body, and how the overhead of delegate invocation can drastically inhibit parallelism. The good news for Parallel LINQ is that it is parallelizing LINQ, which already relies on the use of delegates, so you are not adding as much additional overhead. However, if performance is your ultimate goal, then LINQ is not a great starting point—LINQ was never designed for CPU efficiency. Any LINQ statement could be rewritten using a conventional foreach loop and the necessary filtering inside the loop, and it would outperform the LINQ statement. Having said all that, keep in mind that if your LINQ queries comprise I/O, then it is likely that the time spent doing I/O will swamp the time spent doing computing. If you want to use LINQ to keep code simple to maintain but still get the best possible performance out of it, then PLINQ is still a great choice. The fundamental point here is if you care about maximum performance, LINQ and hence PLINQ are unlikely to be your final destination.

PLINQ is also a great choice for less experienced asynchronous programmers, as lots of the thread safety issues are removed by the functional programming style LINQ promotes. Unlike conventional asynchronous programming, you can now feel confident that the code doesn't have those unexpected race conditions. Perhaps you won't get the ultimate speedup, but you can have confidence in the speedup you do get.

Last, it's worth stating that even though you may request the query to run in parallel, if the runtime deems that the query would not benefit from running in parallel, it will revert to running it on a single thread (you can force it to run parallel—more on that later in section Influencing and Configuring the Query).

Partitioning

In the same way that `Parallel.ForEach` found it harder to partition up the data if it was given a pure `IEnumerable<T>`, the same is true for PLINQ. PLINQ works best with arrays and `IList<T>`. Listing 11-31 benchmarks the filtering of just even numbers from a range of numbers. Running this code produce an overall time of 1.09 seconds. The code is then modified as per Table 11-3 and rerun to obtain the time taken to execute that variant.

Listing 11-31. Timed LINQ Query

```
static void Main(string[] args)
{

    IEnumerable<int> numbers =
                Enumerable.Range(0, 100000000);

    TimeIt(() =>
    {
        var evenNumbers = from number in numbers
            where number%2 == 0
            select number;

        Console.WriteLine(evenNumbers.Count());
    });
}

private static void TimeIt(Action func)
{
    Stopwatch timer = Stopwatch.StartNew();
    func();
    Console.WriteLine("{0}() and took {1}",
        func.Method.Name, timer.Elapsed);
}
```

Table 11-3. *Code Modifications and Associated Times Taken to Execute*

Original Code	Replacement Code	Time Taken (Seconds)
`from number in numbers`	`from number in numbers.AsParallel()`	1.25
`Enumerable.Range(0,100000000);`	`Enumerable.Range(0,100000000).ToList()`	0.70.22
`Enumerable.Range(0,100000000);`	`Enumerable.Range(0,100000000).ToList()`	
`from number in numbers`	`from number in numbers.AsParallel()`	

As shown in Table 11-3, for small, simple queries parallelism only works if PLINQ is able to partition efficiently. This very simple example hopefully tells you not to go through your entire code base modifying all LINQ statements to use AsParallel. Remember: Always benchmark code before attempting to optimize. Just because it is easy to throw on an AsParallel doesn't mean you should.

Does Order Matter?

With conventional LINQ, items are processed in order as they are yielded from the IEnumerable<T> stream. With PLINQ, the processing order and the result order are unknown, just as it was with parallel loops. If you don't care about order, all is good, but if you do need the results to come out in the same order as the source processing, then you need to tell PLINQ to preserve order. For example, consider a piece of PLINQ processing a CSV file row by row: its job is to take each row in turn, add a row total column, and then output the row to a new file. The order of the output CSV file should match that of the input CSV file. If you were to process this with just AsParallel(), then the output order could be different from that of the input. To preserve its order, call AsOrdered() as per Listing 11-32.

Listing 11-32. Ordered Parallel Query

```
IEnumerable<string[]> csvRows = GetRows(@"..\..\data\stockData.csv").Skip(1);

var rowWithTotalColumn =
    from row in csvRows.AsParallel().AsOrdered()
    let total = row.Skip(1).Select(c => decimal.Parse(c)).Sum()
    select row.Concat(Enumerable.Repeat(total.ToString(), 1)).ToArray();

WriteCsvRows(rowWithTotalColumn, "RowsWithTotal.csv");
```

Preserving order comes at a cost, since it means the partitioner is more constrained about how it can partition and has to buffer up results before publishing them. Use AsOrdered for algorithms that need to stream data in, process it, and stream it out in the same order. If only part of the query needs to be ordered, then you can revert back to more efficient behavior by using the AsUnOrdered() method.

If all you need to care about is knowing which input index produced a given output, then a more efficient model is simply to flow an index with the data as per Listing 11-33. An example of running the code is shown in Figure 11-8. While the output order does not match that of the input, the output value does now contain a corresponding index of the input that produced the said output.

Listing 11-33. Associating Result with Input Index

```
IEnumerable<string> values = new List<string>() { "one","two","three","four","five","six"};

var upperCases = values
    .Select((value, index) => new {Index = index, Value = value})
    .AsParallel()
    .Select(valueIndexPair => new {valueIndexPair.Index,Value=valueIndexPair.Value.ToUpper()});
```

```
foreach (var upperCase in upperCases)
{
    Console.WriteLine("{0}:{1}",upperCase.Index,upperCase.Value);
}
```

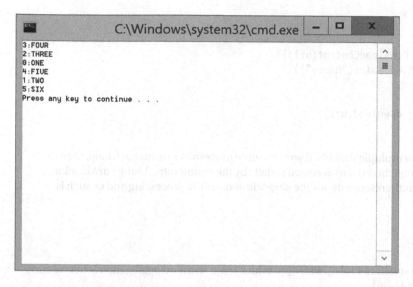

Figure 11-8. *Data with index+*

Influencing and Configuring the Query

Rather than relying completely on PLINQ default behavior, we can provide various additional bits of configuration to influence how the parallelism takes place. This is achieved through a series of extension methods. Listing 11-34 shows a parallel query that will use two tasks, will always run in parallel, and has been supplied with a cancellation token to allow early cancellation of the query.

Listing 11-34. Configuring the Query

```
var cts = new System.Threading.CancellationTokenSource();

var upperCases = values
    .Select((value, index) => new {Index = index, Value = value})
    .AsParallel()
    .WithDegreeOfParallelism(2)
    .WithExecutionMode(ParallelExecutionMode.ForceParallelism)
    .WithCancellation(cts.Token)
    .Select(valueIndexPair => new {valueIndexPair.Index,Value=valueIndexPair.Value.ToUpper()});
```

ForAll

The ForAll method seems an odd addition to PLINQ as it provides virtually identical functionality to that of foreach. The differentiator is that it does allow you to define and consume the parallel query as a single block statement, which can look pretty elegant as shown in Listing 11-35.

Listing 11-35. Define and Consume the Query

```
new string[] { "http://www.bbc.co.uk",
               "http://www.rocksolidknowledge.com",
               "http://www.nsa.gov",
               "http://www.cia.gov",
}
.AsParallel()
.Select(url => new {url, content = DownloadContent(url)})
.Where(download => download.content.Contains("happy"))
.ForAll(download =>
{
  Console.WriteLine("{0} is happy", download.url);
});
```

Although PLINQ executes a query on multiple threads, if you consume the results in a foreach loop, then the query results must be merged back into one thread and accessed serially by the enumerator. Using ForAll allows the results to be processed in parallel; this therefore extends the parallelization of the processing and as such is encouraged.

Aggregating Results

The classic Map/Reduce problem is well suited to PLINQ. PLINQ provides some standard aggregation schemes such as Sum, Min, Max, and Average (see Listing 11-36).

Listing 11-36. Parallel Sum

```
int sum = GenerateNumbers(100000000)
          .AsParallel()
          .Sum();
```

For more complex aggregations PLINQ provides its own unique variant of the LINQ Aggregation method to define your own reduce function. The Aggregate method takes four arguments:

- The initial seed value used for each task involved in the aggregation

- A method used to create a localized aggregation. This method initially receives the seed from Step 1, plus the first value to be aggregated by a given task.

- A method used to combine all the localized aggregations

- A method that takes the combined result and provides the final processing before publication of the aggregation

Listing 11-37 shows an example of customized aggregation for calculating the standard deviation of a set of random numbers.

Listing 11-37. Parallel Implementation of Standard Deviation

```
private static void Main(string[] args)
{
    // http://en.wikipedia.org/wiki/Standard_deviation
    List<int>  values = GenerateNumbers(100000000).ToList();
```

```csharp
        double average = values.AsParallel().Average();

        double std = values
                .AsParallel()
                .Aggregate(
                    0.0,
                    // produces local total
                    (subTotal, nextNumber) => subTotal += Math.Pow(nextNumber - average, 2),
                    // sum of all local totals
                    (total, threadTotal) => total += threadTotal,
                    // final projection of the combined results
                    grandTotal => Math.Sqrt(grandTotal / (double)(values.Count - 1))
                );

        Console.WriteLine(std);

    }

    private static IEnumerable<int> GenerateNumbers(int quantity)
    {
        Random rnd = new Random();
        for (int i = 0; i < quantity; i++)
        {
            yield return rnd.Next(1,100);
        }
    }
}
```

Summary

TPL's parallel extensions provide a relatively high-level form of abstraction to implement parallel algorithms. `Parallel.For` and `Parallel.ForEach` have a syntax very close to the regular loop constructs; this helps to maintain the structure of the algorithm but still execute in parallel. What can't be ignored is the fact that the body of the loop is running over multiple threads, and as such thread safety matters. Solving the thread safety issues through synchronization will often result in poor performance. Ideally you should remove the need to use synchronization by writing loop bodies that have no shared state with other iterations. Refactoring the code to remove the shared state can often introduce extra complexity, making the code far harder to understand than the original single-threaded loop. Further, the size of the loop body may not be of sufficient computational size to justify the effort of parallelism, and again require refactoring through the introduction of nested loops. The final result of all this refactoring is that your code will be a long way from its simple roots. Parallel loops are certainly a huge step forward in enabling multicore programming, but still require the developer to have deep knowledge of multithreaded programming—not the free lunch we had hoped for.

PLINQ offers the best prospect of a free lunch—the declarative and functional nature of LINQ makes it ideal for parallelism. The structure of the LINQ statement varies very little with the introduction of parallelism. Preserving the original structure means we have code that not only performs well, but is also easier to maintain. Ensuring that the PLINQ statement is built purely along functional programming principles means that there is no need to consider thread safety issues, making the code less likely to suffer those sometimes rare but painful race conditions. PLINQ is therefore ideal for less experienced asynchronous programmers. However, remember that LINQ is not designed for performance, so if max performance at all costs is what you desire, then prefer other forms of parallelism.

However you decide to parallelize, remember to benchmark your code before you start. You need to be confident that what you have is faster and produces the correct results.

CHAPTER 12

Task Scheduling

You saw in Chapter 6 how, when creating a continuation, you can pass a scheduler on which to execute the task. The example in the chapter used the out-of-the-box SynchronizationContextTaskScheduler to push task execution on to the UI thread. It turns out, however, that there is nothing special about the SynchronizationContextTaskScheduler; the task scheduler is a pluggable component. .NET 4.5 introduced another specialized scheduler, but beyond that you can write task schedulers yourself. This chapter looks at the new sch eduler introduced in .NET 4.5 and how to write a custom task scheduler. Writing custom task schedulers can be fairly straightforward, but there are some of the issues that you need to be aware of.

ConcurrentExclusiveSchedulerPair

.NET 4.5 introduced a new scheduler—a pair of schedulers, in fact, that work together to simplify concurrency over shared mutable state. This pair of schedulers is called the ConcurrentExclusiveSchedulerPair. The idea is that one scheduler in the pair allows multiple read-based tasks to run concurrently while the other ensures that only a single read/write-based task can run at any one time. If you recall Chapter 4, you will see that the semantics are the same as a reader/writer lock. Consider the code in Listing 12-1, which models a small business. This implementation is not thread safe, as one thread can calculate NetWorth while another is processing a payment. If the payment thread has updated the income field but has not yet decremented the receivables, then an incorrect NetWorth is produced.

Listing 12-1. Non-Thread-Safe SmallBusiness Class

```
public class SmallBusiness
{
  private decimal income;
  private decimal receivables;

  public virtual decimal NetWorth
  {
   get { return income + receivables; }
  }
  public virtual void RaisedInvoiceFor(decimal amount)
  {
      receivables += amount;
  }

  public virtual void ReceivePayments(decimal payment)
```

263

```
  {
    income += payment;
    receivables -= payment;
  }
}
```

This thread safety problem can be fixed using a monitor or a reader/writer lock. Assuming NetWorth is called very often, it is more efficient to use a reader/writer lock. Listing 12-2 shows a class, derived from SmallBusiness, that implements the necessary thread safety measures using ReaderWriterLockSlim. The SmallBusinessRWLock class is now able to have multiple threads reading its NetWorth, but only one thread has access when an update is taking place by calling either RaisedInvoiceFor or ReceivePayments.

Listing 12-2. Reader/Writer Lock, Thread-Safe SmallBusinessRWLock Class

```
public class SmallBusinessRWLock : SmallBusiness
{
    private ReaderWriterLockSlim rwLock = new ReaderWriterLockSlim();

    public override decimal NetWorth
    {
      get
      {
        rwLock.EnterReadLock();
        try{return base.NetWorth;}
        finally { rwLock.ExitReadLock(); }
      }
    }
    public override void RaisedInvoiceFor(decimal amount)
    {
       rwLock.EnterWriteLock();
       try { base.RaisedInvoiceFor(amount);}
       finally{ rwLock.ExitWriteLock();}
    }
    public override void ReceivePayments(decimal payment)
    {
       rwLock.EnterWriteLock();
       try { base.ReceivePayments(payment);}
       finally{rwLock.ExitWriteLock();}
    }
}
```

However, rather than blocking, another way to achieve thread safety would be to schedule the update or read operation to occur in the future when it is safe to do so—in other words, asynchronously. A scheduler could safely allow many read-style operations to occur concurrently, and when a write operation is requested, it could ensure it is only executed when it is the only operation running. The code shown in Listing 12-3 provides such an implementation. Each instance of the SmallBusinessAsync class has its own scheduler, an instance of ConcurrentExclusiveSchedulerPair. This class, as the name suggests, provides two schedulers: one for exclusive accesses, the other for concurrent. When a request is made against the SmallBusinessAsync class, the operation is executed asynchronously using the appropriate scheduler. If the operation is only reading state it will use the concurrent scheduler, and if it is updating state it will use the exclusive scheduler. The concurrent scheduler will run its tasks concurrently, but only if the exclusive scheduler is not running a task. The exclusive scheduler ensures that it only runs one task at a time and that the concurrent scheduler is not running tasks.

Listing 12-3. Thread-Safe Asynchronous SmallBusinessAsync Class

```
public class SmallBusinessAsync
{
  private decimal income;
  private decimal receivables;

  private ConcurrentExclusiveSchedulerPair rwScheduler =
                    new ConcurrentExclusiveSchedulerPair();
  public Task<decimal> NetWorthAsync
  {
    get
    {
      return Task.Factory.StartNew<decimal>( () => income + receivables,
          CancellationToken.None,
          TaskCreationOptions.None,
          rwScheduler.ConcurrentScheduler);
    }
  }

  public Task RaisedInvoiceForAsync(decimal amount)
  {
      return Task.Factory.StartNew(() => receivables += amount,
          CancellationToken.None,
          TaskCreationOptions.None,
          rwScheduler.ExclusiveScheduler);
  }

  public Task ReceivePaymentsAsync(decimal payment)
  {
      return Task.Factory.StartNew(() =>
      {
          income += payment;
          receivables -= payment;
      }, CancellationToken.None,
        TaskCreationOptions.None,
        rwScheduler.ExclusiveScheduler);
  }
}
```

Using the ConcurrentExclusiveSchedulerPair scheduler gives you an alternative mechanism to blocking synchronization primitives, which for asynchronous operations provides a more natural and efficient thread safety model.

Why Write a Task Scheduler?

As you have seen, the .NET framework ships with three task schedulers: ThreadPoolTaskScheduler (the default), SynchronizationContextTaskScheduler, and ConcurrentExclusiveSchedulerPair. Therefore, the first question you need to answer is, "Why would I want to write a task scheduler?" After all, as you have seen over the last few chapters, the ones that come out of the box seem to be very flexible. The task scheduler provides an execution context for the task, allowing you to take control over which thread or threads are used for task execution. Some reasons to build a scheduler are

- You have a set of components with high thread affinity that need to be run asynchronously but all on the same thread.

- You have a set of legacy components written in VB6 or MFC and need to execute these asynchronously. To be able to execute concurrently, these components need to be executed on threads with an ApartmentState of STA, which is not the case with normal thread pool threads.

- You have a set of work that should always be scheduled on low-priority threads as it shouldn't interrupt the normal processing on the machine.

The second of these is the scenario we will use to show you an example of a custom task scheduler.

The TaskScheduler Abstraction

The out-of-the-box schedulers both inherit from the TaskScheduler abstract class. If you want to be able to use our own task scheduler for Task execution, then you also need to create a class that derives, directly or indirectly, from TaskScheduler.

The minimum requirement to implement a scheduler is twofold:

1. Provide an implementation of the three abstract methods of TaskScheduler: QueueTask, GetScheduledTasks, and TryExecuteTaskInline.

2. Have some mechanism of actually executing the tasks.

Let's look at what these requirements involve.

Implementing QueueTask

QueueTask is one of the two core pieces of functionality in implementing a task scheduler (the other being actually executing the tasks, as you shall see hereafter). This is its signature:

```
protected abstract void QueueTask(Task task);
```

As its name suggests, it is called when a new task has Start called on it explicitly or implicitly by Task.Factory.StartNew or Task.Run. The scheduler must make sure that it does not lose the fact that it must execute the task; therefore, unless it is going to execute it directly, it should store task in a collection. Notice that this member is protected, so you cannot call it directly in unit tests, instead, you will have to exercise the task infrastructure to cause it to be executed.

Implementing GetScheduledTasks

GetScheduledTasks is not called during normal task scheduling. It is there for debugger support so the debugger can show all of the scheduled tasks. GetScheduledTasks signature is as follows:

```
protected abstract IEnumerable<Task> GetScheduledTasks();
```

Assuming you have been storing the tasks in a collection, you can simply return the items in the collection. Again, because the method is protected you cannot unit test it directly.

Implementing TryExecuteTaskInline

When the task infrastructure wants to try to execute a task directly, it calls TryExecuteTaskInline. Here is the signature for the method:

```
protected abstract bool TryExecuteTaskInline(Task task, bool taskWasPreviouslyQueued);
```

When you implement TryExecuteTaskInline you need to assess whether it is appropriate to execute the task in the context of the calling thread and, if so, you need to run the task. As you shall see, the task may or may not have already been queued via QueueTask, and TryExecuteTaskInline is informed of this via the taskWasPreviouslyQueued parameter. The return value for the method is whether or not the task was executed.

TryExecuteTaskInline is called in two situations:

1. When RunSynchronously is called on a task, the calling code is saying that it wants to execute the task on its thread. TryExecuteTaskInline is called on the scheduler to attempt this execution. In this case Start is never called, so the task will not have been queued.

2. Wait is called on a task with no timeout or cancellation token. If the task has not yet been scheduled, then TryExecuteTaskInline is called in an attempt to allow Wait to return as quickly as possible. In this case Start will have been called, so the task will already have been queued.

Executing Tasks

The core responsibility of a task scheduler is to execute tasks. Fortunately, the TaskScheduler base class already wraps up the mechanics and you, as the scheduler implementer, just need to decide how and when to trigger that execution. To execute a task from a scheduler you call the base class method TryExecuteTask, which has the following signature:

```
bool TryExecuteTask(Task task);
```

Pass the task you want to execute to TryExecuteTask, and it returns a Boolean indicating whether or not the task was executed. TryExecuteTask will also return true if the task has already been cancelled.

Implementing a Custom Scheduler

As stated earlier, we'll examine building an STA thread scheduler to illustrate the requirements and some of the complexities of implementing a custom scheduler.

COM AND THREADING

Why might COM interop work require a custom scheduler? This comes down to how COM components interact with threads. COM threading was always one of the more complex aspects of COM, which results from COM being a binary standard whose components can be built from a variety of technologies. Some of these technologies have a high level of thread affinity (particularly VB6 and MFC). You must therefore make sure that

---

these components, known as apartment threaded components, are always executed on a specific thread. This drives the concept of apartments, and in threading terms there are two kinds: Single Threaded Apartments (STAs) and the Multithreaded Apartment (MTA). A thread elects either to enter the MTA or to have its own STA. If a component with high thread affinity is created from an STA thread, then in lives in that STA. However, if it is created from an MTA thread, it lives in a special STA, known as the host STA.

By default .NET threads are MTA threads, so if you create an apartment-threaded component from one it will always run the host STA—in other words, all the COM components will execute on a single thread, removing any potential concurrency you may be trying to achieve. To achieve concurrency with apartment-thread COM components, you need to run a pool of STA threads on which to execute them.

Creating a Basic Implementation

To begin with, you need to create a class that derives from TaskScheduler and implements the abstract members of the base class. This can be seen in Listing 12-4.

Listing 12-4. Deriving from TaskScheduler

```
public class STATaskScheduler : TaskScheduler
{
    protected override IEnumerable<Task> GetScheduledTasks()
    {
        throw new NotImplementedException();
    }

    protected override void QueueTask(Task task)
    {
        throw new NotImplementedException();
    }

    protected override bool TryExecuteTaskInline(Task task, bool taskWasPreviouslyQueued)
    {
        throw new NotImplementedException();
    }
}
```

Next you will need somewhere to store the tasks that are enqueued. As this is an inherently concurrent component, use a ConcurrentQueue; also, a BlockingCollection will give you a fairly simple programming model. Remember that a BlockingCollection defaults to wrapping a ConcurrentQueue unless you give it a different data structure. Having somewhere to store tasks will allow you to implement QueueTask and GetScheduledTasks. You also need to be able to call CompleteAdding on the BlockingCollection; to give yourself a place to do that, implement IDisposable. You can see this code in Listing 12-5.

Listing 12-5. Adding Storage for Enqueued Tasks

```
public class STATaskScheduler : TaskScheduler, IDisposable
{
    private readonly BlockingCollection<Task> tasks = new BlockingCollection<Task>();
```

```
protected override IEnumerable<Task> GetScheduledTasks()
{
    return tasks.ToArray();
}

protected override void QueueTask(Task task)
{
    tasks.Add(task);
}

protected override bool TryExecuteTaskInline(Task task, bool taskWasPreviouslyQueued)
{
    throw new NotImplementedException();
}

public void Dispose()
{
    tasks.CompleteAdding();
}
}
```

■ **Note** Calling `Dispose` on the `BlockingCollection` calls `Dispose` on its internal `Semaphores`. If threads are already running this might end up causing an `ObjectDisposedException`. Therefore, the safest way to clean up in this scenario is simply to ensure that any waiting tasks know that no more items are to be added so they can exit cleanly.

You can now store the tasks, but you have yet to implement a way to run them—this is next on our agenda. You are going to need a set of STA threads whose job it is to dequeue the tasks and execute them. As your scheduler will be in full control of when this group of threads is manipulated, you can use a simple `List<Thread>` to store them. The STA threads will need to call `TryExecuteTask` to run the tasks. How many threads should you use? You will pass this value in to the scheduler's constructor. Listing 12-6 shows the code for creating the threads and executing the tasks.

Listing 12-6. Creating the STA Threads

```
private readonly List<Thread> threads;

public STATaskScheduler(int numberOfThreads)
{
    threads = new List<Thread>(numberOfThreads);

    for (int i = 0; i < numberOfThreads; i++)
    {
        var thread = new Thread(() =>
            {
                foreach (Task task in tasks.GetConsumingEnumerable())
                {
                    TryExecuteTask(task);
                }
            });
```

```
        thread.SetApartmentState(ApartmentState.STA);

        threads.Add(thread);
        thread.Start();
    }
}
```

Last, you need to implement TryExecuteTaskInline. As this is an STA thread scheduler, you should only execute the task if the scheduler is being called on an STA thread. This implementation is shown in Listing 12-7.

Listing 12-7. Implementing TryExecuteTaskInline

```
protected override bool TryExecuteTaskInline(Task task, bool taskWasPreviouslyQueued)
{
    if (Thread.CurrentThread.GetApartmentState() == ApartmentState.STA)
    {
        return TryExecuteTask(task);
    }

    return false;
}
```

You now have a fairly basic STA task scheduler. In fact, the PFx team built something similar in the Parallel Extensions Extras samples. However, there are a number of issues with this implementation regarding the management of the threads. If you ever need a large number of threads, there will be a big overhead in allocating them all up front when you may not end up using them. Also, even if you have used a large number of threads, if the amount of work the scheduler needs to do shrinks, then you really should remove the idle threads.

Adding Threads on Demand

If you are going to add threads as they are needed, then you cannot spin them up in the constructor; something about QueueTask must trigger thread creation. However, the maximum number of threads must still be capped so you don't consume too many resources. You therefore need to base the decision whether to create a new thread on whether you already have an available thread to process the task, and whether the maximum number of threads has already been hit. You can see the changes in Listing 12-8.

Listing 12-8. Creating Threads on Demand

```
private readonly int maxThreads;
private int threadsInUse;

public STATaskScheduler(int numberOfThreads)
{
    threads = new List<Thread>(numberOfThreads);
    maxThreads = numberOfThreads;
}

private void StartNewPoolThread()
{
    var thread = new Thread(() =>
```

```
    {
        foreach (Task task in tasks.GetConsumingEnumerable())
        {
            Interlocked.Increment(ref threadsInUse);
            TryExecuteTask(task);
            Interlocked.Decrement(ref threadsInUse);
        }
    });

    thread.SetApartmentState(ApartmentState.STA);

    threads.Add(thread);
    thread.Start();
}

protected override void QueueTask(Task task)
{
    tasks.Add(task);

    int threadCount = threads.Count;
    if (threadCount == threadsInUse && threadCount < maxThreads)
    {
        StartNewPoolThread();
    }
}
```

However, there is now a nasty race condition in the code. When you spawn the new thread, it does not yet appear to be in use. If another task is queued before the first thread starts processing its task, then QueueTask will think there is a free thread and so will not spawn a new thread. If there is some dependency between the two tasks, then this could prevent the second task from ever executing. To fix this you need to increment the threadsInUse count before you spawn the thread and then, in the thread-processing loop, increment the threadsInUse count only if the thread has executed its first task. You can see the amended code in Listing 12-9.

Listing 12-9. Fixing the Race Condition

```
private void StartNewPoolThread()
{
    var thread = new Thread(() =>
        {
            bool firstTaskExecuted = false;

            foreach (Task task in tasks.GetConsumingEnumerable())
            {
                if (firstTaskExecuted)
                {
                    Interlocked.Increment(ref threadsInUse);
                }
                else
                {
                    firstTaskExecuted = true;
                }
                TryExecuteTask(task);
                Interlocked.Decrement(ref threadsInUse);
```

```
        }
    });

    thread.SetApartmentState(ApartmentState.STA);

    threads.Add(thread);
    thread.Start();
}

protected override void QueueTask(Task task)
{
    tasks.Add(task);

    int threadCount = threads.Count;
    if (threadCount == threadsInUse && threadCount < maxThreads)
    {
        Interlocked.Increment(ref threadsInUse);
        StartNewPoolThread();
    }
}
```

You may have spotted that there is still a potential issue where the thread has been marked as in use, but another thread becomes free and runs the newly queued task. In that case it won't actually end up doing anything and will instead block on the empty queue. However, this issue will resolve itself when the next task is enqueued as the blocked thread can pick up the new task.

Removing Idle Threads

If you are to remove idle threads, there are a number of factors you need to consider:

1. What is meant by *idle*?

2. What should trigger you to look for idle threads?

3. How do you know if a thread has been idle?

4. How do you stop an idle thread?

5. How do you implement this in a way that you can test the functionality?

An idle thread is one that hasn't performed any work for a period of time. You should periodically look for these. It makes sense, therefore, that the first two items should be time based. However, this presents an issue with Item 5 as unit tests would have to rely on timeouts. To solve this, you will model the idle processing via an abstraction, as you can see in Listing 12-10. The CheckIdle event signals the scheduler to look for idle threads, and the IdleTimeout specifies how long a thread should be idle before it should be removed from the pool.

Listing 12-10. Idle Detection Abstraction

```
public interface IIdleTrigger : IDisposable
{
    event EventHandler CheckIdle;
    TimeSpan IdleTimeout { get; }
}
```

Remember, you are using this abstraction to be able to provide a test version of the idle trigger, but you will of course require a timer-based one for normal execution. You can see this in Listing 12-11.

Listing 12-11. Timer-Based Idle Trigger

```
class TimerIdleTrigger : IIdleTrigger
{
    private readonly TimeSpan idleTimeout;
    private readonly Timer idleTimer;

    public TimerIdleTrigger(TimeSpan checkFrequency, TimeSpan idleTimeout)
    {
        this.idleTimeout = idleTimeout;
        idleTimer= new Timer(_ => CheckIdle(this, EventArgs.Empty),
                             null,
                             TimeSpan.Zero,
                             checkFrequency);
    }

    public event EventHandler CheckIdle = delegate { };

    public TimeSpan IdleTimeout
    {
        get { return idleTimeout; }
    }

    public void Dispose()
    {
        idleTimer.Dispose();
    }
}
```

The next task is to inject an implementation of the idle trigger into the constructor of the scheduler to be able to unit test effectively. However, normally you will want the timer-based idle trigger, so you'll have two constructors: one that takes an idle trigger and one that defaults to the timer one. During construction you will subscribe to the CheckIdle event of the idle trigger—although we will look at the implementation of the event handler after we have discussed how to recognize a thread is idle. Listing 12-12 shows the code necessary to inject the idle trigger.

Listing 12-12. Injecting the Idle Trigger

```
private const int IDLE_CHECK_FREQUENCY = 5;
private const int IDLE_TIMEOUT = 30;

private readonly int maxThreads;
private readonly IIdleTrigger idleTrigger;

public STATaskScheduler(int maxThreads)
    : this(maxThreads,
           new TimerIdleTrigger(TimeSpan.FromSeconds(IDLE_CHECK_FREQUENCY),
                                TimeSpan.FromSeconds(IDLE_TIMEOUT)))
{
}
```

```
public STATaskScheduler(int maxThreads, IIdleTrigger idleTrigger)
{
    this.maxThreads = maxThreads;
    this.idleTrigger = idleTrigger;

    this.idleTrigger.CheckIdle += CheckForIdleThread;
}
```

You have now dealt with three of the five issues you needed to consider when removing idle threads. However, there are still two outstanding:

- How do you know if a thread is idle?

- How do you stop a thread you want to remove from the pool?

To track the last time a thread is used, you need to record that somewhere. You also need to track whether the thread is currently in use in case it is performing a long-running action whose duration exceeded the idle timeout. Last, you need to encapsulate the mechanism to stop the thread. When a thread is idle it will be waiting on the blocking collection, so you can use a CancellationToken to break out of this wait if you need to stop the thread. You can create a ThreadControl class that encapsulates these pieces of information; it is shown in Listing 12-13.

Listing 12-13. The ThreadControl Class

```
class ThreadControl
{
    private readonly CancellationTokenSource cts;
    public ThreadControl()
    {
        LastUsed = DateTime.UtcNow;
        cts = new CancellationTokenSource();
    }

    public DateTime LastUsed { get; private set; }
    public bool InUse { get; private set; }
    public CancellationToken CancellationToken { get { return cts.Token; } }

    public bool CancelIfIdle(TimeSpan idleTimeout)
    {
        if (!InUse && DateTime.UtcNow - LastUsed > idleTimeout)
        {
            cts.Cancel();
        }

        return cts.IsCancellationRequested;
    }

    public void SetNotInUse()
    {
        LastUsed = DateTime.UtcNow;
        InUse = false;
    }
```

```
public void SetInUse()
{
    InUse = true;
}
}
```

You are going to need to associate the ThreadControl object with the thread so you will have to change the existing data structure that holds the threads from a List<Thread> to a dictionary. However, this is highly concurrent code now, so use a ConcurrentDictionary<ThreadControl, Thread> to simplify the scheduler. The running thread will also now be responsible for updating the ThreadControl's usage status, so the implementation of StartNewPoolThread needs to change to reflect this, as shown in Listing 12-14. The listing also shows the use of the ThreadControl CancellationToken to stop the idle thread when it is blocked waiting on the BlockingCollection.

Listing 12-14. StartNewPoolThread Tracking Thread Usage

```
private void StartNewPoolThread()
{
    bool firstTaskExecuted = false;
    var thread = new Thread(o =>
    {
        try
        {
            var currentThreadControl = (ThreadControl) o;
            foreach (TaskWrapper taskWrapper in
                    taskQueue.GetConsumingEnumerable(currentThreadControl.CancellationToken))
            {
                currentThreadControl.SetInUse();
                // if this is the first task executed then the thread was already
                // marked in-use before it was created
                if (firstTaskExecuted)
                {
                    Interlocked.Increment(ref threadsInUse);
                }
                else
                {
                    firstTaskExecuted = true;
                }
                TryExecuteTask(task);

                currentThreadControl.SetNotInUse();
                Interlocked.Decrement(ref threadsInUse);
            }
        }
        catch (OperationCanceledException)
        {
            // if we haven't yet run a task when cancelled
            // then need to decrement the threadsInUse count as
            // it won't yet have been reset
            if (!firstTaskExecuted)
            {
                Interlocked.Decrement(ref threadsInUse);
            }
```

```
        }
    });

    thread.SetApartmentState(ApartmentState.STA);

    var threadControl = new ThreadControl();
    threads.TryAdd(threadControl, thread);

    thread.Start(threadControl);
}
```

Last, you need to implement CheckForIdleThread, the event handler wired up to the idle trigger. This method's job is to look at each thread and verify whether it has now been idle longer than the timeout in the idle trigger and, if so, to stop the thread using the CancellationToken (this is handled internally by the ThreadControl CancelIfIdle method). You can see the implementation of CheckForIdleThread in Listing 12-15.

Listing 12-15. Checking for Idle Threads

```
private void CheckForIdleThread(object sender, EventArgs e)
{
    TimeSpan timeoutToCheck = idleTrigger.IdleTimeout;

    foreach (ThreadControl threadControl in threads.Keys)
    {
        bool cancelled = threadControl.CancelIfIdle(timeoutToCheck);
        if (cancelled)
        {
            Thread thread;
            threads.TryRemove(threadControl, out thread);
            thread.Join(TimeSpan.FromSeconds(5));
        }
    }
}
```

This completes the functionality to remove threads from the pool of STA threads if they have been idle for an extended period of time. The ThreadControl class manages the concept of idle, the thread function tells the ThreadControl when the thread is in use, and the idle event handler triggers the examination of each thread to see whether it should be stopped.

Unit Testing Custom Schedulers

There are a number of issues in writing unit tests for custom schedulers:

- You cannot call the significant scheduler methods directly as they are protected rather than public.

- If you directly invoke the methods, say by reflection, the execution environment may be substantially different from the one the task infrastructure puts in place—so the tests may be meaningless.

- Invoking the scheduler indirectly, via the task infrastructure, makes it difficult to verify the expected outcome.

- The test must not complete before the scheduler as completed its work. Therefore, you require some way of synchronizing the behavior of the test and the scheduler.

However, there are big advantages to being able to create quality tests for schedulers as they have an inherent complexity. As you evolve their functionality it is comforting to be able to verify that you have not inadvertently changed unrelated behavior. So how do you write tests against an asynchronous component that you can't directly invoke? There are three approaches you can take:

1. Use constrained numbers of threads and synchronization primitives in your tasks to ensure execution order in the scheduler.

2. Add members to the scheduler (e.g., events and properties) to provide insight into the scheduler's behavior.

3. Derive a class from the scheduler that allows you to verify behavior that only the task infrastructure would normally see.

These approaches should not be seen as mutually exclusive but rather as different tools you can use to elicit and verify different behavior. Let's look at an example of each of them.

Controlling Execution Order with Synchronization Primitives

If you restrict the number of threads available to the scheduler, you can use synchronization primitives to control whether or not these threads are available to perform multiple tasks. For example, to verify that the STATaskScheduler does execute tasks on STA threads, you need to make sure that the task has executed before attempting that verification. Listing 12-16 shows the use of a ManualResetEventSlim to ensure that the ApartmentState of the task's thread is captured before you perform the assertion. In this specific example you could also wait on the task itself. However, it is also a good idea to make sure that any wait is given a timeout. If you don't provide a timeout, and the scheduler doesn't actually execute the task, then the test would never end and the failure would be not be obvious.

Listing 12-16. Contolling Execution Order with ManualResetEventSlim

```
[TestMethod]
public void QueueTask_WhenQueuesFirstTask_ShouldExecuteTaskOnSTAThread()
{
    using (var scheduler = new STATaskScheduler(1, new StubIdleTrigger()))
    {
        ApartmentState apartment = ApartmentState.MTA;
        var evt = new ManualResetEventSlim();

        Task t = new Task(() =>
            {
                apartment = Thread.CurrentThread.GetApartmentState();
                evt.Set();
            });

        t.Start(scheduler);
```

```
        if (evt.Wait(1000))
        {
            Assert.AreEqual(ApartmentState.STA, apartment);
        }
        else
        {
            Assert.Fail();
        }
    }
}
```

A more complex situation is verifying that if the scheduler does not have an available thread when the task is enqueued, then it will wait for the thread to become available before executing the task. This test can be seen in Listing 12-17. The test uses multiple synchronization primitives to ensure control of the precise execution order: evt makes sure that you don't decrement the currentConcurrency until the maxConcurrency has been captured, incrementDoneEvt ensures that the increment has taken place, and countdownDone ensures that both tasks have finished their work (you could also use Task.WaitAll for this purpose).

Listing 12-17. Using Multiple Primitives for Controlling Execution

```
[TestMethod]
public void QueueTask_WhenQueuesTaskAndAllThreadsBusy_ShouldWaitUntilThreadFree()
{
    using (var scheduler = new STATaskScheduler(1, new StubIdleTrigger()))
    {
        int maxConcurrency = 0;
        int currentConcurrency = 0;
        var evt = new ManualResetEventSlim();
        var countdownDone = new CountdownEvent(2);
        var incrementDoneEvt = new ManualResetEventSlim();

        Task t = new Task(() =>
            {
                maxConcurrency = Interlocked.Increment(ref currentConcurrency);
                incrementDoneEvt.Set();
                evt.Wait();
                Interlocked.Decrement(ref currentConcurrency);
                countdownDone.Signal();
            });
        Task t2 = new Task(() =>
            {
                maxConcurrency = Interlocked.Increment(ref currentConcurrency);
                incrementDoneEvt.Set();
                evt.Wait();
                Interlocked.Decrement(ref currentConcurrency);
                countdownDone.Signal();
            });

        t.Start(scheduler);
        t2.Start(scheduler);
```

```
        incrementDoneEvt.Wait();
        evt.Set();

        if (countdownDone.Wait(1000))
        {
            Assert.AreEqual(1, maxConcurrency);
        }
        else
        {
            Assert.Fail();
        }
    }
}
```

Adding Members to the Scheduler to Provide Insight

It may seem inappropriate to change the public interface of a class to be able to test it, but if testability is a priority then it is a useful technique. In this case the issue is also mitigated by the fact that only the task infrastructure will ever normally invoke methods on the scheduler. As an example, how do you verify that a task is not inlined when Wait is called on it from a non-STA thread? If you add an event to the STATaskScheduler that gets fired if the task is not inlined, then the test becomes fairly straightforward, as Listing 12-18 demonstrates.

Listing 12-18. Adding a Member to Aid Testability

```
[TestMethod]
public void TryExecuteTaskInline_WhenTriggeredFromNonSTAThread_ShouldNotExecuteTask()
{
    var evt = new ManualResetEventSlim();
    var notInlinedEvent = new ManualResetEventSlim();
    int callingThread = -1;
    int executionThread = -1;
    using (var scheduler = new STATaskScheduler(1))
    {
        scheduler.TaskNotInlined += (s, e) =>
            {
                notInlinedEvent.Set();
            };

        var t1 = new Task(() =>
        {
            evt.Wait();
        });

        var t2 = new Task(() =>
        {
            executionThread = Thread.CurrentThread.ManagedThreadId;
        });

        t1.Start(scheduler);
        t2.Start(scheduler);
```

```
        var staThread = new Thread(() =>
            {
                callingThread = Thread.CurrentThread.ManagedThreadId;
                t2.Wait();
            });
        staThread.SetApartmentState(ApartmentState.MTA);
        staThread.IsBackground = true;
        staThread.Start();

        notInlinedEvent.Wait();

        evt.Set();

        t2.Wait();
    }

    Assert.AreNotEqual(callingThread, executionThread);
}
```

Deriving a Testable Class from the Scheduler

One of the methods you need to test is GetScheduledTasks. The problem is that it is protected and so you cannot access it directly from the test code (unless you resort to reflection). You can, however, derive from your scheduler and expose the information you need from the derived class. Listing 12-19 shows a SpySTAScheduler class that derives from STATaskScheduler and allows you to see what the STATaskScheduler returns from GetScheduledTasks via its public GetTasks method.

Listing 12-19. Deriving from the Scheduler to Expose Information

```
class SpySTAScheduler : STATaskScheduler
{
    public SpySTAScheduler(int maxThreads, IIdleTrigger idleTrigger)
        : base(maxThreads, idleTrigger)
    {
    }

    public IEnumerable<Task> GetTasks()
    {
        return GetScheduledTasks();
    }
}
```

You can now use the SpySTAScheduler in a test to verify behavior of the STATaskScheduler as can be seen in Listing 12-20.

Listing 12-20. Using the SpySTAScheduler in a Test

```
 [TestMethod]
public void GetScheduledTasks_WhenCalled_ShouldReturnAllTasksNotYetExecuting()
{
    IEnumerable<Task> tasks;
```

```
Task t2;
Task t3;

using (var scheduler = new SpySTAScheduler(1, new StubIdleTrigger()))
{
    var evt = new ManualResetEventSlim();

    Task t1 = new Task(() =>
    {
        evt.Set();
    });

    t1.Start(scheduler);

    t2 = new Task(() =>
    {
    });

    t2.Start(scheduler);
    t3 = new Task(() =>
    {
    });

    t3.Start(scheduler);

    tasks = scheduler.GetTasks();

    evt.Set();
}

Assert.IsNotNull(tasks.SingleOrDefault(t => t == t2));
Assert.IsNotNull(tasks.SingleOrDefault(t => t == t3));
}
```

Summary

As you have seen, the pluggable model of task scheduling means that as new releases of the .NET framework occur, richer models of task scheduling can be introduced. However, more importantly, you can create customer task schedulers that meet your requirements. You saw that creating the essential behavior of a custom task scheduler is fairly straightforward. Adding features to make the scheduler more efficient in its use of threads does add some complexity, but is also very achievable. One of the biggest challenges with asynchronous code in general, and custom schedulers in particular, is writing effective unit tests. However, as described in this chapter, there are techniques you can use to alleviate some of the issues.

CHAPTER 13

■ ■ ■

Debugging Async with Visual Studio

Debugging multithreaded applications is often nontrivial. This is because they have multiple threads of execution running asynchronously and, to some degree, independently. These threads can sometimes interact in unexpected ways, causing your code to malfunction. However, exactly when the threads execute depends on the Windows thread scheduler. It is therefore possible that one instance of a program will run perfectly fine whereas another will crash—and the only thing that is different is how and when the different threads were scheduled.

Not only is identifying bugs harder with multithreaded applications, but the actual type of bug can be something you do not experience in a single-threaded application. Multithreaded applications are subject to whole new classes of bugs that can be confusing when first encountered. Let's have a look at some of the potential issues.

Types of Multithreading Bugs

There are four main classes of bugs in multithreaded applications:

1. data corruption

2. race conditions

3. deadlocks

4. runaway threads

We've mentioned these over the course of the book, but what do they actually mean? Let's look at the nature of these bugs before we move on to how Visual Studio can help you track them down and fix them.

Data Corruption

In Chapter 4 you looked at how non-atomic updates of shared data, when executed on multiple threads, can cause data corruption. On modern hardware it is fairly straightforward to demonstrate that this is happening by rapidly performing non-atomic increments of a value from more than one thread simultaneously. However, in most applications unsynchronized updates would only very occasionally collide, and so these kind of bugs are often hard to spot, with infrequent aberrant behavior that cannot be easily reproduced.

Race Conditions

A race condition is an issue in software where, depending on the sequencing of instructions on different threads, incorrect behavior may result. In some ways these are a superset of data corruption as data only get corrupted when two non-atomic updates interleave. Race conditions, however, go beyond data corruption to pure timing issues. For example, if you have a controller thread and a processing thread, the processing thread may be expecting the controller to have set up some execution parameters before it runs. However, without synchronization, the processor may start processing before the execution parameters have been set.

Deadlocks

Deadlocks (sometimes referred to as deadly embraces) occur when two or more threads need to acquire resources that, for some reason, cannot be released. As a result the affected threads block and will not continue execution. Sometimes deadlocks can be fairly obvious as the application freezes, but other kinds of deadlocks can be more difficult to detect.

Imagine a web application where different threads are executing requests. Assume that as part of the execution they have to obtain multiple, concurrent locks on synchronization objects. If one thread tries to get Lock A, then Lock B and another wants Lock B, then Lock A, then they will deadlock if the first thread gets Lock A and the second gets B, as neither will be able to proceed (see Figure 13-1).

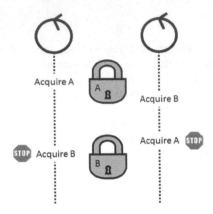

Figure 13-1. *Two threads deadlocking*

Assume this deadlock is happening occasionally in the application, causing you to gradually lose request threads as they become stuck in deadlocks. The problem is that, in terms of visible symptoms, the web application will have occasional request timeouts and will generally just get slower and slower as you end up with fewer and fewer available request threads. Operations staff will spot that a reboot cures the problem but they will not be able to identify deadlocks as the underlying cause. The performance degradation could be deadlocks but could also be GC thrashing, network issues, large numbers of exceptions being thrown, and many other causes. This is why you should generally use timeouts when waiting for locks, as you will be able to proactively log that there is an issue.

Runaway Threads

A runaway thread is one that consumes a lot of CPU for no real benefit. A common cause is when a thread ends up in a tight processing loop due to a bug in the code (maybe a wait is being skipped, or the loop's exit condition is never being hit). If you have a small number of cores available, then it is fairly obvious when this happens (assuming you are not trying to saturate the CPU with a parallel algorithm), as Task Manager will show a high-percentage CPU usage. When you have a large number of cores, however, it is far less obvious, as even with one core being consumed by the runaway thread, the overall machine load on a 16-core machine would be 6.25 percent, which is unlikely to raise alarm bells.

The Limitations of Using Visual Studio for Debugging

Visual Studio is a very powerful debugging tool, and shortly we will look at a number of features that can assist with debugging multithreaded applications. However, before we do, it is worth noting the limitations of using Visual Studio in this situation.

The Interactive Debugger

Although a very convenient tool in your debugging toolbox, an interactive debugger is quite invasive to program execution. As a result, particularly with timing-related issues, you may never be able to reproduce a bug inside a debugging session (at least not without taking explicit control of instruction ordering, as you will see hereafter).

It Works on My Machine

It is not uncommon for problems to occur in production that are very hard, if not impossible, to reproduce on a development machine. This happens for a variety of reasons: the hardware is different, the data volumes are different, or a different mix of software is executing on the machine. You are extremely unlikely to be able to install Visual Studio on the production machine, and even if you are allowed you shouldn't. Visual Studio brings with it a lot of extra components and system DLLs that could alter the behavior of the production systems. In addition, even using remote debugging is going to be a problem, as the interactive debugger will halt execution of the production system. So in the case of production debugging, you need to take another approach, and that is covered in Chapter 14.

Multithreaded Visual Studio Debugging Basics

There are quite a few tools inside Visual Studio to help you debug multiple threads. However, before we get there we should go through a few basics of how the interactive debugger interacts with threads and what the most familiar tools show you.

Breakpoints and Threads

If you set a breakpoint on a line of code, then by default any thread that hits that breakpoint will halt execution. However, it is not only the thread that hit the breakpoint that halts in the debugger, but *all* of threads in the process will break. This makes sense as otherwise, while you are looking at various aspects of the program, values would be changing under your feet.

It is possible to add a filter to a breakpoint so that it only breaks on one or more specific threads. Right-click on the breakpoint and select `Filter....` This will show the Breakpoint Filter dialog shown in Figure 13-2.

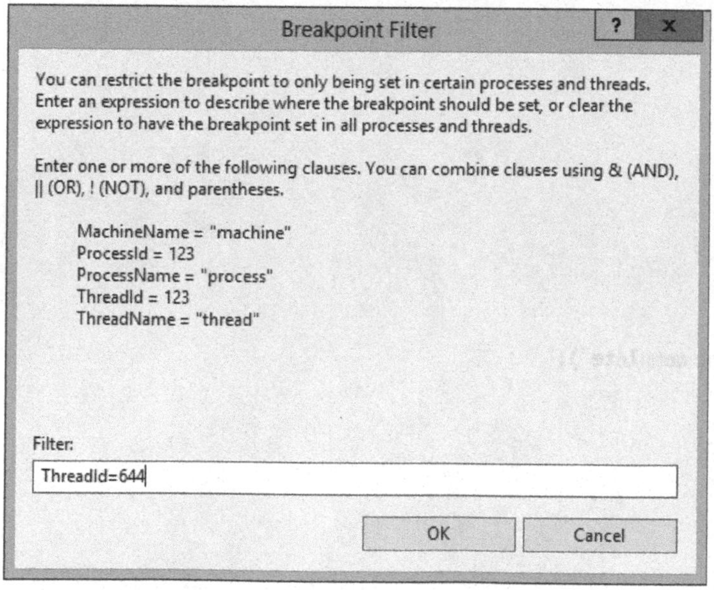

Figure 13-2. *The Breakpoint Filter dialog*

Not only can you restrict the breakpoint to specific threads, but also to specific processes and machines (useful if debugging multiple processes or multiple machines using remote debugging). Note that the ThreadId in the Breakpoint Filter dialog uses the unmanaged Windows thread id and not the .NET thread ManagedThreadId.

Now you are stopped on a breakpoint—what happens when you single-step using F10 or F11? At this point things get a bit trickier; the current thread will single-step, but all of the other threads will leap forward at full speed until the current thread breaks at the next instruction. This means that you can't really use breakpoints, on their own, to control the sequencing of instructions across different threads.

Locals, Autos, and Watch Windows

The Locals, Autos, and Watch debug windows are for examining the state of variables. The Watch windows (you can have up to four of them) and the Locals and Autos show the values of variables in the context of the thread currently in scope. If, in the Watch windows, you are watching variables that are not applicable to the current thread, or are not in scope generally, the debugger will report that those variables are not recognized in the current context.

The Call Stack Window

As you saw in Chapter 1, each thread has its own stack. This means the call stack is specific to a thread. The Call Stack window shows the call stack for the thread that is currently in focus. For much async work this is fairly straightforward, but in .NET 4.5 the C# team introduced the new async and await keywords (see Chapter 7), which create an issue for debugging. As Chapter 7 noted, async and await allow you to describe your intent with asynchrony while the compiler takes care of the mechanics for you. However, the debugger works against the compiled code rather than the source and will reflect the reality of execution. Consider the code in Listing 13-1. If you put a breakpoint on the second Console.WriteLine in RunWorkAsync (the line in bold) and then run in the debugger, what does the call stack look like?

Listing 13-1. A Simple Async Wait Using await

```csharp
class Program
{
    static void Main(string[] args)
    {
        DoWork();

        Console.ReadLine();
    }

    static async Task RunWorkAsync()
    {
        Console.WriteLine("Starting work");

        await Task.Delay(2000);

        Console.WriteLine("background work complete");
    }

    static async Task DoWork()
    {
        await RunWorkAsync();

        Console.WriteLine("DoWork");
    }
}
```

Considering the amount of work the compiler has done behind the scenes, it is somewhat surprising that there appears to be very little on the call stack. You can see the default output in Figure 13-3. By default, a feature called Just My Code is enabled in the IDE, which provides a simplified view of the call stack.

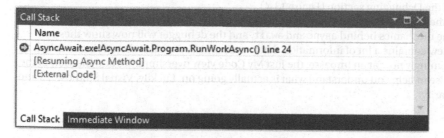

Figure 13-3. *Async call stack with Just My Code enabled*

Just My Code

Just My Code, as the name suggests, only shows you code that is in the solution you are debugging. Any external code is identified as such and hidden from you. If you look at the same call stack from Listing 13-1 with Just My Code enabled (Figure 13-4), you have a much cleaner picture of what is happening in your application. However, things aren't perfect; the breakpoint is in a method that is in turn invoked by an asynchronous method. This level of indirection is lost in the Call Stack window.

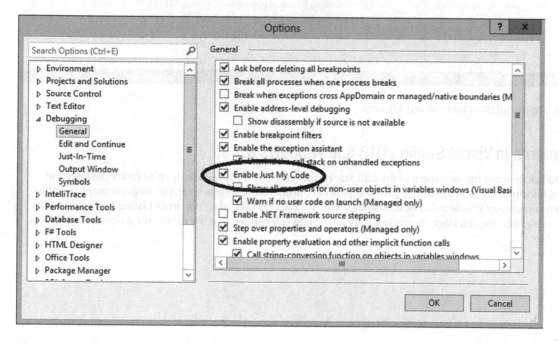

Figure 13-4. *Changing the Just My Code settings*

Just My Code can certainly help with clarity, but it can also obscure the cause of bugs in your code. For example, a thread blocked in Monitor.Enter could be an indication of a deadlock. Because Monitor.Enter is not part of your code, the call will be hidden if you have Just My Code enabled. In general, remember that Just My Code is a setting you can change if the feature will help or hinder the debugging task at hand. The toggle for this debugging setting is in the options under the Tools menu, in the Debugging section (Figure 13-4).

If you disable Just My Code, the Call Stack window now looks like Figure 13-5. This is because the compiler has done a lot of work to create the mechanics behind async and await, and the debugger will now show these mechanics. This unadulterated view contains a lot of information that is unlikely to be useful when trying to debug a problem in your code. You are seemingly now at an impasse: the Just My Code view oversimplifies and the view of the mechanics contains too much noise to help you understand what is actually going on. Luckily, Visual Studio 2013 and Windows 8.1 have added some clarity.

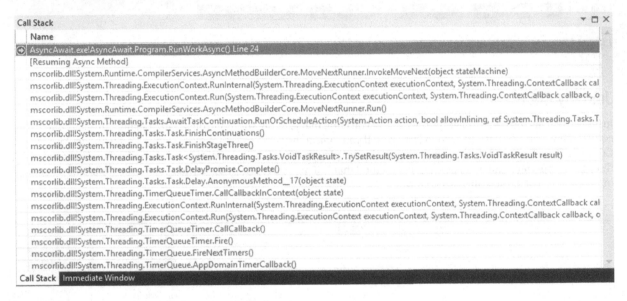

Figure 13-5. *Async call stack without Just My Code*

Improvements in Visual Studio 2013 and Windows 8.1

Visual Studio brings some improvement to the Call Stack window to show the missing level of indirection seen in Figure 13-3. Unfortunately, due to some required support at the operating system level, this improvement can only be seen when running on Windows 8.1 or Windows Server 2012 R2. Running the code from Listing 13-1 in this new environment gives you the call stack shown in Figure 13-6. Here you can see that the previous async call in DoWork is now also visible.

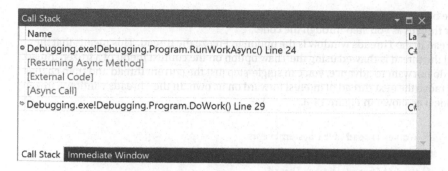

Figure 13-6. *Improved async Call Stack window in Visual Studio 2013*

The Threads Window

The Threads window has been a feature of managed debugging with Visual Studio since .NET 1.0. When the application is stopped in the debugger, the Threads window shows all of the threads currently running in the process. However, this is not limited to managed threads but all of the operating system threads. In Figure 13-7 you can see the call stack from the code in Listing 13-1. From the managed code perspective there are really only two interesting threads: those with the Managed IDs of 10 and 11. The rest of the threads are from the infrastructure controlling the managed execution in the debugger.

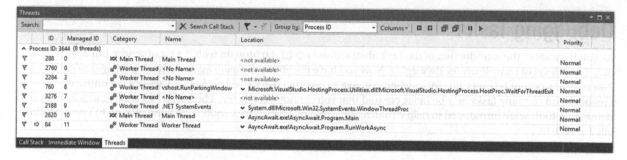

Figure 13-7. *The Threads window in action*

Flagging and Filtering

Although the picture is muddied by the infrastructure threads it is possible to filter out the ones that are concerned with your code. You can manually flag them by clicking on the flag symbol on the left of the thread's row, or you can click the flag symbol on the Thread window's toolbar. Once threads are flagged a double flag toolbar button becomes enabled, which will constrain the visible threads to only those that are flagged. You remove the flag on a thread by clicking the flag symbol on the left of the thread's row again.

Freezing and Thawing

You saw earlier that, by their very nature, race conditions are difficult to reproduce reliably. Analyzing the different code paths and how they might be interleaved is an important step to creating a hypothesis for the cause of the bug, but how do you prove the hypothesis? You need to force a specific sequencing of operations that, hopefully, will display the same symptoms as the bug. But you also saw that simply setting a breakpoint on one thread will not give you precise control over the other threads as you step through the code.

On the context menu of a thread in the Threads window is the option to Freeze the thread. This means that the thread will not be scheduled until the thread is thawed using the Thaw option on the context menu of a frozen thread. If you freeze the threads that you do not want to advance, you can single-step just the current thread and then change the frozen and thawed threads to move the next thread of interest forward on its own. In the Threads window a frozen thread has a "pause" symbol beside it as shown in Figure 13-8.

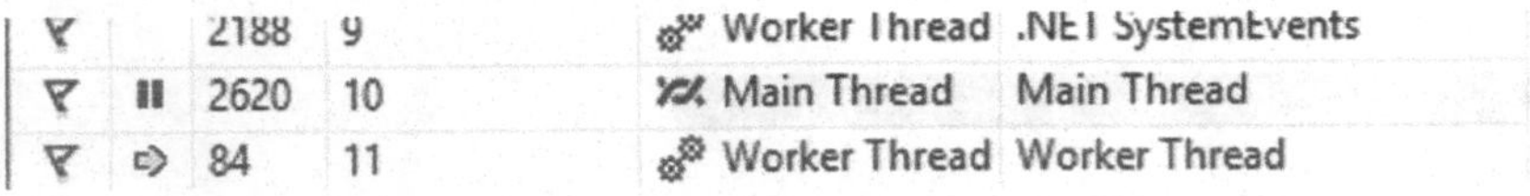

▼		2188	9	⚙ Worker Thread	.NET SystemEvents
▼	‖	2620	10	✖ Main Thread	Main Thread
▼	⇨	84	11	⚙ Worker Thread	Worker Thread

Figure 13-8. A frozen thread in the Threads window

Although freezing and thawing threads does allow you to control, precisely, the sequencing of instruction execution on different threads, it is still very error prone in nontrivial situations.

■ **Caution** Beware of freezing threads that are explicitly or implicitly holding locks. Your application may deadlock during debugging because the frozen thread will be unable to release its lock as it is not being scheduled.

Debugging Tasks

As you have seen, the introduction of the Task abstraction in .NET 4.0 brought with it a lot of power, but also, it turns out, a new level of complexity for debugging. Now you have the ability to create asynchronous packages of code that may or may not be executing. Also, when you use a construct like Parallel.For you are not in control of Task creation, and so many tasks may be being created that you cannot directly see. Therefore, in Visual Studio 2010 new debugging tools were introduced to help visualize the world of Tasks. These tools have been refined in Visual Studio 2012 and 2013.

The Parallel Tasks / Tasks Window

Playing a role similar to the one that the Threads window does for threads, the Parallel Tasks window, introduced in Visual Studio 2010, allowed you to see all of the noncompleted tasks in the process—including those that had not been committed to a thread by the scheduler. In Visual Studio 2013 this debugging window has been renamed, simply, the Tasks window, and its functionality has been expanded. Figure 13-9 shows the Visual Studio 2013 Tasks window when a Parallel.ForEach is in progress. Notice that the one of the tasks has yet to be mapped to a thread and so is shown as Scheduled.

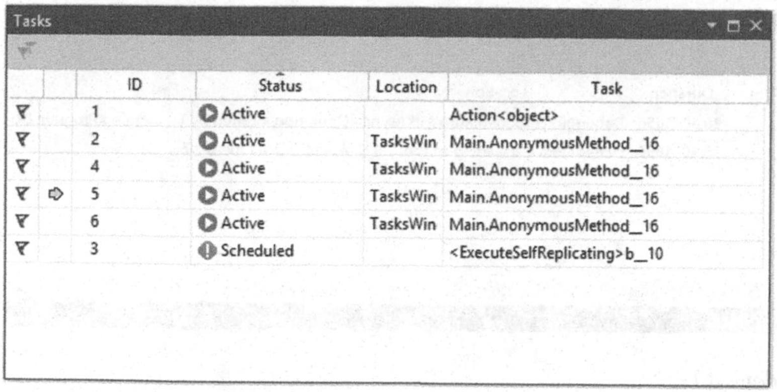

		ID	Status	Location	Task
▽		1	▶ Active		Action<object>
▽		2	▶ Active	TasksWin	Main.AnonymousMethod__16
▽		4	▶ Active	TasksWin	Main.AnonymousMethod__16
▽	⇨	5	▶ Active	TasksWin	Main.AnonymousMethod__16
▽		6	▶ Active	TasksWin	Main.AnonymousMethod__16
▽		3	⏸ Scheduled		<ExecuteSelfReplicating>b__10

Figure 13-9. The Tasks window

When running on Windows 8.1 the Tasks window has even more information available, as can be seen in Figure 13-10. Here you get the start time relative to the start of the debugging session and how long the task has been running.

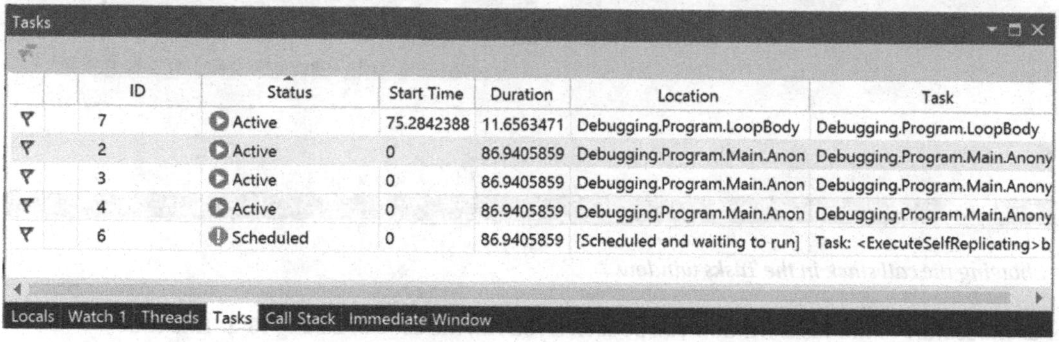

	ID	Status	Start Time	Duration	Location	Task
▽	7	▶ Active	75.2842388	11.6563471	Debugging.Program.LoopBody	Debugging.Program.LoopBody
▽	2	▶ Active	0	86.9405859	Debugging.Program.Main.Anon	Debugging.Program.Main.Anony
▽	3	▶ Active	0	86.9405859	Debugging.Program.Main.Anon	Debugging.Program.Main.Anony
▽	4	▶ Active	0	86.9405859	Debugging.Program.Main.Anon	Debugging.Program.Main.Anony
▽	6	⏸ Scheduled	0	86.9405859	[Scheduled and waiting to run]	Task: <ExecuteSelfReplicating>b

Locals | Watch 1 | Threads | **Tasks** | Call Stack | Immediate Window

Figure 13-10. The Tasks window on Windows 8.1

If you look at the code from Listing 13-1 in the Tasks window, you see another striking difference between Visual Studio 2013 running on Windows 8 and Windows 8.1. On Windows 8 the Tasks window shows no tasks at all. However, the Tasks window on Windows 8.1 shows you some very useful information, as you can see in Figure 13-11. Here you can see a big difference between the Location column and the Task column. The Location column shows where the executing code is, and the Task column shows some context about the origins of the task.

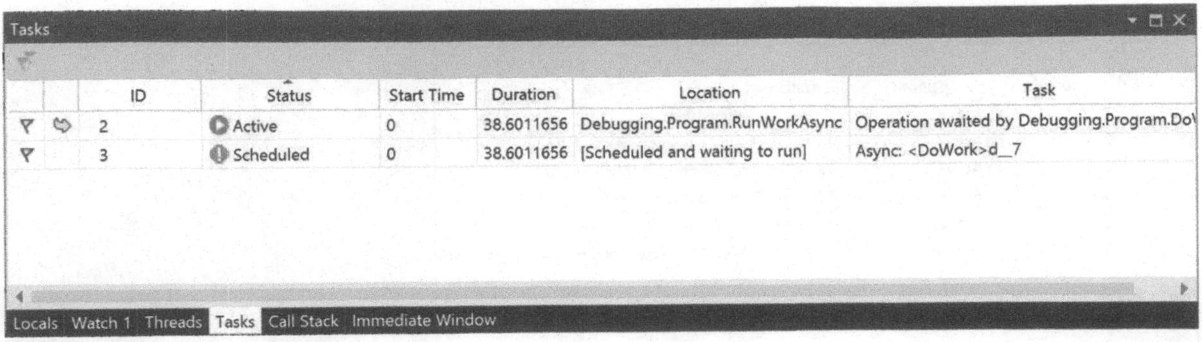

Figure 13-11. *Awaited operations on Windows 8.1*

To give further context to a task, hovering the mouse over a task's location shows the call stack for that task (Figure 13-12).

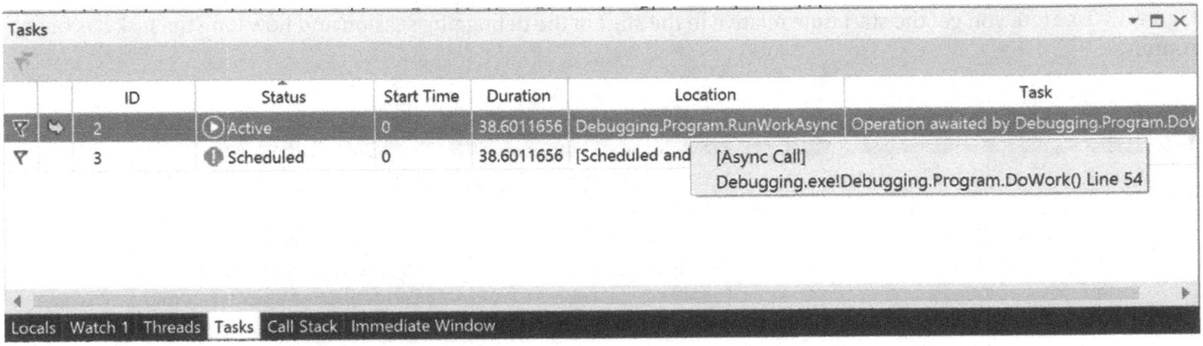

Figure 13-12. *Showing the call stack in the Tasks window*

One other useful feature of the Tasks window can be seen if you run the code in Listing 13-2. This code deliberately forces a deadlock by two tasks taking locks, then waiting for the other task's lock.

Listing 13-2. Forcing a Deadlock

```
static void Main(string[] args)
{
    object guard1 = new object();
    object guard2 = new object();

    Task.Run(() =>
        {
            lock (guard1)
            {
                Thread.Sleep(10);
                lock (guard2)
                {
                }
            }
        });
```

```
    Task.Run(() =>
    {
        lock (guard2)
        {
            Thread.Sleep(10);
            lock (guard1)
            {
            }
        }
    });

    Console.ReadLine();
}
```

The Tasks window notices that the two tasks are deadlocked, as can be seen in Figure 13-13.

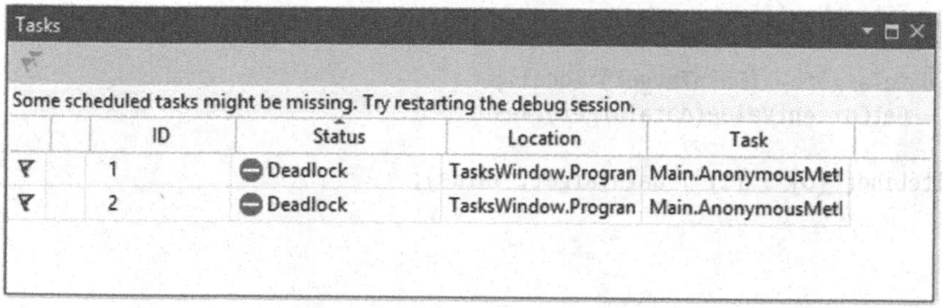

	ID	Status	Location	Task	
▼	1	⊖ Deadlock	TasksWindow.Progran	Main.AnonymousMetl	
▼	2	⊖ Deadlock	TasksWindow.Progran	Main.AnonymousMetl	

Figure 13-13. *Tasks window showing a deadlock*

The Parallel Stacks Window

The Tasks window shows a snapshot of what is happening in the process at this exact moment. To get a more historical view you can use the Parallel Stacks window. This shows, either in terms of threads or tasks, the origins of all executing code. Consider the code in Listing 13-3 with a breakpoint on the bold line of code in CreateChildWorker.

Listing 13-3. Application with Many Tasks

```
class Program
{
    static Dictionary<DataTarget, string[]> dataTargetMap =
                                    new Dictionary<DataTarget, string[]>();
    static void Main(string[] args)
    {
        PopulateMap();
        CheckForCancellation();
        PrintValues().Wait();
    }

    private static void CheckForCancellation()
    {
        // details omitted for brevity
    }
```

```csharp
private static void PopulateMap()
{
    // details omitted for brevity
}

static string[] GetUrls(DataTarget target)
{
    return dataTargetMap[target];
}

static async Task PrintValues()
{
    List<Task> tasks = new List<Task>();
    for (int i = 0; i < 4; i++)
    {
        int locali = i;
        Task t = Task.Factory.StartNew(() =>
            {
                DataTarget dataTarget = (DataTarget) locali;
                long value = GetCurrentValue(dataTarget).Result;

                Console.WriteLine("{0} : {1}", dataTarget, value);
            });

        tasks.Add(t);
    }
    await Task.WhenAll(tasks);
}

static async Task<long> GetCurrentValue(DataTarget dataTarget)
{
    var bag = new ConcurrentBag<long>();
    Task parent = Task.Factory.StartNew(() =>
        {
            foreach (string url in GetUrls(dataTarget))
            {
                CreateChildWorker(url, bag);
            }
        });

    await parent;

    return bag.Max(i => i);
}
```

```
    private static void CreateChildWorker(string url, ConcurrentBag<long> bag)
    {
        WebRequest req = WebRequest.Create(url);
        Task.Factory.StartNew(() =>
            {
                WebResponse resp = req.GetResponse();
                bag.Add(resp.ContentLength);
            }, TaskCreationOptions.AttachedToParent);
    }
}

enum DataTarget
{
    DowJones,
    FTSE,
    NASDAQ,
    HangSeng
}
```

If you bring up the Parallel Stacks window, you will see something along the lines of Figure 13-14 with the various tasks running and their call stacks. You also see the relationship between the different tasks (which paths of execution spawned new tasks). However, here you see a limitation of Just My Code in that the "External Code" hides the full picture of what is going on.

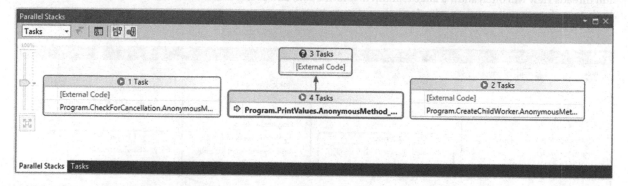

Figure 13-14. *Parallel stacks in Task view using Just My Code*

Turning off Just My Code shows you a far more comprehensive picture where you can see what the "External Code" execution relates to (Figure 13-15). Here you can see that two of the tasks are doing various web calls and three of the tasks are waiting to retrieve the results of other tasks they have spawned. The other thing to notice, generally, about the Parallel Stacks window in Task mode is that you get icons on each task showing the status of the task (running, blocked, deadlocked, etc.).

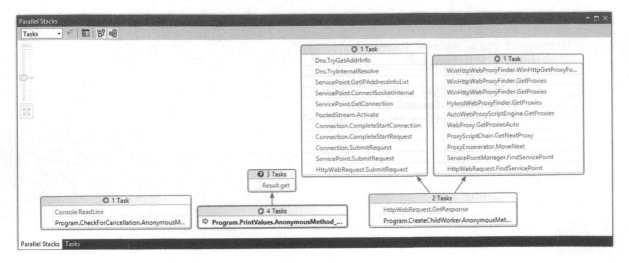

Figure 13-15. *Parallel stacks in Task view without using Just My Code*

In the Parallel Stacks window you can change the view from being task based to showing all of the threads in the process. This is achieved using the drop-down in the top right of the window. Especially when not using Just My Code, you get a very full picture of the state of the process including, potentially, what the finalizer thread is doing. Using this full threads view will often show a large amount of information, and so it is useful that the Parallel Stacks window has both zoom functionality and a navigation helper (Figure 13-16).

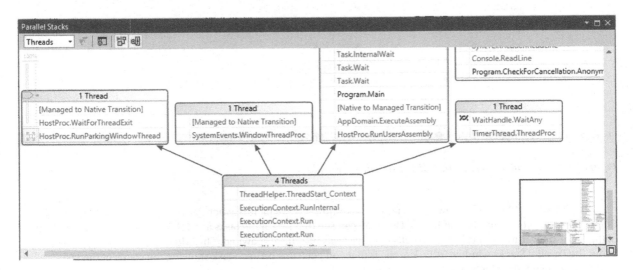

Figure 13-16. *Parallel Stacks windows in Threads mode*

The Concurrency Visualizer

So far we have talked about various ways of viewing an asynchronous application in terms of gaining insight into particular areas of behavior. The Concurrency Visualizer, first introduced in Visual Studio 2010, provides a more holistic view of the application while allowing you to drill down into the specifics where necessary. It is essentially a concurrency profiler (in fact it initially shipped as part of the built-in Visual Studio profiler), so you run it against an application and then examine, in a historical sense, the behavior of the application in terms of its use of multiple threads and cores.

Where you find the Concurrency Visualizer depends on which version of Visual Studio you are using. In Visual Studio 2010 it was packaged as part of the profiler in the Premium and Ultimate editions. In Visual Studio 2012 it had its own menu item in the Analyze menu in the Premium and Ultimate editions. In Visual 2013 it doesn't come packaged in the out-of-the-box IDE, but is a download for all editions from the Visual Studio Gallery.

The Concurrency Visualizer distinguishes different states of a thread by color. Therefore, it is not the most photogenic component of Visual Studio for this medium. However, as Figure 13-17 shows (when converted to grayscale), it can highlight important information.

Figure 13-17. *Thread contention in the Concurrency Visualizer*

Figure 13-17 shows a situation where you have your code locking at a very coarse-grained level. Each thread has to wait for another to leave the lock before it can do its part of the work. In effect you have lost all of the benefits of concurrency in the name of making sure no data get corrupted.

The Concurrency Visualizer is a powerful tool that can show many things, including lack of CPU usage during parallelization, lock contention, threads waiting for I/O, and much more. As such it is an important tool for any async developer.

Summary

Visual Studio is a very powerful debugging tool for software development in general. It has many tools specifically designed to assist with multithreaded debugging and thus should never be dismissed as an aid in resolving issues with multithreaded code. In general, however, Visual Studio assumes you are able to attach an interactive debugger to resolve any bugs that you are seeing. This is not always practical:

- The system may be in production, and attaching an interactive debugger will halt the production system.

- Attaching an interactive debugger to an application is an invasive operation that will change the behavior of the application. With luck that change will not be significant, but all too often it is.

In both of these situations you need an alternative to interactive debugging, and that is the subject of the next chapter.

CHAPTER 14

Debugging Async—Beyond Visual Studio

Visual Studio is a very powerful debugging tool. However, by its very nature, it struggles to provide insight into issues experienced on production machines. Developers cannot install development tools on production machines or attach an interactive debugger; as you have seen, hitting a breakpoint halts execution of all threads in the process, which means the production system halts. Instead, we need an approach that gives us data that we can mine, offline, to discover the root cause of a bug or performance issue. Generally this means using memory dumps.

Memory Dumps

A memory dump is a file containing a copy of the address space of a process. There are, in fact, two types of memory dumps: full dumps and mini dumps. Full dumps contain the entire virtual address space of the process, whereas mini dumps contain only a subset of those data, possibly down to only the stacks of the threads in the process. For native code a mini dump can prove very useful for the issue being investigated, especially if the interesting state resides on the stack. However, managed code heavily relies on heap-based resources—for example, thrown exceptions are allocated on the heap. This means that even though the process may have terminated due to an unhanded exception, with a mini dump you cannot discern the actual cause. Therefore, using memory dumps for debugging managed code generally requires a full dump.

Generating a Memory Dump

To many people the most familiar way of getting a dump file for a process is via Dr. Watson for Windows; however, this only produces mini dumps. Luckily there are a number of alternative techniques that will create full dumps, or at least heavily augmented mini dumps that are useful for managed code debugging.

A QUESTION OF "BITNESS"

Modern versions of Windows are 64 bit. When you write managed code it is commonly compiled for "Any CPU"—in other words, the JIT compiler will compile the code for 64 bit when loaded into the 64-bit subsystem and 32 bit when loaded into the 32-bit subsystem. Sometimes, however, through interop, your managed code is dependent on 32-bit or 64-bit native DLLs. If that is the case you need to ensure your code is always loaded into the correct subsystem, such that the native DLLs can be loaded successfully. You can control this via the Build tab in the project properties where the Platform Target drop-down allows you to specify how the JIT compiler should behave.

Dump files, and the tools you use to analyze them, need to match the "bitness" of the process you are debugging. Fortunately all of the tools used for generating dump files have the potential to create a dump file with the correct bitness.

Sometimes you have to work with what you have—for example, a customer has generated a mismatched dump file and it can't easily be recreated. Fortunately, all is not lost and workarounds for mismatches can sometimes be found. Generally, however, life is always far smoother if the tools and the application are aligned.

Task Manager

Since Windows Vista we have been able to right-click on a process in Task Manager and select Create Dump File. This will generate a dump file in the current user's profile in the \AppData\Local\Temp directory. As long as you are simply trying to take a snapshot of a process, this is probably the simplest method of generating a dump file. However, because Task Manager is part of the operating system, it is easy to forget that it is bound to either 32 bit or 64 bit. On a 64-bit operating system the Task Manager you will normally see is a 64-bit application. As the "A Question of 'Bitness'" sidebar explains, this is not a problem for 64-bit applications but will cause issues with 32-bit applications. So how do you know whether the application for which you want to create a dump file is a 32-bit or 64-bit application?

By default Task Manager doesn't show the subsystem a process is running in. To see this information you have to show an extra column in the Details view of Task Manager. You can do this by right-clicking on the column headers and selecting Select Columns. If you click the Platform check box you will see a new Platform column showing either 32 bit or 64 bit (Figure 14-1).

Name ▲	PID	Status	User name	CPU	Memory (p...	Platform	Description	
armsvc.exe	1288	Running	SYSTEM	00	812 K	32 bit	Adobe Acro....	
cmd.exe	4580	Running	richard	00	756 K	64 bit	Windows C...	
cmd.exe	5020	Running	richard	00	504 K	32 bit	Windows C...	
cmd.exe	984	Running	richard	00	1,336 K	64 bit	Windows C...	≡
conhost.exe	3704	Running	richard	00	604 K	64 bit	Console Wi...	
conhost.exe	3188	Running	richard	00	904 K	64 bit	Console Wi...	
conhost.exe	1368	Running	richard	00	600 K	64 bit	Console Wi...	
conhost.exe	4268	Running	richard	00	864 K	64 bit	Console Wi...	
conhost.exe	516	Running	richard	00	620 K	64 bit	Console Wi...	
conhost.exe	68	Running	richard	00	908 K	64 bit	Console Wi...	
csrss.exe	380	Running	SYSTEM	00	1,084 K	64 bit	Client Serve...	
csrss.exe	456	Running	SYSTEM	00	1,616 K	64 bit	Client Serve...	
Deadlocks.exe	4304	Running	richard	00	8,520 K	32 bit	Deadlocks	
Deadlocks.vshost.exe	5004	Running	richard	00	4,284 K	32 bit	vshost32-cl...	
devenv.exe	3708	Running	richard	00	251,340 K	32 bit	Microsoft V...	
dllhost.exe	2764	Running	SYSTEM	00	3,136 K	64 bit	COM Surro...	
dwm.exe	796	Running	DWM-1	00	10,512 K	64 bit	Desktop Wi...	
explorer.exe	3388	Running	richard	00	49,240 K	64 bit	Windows Ex...	
IntelliTrace.exe	324	Running	richard	00	21,964 K	32 bit	IntelliTrace....	
JabberVideo.exe	3160	Running	richard	00	20,432 K	32 bit	Jabber Video	
JetBrains.TrayNotifie...	3252	Running	richard	00	928 K	32 bit	TeamCity T...	
jusched.exe	1660	Running	richard	00	744 K	32 bit	Java(TM) U...	
lsass.exe	556	Running	SYSTEM	00	4,156 K	64 bit	Local Securi...	∨

Figure 14-1. Task Manager showing Platform

If the process is 64 bit, then you can happily create the dump file directly and it will be perfectly usable. However, if the process is 32 bit, then to get a usable dump file you need to run the 32-bit version of Task Manager and capture the dump using that. On a 64-bit machine you will find the 32-bit version of Task Manager (`taskmgr.exe`) under the `Windows` directory in the `SysWOW64` subdirectory.

DebugDiag

If you call Microsoft Product Support with a server problem, and they need a memory dump to aid their diagnosis, they will very likely ask you to install a tool called DebugDiag on the machine. They will then walk you through configuring it to create one or more dump files. DebugDiag is a free download from Microsoft's website. It installs as a Windows service and monitors applications, generating dump files according to a set of configurable rules.

Adding Rules

Rules are added using a wizard. By default, this wizard starts automatically when the DebugDiag Collection application is started. However, if you have turned this off it can be found as the Tools ➤ Rule Actions ➤ Add Rule menu option. The initial page of the wizard is shown in Figure 14-2.

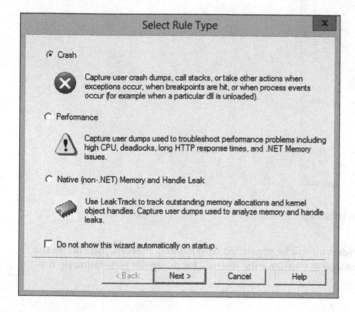

Figure 14-2. *The Add Rule Wizard*

There are three types of rules that you can add: Crash, Performance, and Native (non-.NET) Memory and Handle Leak. These labels, however, don't tell the whole story. For example, the Crash option allows you to create dumps on a far more flexible basis than simply if the application crashes. Let's look at the options in more detail.

Crash

Certainly the crash option can be used for capturing a memory dump when an application crashes, but as you have seen, threading bugs rarely manifest themselves as program crashes. Fortunately, the Crash option is far more flexible than just capturing simple crashes. First you need to select the process to monitor, and again you have a choice. When you click the Next button with the Crash option selected you are presented with the Select Target Type wizard (Figure 14-3). Of these options, only three really apply to managed code: a process (for standard applications), an IIS web application pool (for ASP.NET web applications or services), and an NT service (for code deployed as a service). Select the most appropriate option for your needs and you will be presented with the corresponding list of targets (processes, application pools, or services). One option to note when selecting a process is that you can opt to monitor just one running instance of a process or all instances of that process (including ones that have yet to be started).

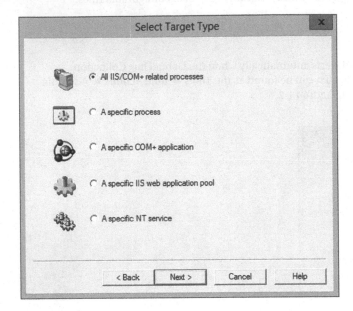

Figure 14-3. *The Select Target Type page of the Crash Wizard*

Once you have selected the target and pressed Next you will be presented with a dialog that lets you choose the process, service or IIS application pool. Once this is selected, you can tune the rule for dump file generation on the Advanced Configuration Dialog (Figure 14-4).

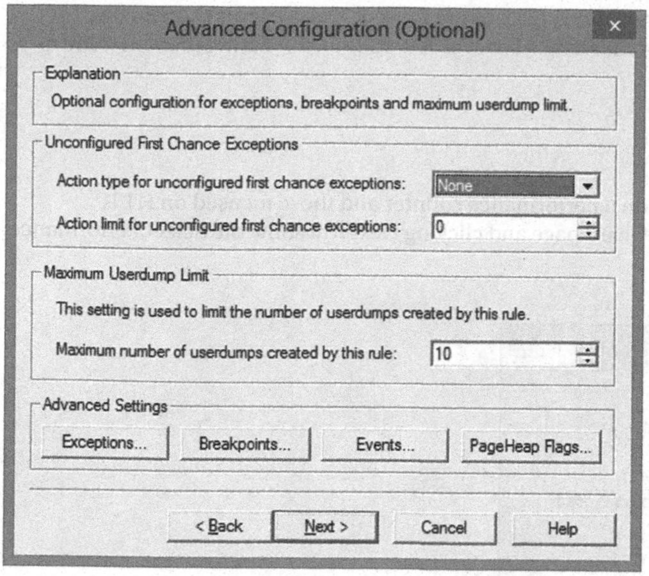

Figure 14-4. *The Advanced Configuration dialog*

If you simply click Next, you will create a rule that generates a single dump file if the process terminates unexpectedly. However, for multithreaded debugging there is another useful option you can enable. In the Events part of the advanced configuration you can add events to monitor for thread creation and exit (Figure 14-5). This means that you can auto-generate a dump file every time a new thread is created or exits (remember to select the option to generate a full dump).

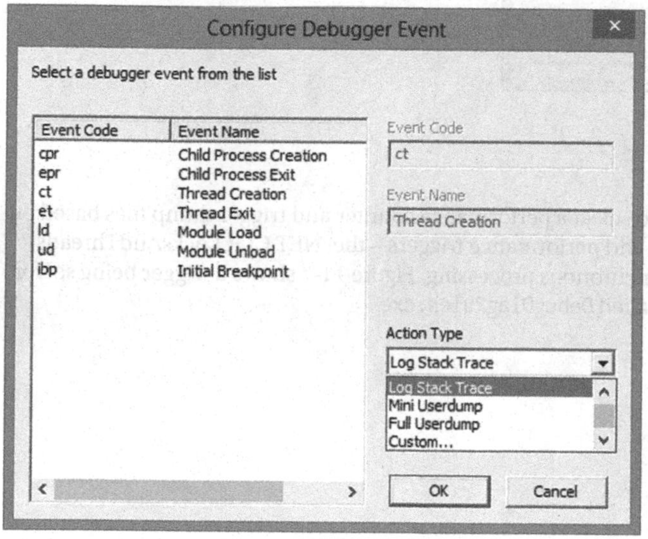

Figure 14-5. *The Add Event dialog*

One thing to consider, however, is that with the thread pool, threads are reused. These events therefore will not necessarily map to new items of work being executed or finishing. However, it is still worth bearing them in mind as one way to trigger dump file creation.

Performance

There are two types of performance rules: those based on a performance counter and those focused on HTTP. Selecting the Performance option on the initial Crash Wizard page and clicking Next will show the Select Performance Rule Type page (Figure 14-6).

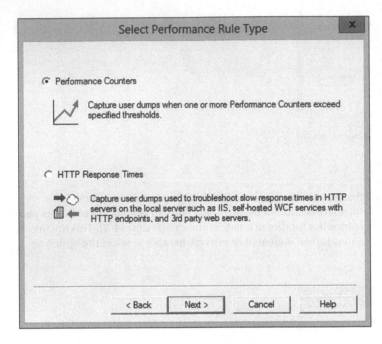

Figure 14-6. *Selecting the performance rule type*

The performance-counter-based rules allow you to select a performance counter and trigger dump files based on that counter breaching specified values. To get started, add performance triggers—the .NET CLR LocksAndThreads category contains useful counters for working with asynchronous processing. Figure 14-7 shows a trigger being set for the Contention Rate/sec for all instances of a process called DebugDiagRules.exe.

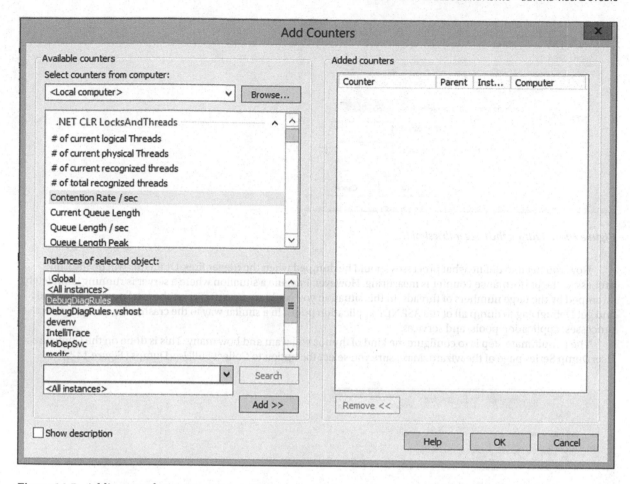

Figure 14-7. Adding a performance counter trigger

Once you have added the trigger, you can set trigger points for the counter by selecting the created trigger and clicking the Edit Thresholds button. This shows the properties of the trigger (Figure 14-8). On this dialog you can specify what the threshold is and for how long it must be breached before a dump file is generated.

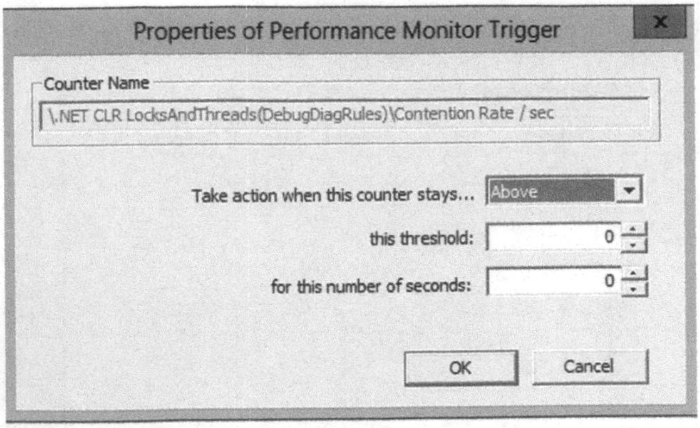

Figure 14-8. *Editing the trigger thresholds*

Now you need to define what processes should be dumped when the trigger fires. Often this will be the same process as the performance counter is measuring. However, imagine a situation where a server is running completely swamped by the large numbers of threads. In this situation you could set up a trigger on the total number of threads and get DebugDiag to dump all of the ASP.NET application pools. In a similar way to the crash rules, you can select processes, application pools, and services.

The penultimate step is to configure the kind of dumps you want and how many. This is done on the Configure UserDump Series page of the wizard. Make sure you select the option to Collect FullUserDumps (Figure 14-9).

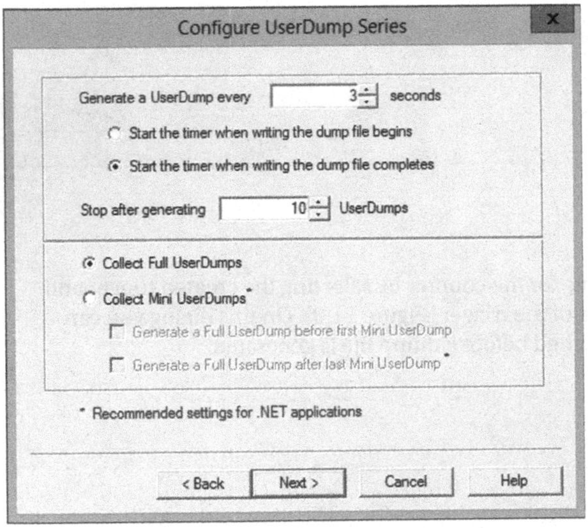

Figure 14-9. *Configuring the UserDumps*

Last, name the rule and specify an output directory for the generated dump files and the rule is complete.

■ **Tip** You may be thinking, "I know when my issue occurs but I can't work out a rule." Remember that you can create your own performance counters. There is a whole API around `System.Diagnostic.PerformanceCounter` that allows you to create and increment counters. So if you need a counter that doesn't exist to hook your debugging around, you can always create your own counters in your application that surface behavior to aid debugging. Just bear in mind that you have to deploy a new version of your code to introduce your own performance counters (not the registration of them, but your application code needs to increment them at appropriate times).

Native (non-.NET) Memory and Handle Leak

Despite the name of this rule, it is a useful rule type for .NET code when trying to track down a memory leak, as you can trigger the generation of a series of dump files as the memory of a process increases (in managed code you can assess which objects are growing in size and number and therefore the likely root of the leak). However, our focus is threading and so we will not go into detail on this option.

Executing Rules

Unless you state otherwise, rules are enabled once created. Rules will be active until they have generated the dump files they were designed to produce, at which time they deactivate. DebugDiag shows a list of configured rules in its main window. These rules have one of three statuses: `Active` means the rule is monitoring and potentially going to generate dump files; `Completed` means the rule has generated its required dumps and has deactivated; and `Not Active` means the rule has not yet been activated since being created. `Not Active` and `Completed` rules can be set to `Active` using the rule's context menu.

ADPLUS

Task Manager can generate a user dump of a running process on demand and DebugDiag can create user dumps based on a set of configurable rules. However, it can also be useful to be able to generate a dump file on an ad hoc basis when an application is terminating unexpectedly—either when certain actions are performed or on startup. This is the gap that a tool called ADPLUS fulfils.

ADPLUS comes as part of Debugging Tools for Windows which, at the time of writing, ships as part of the Windows SDK (previously it has been a stand-alone install). Its origins are based on issues experienced in Microsoft support when trying to explain to customers how to generate a dump file. The tool that actually does the work is the command line debugger (or `cdb.exe`), but the configuration of `cdb.exe` is nontrivial, and so Microsoft support created a VBScript file, `ADPLUS.VBS`, which presented a much simpler façade to enable dump file generation. These days the VBScript file has been turned into an executable, `adplus.exe`.

With all the tools in Debugging Tools for Windows, you need to ensure that you use the correct "bitness" of tool for the running executable. Fortunately, with the latest installations, both 32-bit and 64-bit versions are installed when you install the tools (assuming you are installing on a 64-bit machine). At the time of writing, Debugging Tools for Windows is installed in the `Program Files(x86)\Windows Kits\<version>\Debuggers` directory and the 32-bit and 64-bit versions are in the x86 and x64 subdirectories, respectively.

There are three ways to run ADPLUS, depending on the circumstances in which you want the dump file generated.

Crash Mode

If you are trying to capture a dump file when an application is crashing, Task Manager cannot help. This is somewhere ADPLUS can really shine as you do not have to install DebugDiag and configure rules. You simply run the following command (obviously, as an executable, you will need to run this in a context where adplus.exe is on path).

```
adplus -crash -pn <name of executable> -o <directory in which to generate the dump files>
```

Here -pn identifies the process, although it is possible to use -p and provide the process ID, which is useful if you have more than one instance of the application running. At the point when the specified process exits unexpectedly, cbd.exe (which has spawned in the background) will create the crash dump.

Spawning Mode

Crash Mode works well when the process is already running. However, if the application crashes when you start it, then you will not get an opportunity to run ADPLUS in Crash Mode. This is the situation for which Spawning Mode (a refinement of Crash Mode) exists. You trigger Spawning Mode by adding the -SC flag to the preceding command line. In this case the executable needs to be on path or you need to provide the path to it.

```
adplus -crash -SC -pn <path to executable> -o <directory in which to generate the dump files>
```

Hang Mode

Although its name suggests it, hang mode is not about the application hanging as such (as it would if every thread was deadlocked), but rather that you need a snapshot of the process as it is at this point in time. For completeness the syntax is included, although if you are running on Windows Vista or later you can simply use Task Manager to achieve the same effect.

```
adplus -hang -pn <name of executable> -o <directory in which to generate the dump files>
```

IMPROVING DUMP QUALITY

The JIT compiler performs a number of optimizations that can obscure the information in the dump file (such as inlining and using registers instead of the stack for parameters in method calls). You can turn off optimization by creating an .INI file matching the application or DLL for which you want to disable optimization. Enter the following in the .INI file before starting the process.

```
[.NET Framework Debugging Control]
GenerateTrackingInfo=1
AllowOptimize=0
```

Obviously, here you are changing the executing code, and so there is always a chance that the behavior you are trying to debug suddenly no longer happens—especially with race conditions. However, it can be a useful technique to make analyzing the dump file easier.

Analyzing Memory Dumps

You have seen a number of ways to generate a memory dump, but what do you do with it once you have it? Since .NET 4.0 and Visual Studio 2010 (note that both are necessary), you can load a dump file into Visual Studio and use its visual tools (Call Stack, Threads, and Parallel Stacks windows) to gain insight. Also, if the PDB file was available when the dump was produced and you have access to the source code, you can synchronize the point in the source when the dump was produced. While Visual Studio can provide some insight, the main tool we tend to use for dump analysis is WinDbg (normally pronounced either "Win Debug" or "Wind Bag").

WinDbg

WinDbg is part of the Debugging Tools for Windows tool set. As such there is are 32-bit and 64-bit versions and, again, the right one must be used. WinDbg is traditionally used with native code and especially device driver debugging. However, it can also provide powerful insight into bugs in managed applications.

To load a dump file, simply open WinDbg and select File ➤ Open Crash Dump (or press Ctrl-D). You will notice that WinDbg is, basically, a windowed view of command line output (Figure 14-10).

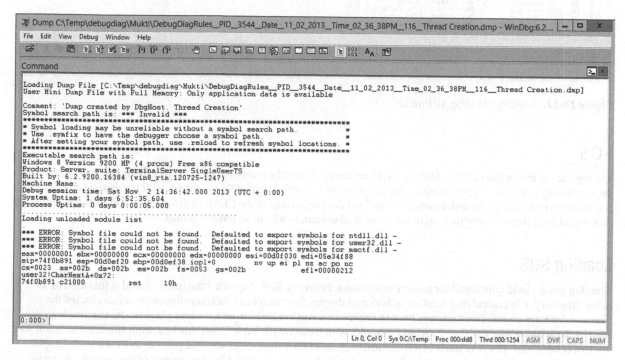

***Figure 14-10.** WinDbg with a loaded dump file*

WinDbg has a fairly arcane syntax for entering commands which, at first, can seem very obscure. However, once learned, it provides a concise and powerful way to run commands showing information from the memory dump. To show all of the threads in the dumped process, use the ~ command (the logic is that it looks a little like a stitch); you can see the output in Figure 14-11. However, there is a problem: much of what happens in the native world is not significant to managed code, and this is especially true in the case of threads. WinDbg on its own has a purely native view of the world. You need to provide WinDbg with a managed code "filter," and this is the job of sos.dll.

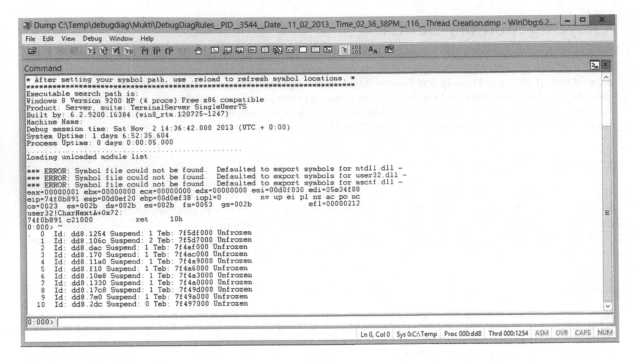

Figure 14-11. *WinDbg showing all threads*

SOS

During the development of .NET, Microsoft had an internal WinDbg extension called Strike. Realizing that this would be a generally useful tool, they created a derivative version that they called Son of Strike, which ships as sos.dll. SOS is a WinDbg extension that understands the internal data structures of the CLR and provides commands to interrogate those data structures to provide insight into managed execution within a memory dump.

Loading SOS

WinDbg has a .load command for loading extensions. However, SOS ships with the runtime and is installed in the same directory. It is critical that versions of SOS and the runtime match, as each runtime release can change the internal data structures. You therefore have to ensure that you load SOS from the same place as the runtime was loaded. To achieve this, use the .loadby command, which essentially says, "Load this DLL from the same location you got this other DLL." The core parts of the runtime ship in a DLL called mscorwks.dll prior to .NET 4.0 and clr.dll from version 4.0 onward. It is important therefore to use the right command for the version of the runtime that was loaded when the dump file was generated.

To load SOS prior to .NET 4.0, issue the following command.

.loadby sos **mscorwks**

And for .NET 4.0 and later, issue this command.

.loadby sos **clr**

Fortunately, if you choose the wrong command WinDbg will simply say that it cannot find the module. If the `.loadby` command works, you will see no output as WinDbg only notifies you of failures. Now that you have SOS loaded, you have a new, richer set of commands that understand managed code. All of the SOS commands start with the symbol `!` and can be listed using `!help`.

Examining Threads via SOS

You can see the difference between the native and managed views of the world by running the `!threads` command on the dump file from Figure 14-10. Figure 14-12 shows the `!threads` output.

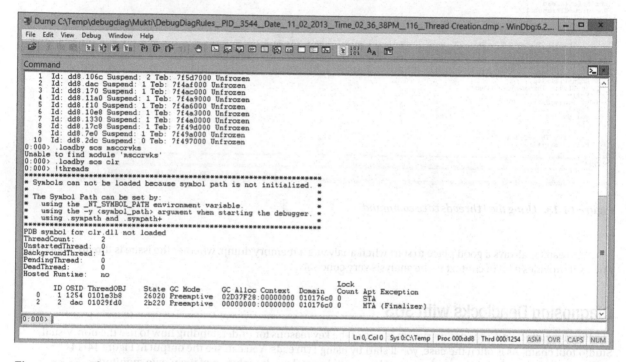

Figure 14-12. *The output from* `!threads`

`!threads` shows, among other things, the WinDbg thread identifier (the first column), which will be useful shortly; the managed thread ID; the operating system thread ID; the address of the associated thread object; a set of bit flags called `State`; the AppDomain in which the thread is executing (`Domain`); the number of `Monitors` owned (`Lock Count`); the COM apartment type of the thread (`Apt`); and any unhandled exception objects.

The `State` bit flags can be interpreted using the `!threadstate` command passing the `State` value (see Figure 14-13).

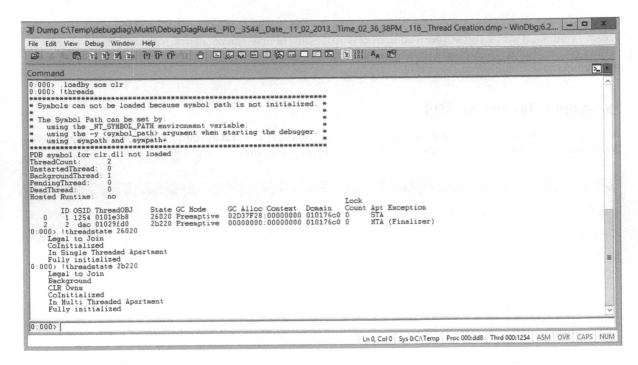

Figure 14-13. Using the !threadstate command

!threads is always a good place to start when analyzing a memory dump, whether the issue is thread related or not, as it provides a lot of context to the analysis very concisely.

Diagnosing Deadlocks with SOS

Finding a deadlock in a production system is one of the key reasons for understanding how to use the non-Visual Studio tool chain. As is often the case, you'll start by using !threads. You can see the output in Figure 14-14 and you may notice that although there are a large number of threads, only two of them own monitors (the Lock Count column).

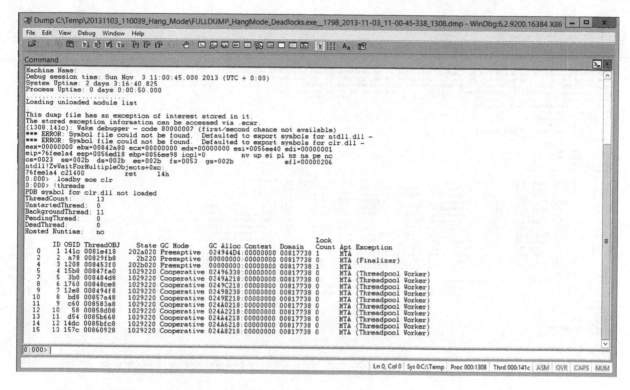

Figure 14-14. *!threads when threads own monitors*

Threads owning monitors, however, isn't necessarily an issue, so you need to understand what monitors are being held. You can use the !syncblk command to show which threads own which monitors. You can see the output from !syncblk in Figure 14-15; it shows that thread 0 owns the monitor for the object at the address 024923ac and thread 4 owns the monitor for the object at address 024923b8.

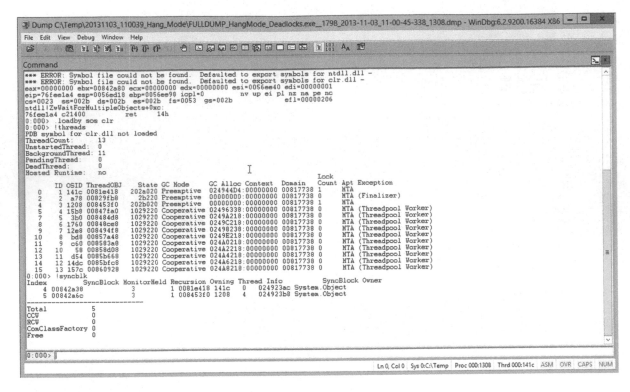

Figure 14-15. *Output from* `!syncblk`

Knowing which threads own which monitors is only half of the story; you also need to know if those threads are trying to acquire monitors and, if so, which ones. `!clrstack` shows the call stack for a thread and with the `-a` flag can also show parameters that were passed to the methods. However, the JIT compiler can introduce optimizations that hide the parameter information so using the .INI file as described in the "Improving Dump Quality" sidebar may be necessary to get full visibility.

The call stack is obviously thread specific, so how do you get the call stack from threads other than the main thread? If you look at the bottom left of the WinDbg display you will see, by default, the number 0. This is the thread the current commands are executing against. You can use the command `~#s`, where # is the thread number, to switch the current thread (the number in the bottom left changes as a result). You can also use `~#e` to execute a specific command against a specific thread (e.g. `~3e !clrstack` to run `!clrstack` against thread number 3).

Running `!clrstack -a` against both threads that own monitors shows that both threads are in the process of calling `Monitor.Enter`, so if you can verify that they are trying to acquire each other's owned monitor, you have found your deadlock. However, if optimization is on, or depending on which version of the runtime is being used, `!clrstack -a` may not show which object was being passed to it. Fortunately those parameters will be at the top of the stack, and it turns out you can show the objects on the stack using `!dso` against the thread (Figure 14-16).

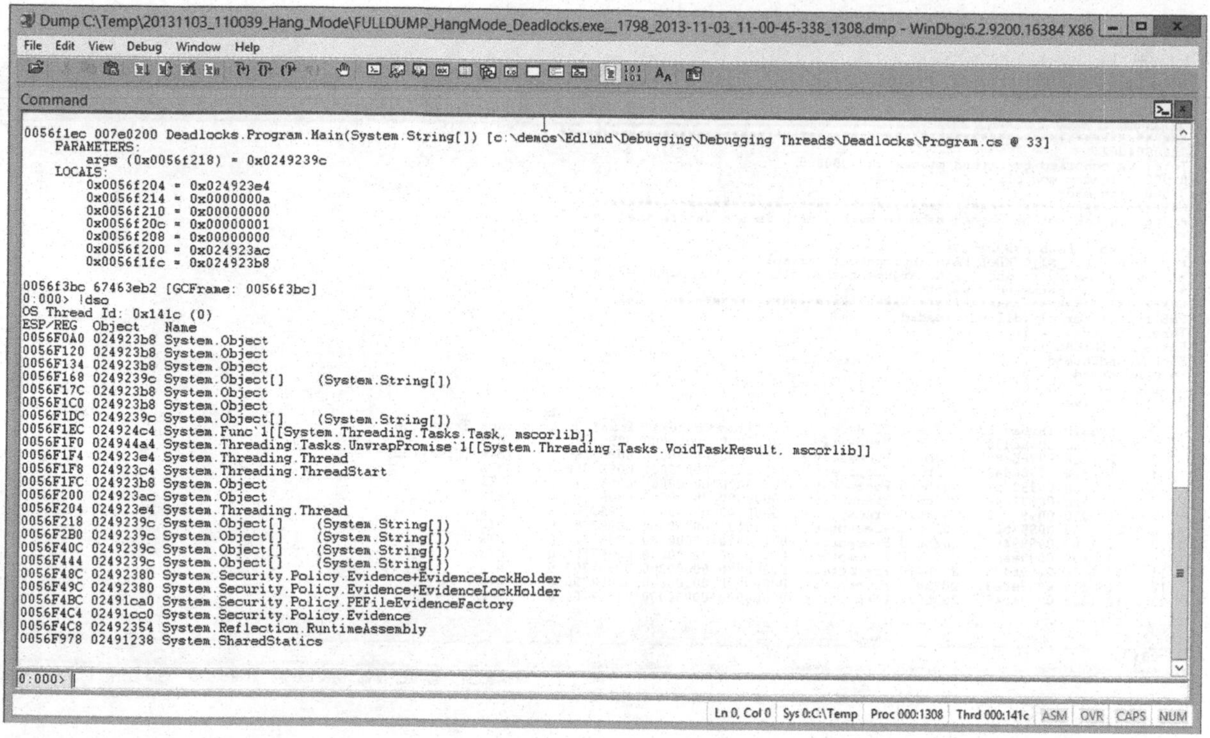

Figure 14-16. *The output from !dso*

By putting this information together you can see that the data in Figure 14-17 clearly show a thread deadlock.

Figure 14-17. *Diagnosing the deadlock*

Finding Runaway Threads

A runaway thread is one that, for some reason, has started to consume a lot of CPU power on an unproductive task—normally from accidentally ending up spinning in a tight loop. The more cores you have, the harder it is to spot a runaway thread as the percentage of CPU consumed can look quite small. However, with SOS you can see the amount of CPU each thread in a process has used. But as your starting point, use !threads (Figure 14-18).

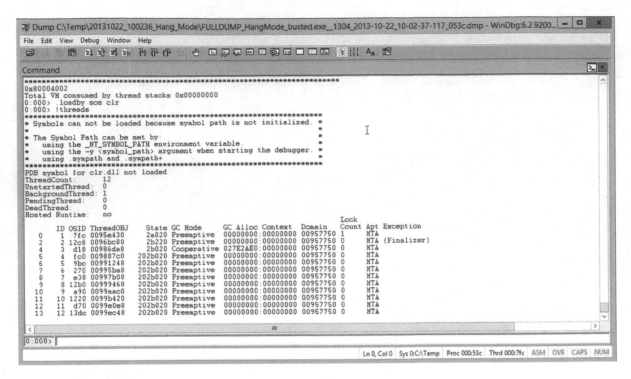

Figure 14-18. *Looking for runaway threads*

There are a lot of threads running, but Thread 4 does look a little different to the others. If you use the command !runaway you get the CPU usage statistics for each thread, as you can see in Figure 14-19—Thread 4 is definitely spinning in a tight loop. Now, by using !clrstack -a you can start to dig into the thread to work out why it is behaving as it is. Hopefully, with that context, you can look at the code and understand what went wrong.

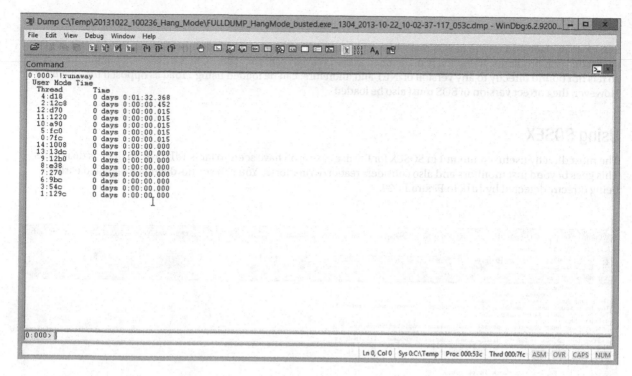

Figure 14-19. Output from `!runaway`

Other Useful SOS Commands

You've seen most of the SOS commands that are critical to analyzing threads. However, there are many more commands that provide useful information, and some of these can be seen in Table 14-1.

Table 14-1. Useful SOS Commands

Command	Result
`!dumpheap -stat`	Shows all of the types of objects allocated on the managed heap, how many, and how much memory they jointly consume. Can be filtered with -type (`!dumpheap -stat -type Exception` to find all types with Exception in their name)
`!dumpheap -MT <address>`	Shows all instances of a type identified by the Method Table address shown in `!dumpheap -stat`
`!do <address>`	Shows all of the fields in specific object
`!objsize <address>`	Shows how much memory an object is directly and indirectly responsible for
`!pe`	Prints details of an unhandled exception object on the current thread
`!gcroot <address>`	Identifies the live roots that are keeping the object from being garbage
`!threadpool`	Shows the number of threads in the pool, the depth of the queue, and how many threadpool timers are running

SOSEX

SOSEX is an extension on top of SOS that wraps up a series of low-level commands into higher-level operations to solve common problems. It is actively maintained at www.stevestechspot.com. SOSEX drives SOS behind the scenes so it is not bound directly to any version of .NET and, therefore, can be loaded using .load as opposed to .loadby. However, the correct version of SOS must also be loaded.

Using SOSEX

The most directly useful command in SOSEX for the use cases you have seen so far is !dlk, which detects deadlocks. This goes beyond just monitors and also considers reader/writer locks. You can see the deadlock depicted earlier being directly detected by !dlk in Figure 14-20.

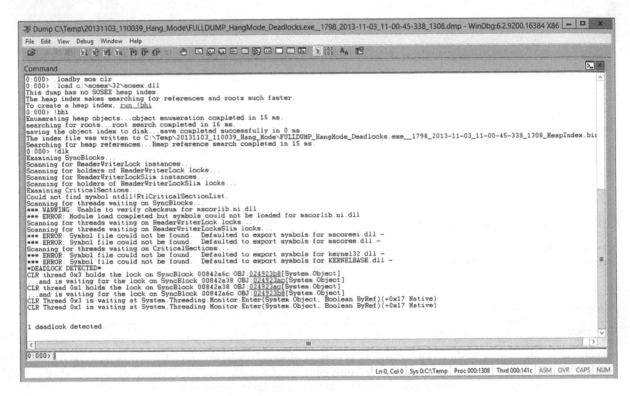

Figure 14-20. *!dlk in action detecting a deadlock*

Useful SOSEX Commands

There are a number of useful commands in SOSEX to aid in tracking down threading-related issues. Some useful SOSEX commands are listed in Table 14-2.

Table 14-2. *Useful SOSEX Commands*

Command	Result
!dlk	Automates deadlock detection
!mlocks	Finds owned locks for monitors, `ReaderWriterLock`, `ReaderWriterLockSlim`, and native critical sections
!mdso	Does the same as !dso but provides extra options for filtering to make locating objects on the stack easier
!rwlock	Shows details of owned reader/writer locks
!mk	Shows stack frames, including transition to native code, which can help if debugging memory dumps that include interop
!mwaits	Lists all threads waiting for synchronization primitives and the object on which they are waiting

PSSCOR

PSSCOR is an alternative to SOS. Its commands are a superset of SOS and some commands display extra useful information. In general it is a good idea to use PSSCOR in preference to SOS; however, its release always lags behind that of SOS, which ships with the runtime. You always know that you can use SOS regardless of whether the runtime version is in beta or just recently released. However, because the responsible team at Microsoft is not bound to the same release cycle as SOS, they can release fixes to bugs far more rapidly. In particular, PSSCOR has extra commands to assist with debugging ASP.NET applications.

Summary

Understanding how to capture memory dumps and then how to analyze them is an important skill for developers who spend a lot of time debugging multithreaded applications. After Visual Studio, this tool chain can seem primitive and obscure. However, there is a lot of power in working at this lower level, and memory dumps can highlight issues that interactive debugging cannot.

Index

Get the eBook for only $10!

> Now you can take the weightless companion with you anywhere, anytime. Your purchase of this book entitles you to 3 electronic versions for only $10.

This Apress title will prove so indispensible that you'll want to carry it with you everywhere, which is why we are offering the eBook in **3 formats** for only $10 if you have already purchased the print book.

Convenient and fully searchable, the PDF version enables you to easily find and copy code—or perform examples by quickly toggling between instructions and applications. The MOBI format is ideal for your Kindle, while the ePUB can be utilized on a variety of mobile devices.

Go to www.apress.com/promo/tendollars to purchase your companion eBook.